I'm really happy with what Luebke et al. have created. It's exactly what I would want to find on the shelf if I needed to implement some LOD techniques in a game. The book gives both a survey of existing techniques and some specific examples of LOD use, which is what makes it uniquely valuable. If you're a game developer who is just starting out, and you want to come up to speed on the state of the art in LOD, you can read through the initial chapters to familiarize yourself with the important concepts. On the other hand, if you're familiar with LOD techniques but perhaps not how to use them in a real-time system, you can jump straight to the game development and terrain rendering chapters. Great stuff!

The extensive set of references at the end of the book is quite nice to have as well. One of the challenges in implementing a cutting-edge technique and altering it to suit your application is understanding the algorithm to its core. It's invaluable having all of those references in one place, so that you can easily find the exact paper where the technique you want to implement was first detailed.

Mark DeLoura
Manager of Developer Relations, Sony Computer Entertainment America
Creator, Game Programming Gems series

A fantastic and well-written book, filled with a lot of very useful information. There is no other like it on the market.

The concept of level of detail is an important one in the field of computer graphics, dating back to James Clark's 1976 Communications of the ACM paper entitled "Hierarchical Geometric Models for Visible Surface Algorithms." Current books on graphics discuss only the basics of level of detail and present one or more of a small number of algorithms on the topic. The field has evolved over the last decade to the point where there is a lot more to say about it.

Level of Detail for 3D Graphics says it all! This is the first and only book that provides a comprehensive coverage about level of detail. At a high level, the book is organized into three parts. The first concerns theory and algorithms for generation of level of detail. The second discusses applications, including optimizations for game programming and level of detail for terrain. The third details advanced issues, including a discussion on visual systems and on temporal level of detail. At a low level, the book is well written and the authors cover the topics in meticulous detail. Not only are the algorithms themselves presented but comparisons are made between them so you know which one is the best choice for your application. This book is packed with information. When you are finished reading it, all you will be able to say is "Wow!"

Level of Detail for 3D Graphics is absolutely a must-have book for practitioners in any graphics field including game programming, scientific or medical visualization, computer aided design, or virtual reality systems.

Dave Eberly
President, Magic Software, Inc.

A comprehensive presentation of the terminology, theory, and practice of mesh simplification. Includes extensive references to Web-accessible source code and data. This book will find a choice spot on my bookshelf.

Will Schroeder
Cofounder, Kitware, Inc.

I like the writing style of the book! The first three chapters nicely outline and divide concepts that have been floating around the literature. The book presents a good classification of algorithms and their general strategies and variations. I hope this classification extends to the research community and fosters better communication among researchers.

The applications section gives a solid glimpse into the issues and complexities that arise when developing geometry-rendering systems for real and large applications.

The advanced issues section is very enlightening! The summary of perceptual issues and the ideas for measuring visual fidelity will help both new and experienced researchers develop novel and revolutionary algorithms to take level-of-detail work to the next stage.

The book does a great job of piecing together years of work and presenting it in an organized fashion. This betters the understanding for both new and experienced researchers, and it provides a mechanism to put researchers on the same wavelength, thus promoting better communication. In addition, the advanced issues section of the book contains several forward-looking concepts that hopefully will take level-of-detail work to the next stage!

Daniel Aliaga
Computer Graphics Researcher
Bell Laboratories

LEVEL OF DETAIL FOR 3D GRAPHICS

LEVEL OF DETAIL
FOR 3D GRAPHICS

DAVID LUEBKE — *University of Virginia*

MARTIN REDDY — *SRI International*

JONATHAN D. COHEN — *Johns Hopkins University*

AMITABH VARSHNEY — *University of Maryland*

BENJAMIN WATSON — *Northwestern University*

ROBERT HUEBNER — *Nihilistic Software*

MORGAN KAUFMANN PUBLISHERS

AN IMPRINT OF ELSEVIER SCIENCE

AMSTERDAM   BOSTON   LONDON   NEW YORK
OXFORD   PARIS   SAN DIEGO   SAN FRANCISCO
SINGAPORE   SYDNEY   TOKYO

Publishing Director   Diane Cerra
Publishing Services Manager   Edward Wade
Production Editor   Howard Severson
Senior Developmental Editor   Marilyn Alan
Cover Design   Frances Baca
Cover Image   Laughing gulls, TX/Doug Plummer/Photonica
Text Design   Rebecca Evans & Associates
Illustration   Dartmouth Publishing Industries
Composition   Windfall Software, using ZzTEX
Copyeditor   Barbara Kohl
Proofreader   James Gaglione
Indexer   Bill Meyers
Printer   Maple-Vail Book Manufacturing Group

Designations used by companies to distinguish their products are often claimed as trademarks or registered trademarks. In all instances in which Morgan Kaufmann Publishers is aware of a claim, the product names appear in initial capital or all capital letters. Readers, however, should contact the appropriate companies for more complete information regarding trademarks and registration.

Morgan Kaufmann Publishers
An imprint of Elsevier Science
340 Pine Street, Sixth Floor
San Francisco, CA 94104-3205, USA
www.mkp.com

Library of Congress Control Number: 2002107328
ISBN: 1-55860-838-9

This book is printed on acid-free paper.

To Emily Luebke,
Genevieve Vidanes,
Suzy Maska,
Poonam Gupta, and
Polly Watson

FOREWORD

Frederick P. Brooks, Jr.
Kenan Professor of Computer Science
University of North Carolina at Chapel Hill

A perennial goal (by no means the only one) of computer graphics is to produce visual evocations of virtual worlds that *look real*. This is a formidable challenge for modeling, for illumination, and then for rendering on displays of limited resolution and limited dynamic range.

For interactive computer graphics, this challenge is aggravated by the necessity of rendering a new picture 25–30 times per second for each eye so that the whole task must be done in 17 milliseconds or so.

Modeling and model management is perhaps the biggest part of the challenge. The God-made world looks real because it is everywhere and is dense in detail, far below visual resolution. Any of our models of real world scenes are limited to fewer than a billion primitives (usually colored, shaded triangles).

The strategy by which the overall challenge has been tackled is conceptually very simple: People devise algorithms so that the primitives actually fed into the graphics pipeline are (almost) only those that will be seen and noticed by the viewer of the final image.

Thus, view-frustum culling eliminates primitives outside the field of view, recalculated frame by frame. Back-facing triangles are eliminated by a simple test. Obscuration culling calculates, for each new image, those triangles completely behind others. Texture mapping enables detailed 2D patterns to be carried by a single triangle.

Many unobscured triangles in a field of view will nevertheless be invisible to the viewer. At their distance to the viewpoint, their projection on the final image will be substantially less than the pixel resolution of the display. So there is no need to burden the graphics pipeline with those.

Instead, one wants to manage the world model so that fine levels of detail are grouped together into a single primitive when, and only when, they would not be seen separately. This fine book is an exposition of the concepts, algorithms, and data structures for doing this grouping. The authors have developed many of the techniques described here. The book provides both a treatment of the underlying theory and a valuable practical reference for the graphics practitioner.

Contents

PART I

GENERATION

CHAPTER 1

CHAPTER 2

CHAPTER
3

SIMPLIFICATION ERROR METRICS 　　　　　　　　　　　　　　47

PART II

APPLICATION

CHAPTER 4

RUN-TIME FRAMEWORKS   87

CHAPTER 5

A CATALOG OF USEFUL ALGORITHMS   121

CHAPTER
6

GAMING OPTIMIZATIONS 151

CHAPTER

7

TERRAIN LEVEL OF DETAIL   185

PART III

ADVANCED ISSUES

CHAPTER 8

PERCEPTUAL ISSUES

231

PREFACE

Managing level of detail (LOD) is at once a very current and a very old topic in computer graphics. As early as 1976 James Clark described the benefits of representing objects within a scene at several resolutions, and flight simulators have long used handcrafted multiresolution models of airplanes to achieve a constant frame rate. Recent years have seen many algorithms, papers, and software tools devoted to generating and managing such multiresolution representations of objects automatically. Indeed, an entire field of computer graphics dedicated to regulating level of detail virtually exploded into existence in the early 1990s. This book presents a detailed treatment of that field.

COVERAGE AND AUDIENCE

In this book we cover the following:

- We survey the state of the art, describing past and current research as well as trends and open questions in the field to date.

- We discuss the theoretical underpinnings of the field, such as visual perception, how to measure geometric error, and how to evaluate temporal factors such as frame rate and latency.

- We provide an applied resource for graphics developers, detailing a host of useful algorithms and addressing two applications of particular interest: video games and terrain visualization.

By covering both theory and application, we hope to create a useful resource for graphics researchers as well as developers of any real-time graphics application: video games, flight and driving simulators, visualization engines for scientific, medical, and CAD applications, and virtual reality systems for training and entertainment. Nor is level of detail strictly limited to the realm of interactive graphics; the same techniques have long been used to accelerate offline rendering for animation. Readers interested in this topic may find particularly interesting those simplification techniques that prioritize preserving the appearance of simplified models, as well as the chapters on perception and the perceptibility of simplification.

This book should be accessible to anyone familiar with the essentials of computer science and interactive computer graphics. For example, we assume knowledge of graphics fundamentals such as transformations and texture mapping, but we do not presuppose a working knowledge of a specific graphics library such as DirectX or OpenGL. In general we presume no advanced math beyond what any introductory computer graphics text will cover: the basics of linear algebra, such as vectors, matrices, and so on, and the basics of three-dimensional geometry, such as the equation of a plane and the distance between two points. We provide simple pseudocode for some algorithms but do not assume knowledge of any particular programming language. We also provide an extensive glossary to define unfamiliar terms, academic jargon, and formal notation. In short, we have tried to make this book useful to everybody from aspiring game developers to researchers in mesh simplification.

WHY WE WROTE THIS BOOK

This book grew out of a course titled "Advanced Issues in Level of Detail" that we have taught at ACM SIGGRAPH starting in 2000. We felt that that there was a need for an advanced course on LOD; many courses, tutorials, and books on high-performance interactive rendering cover the basics of LOD, but only the basics. A great deal more information is available on the Web, from the latest research results to implementations for sample video game engines, but that information is hard to find, everchanging, and sometimes unreliable. Where could a graphics developer go to learn about the state of the art in LOD, or to learn the basics of supporting fields such as visual perception? Answer: nowhere. We set out to create a course targeted toward serious graphics developers that serves as a vehicle for reviewing and disseminating the latest research results as well as the underpinning theory of our field. As we prepared, taught, and refined the SIGGRAPH course, we began to perceive a real gap in the computer graphics market.

LOD is a vital technique for real-time graphics, an essential tool in the developer's grab bag. Probably every high-performance graphics application or toolkit built in the last five years includes some support for LOD, whether simple or sophisticated. The last decade saw a flurry of research and development around the problem of taking a detailed object and creating simple yet faithful versions. Many algorithms, mechanisms, and metrics were tossed around in a frenzy of experimentation. Now the field appears to be approaching maturity. Many questions remain open, but many have been settled. Some excellent algorithms now exist for creating simple, yet faithful, LODs. A graphics developer can choose from a buffet of excellent algorithms for creating LODs, each with particular strengths: some are simple, some are fast, and some create remarkably high-fidelity simplifications. Yet no graphics text gives the field more than a handful of pages. Right now a developer seeking information on this field must root through conference proceedings and journal articles, follow references, and generally do a full-scale research dig.

We decided that the time was ripe to write a book. Our goals were the following:

1. To become the seminal reference for issues surrounding level of detail management.

2. To describe and review state-of-the-art advances in the field of level of detail, and to distill the breadth of cutting-edge research into a coherent, accessible treatise.

3. To develop an applied resource that researchers and software developers alike could use to assess and implement the best solution for their graphics application.

You hold the result in your hands. We hope you will find it useful!

ACKNOWLEDGMENTS

We would like to thank a few of the great many people whose contributions were instrumental in taking this book from an initial suggestion to a final product. First, we would like to express our gratitude to Dr. Frederick P. Brooks, Jr. of the University of North Carolina for writing the preceding foreword. Dr. Brooks has made outstanding contributions to our field over several decades, and we are honored and delighted by his involvement in our own modest effort.

Several reviewers provided many invaluable pages of feedback and suggestions: Jarek Rossignac (Georgia Institute of Technology), Michael Garland (University of Illinois at Urbana-Champaign), Leila De Floriani (University of Genova), Peter Lindstrom (Lawrence Livermore National Laboratory), David Duchaineau (Lawrence Livermore National Laboratory), Thomas True (SGI), Colin Ware (University of New Hampshire), Ben Discoe (Virtual Terrain Project), Ian Ashdown (byHeart Consultants Limited), Steven Woodcock (National Missile Defense System), and Mike Lucas (Victor Valley College Academy of Digital Animation).

Also deserving thanks are our many colleagues and peers who gave us support, offered constructive criticisms, or provided illustrations to include in the book. These include Jack Tumblin (Northwestern University), Hugues Hoppe (Microsoft Research), Thomas Funkhouser (Princeton University), Yvan Leclerc and Bob Bolles (SRI International), Cliff Woolley and Nathaniel Williams (University of Virginia), Toshikazu Ohshima and Hiroyuki Yamamoto (Canon, Japan), James Ferwerda (Cornell University), Thomas Gerstner (University of Bonn), and Leila de Floriani and Paola Magillo (University of Genova).

We would also like to acknowledge the prodigious work of the people at Morgan Kaufmann Publishers. They were always quick to answer queries and provided the utmost support during the publishing process. In particular, we would like to recognize our valued relationships with Diane Cerra, our executive editor; Marilyn Alan, our senior developmental editor; Howard Severson, our production editor; and Sarah E. O'Donnell, our marketing manager, among many others at Morgan Kaufmann. They made this process a smooth and enjoyable ride.

ABOUT THE WEB SITE

We have developed a Web site to accompany this book at *http://LODBook.com/*. Here you will find various helpful resources, such as source code to many of the systems described in the text, links to polygon simplification products, tools, 3D models, and documentation. Our aim is to supplement the descriptions here with practical material that developers can use today in their applications. We will also use this site to publish updated information about the book such as errata or revision announcements. This Web site provides us with a more timely mechanism to keep you, the reader, up to date with the latest developments in the field of level of detail.

ABOUT THE AUTHORS

David Luebke is an Assistant Professor in the Department of Computer Science at the University of Virginia. His principal research interest is the problem of rendering very complex scenes at interactive rates. His research focuses on software techniques such as polygonal simplification and occlusion culling to reduce the complexity of such scenes to manageable levels. Luebke's dissertation research, summarized in a SIGGRAPH '97 paper, introduced a dynamic, view-dependent approach to polygonal simplification for interactive rendering of extremely complex CAD models. He earned his Ph.D. at the University of North Carolina, and his bachelor's degree at the Colorado College. David's email address is <luebke@cs.virginia.edu>.

Martin Reddy is a Research Engineer at SRI International where he works in the area of terrain visualization. This work involves the real-time display of massive terrain databases that are distributed over wide-area networks. His research interests include level of detail, visual perception, and computer graphics. His doctoral research involved the application of models of visual perception to real-time computer graphics systems, enabling the selection of level of detail based on measures of human perception. He received his B.Sc. from the University of Strathclyde and his Ph.D. from the University of Edinburgh, UK. He is on the board of directors of the Web3D Consortium and chair of the GeoVRML Working Group. Martin's email address is <reddy@ai.sri.com>.

Jonathan D. Cohen is an Assistant Professor in the Department of Computer Science at The Johns Hopkins University. He earned his doctoral and master's degrees from the University of North Carolina at Chapel Hill and earned his bachelor's degree from Duke University. His interests include polygonal simplification and other software acceleration techniques, parallel rendering architectures, collision detection, and high-quality interactive computer graphics. Jon's email address is <cohen@cs.jhu.edu>.

Amitabh Varshney is an Associate Professor in the Department of Computer Science at the University of Maryland. His research interests lie in interactive computer graphics, scientific visualization, molecular graphics, and CAD. Varshney has worked on several aspects of level of detail, including topology-preserving and topology-reducing simplification, view-dependent simplification, parallelization of simplification computation, as well as using triangle strips in multiresolution rendering. Varshney received his Ph.D. and master's degrees from the University of North Carolina at Chapel Hill in 1994 and 1991, respectively. He received his bachelor's degree in computer science from the Indian Institute of Technology at Delhi in 1989. Amitabh's email address is <varshney@cs.umd.edu>.

Benjamin Watson is an Assistant Professor in computer science at Northwestern University. He earned his doctoral and master's degrees at Georgia Tech's GVU Center, and his bachelor's degree at the University of California, Irvine. His dissertation focused on user-performance effects of dynamic level of detail management. His other research interests include object simplification, medical applications of virtual reality, and 3D user interfaces. Ben's email address is <watsonb@cs.nwu.edu>.

Robert Huebner is the Director of Technology at Nihilistic Software, an independent development studio located in Marin County, California. Prior to cofounding Nihilistic, Robert has worked on a number of successful game titles including "Jedi Knight: Dark Forces 2" for LucasArts Entertainment, "Descent" for Parallax Software, and "Starcraft" for Blizzard Entertainment. Nihilistic's first title, "Vampire The Masquerade: Redemption" was released for the PC in 2000 and sold over 500,000 copies worldwide. Nihilistic's second project will be released in the winter of 2002 on next-generation game consoles. Robert has spoken on game technology topics at SIGGRAPH, the Game Developer's Conference (GDC), and Electronic Entertainment Expo (E3). He also serves on the advisory board for the Game Developer's Conference and the International Game Developer's Association (IGDA). Robert's email address is <innerloop@nihilistic.com>.

PART I
GENERATION

INTRODUCTION

Practitioners of computer graphics have always struggled with the tradeoff between complexity and performance. Every graphics programmer knows the tension between realism and speed, between fidelity and frame rate, between rich, highly detailed graphical worlds and smooth, flowing animation. An entire field has grown out of this tension. Known as *level of detail*, or *LOD* for short, this discipline of interactive computer graphics attempts to bridge complexity and performance by regulating the amount of detail used to represent the virtual world. This book is devoted to the field of LOD—its mechanisms and underpinnings, its principles and practices, its application and theory.

Level of detail is as relevant today as ever, for despite tremendous strides in graphics hardware, the tension between fidelity and speed continues to haunt us. The complexity of our 3D models—measured most commonly by the number of polygons—seems to grow faster than the ability of our hardware to render them. No matter how powerful our platform, the number of polygons we want always seems to exceed the number of polygons we can afford. The problem may be sheer complexity: for example, Figure 1.1 shows several massive models ranging from handmade CAD, to procedurally generated geometry, to laser scans of real objects. All are too complex to render interactively with any machine available to date. The problem may be

3

(a)

(b)

(c)

Figure 1.1   A variety of large models, all well beyond the interactive rendering capabilities of today's hardware. (a) The UNC Powerplant ($\approx$13 million polygons), (b) the Digital Michelangelo scan of David ($\approx$56 million polygons), and (c) a model produced by a plant ecosystem simulation ($\approx$16 million polygons) (University of North Carolina [Aliaga 99] and Stanford University [Levoy 00][Deussen 98]). Copyright © 2000 and 1998 Association for Computing Machinery, Inc.

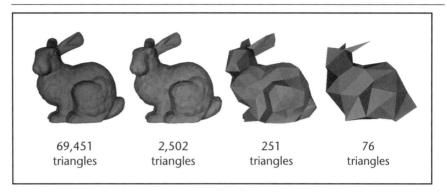

69,451
triangles

2,502
triangles

251
triangles

76
triangles

(a)

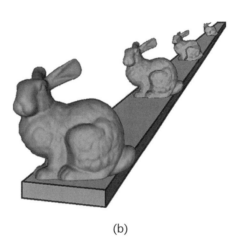

(b)

Figure 1.2   The fundamental concept of LOD. (a) A complex object is simplified, (b) creating levels of detail or LODs to reduce the rendering cost of small, distant, or unimportant geometry [Luebke 01a]. Copyright © 2001 IEEE.

unsegmented or poorly segmented data, which is often the case for surfaces generated in scientific and medical visualization. Or the problem may be limited rendering resources, a challenge well known to video game developers who must support last year's hardware. Even offline rendering of animation and visual effects, which does not require interactive rates, can benefit from regulating level of detail.

The fundamental concept of LOD, summed up in Figure 1.2, is almost embarrassingly simple: when rendering, use a less detailed representation for small, distant, or unimportant portions of the scene. This less detailed representation typically consists of a selection of several versions of objects in the scene, each version less detailed and faster to render than the one before. Generating and rendering these progressively coarser versions of objects, known themselves as *levels of detail* or *LODs*, has become an extremely hot topic over the last decade. Dozens of LOD algorithms have been published, and dozens more have undoubtedly been whipped up by developers unaware of or confused by the menagerie of techniques available. This book presents a detailed treatment of the field of LOD, distilling into a single volume research, theory, and algorithms from journals and conferences spanning several countries and several years. The book also aims to provide an applied resource that will help developers integrate state-of-the-art LOD into their games, simulations, and visualizations. In our field an unfortunate gulf separates much research from implementation; many excellent algorithms have never made it from the ivory towers of academia to the practical world of industrial development. This book aims to bridge that gulf.

1.1 COVERAGE AND ORGANIZATION

We cover a wide gamut of topics in LOD, broadly categorized into three areas reflected in the three parts of the book: Generation, Application, and Advanced Issues.

- *Generation.* Part I discusses frameworks and algorithms for generating levels of detail. We focus here on the most common task in LOD: starting from a complex polygonal model, create a series or spectrum of simpler models that resemble the original but use fewer polygons. Once an entirely manual process, a great many algorithms have been proposed in the last decade to perform this simplification. In Chapter 2 we categorize and discuss work on mesh simplification, emphasizing the underlying similarities and differences among algorithms: what local simplification operation removes polygons, in what order that operation is applied, what metric guides simplification. We also discuss issues of mesh topology, since modifying that topology (e.g., closing holes in the mesh) can permit more drastic simplification, but can also lead to poor fidelity. Finally, in Chapter 3 we focus on error metrics in simplification. We examine not only geometric error but also analytic and image-based measures of error for surface attributes, such as colors, normals, and texture coordinates.

- *Application.* Part II focuses on the task of managing the level of detail used to render a scene. Here the tradeoff between fidelity and performance becomes concrete: the system must choose or generate LODs to represent the objects in the scene, and their total complexity will determine the rendering performance. We move from the general to the specific, opening with a discussion of run-time frameworks for level of detail in Chapter 4. Such frameworks may assemble the scene from LODs created ahead of time, or they may generate LODs on the fly, tailoring them to the particular viewing scenario. Chapter 5 provides a catalog of useful algorithms related to LOD, including several approaches to mesh simplification. We have chosen algorithms that span the gamut of simplification research: some are particularly fast, some particularly robust, and others produce particularly high-fidelity simplifications. Chapter 6 addresses special topics of particular applied interest: video game programming, and the implementation issues and practical realities of managing level of detail in video games. The most mainstream application of computer graphics, video games impose unique constraints, such as tight polygon and computation budgets, as well as unique opportunities, such as a staff of full-time artists to manually create or optimize LODs. Chapter 7 is devoted to the special case of terrain simplification. Terrains and height fields have a specific structure and often tremendous complexity that enable and require specialized algorithms. Many innovations in mesh simplification were first invented for the particular case of terrains.

- *Advanced Issues.* Part III turns to more theoretical, but no less important, topics. These are the deeper questions underlying level of detail management. What principles of visual perception can help us design better LOD algorithms? How can we evaluate the perceptual error introduced by our simplifications? What is an appropriate frame rate, and how does it vary by task? In Chapter 8, we begin with an overview of human visual perception, present a simple model of low-level vision suitable for driving LOD, and describe some algorithms based on variations of that model. In Chapter 9, we examine techniques to evaluate visual fidelity in level of detail. We describe automatic and experimental measures of visual fidelity, and discuss the implications of recent research comparing these measures. Finally, in Chapter 10, we consider temporal issues. What is an appropriate frame rate, and how does it vary by task? How do the effects of latency, frame rate, and overall system responsiveness differ? Is a fixed frame rate always best?

1.2 HISTORY

No introduction to the use of LOD in real-time 3D graphics would be complete without acknowledging the seminal work of James Clark. In a 1976 paper titled "Hierarchical Geometric Models for Visible Surface Algorithms," Clark codified the basic principles behind level of detail [Clark 76]. Recognizing the redundancy of using many polygons to render an object covering only a few pixels, Clark described a hierarchical scene graph structure that incorporated not only LOD but other now common techniques, such as view-frustum culling. Many advanced topics in current level of detail research first surfaced in Clark's paper, including keeping a graphical working set in immediate-access store (what we now term out-of-core simplification and rendering), parallel processing of scene graphs, and perceptual metrics for LOD such as the eccentricity and velocity criteria described in Chapter 8. We highly recommend this paper to readers interested in the historical genesis of computer graphics.

Flight simulators were probably the earliest applications to make extensive use of LOD [Cosman 81]. In these early days, LODs were created by hand—considering the overall cost of a flight simulator system, the cost of paying a designer or artist to create multiple models of each object was insignificant. The early 1990s saw a sudden interest in automating this process, and researchers published a flurry of papers describing algorithms for simplifying a highly detailed model while still capturing its visual appearance. Some of those first algorithms, such as vertex decimation [Schroeder 92] and gridded vertex clustering [Rossignac 92], remain among the most important and useful; we describe them in detail in Chapter 5. Over the years other algorithms and frameworks for LOD have been developed. The many key developments, which we will elucidate throughout the book, include optimization-based predictive schedulers for selecting LODs [Funkhouser 93b], progressive meshes for continuous LOD [Hoppe 96], vertex hierarchies for view-dependent LOD [Hoppe 97][Luebke 97][Xia 96], quadric error metrics for measuring simplification error [Garland 97], guaranteed bounds on surface and texture distortion [Cohen 96][Cohen 98a], and principled simplification of topology [He 96][El-Sana 99b]. Today the graphics developer faces a bewildering array of choices. Simplification algorithms range from simple and fast to sophisticated and slow, and the resulting LODs range from crude to excellent. This book should provide a guide to the many techniques for creating and managing LODs, as well as an understanding of the deeper underlying principles.

1.3   Simplifications in Computer Graphics

Geometric mesh simplification is not the only form of LOD management. Some simplifications are so woven into the practice of computer graphics that we tend to forget about them, such as the quantization of color to 24 bits or the use of three-color channels (red, green, and blue) to represent the spectral response of the virtual scene. Even storing a polygonal mesh may involve simplification, since we clamp the precision of the coordinates and normals (typically to 32 bits each for X, Y, and Z). Although useful and long-used approximations, especially in interactive graphics, the quantization of color and geometric attributes is indeed simplification, and recognizing this can lead to many benefits. For example, game programmers once commonly optimized storage and computation by using fixed-point arithmetic and fewer bits of precision for vertex coordinates, and Michael Deering's seminal work on geometry compression introduced many ways of controlling precision to optimize storage and transmission of 3D models [Deering 95]. In general the line between simplification and lossy compression techniques, which include quantization in its various forms, can be blurry. In the main, however, we will define LOD and simplification throughout this book as processes that reduce the complexity of polygonal meshes, not their precision or storage size.

Shading and illumination form another spectrum of simplification in computer graphics. Many packages let the user control rendering performance with the familiar progression from wireframe to flat shading, to Gouraud shading, to texture mapping, and finally to per-pixel effects, such as Phong shading, bump mapping, and environment mapping. Lighting calculations range from simple local illumination techniques, such as the Phong model (still used for the majority of interactive graphics, since this is what most hardware supports), to sophisticated global illumination methods such as radiosity and path tracing. Designers have long recognized the possibility of managing rendering performance by varying the complexity of shading and illumination applied to objects within the scene. The connection between texture mapping and level of detail deserves particular mention. One can think of MIP mapping and other texture filtering techniques as a form of LOD management. For example, Dumont et al. manage texture memory (and hence rendering performance) with a perceptually motivated metric by varying the maximum-resolution MIP map used [Dumont 01]. A more frequent technique, however, replaces geometric detail in LODs with texture maps. Termed *imposters* by Maciel and Shirley [Maciel 95], these textured LODs are especially common in video games and visual simulation applications. Although we chiefly focus on geometric level of detail management, we discuss the use of textured imposters and backdrops in Chapter 6.

1.4 LOD FRAMEWORKS

The rest of this chapter introduces some important concepts and terminology in LOD, providing a brief overview of the field as context for the remainder of the book. We begin with an overview of three basic frameworks for managing level of detail: discrete, continuous, and view-dependent LOD.

1.4.1 DISCRETE LOD

We refer to the traditional approach to LOD as *discrete LOD*. The original scheme proposed by Clark in 1976 and used without modification in most 3D graphics applications today, this approach creates multiple versions of every object, each at a different level of detail, during an offline preprocess. At run-time the appropriate level of detail, or LOD, is chosen to represent the object. Since distant objects use coarser LODs, the total number of polygons is reduced and rendering speed increased. Because LODs are computed offline during preprocessing, the simplification process cannot predict from what direction the object will be viewed. The simplification therefore typically reduces detail uniformly across the object, and for this reason we sometimes refer to discrete LOD as *isotropic* or *view-independent LOD*.

Discrete LOD has many advantages. Decoupling simplification and rendering makes this the simplest model to program: the simplification algorithm can take as long as necessary to generate LODs and the run-time rendering algorithm simply needs to choose which LOD to render for each object. Furthermore, modern graphics hardware lends itself to the multiple model versions created by static level of detail, because individual LODs can be compiled during preprocessing to an optimal rendering format. For example, depending on the particular hardware targeted, developers may convert models to use features such as triangle strips, display lists, and vertex arrays. These will usually render much faster than simply rendering the LODs as an unordered list of polygons.

1.4.2 Continuous LOD

Continuous LOD[1] departs from the traditional discrete approach. Rather than creating individual LODs during the preprocessing stage, the simplification system creates a data structure encoding a continuous spectrum of detail. The desired level of detail is then extracted from this structure *at run-time*. A major advantage of this approach is better granularity: since the level of detail for each object is specified exactly rather than selected from a few precreated options, no more polygons than necessary are used. This frees up more polygons for rendering other objects, which in turn use only as many polygons as needed for the desired level of detail, freeing up more polygons for other objects, and so on. Better granularity thus leads to better use of resources and higher overall fidelity for a given polygon count. Continuous LOD also supports streaming of polygonal models, in which a simple base model is followed by a stream of refinements to be integrated dynamically. When large models must be loaded from disk or over a network, continuous LOD thus provides progressive rendering and interruptible loading—often very useful properties.

1.4.3 View-Dependent LOD

View-dependent LOD extends continuous LOD, using view-dependent simplification criteria to dynamically select the most appropriate level of detail *for the current view*. Thus view-dependent LOD is *anisotropic:* a single object can span multiple levels of simplification. For instance, nearby portions of the object may be shown at higher resolution than distant portions, or silhouette regions of the object shown at higher resolution than interior regions (Figures 1.3 and 1.4). This leads to still better granularity: polygons are allocated where they are most needed within objects, as well as among objects. This in turn leads to still better fidelity for a given polygon count, optimizing the distribution of this scarce resource.

Indeed, very complex models representing physically large objects, such as terrains, often cannot be adequately simplified without view-dependent techniques. Creating discrete LODs does not help: the viewpoint is typically quite close to part of the terrain and distant from other parts, so a high level of detail will provide good fidelity at unacceptable frame rates, while a low level of detail will provide

---

1. This class of algorithms is often termed "progressive LOD" after Hoppe's groundbreaking *progressive mesh* data structure [Hoppe 96]. However, we prefer the term "continuous LOD" to emphasize the contrast with "discrete LOD."

Figure 1.3   View-dependent LOD: a birds-eye view of a terrain model simplified in view-dependent fashion. The field of view is shown by the two lines. The model is displayed at full resolution near the viewpoint and at drastic simplification far away [Luebke 01a]. Copyright © 2001 IEEE.

good frame rates but terrible fidelity. Unsegmented or poorly segmented data, such as the skeleton extracted from an MRI scan shown in Figure 1.5, may also require view-dependent LOD. Here almost the entire data set forms one connected surface, preventing the use of discrete LODs to speed rendering and preserving detail in the area of interest. Another source of difficult models is scientific visualization, which tends to produce extremely large data sets that are rarely organized into conveniently sized objects. Again, view-dependent LOD can enable interactive rendering without manual intervention or extra processing for segmentation.

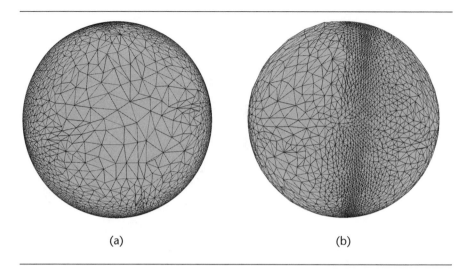

(a)   (b)

Figure 1.4   A sphere simplified with silhouette preservation, seen (a) head-on and (b) from the side. Note that the polygons facing away from the viewer, shown here for clarity, would typically be culled away by backface culling.

1.4.4 LOD IN PRACTICE

Despite advances in continuous and view-dependent LOD, traditional discrete LOD remains by far the most common approach in practice. View-dependent LOD, despite its advantages, also comes with some significant drawbacks. The extra processing required for evaluating, simplifying, and refining the model at run-time, and the extra memory required by the view-dependent data structures, steer many developers away from this approach. Video games, often the most demanding and tightly optimized of graphics applications, have been notably reluctant to adopt view-dependent LOD outside of situations that almost require it, such as terrain rendering. Continuous LOD also imposes a cost in processing and memory, but has fared somewhat better in game usage. For example, the Unreal game engine pictured in Figure 4.1 uses a continuous LOD scheme to manage player objects.

To summarize, the traditional static approach of creating multiple discrete LODs in a preprocess is simple and works best with most current graphics hardware. Continuous simplification supports progressive streaming of polygonal models and provides better granularity, which in turn can provide better fidelity. View-dependent simplification can provide even better fidelity for a given polygon count, and can handle models (such as terrains) containing very large or poorly segmented individual objects, but it increases the run-time processing and memory requirements. If the

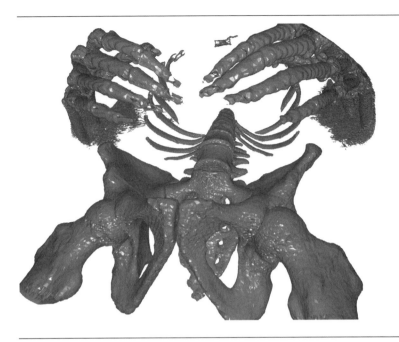

Figure 1.5   An isosurface generated from a medical visualization.

rendering system is CPU-bound, or memory is particularly tight, this additional load can decrease the frame rate and cut into the speedup provided by regulating level of detail.

1.5 POLYGONAL MESHES

The essential concepts of LOD management apply to any model representation. Polygonal meshes, splines, voxels, implicit surfaces, and even point- and image-based representations are all compatible with the notions of static, continuous, and view-dependent LOD. All of these representations are important for certain applications or problem domains. For example, 3D design systems ranging from mechanical engineering to character animation rely on nonuniform rational B-splines (NURBS). Medical visualization and scientific simulations often use volumetric models stored as voxels, while the QSplat system by Rusinkiewicz and Levoy applies view-dependent techniques to point-based rendering of massive scanned models [Rusinkiewicz 00]. However, the most common and important application of LOD remains the simplification of polygonal meshes.

Polygonal models currently dominate interactive 3D computer graphics. This is chiefly due to their mathematical simplicity: by providing a piecewise linear approximation to shape, polygonal meshes lend themselves to simple, regular rendering algorithms in which the visibility and colors of most pixels are determined by interpolating across the polygon's surface. Such algorithms embed well in hardware, which has in turn led to widely available polygon rendering accelerators for every platform. In addition, polygons serve as a sort of lowest common denominator for computer models, since most model representations (spline, implicit-surface, volumetric isosurface) may be converted with arbitrary accuracy to a polygonal mesh. For these and other reasons, polygonal models are the most common representation for every application from video games to visualization of medical, scientific, and CAD data sets. A great deal of LOD research has therefore focused on the specific problem of simplifying polygonal meshes.

Informally, we define a polygonal model as a collection of vertices and polygons that connect those vertices. This definition is intentionally loose; for example, we do not necessarily assume that all polygons form a single connected component, or that all edges between vertices are shared by two polygons. Most LOD algorithms actually simplify the problem by assuming that polygonal meshes have been fully triangulated. The constant memory requirements and guaranteed planarity of triangles make them preferable to generic polygons. We will often use "polygon" interchangeably with "triangle," or refer to polygonal models without making the additional distinction that most algorithms assume those models are triangulated. Polygon triangulation is a well-studied problem; we present one practical algorithm for triangulation in Chapter 5.

1.5.1 Topology

The treatment of mesh topology during simplification provides an important distinction among algorithms. First, a word on terminology: mesh topology is a formal and rigorous mathematical topic. For readability we have elected to use loose informal language when discussing topology in this book, and in particular have avoided the use of *simplicial complex* notation. For example, we prefer language such as "the set of triangles surrounding edge e" to the terser notation $\lceil\lceil\lfloor e\rfloor\rceil\rceil$. However, our definitions are of necessity less precise as a result, and the interested reader is encouraged to consult [Edelsbrunner 01a] for a good introduction to and a more rigorous treatment of this very important field.

With this disclaimer in mind, let us define a few terms: in the context of polygonal simplification, *topology* refers to the structure of the connected polygonal mesh. The *genus* is the number of holes in the mesh surface. For example, a sphere and a cube have a genus of zero, while a doughnut and a coffee cup have a genus of one. The *local topology* of a face, edge, or vertex refers to the connectivity of that feature's immediate neighborhood. The mesh forms a *2D manifold* if the local topology is everywhere equivalent to a disc, that is, if the neighborhood of every feature consists

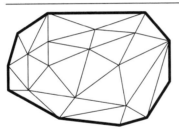

Figure 1.6   A 2D manifold with boundary (boundary edges bold). Each edge is shared by one or two triangles, and each vertex is shared by a connected ring of triangles.

of a connected ring of polygons forming a single surface. In a triangulated mesh displaying manifold topology, every edge is shared by exactly two triangles, and every triangle shares an edge with exactly three neighboring triangles. A *2D manifold with boundary* permits boundary edges, which belong to only one triangle (Figure 1.6).

Manifold meshes make for well-behaved models; virtually any simplification algorithm can successfully operate on a manifold object. Manifold meshes are also desirable for many other applications, such as finite element analysis (a common tool in engineering and scientific simulations) and radiosity (an illumination algorithm that computes shadows and interreflections between surfaces). Some algorithms and modeling packages are guaranteed to produce manifold output; for example, the Marching Cubes algorithm [Lorensen 87] can construct manifold isosurfaces (such as the skeletal model pictured in Figure 1.5) from volumetric data. Unfortunately, many models encountered in actual practice are not perfectly manifold, with topological flaws such as cracks, T-junctions, and nonmanifold points or edges (Figure 1.7). These problematic defects are particularly common in handmade models, such as those created by artists for a video game, or engineers in a CAD system.

A *topology-preserving* simplification algorithm preserves manifold connectivity at every step. Such algorithms do not close holes in the mesh, and therefore preserve the overall genus. Since no holes are appearing or disappearing during simplification, the visual fidelity of the simplified object tends to be relatively good. This constraint limits the simplification possible, however, since objects of high genus cannot be simplified below a certain number of polygons without closing holes in the model (Figure 1.8). Nor can a topology-preserving algorithm eliminate or merge small objects, since both operations would violate the manifold connectivity property. A topology-preserving approach also presumes that the initial mesh has manifold topology. Some algorithms are *topology tolerant:* they ignore regions in the mesh with nonmanifold local topology, leaving those regions unsimplified. Other algorithms, faced with nonmanifold regions, may simply fail.

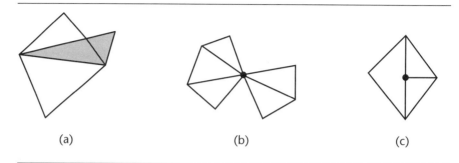

Figure 1.7   Examples of nonmanifold meshes: (a) An edge shared by three triangles. (b) A vertex shared by two otherwise unconnected sets of triangles. (c) A *T-junction*, in which the edge of one triangle is spanned by edges from two other triangles.

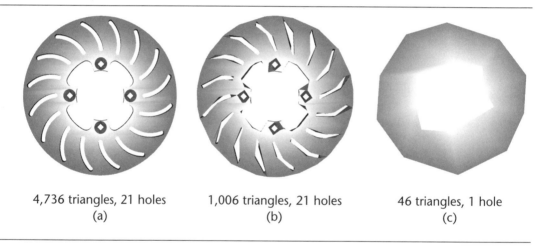

| 4,736 triangles, 21 holes | 1,006 triangles, 21 holes | 46 triangles, 1 hole |
| (a) | (b) | (c) |

Figure 1.8   Preserving genus limits drastic simplification. (a) The original model of a brake rotor is shown (b) simplified with a topology-preserving algorithm and (c) a topology-modifying algorithm [Luebke 01a]. Copyright © 2001 IEEE. Courtesy Alpha_1 Project, University of Utah.

Topology-modifying algorithms do not necessarily preserve manifold topology. The algorithms can therefore close up holes in the model and aggregate separate objects into assemblies as simplification progresses, permitting drastic simplification beyond the scope of topology-preserving schemes. This drastic simplification often comes at the price of poor visual fidelity, and distracting popping artifacts as holes appear and disappear from one LOD to the next. Most topology-modifying algorithms do not require valid topology in the initial mesh, which greatly increases their utility in real-world CAD applications. Some topology-modifying algorithms attempt to regulate the change in topology, but many are *topology-insensitive*, paying no heed to the initial mesh connectivity at all.

As a rule, topology-preserving algorithms work best when visual fidelity is crucial, or with an application such as finite element analysis, in which surface topology can affect results. Preserving topology also simplifies some applications, such as multiresolution surface editing, which require a correspondence between high- and low-detail representations of an object. Real-time visualization of very complex scenes, however, requires drastic simplification, and here topology-modifying algorithms have the edge. We will return to the questions of when and how to modify topology in Section 2.3.

1.6 Fidelity Metrics

Methods for creating LODs can also be characterized by how they use a fidelity metric to guide simplification. Many early algorithms used no metric at all, but instead required the user to run the algorithm with different settings and manually decide when each LOD should represent the original object. For large databases, however, this degree of user intervention is simply not practical. Those algorithms that regulate simplification with a fidelity metric fall into two categories. *Fidelity-based simplification* techniques allow the user to specify the desired fidelity of the simplification in some form, and then attempt to minimize the number of polygons without violating that fidelity constraint. *Budget-based simplification* techniques allow the user to specify a target number of polygons or vertices, and attempt to maximize the fidelity of the simplified model without exceeding the specified budget.

To be most useful, an LOD algorithm needs to support both fidelity- and budget-based operation. Fidelity-based approaches are important for generating accurate images, whereas budget-based approaches are crucial for time-critical rendering. The user may well require both of these tasks in the same system.

Of course, how to measure fidelity is a profound question to which much of this book is devoted. Most algorithms to date have considered various measures of the geometric error introduced by simplification; some also consider the effect of simplification on surface attributes such as colors, normals, and texture coordinates. Chapter 3 examines such error metrics in detail. However, often the crucial measure of fidelity is not geometric but perceptual: does the simplification *look* like the original? We return to this higher-level question in Part III of the book, which considers advanced perceptual issues in LOD management.

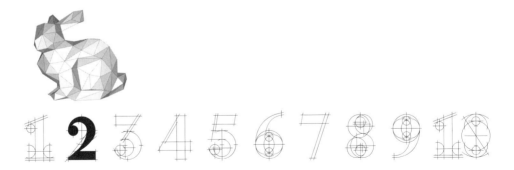

MESH
SIMPLIFICATION

This chapter provides a high-level overview of various mesh simplification algorithms. We describe mesh simplification as an optimization process under fidelity-based or triangle–budget-based constraints, to be achieved by the application of local and global mesh simplification operators. Local operators simplify the geometry and connectivity in a local region of the mesh, reducing the number of polygons, while global operators operate over much larger regions and help simplify the mesh topology. We also briefly address the desirability of topology simplification for different applications. After describing the range of mesh simplification operators available, we conclude with a discussion of the various optimization frameworks in which these operators are chosen and applied to the mesh.

2.1 OVERVIEW

A mesh in 3D graphics has two components: the *mesh geometry*, represented by the vertices, and the *mesh connectivity*, represented by the edges or faces that connect the vertices. The mesh connectivity encodes the topology of the mesh, that is, the number of holes, tunnels, and cavities in that mesh. Simplification of the mesh geometry may or may not result in simplification of the mesh topology.

Before we start describing the various approaches to the simplification of mesh geometry, we should reemphasize that algorithms for mesh simplification deal almost exclusively with triangle meshes. If your mesh is composed of nontriangulated polygons, you will almost certainly wish to triangulate them in a preprocessing step. Many triangulation algorithms exist; one example is Seidel's incremental randomized algorithm to triangulate a non–self-intersecting polygon with n vertices in time $O(nlog^*n)$ [Seidel 91]. We describe this algorithm at a high level in Chapter 5 and include source code by Narkhede and Manocha on this books' accompanying Web site [Narkhede 95]. O'Rourke provides an excellent introduction to the topic of triangulation algorithms for the interested reader [O'Rourke 94].

2.1.1 FIDELITY-BASED SIMPLIFICATION

In fidelity-based simplification the user provides a fidelity constraint that the simplified mesh must satisfy with respect to the original input mesh. The simplification algorithm then generates a simplified mesh, attempting to minimize the number of triangles while respecting the fidelity constraint. The simplifications that these methods produce are typically best suited for applications in which visual fidelity is more important than interactivity. The fidelity constraint is usually specified as some measure of the difference between the simplified mesh and the input mesh, denoted by the simplification error ϵ. This error can be measured many ways; Chapter 3 discusses various error metrics in detail. Solving this minimization problem optimally is suspected to be NP-hard. Graphics practitioners therefore settle for algorithms that generate mesh simplifications with a small (instead of the minimum) number of triangles that satisfy the given error tolerance ϵ.

Given a fidelity-based simplification algorithm, one can generate successive simplifications, for example with errors of ϵ, 2ϵ, 4ϵ, 8ϵ, and so on. LOD management techniques (described in Part II of this book) can then be used to assess the permissible rendering error for an object at run time, and determine the appropriate level of detail for rendering.

2.1.2 BUDGET-BASED SIMPLIFICATION

In budget-based simplification the user specifies the maximum number of triangles, and the algorithm attempts to minimize the error ϵ without exceeding that constraint. Since this approach allows us to generate a fixed number of triangles, it is appropriate for time-critical applications where a desired frame rate dictates the per-frame triangle budget. Thus, this approach is often used for applications where interactivity is paramount. Since the error ϵ is not controllable by the end user, this approach does not guarantee visual fidelity. Solving the budget-based simplification problem optimally is also difficult. Comparisons across different budget-based algorithms are often based on empirical observations on a few data sets that have become de facto benchmarks in the field. We will return to the topic of evaluating visual fidelity in Chapter 9.

2.2 LOCAL SIMPLIFICATION OPERATORS

In this section we discuss the various low-level local operators that have been used for simplification of meshes. Each of these operators reduces the complexity of a mesh by some small amount. Section 2.4 will describe how to combine these low-level operators into a high-level simplification algorithm.

2.2.1 EDGE COLLAPSE

Hoppe first proposed using the *edge collapse* operator for mesh simplification [Hoppe 93]. This operator collapses an edge (v_a, v_b) to a single vertex v_{new}. This causes the removal of the edge (v_a, v_b) as well as the triangles spanning that edge. The inverse operator of an edge collapse is a *vertex split,* which adds the edge (v_a, v_b) and the triangles adjacent to it. Thus, the edge collapse operator simplifies a mesh and the vertex split operator adds detail to the mesh. Figure 2.1 illustrates the edge collapse operator and its inverse, the vertex split.

The edge collapse operator has been widely used in view-independent simplification [Hoppe 96], view-dependent simplification [Xia 96] [Hoppe 97], progressive compression [Bajaj 99], as well as progressive transmission [Bajaj 99] [Guéziec 99b]. There are two variants of the edge collapse operator: *half-edge collapse* and *full-edge collapse.* In the half-edge collapse (Figure 2.2), the vertex to which the edge collapses to is one of its end points, that is, $v_{new} = v_a$ or v_b. In the more general full-edge collapse (often abbreviated as simply edge collapse) the collapsed vertex v_{new} may be a newly computed vertex.

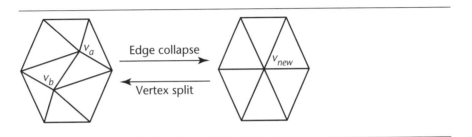

Figure 2.1   An edge collapse and its inverse vertex split.

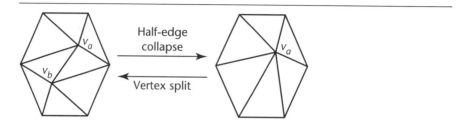

Figure 2.2   A half-edge collapse and its vertex split inverse.

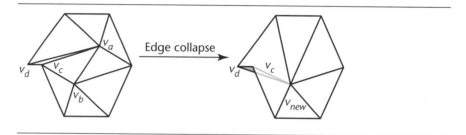

Figure 2.3   A mesh foldover arising from an edge collapse.

Although the edge collapse operator is simple to implement, care must be taken not to apply an edge collapse if it would cause a mesh foldover or a topological inconsistency, as described in the next section.

Mesh Foldover

Mesh foldovers are an undesirable side effect of some edge collapses [Xia 97]. In Figure 2.3, consider the triangle (v_d, v_c, v_a). When the edge (v_a, v_b) collapses to the new vertex v_{new}, the mesh around the vertex v_{new} gets a folded crease or a foldover due to the newly created triangle (v_d, v_c, v_{new}). This can be detected by measuring the change in the normals of the corresponding triangles before and after an edge collapse: a mesh foldover is characterized by a large change in the angle of the normal, usually greater than 90°. Mesh foldovers result in visual artifacts, such as illumination and texture discontinuities, where none existed before.

Topological Inconsistency

If the neighborhoods of vertices v_a and v_b share three or more vertices (as shown in Figure 2.4), the collapse of the edge (v_a, v_b) will create one or more nonmanifold

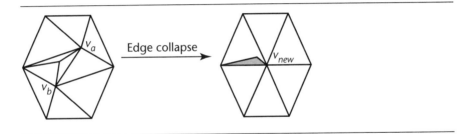

Figure 2.4   A manifold mesh becoming nonmanifold due to an edge collapse.

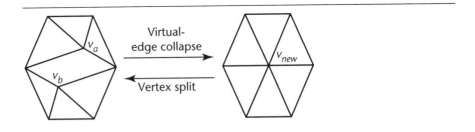

Figure 2.5   Virtual-edge or vertex-pair collapse.

edges. Nonmanifold edges have one, three, or more adjacent triangles; since many algorithms rely on manifold connectivity, introducing such edges can create problems later in the simplification process.

2.2.2 VERTEX-PAIR COLLAPSE

A *vertex-pair collapse* operator [Schroeder 97] [Garland 97] [Popovic 97] [El-Sana 99a] collapses two unconnected vertices v_a and v_b. Since these vertices do not share an edge, no triangles are removed by a vertex-pair collapse, but the triangles surrounding v_a and v_b are updated as if an imaginary edge connecting v_a and v_b underwent an edge collapse (Figure 2.5). For this reason, the vertex-pair collapse operator has also been referred to as a *virtual-edge* collapse. Collapsing unconnected vertices enables connection of unconnected components as well as closing of holes and tunnels.

In general, for a mesh with n vertices there can be potentially $O(n^2)$ virtual edges, so an algorithm that considers all possible virtual edges will run slowly. Most of the topology simplification algorithms that rely on virtual-edge collapses therefore use some heuristic to limit the candidate virtual edges to a small number. One such heuristic chooses virtual edges only between nearby vertices, considering virtual-edge collapses from each vertex v_a to all vertices within a small distance δ from v_a

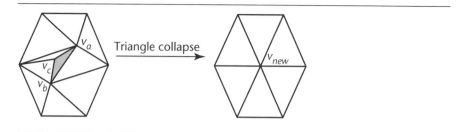

Figure 2.6   A triangle collapse operator.

[Garland 97] [El-Sana 99a]. In practice this reduces the number of candidate edges to a linear factor of the model size, though care must be taken to choose δ small enough.

2.2.3 TRIANGLE COLLAPSE

A triangle collapse operator simplifies a mesh by collapsing a triangle (v_a, v_b, v_c) to a single vertex v_{new} [Hamann 94] [Gieng 98]. The edges that define the neighborhood of v_{new} are the union of edges of the vertices v_a, v_b, and v_c. The vertex v_{new} to which the triangle collapses can be either one of v_a, v_b, or v_c or a newly computed vertex. This is shown in Figure 2.6. A triangle collapse is equivalent to two edge collapses. A triangle collapse-based hierarchy is shallower than an equivalent edge collapse-based hierarchy and thus requires less memory. However, triangle collapse hierarchies are also less adaptable, since the triangle collapse is a less fine-grained operation than an edge collapse.

2.2.4 CELL COLLAPSE

The cell collapse operator simplifies the input mesh by collapsing all the vertices in a certain volume, or cell, to a single vertex. The cell undergoing collapse could belong to a grid [Rossignac 93], or a spatial subdivision such as an octree [Luebke 97], or could simply be defined as a volume in space [Low 97]. The single vertex to which the cell collapses could be chosen from one of the collapsed vertices or newly computed as some form of average of the collapsed vertices.

We present the cell collapse operator here following the discussion in [Rossignac 93]. Consider a triangle mesh object as shown in Figure 2.7(a). The vertices of the mesh are placed in a regular grid. All the vertices that fall in the same grid cell are then unified into a single vertex. The vertices are identified in Figure 2.7(b). All triangles of the original mesh that have two or three of their vertices in a single cell are either simplified to a single edge or a single vertex. This is shown in Figure 2.7(c). The final mesh is shown in Figure 2.7(d). Note that such a simplification does not preserve

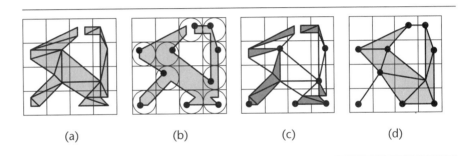

(a)   (b)   (c)   (d)

Figure 2.7   A cell collapse. (a) A regular grid classifies the vertices. (b) A single vertex is selected to represent all vertices within each cell. (c) Triangles with 2 or 3 corner vertices in the same cell simplify to a single edge or vertex, respectively. (d) The final simplification [Rossignac 92].

the topology of the input mesh, and that the level of simplification depends on the resolution of the grid.

2.2.5 VERTEX REMOVAL

The vertex removal operator removes a vertex, along with its adjacent edges and triangles, and triangulates the resulting hole. Schroeder et al. [Schroeder 92] were the first to propose this approach. As shown by Klein and Kramer [Klein 97], triangulation of the hole in the mesh resulting from removal of the vertex v can be accomplished in several ways and one of these triangulations is the same as a half-edge collapse involving the vertex v. In this respect at least, the vertex removal operator may be considered to be a generalization of the half-edge collapse operator. Figure 2.8 illustrates such a vertex removal operation.

As an aside, the number of possible ways to fill such a hole (i.e., to triangulate a polygon) is bounded by the elements of the *Catalan sequence* [Dörrie 65] [Plouffe 95]:

$$C(i) = \frac{1}{i+1} * \binom{2i}{i} = \frac{1}{i+1} * \frac{(2i)!}{i!(2i-i)!} = \frac{1}{i+1} * \frac{(2i)!}{i!i!} = \frac{(2i)!}{(i+1)!i!}$$

$C(i)$ is the number of ways to fill a convex, planar hole with $i+2$ sides. We can think of choosing from among these possible ways as a discrete optimization problem.

2.2.6 POLYGON MERGING

In one of the earliest papers on simplification, Hinker and Hansen [Hinker 93] proposed merging nearly coplanar and adjacent polygons into larger polygons, which

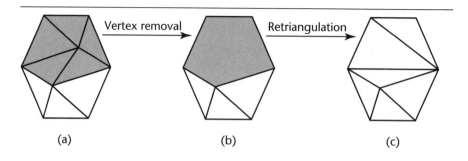

Figure 2.8   A vertex removal operation. (a) A vertex *va* is chosen for removal. (b) The vertex and all surrounding triangles are removed, leaving a hole in the mesh. (c) The hole is retriangulated with two fewer triangles than the original mesh.

are then triangulated. As an example, we can consider the shaded triangles in Figure 2.8(a) to have been merged in (b) and then retriangulated in (c). Polygon merging is, however, more general than vertex removal since it can combine polygons (not just triangles), can result in removal of several vertices at once, and may even result in merged polygons with holes. Polygon merging as a simplification operator has been used in different applications under different names, such as *superfaces* [Kalvin 96] and *face clustering* [Garland 01]. Figure 2.9 illustrates face clustering from [Garland 01].[1]

2.2.7   GENERAL GEOMETRIC REPLACEMENT

The general geometric replacement operator proceeds by replacing a subset of adjacent triangles by another set of (simplified) triangles, such that their boundaries are the same. DeFloriani et al. [DeFloriani 97] [DeFloriani 98] have proposed this operator (they call it the *multi-triangulation*), which is the most general of the mesh simplification operators. It can encode edge collapses and vertex removals. It can also encode an edge flip, in which the common edge between two triangles is replaced by another edge that joins the two other opposite vertices. It has been shown that edge collapses and edge flips are sufficient to generate any simplification of mesh geometry and hence the general geometric replacement operator suffices for encoding all mesh

---

1. Garland et al. [Garland 01] consider face clustering to be the graph dual of the edge collapse operator. This concept involves the graph-theoretic dual of a triangle mesh, in which the triangles correspond to the nodes and the vertices correspond to the faces. An edge connects two nodes if the corresponding triangles in the original mesh shared an edge. Therefore, an edge collapse operator in the primal representation will correspond to a face-clustering operator in its dual representation.

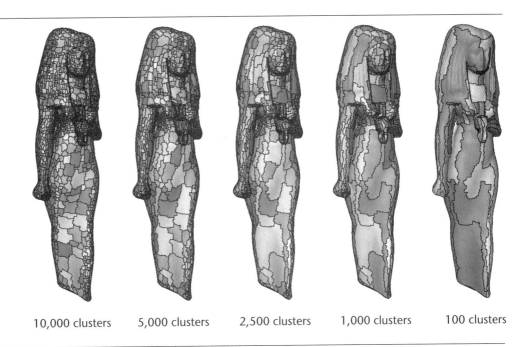

10,000 clusters	5,000 clusters	2,500 clusters	1,000 clusters	100 clusters

Figure 2.9   Face clustering simplifications [Garland 01]. Copyright © 2001 Association for Computing Machinery, Inc.

geometry simplifications. This general operator can even be used to replace geometry of one primitive type with geometry of another primitive type. For example, Cohen et al. [Cohen 01] use this operator to describe the substitution of point primitives for triangles primitives.

2.2.8   COMPARING THE LOCAL SIMPLIFICATION OPERATORS

The collapse operators (edge collapse, triangle collapse, and cell collapse) are the simplest to implement. Further, since they can be conceptualized as gradually shrinking the appropriate geometric primitive (edge, triangle, or cell, respectively) to a single vertex, they are well suited for implementing *geomorphing* between successive levels of detail (see Section 4.4.2).

The full-edge collapse operator has greater flexibility in determining the new vertex after edge collapse than the half-edge collapse operator, and in practice, this means that one can compute higher-fidelity simplifications using full-edge collapses than using half-edge collapses. However, the advantage of the half-edge collapse operator is that the vertices of the simplified mesh are a subset of the high-detail input mesh. This simplifies the bookkeeping associated with keeping track of the vertices and results in substantial storage savings since no new vertices must be stored. Finally, the number of triangles modified by a half-edge collapse is smaller than the number modified by a full-edge collapse. This may lead to more efficient simplification since fewer triangles need to be updated.

The cell collapse operator has many advantages: it provides both geometry and topology simplification, it is robust, and it is very simple to implement. The cell collapse also has disadvantages. First, it is not invariant with respect to rotation and translation, meaning that an object may be simplified differently depending on its rotation and positioning, since different parts of the object will end up in different grid cells. Second, cell collapse does not simplify topology in a controlled fashion. For example, a small hole that happens to span a cell boundary may be magnified, but if the same hole falls entirely within a cell, it will disappear. We expand on these difficulties in Section 5.1, but despite these disadvantages the cell collapse operator has much to recommend it.

The vertex removal operator requires somewhat more effort than the collapse operators to implement correctly, since it involves triangulating a hole in 3D. Schroeder et al. describe a recursive loop-splitting method for triangulation [Schroeder 92]. If the 3D hole can be projected without self-intersections onto a 2D plane, an algorithm such as Seidel's randomized method [Seidel 91] may be used for its triangulation. There are several publicly available LOD algorithms based on the vertex removal operator, such as the *Visualization ToolKit* or *VTK* [Schroeder 98] that may serve as a good starting point for the practitioner. The implementation of the general geometric replacement operator takes slightly more effort to capture its full generality, but once implemented offers great flexibility.

The vertex removal operator and the edge collapse operator each have their strengths and weaknesses, but neither is strictly more powerful than the other. Each can produce triangle meshes that the other cannot. Computing the new output vertex of an edge collapse is a continuous optimization problem, whereas choosing from among the possible ways to fill the hole after a vertex removal is a discrete optimization problem. The number of triangles affected by the vertex removal operation is smaller than that of the edge collapse (i.e., those triangles surrounding one vertex as opposed to two), which may be relevant if coherence of the set of primitives rendered from frame to frame is valued. It is interesting to note that there is a subset of the possible edge collapse operations that are equivalent to a subset of the possible vertex removal operations. This common subset is the set of half-edge collapses, which share some of the properties of each of the other two operation types.

2.3 GLOBAL SIMPLIFICATION OPERATORS

The global simplification operators modify the topology of the mesh in a controlled fashion. Since they tend to be more complex than the local simplification operators, which only consider a small portion of the model, our discussion will necessarily be at a higher level. If you do not need to modify topology, you may wish to skip ahead to Section 2.4 on simplification frameworks.

The global simplification operators include methods based on volumetric, digital signal processing [He 96] [Nooruddin 99], Delaunay tetrahedralization and alpha hulls [Edelsbrunner 83] [Edelsbrunner 94] [Popovic 97] [El-Sana 98], and more recently on filtration methods grounded in Morse theory [Edelsbrunner 00] [Wood 01] [Edelsbrunner 01b].

2.3.1 VOLUME PROCESSING

Two schemes have been proposed for simplification of the topology in the volumetric domain [He 96] [Nooruddin 99]. Both schemes proceed by first *voxelizing,* or converting the input objects into a volumetric grid, followed by application of the topology simplifying operations in the volumetric domain, and finally, using an isosurface extraction method to convert the volumetric densities into a triangle mesh. The topology simplifying operators used in the middle stage are low-pass filtering [He 96] and morphological operations of dilation and erosion [Nooruddin 99].

Low-Pass Filtering

He et al. introduced the first algorithm [He 96] to simplify the topology of an input model in the volumetric domain. Their approach first converts the input object into a volumetric data set using an approach such as the one by Wang and Kaufman [Wang 93]. This approach places a filter at each grid value and computes the intersection of the geometric primitive with the extent of the filter kernel. This intersection amount produces a filtered density value for each voxel, enabling data sets derived from polygonal meshes and implicit functions to be treated in the same manner as innate volumetric data sets such as those from CT or MRI scans. Wang and Kaufman's method generates reasonable results for all classes of objects outlined above, but works best for objects that represent volumes with no sharp discontinuities or corners.

The approach of He et al. proceeds by applying a low-pass filter to each of the grid values of the volumetric buffer. Low-pass filtering eliminates fine details in the volumetric model, including topological features such as small holes and tunnels. This is followed by isosurface reconstruction using a method such as the *marching cubes* algorithm [Lorensen 87]. Marching cubes approximates an isosurface by determining its intersections with edges of every voxel in the volume buffer. Up to five triangles are used to approximate the surface within a voxel. Figure 2.10 shows the results of topology simplification using this approach.

From a signal-theoretic point of view, a lower sampling resolution of the volume corresponds to a lower Nyquist frequency, and therefore requires a low-pass filter with wider support for a good approximation. This direct correspondence between the size of the filter support and the resolution of the volume leads to a hierarchical

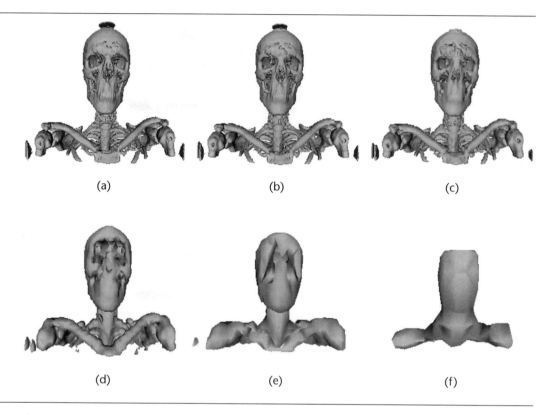

Figure 2.10   LODs of a medical isosurface using volume-domain topology simplifications: (a) 334K triangles, (b) 181K triangles, (c) 76K triangles, (d) 17K triangles, (e) 3K triangles, and (f) 568 triangles [He 96]. Copyright © 1996 IEEE.

representation of the model. The base of such a hierarchy contains the most detailed and the highest resolution version of the object. As one moves up the hierarchy, low-pass filters with wider support are applied, and the top contains the least detailed version of the object. Convolving the original object with a low-pass filter of an appropriate support creates each level of the simplification hierarchy, which in turn is used to create a polygonal LOD. This avoids error propagation from one stage of the simplified volume to the next. A wide variety of low-pass filters can be used, such as the hypercone and the Gaussian.

Morphological Operators

Nooruddin and Turk [Nooruddin 99] describe a different scheme for topology simplification in the volumetric domain. Their scheme voxelizes the input model into

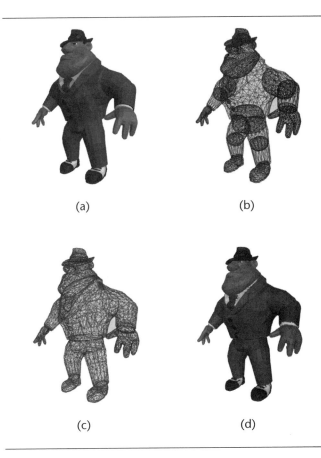

(a)   (b)

(c)   (d)

Figure 2.11   Merging multiple components of the Al Capone model: (a) original model, (b) wire-frame of the original model, (c) wireframe of the model after conversion to a single manifold, and (d) filled rendering of the single manifold model [Nooruddin 99]. Copyright © 1999 Graphics, Visualization, & Usability Center, Georgia Institute of Technology.

a volumetric data set using a parity-count scheme for a single component polygonal model, or a ray stabbing method for polygonal models with multiple intersecting components. The results of voxelization using ray stabbing are shown in Figure 2.11. Note how cleanly this method converts 15 intersecting components into a single manifold.

The next step in Nooruddin and Turk's algorithm is to build a distance field on the volumetric model. Their distance field associates with each voxel a distance to the nearest voxel that lies inside the object. After this, the morphological operators of *erosion* and *dilation* [Jain 89] are applied on the distance field. In the dilation operator with a threshold T, any voxel that has a distance less than the value T is reclassified as being inside the object. Thus, this process effectively ends up enlarging the object, filling up its holes, and connecting the disconnected components that lie within a distance T. The erosion operator is the complement of the dilation operator and ends up shrinking the object. A dilation operator followed by an erosion operator will result in a topologically simplified object with the same dimensions as the original.

Once the model has been simplified in the volumetric domain, the isosurface is extracted using marching cubes. This is followed by a geometry simplification stage in which an algorithm such as *QSlim* by Garland and Heckbert [Garland 97] is used (see Section 5.3). The advantage of this approach is that the dilation and erosion operators are very precise and can be used to control very finely the level of topological simplification of the object. Figure 2.12 shows the results of this approach. Note how well the morphological operators preserve the shape of the model while simplifying the topological detail as shown in Figure 2.12(c), compared with directly simplifying the geometry as shown in Figure 2.12(d).

2.3.2 ALPHA-HULL—BASED TOPOLOGY SIMPLIFICATIONS

Controlled simplification of mesh topology can also be accomplished using the concept of *alpha hulls*. These are best illustrated with a somewhat fanciful example.

Consider a set of points P embedded inside a block made out of styrofoam. Now, you are given a spherical eraser of radius α and you are asked to erase away as much of the styrofoam as possible. The only constraint is that the eraser cannot overlap any point in P. The resulting mass of styrofoam left over after such an erasing process will correspond to an α-*hull* over P. When the value of $\alpha = 0$, the α-hull consists of exactly the points of P. As the value of α is increased from 0, the topological complexity of the α-hull gradually decreases. When $\alpha = \infty$ our spherical eraser becomes a half-plane and the α-hull becomes the convex hull over P. Alpha hulls have been widely used in a number of applications, including reconstruction of surfaces from point data [Bajaj 97] and computation and display of molecular surfaces [Varshney 94b]. For a mathematically precise description of 2D and 3D alpha hulls, see [Edelsbrunner 83] and [Edelsbrunner 94].

El-Sana and Varshney [El-Sana 98] have developed a method to simplify the polygonal meshes by generalizing the concept of α-hulls over polygonal objects. The intuitive idea underlying this approach is to simplify the genus of a polygonal object by rolling a sphere of radius α over it and filling up all the regions that are not accessible to the sphere. Bajaj and Kim [Bajaj 88] have nicely worked out the problem of planning the motion of a sphere amidst polyhedral obstacles in 3D. They show that planning the motion of a sphere S of radius α among triangles is equivalent to planning the motion of a point among triangles "grown" by the radius of the sphere. Mathematically, a grown triangle $T_i(\alpha)$ is the Minkowski sum of the original triangle t_i with the sphere $S(\alpha)$. Formally, $T_i(\alpha) = t_i \oplus S(\alpha)$, where $\oplus$ denotes the Minkowski sum, which is equivalent to the convolution operation. The boundary of $\cup_{i=1}^{n} T_i(\alpha)$, where n is the number of triangles in the data set, will represent the locus of the

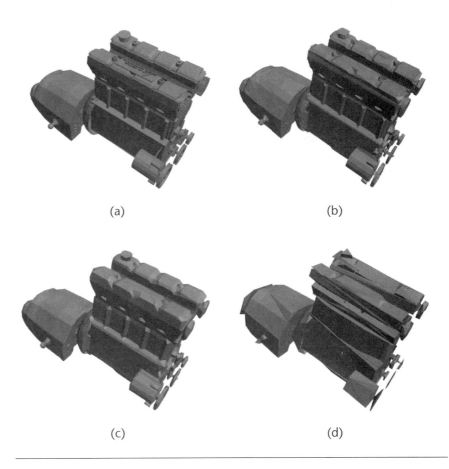

(a)   (b)

(c)   (d)

Figure 2.12   Topology simplifications using morphological operators: (a) original model of a car motor (140K faces), (b) topology simplified (5K faces), (c) geometry of part further simplified by Qslim (3.3K faces), and (d) original model directly simplified by *QSlim* (3.3K faces) [Nooruddin 99]. Copyright © 1999 Graphics, Visualization, & Usability Center, Georgia Institute of Technology.

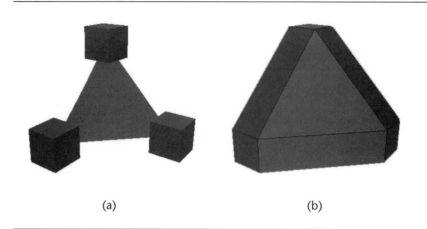

(a)   (b)

Figure 2.13   Convolving a triangle with L_∞ cube in (a) to generate a *grown* triangle convex polyhedron in (b) [El-Sana 98]. Copyright © 1998 IEEE.

center of the sphere as it is rolled in contact with one or more triangles and can be
used in the topology simplification stage. Computing the union of $T_i(\alpha)$, $1 \le i \le n$
can be simplified by considering the offsetting operation in the L_1 or the L_∞ distance
metrics instead of the L_2 distance metric. This is equivalent to convolving the triangle
t_i with an oriented cube (which is the constant distance primitive in the L_1 or the L_∞
metrics, just as a sphere is in the L_2 metric). Each resulting grown triangle forms a
convex polyhedron $T_i(\alpha)$ (Figure 2.13).

Computing the union of the convex polyhedra $T_i(\alpha)$ can be computed from
pairwise intersections. Intersection of two convex polyhedra with p and q vertices
can be accomplished in optimal time $O(p + q)$ [Chazelle 92]. A simpler algorithm to
implement takes time $O((p + q) \log(p + q))$ [Muller 78].

Figure 2.14 provides an overview of the stages involved in this approach. Consider
a hole *abcde* in the mesh shown in Figure 2.14(a). First, we generate the α-grown
triangles in the region of interest (in this case the triangles bordering the hole) and
compute their union (Figure 2.14(b)). Second, this union is used to generate a valid
surface triangulation (Figure 2.14(c)). The result of this process as shown for this
example adds an extra triangle *abe* in the interior of the region *abcde*. This extra
triangle is added in the region where the oriented L_∞ cube of side α could not pass
through.

Although this approach can work on any region of the triangulated mesh, it can
also be selectively applied in the neighborhood of holes. Such holes can be detected
using heuristics, such as finding adjacent triangles which meet at an angle greater
than some threshold (say 70°). Figure 2.15 shows an example in which a hole is filled,
internal triangles detected and deleted, and finally a geometry-simplification stage
yields a simple cube. Another example appears in Figure 2.16.

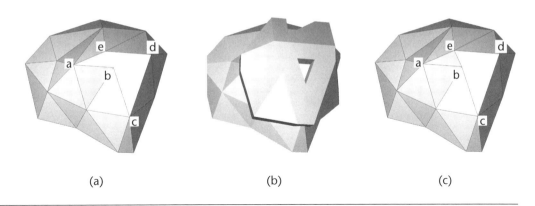

(a)　　　　　　　　　　(b)　　　　　　　　　　(c)

Figure 2.14　Topology simplifications by using generalized α-hulls: (a) original mesh, (b) α-grown triangles, and (c) partially filled mesh [El-Sana 98]. Copyright © 1998 IEEE.

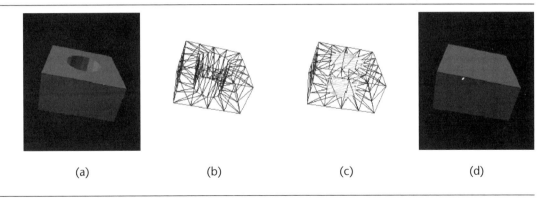

(a)　　　　　　(b)　　　　　　(c)　　　　　　(d)

Figure 2.15　Explicit detection and filling up of holes whose radii are less than threshold α [El-Sana 98]. Copyright © 1998 IEEE.

Let us reconsider the concept of α-hulls in three dimensions. With an increasing value of α, larger and larger concave regions in the external surface get progressively "filled." Finally, when $\alpha = \infty$, all concavities in the external surface are filled and the α-hull is the convex hull of the input points. This leads to the question, what would happen if the sphere were being rolled from inside the object instead of outside? The answer is evident in Figure 2.17—all the protuberances and convexities of the surface are progressively simplified. In the implementation, the rolling of an α-sphere or α-cube on the interior as opposed to the exterior is accomplished by simply inverting the normals of every triangle in the polygonal model, conceptually turning the object inside out.

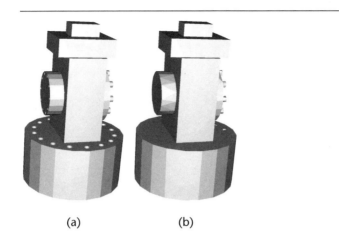

(a)   (b)

Figure 2.16   Topology simplification for a mechanical CAD part: (a) 5180 triangles and (b) 1438 triangles [El-Sana 98]. Copyright © 1998 IEEE.

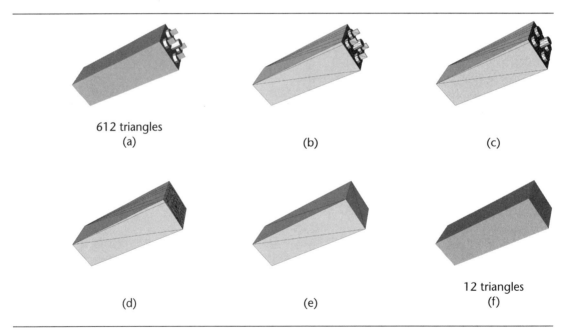

612 triangles
(a)   (b)   (c)

(d)   (e)

12 triangles
(f)

Figure 2.17   (a–f) Alternating simplification of the protuberances and geometry [El-Sana 98]. Copyright © 1998 IEEE.

Figure 2.18   A topology-preserving LOD hierarchy for a rotor from a brake assembly [Cohen 96].
Copyright © 1996 Association for Computing Machinery, Inc.

2.3.3 WHEN IS TOPOLOGY SIMPLIFICATION DESIRABLE?

Topology simplification is compelling—indeed, often vital—for interactive visualization applications. As an example, we return to the brake rotor shown in Figure 1.8. Consider the topology-preserving LODs of this rotor created by the simplification envelopes approach [Cohen 96] shown in Figure 2.18. The closest rotor has 4700 triangles and the farthest rotor has about 1000 triangles. Most of the triangles in the farthest rotor are used for representing the 21 holes in the rotor even though barely one hole is visible. For this example, if the topology for the farthest rotor were simplified to a single hole, it will permit a much more aggressive geometric simplification without sacrificing visual realism. Topology simplifications of sub-pixel holes may also help reduce aliasing artifacts, effectively removing details that will be undersampled.

2.3.4 WHEN IS TOPOLOGY SIMPLIFICATION UNACCEPTABLE?

There are several applications when simplification of the topology is undesirable and leads to unacceptable changes in the structure of the object. For example, topological structures are often of great interest in the study of protein structure and function. For instance, ion-transport channels are highly susceptible to small changes in side chains that border such channels. An example of Gramicidin A, a peptide antibiotic, is shown in Figure 2.19 with a channel. This channel is important for the transport of ions and water molecules across lipid membranes [Edelsbrunner 00]. The figure

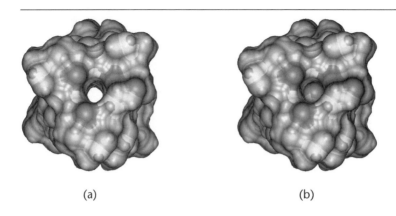

(a)   (b)

Figure 2.19   Gramicidin A's channel accessibility for (a) probe radius < 1.38 Å, and (b) probe radius > 1.38 Å.

shows the accessibility for molecules or ions with radii less than 1.38 Å on the left and greater than 1.38 Å on the right. Topological simplifications for such mesh data sets will obviously lead to the loss of important structural information, such as the channel, and should not be attempted.

Analysis of mechanical CAD models provides another example where unrestricted topological simplification may be undesirable. Finite element analysis to determine the strength or stress at different parts of a mechanical part might require continued presence of certain topological structures such as holes and voids. Topological simplification of such structures may sometimes drastically alter the results of such simulations and should therefore be avoided. Study of tolerances in mechanical CAD also requires that the topology of the models not be simplified. Similarly, in medical imaging the data collected from computer-aided tomography (CT) or magnetic resonance imaging (MRI) scans often have important topological structures that are better left in the data, rather than simplified away. In applications such as these, it is important for an application domain expert to guide the process of topological simplification.

2.4 SIMPLIFICATION FRAMEWORKS

Having described local and global simplification operators, we now turn to the high-level algorithmic framework in which these operators are applied. A typical goal of simplification is to create a hierarchy of meshes with varying numbers of polygons. Most hierarchy-building algorithms can be classified as *top-down* or *bottom-up*. To use tree terminology, top-down approaches start from the root of the hierarchy and work toward the leaves. For polygon simplification, this top-down scheme starts from

```
1  for each level of hierarchy
2      for each possible independent operation op
3          ApplyOp(op)
```

Figure 2.20   The nonoptimizing queuing algorithm for ordering mesh operations.

a simplified version of the mesh and then progressively adds more detail to it by following some refinement rules. Methods such as subdivision surfaces [Catmull 74] and wavelets for meshes [Eck 95] follow this approach. This approach has also been used for simplifying terrains [Fowler 79], and occasionally for more general polygon meshes [Brodsky 00].

Bottom-up approaches start from the leaves of the hierarchy and work upward toward the root. The bottom-up polygon simplification schemes start from a high-detail version of the model and repeatedly apply the simplification operators described in Section 2.3 to generate a sequence of successive simplifications of the mesh. Most of the algorithms described in this book follow this approach, so it is useful to consider it in more detail.

We can classify a simplification algorithm according to the simplification error metric, the simplification operator, and the simplification process that it uses. The typical simplification algorithm uses a nested optimization process: an outer optimization makes a sequence of discrete choices for which operations to perform and in what order, and an inner optimization makes choices in processing the operator, such as which way to fill the hole during a vertex removal or where to place the new vertex during an edge collapse.

In this section we ignore the question of how to measure error and focus on how to choose which simplification operations to perform and in what order to perform them. Most geometry simplification algorithms use just a single simplification operator, so we are left only with the choice of ordering. However, we will see that some algorithms alternate geometry and topology simplification, thus introducing a choice of simplification operator as well. We will first discuss a few of the high-level queuing algorithms for choosing the ordering of the simplification operations and then discuss the choice of simplification operators (as in the case of interleaving geometry and topology simplifications).

2.4.1 NONOPTIMIZING

The simplest algorithm essentially applies all possible simplification operations in an arbitrary order (Figure 2.20). This is often appropriate for a cell-clustering approach, in which any operation may be performed completely independently of any other operation, and all operations produce roughly the same geometric error bound for

```
1   for each possible operation op
2       ComputeCost(op)
3       Q->insert(op)
4   while Q not empty
5       op = Q->extractMin()
6       ApplyOp(op)
7       for each neighbor operation i
8           ComputeCost(i)
9           Q->changeKey(i)
```

Figure 2.21   The greedy queuing algorithm for ordering mesh operations.

the simplified mesh. In the case of multilevel clustering approaches, all the clustering operations from the finest level are performed before all the operations of the next coarser level, and so on. Note that this algorithm is nonoptimizing in the sense that it does not concern itself with the outer optimization problem described previously. It is still possible for some optimization to take place during the actual application of the selected operation (i.e., the inner optimization).

2.4.2   GREEDY

The greedy queuing algorithm solves the outer optimization problem according to some *cost function,* usually a measure or bound on the error ϵ for the simplified mesh after a proposed operation is performed. The pseudocode shown in Figure 2.21 illustrates this approach, evaluating potential mesh operations using ComputeCost and placing them on the priority queue Q in lines 1 to 3. The minimum cost operation is removed from the queue and applied to the current mesh in lines 5 to 6. Applying this mesh operation may affect the cost of other operations in the neighboring mesh, so we update the cost of neighboring operations in lines 7 to 9. Note that the changeKey function may require some sharing of data pointers between the queue and the operation, allowing the priority queue to efficiently find, remove, and reinsert an element that is not the one with minimum cost.

In a typical implementation, ComputeCost and ApplyOp will share a great deal of code, and this shared code amounts to most of the time spent by the simplification process. Thus, reducing the number of calls to ComputeCost will dramatically impact the running time of the simplification algorithm. One way to reduce the number of calls is to choose operations with fewer neighbors. For example, vertex removal and half-edge collapse operations affect fewer triangles than the edge collapse, and thus

```
1   for each possible operation op
2       ComputeCost(op)
3       op->dirty = false
4       Q->insert(op)
5   while Q not empty
6       op = Q->extractMin()
7       if (op->dirty == false)
8           ApplyOp(op)
9           for each neighbor operation i
10              i->dirty = true
11      else
12          ComputeCost(op)
13          op->dirty = false
14          Q->insert(op)
```

Figure 2.22   The lazy queuing algorithm for ordering mesh operations.

they change the costs of fewer neighboring operations. However, many people still prefer the edge collapse for its other desirable properties (discussed in Section 2.2).

2.4.3   LAZY

The lazy queuing algorithm, introduced by [Cohen 97], attempts to reduce the number of calls to ComputeCost as compared to the greedy algorithm, without increasing the error of the resulting meshes too much. It is based on the observation that in the greedy algorithm, many operations will have their cost updated multiple times before they are ever actually applied to the mesh. Thus, many of these cost updates may be a waste of time. To remedy this (Figure 2.22), we avoid recalculating the cost of neighboring operations, instead setting a dirty flag (in line 10) for neighboring operations when we apply an operation. The dirty flag indicates that the cost value used to prioritize this operation is no longer accurate (but is hopefully not too far off). When we extract the minimum cost operation from the priority queue, we check its dirty flag. If the dirty flag is false, we know this operation has the lowest cost *currently known,* and we go ahead and apply the operation. Otherwise, we *clean* the operation by computing its actual cost and reinserting it into the queue. Notice that this process ensures that any operation with a lower actual cost must be currently dirty. This means that such a lower-cost operation had its cost *reduced* when one of its neighbors was applied. Thus, these cost reductions are the only opportunities we miss by performing the cost reevaluations in a lazy fashion.

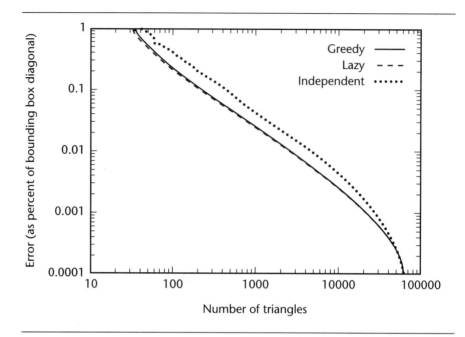

Figure 2.23   Plotting number of triangles versus error for the bunny model using the greedy, lazy, and independent frameworks, measured with the error metric of [Cohen 97].

The number of cost evaluations performed per applied operation depends in part on how accurate the costs of the dirty operations remain as the simplification progresses. If a dirty operation has an inaccurate cost, it will not re-emerge near the head of the queue when it is cleaned, resulting in more cost computations before we find a clean operation at the head of the queue. In Figure 2.23, we see that the lazy queuing algorithm is almost identical to the greedy algorithm for the bunny model. However, the average number of cost evaluations per applied edge collapse is reduced from 39.4 to 12.5 [Cohen 98b], resulting in a significant speedup.

2.4.4   ESTIMATING

Another method for reducing the number of cost computations performed simply replaces these computations with a faster-to-compute estimate. For example, in Figure 2.24, the priority ordering of the operations is determined entirely by estimated costs, whereas the accurate cost computation is performed only once per operation (inside ApplyOp). This method will work well if the ordering generated by the estimated costs is similar to the ordering that would be generated by the accurate costs. [Guéziec 99a] employs this approach to speed up the simplification, using an appro-

```
1   for each possible operation op
2       EstimateCost(op)
3       Q->insert(op)
4   while Q not empty
5       op = Q->extractMin()
6       ApplyOp(op)   // also computes and stores actual cost
7       for each neighbor operation i
8           EstimateCost(i)
9           Q->changeKey(i)
```

Figure 2.24   The estimating queuing algorithm for ordering mesh operations.

priately weighted edge length as the estimated cost. It may also be possible to use cost estimation as part of a lazy queuing algorithm, so that each possible operation has three possible states instead of two—dirty, estimated, or computed.

2.4.5 INDEPENDENT

The independent queuing algorithm (see Figure 2.25), introduced by DeFloriani et al. [DeFloriani 97] and Xia et al. [Xia 97], targets view-dependent LODs in which the goal is to build a *vertex hierarchy* (described in detail in Chapter 4) of simplification operations. The independent algorithm performs operations one level of the hierarchy at a time. It performs a maximum set of independent operations, or operations whose mutual neighborhoods do not overlap, chosen in order of the cost function. Each pass defined by the outer loop of line 3 creates one level of the simplification hierarchy. Within a pass, only operations affecting independent mesh neighborhoods are applied, with the remaining operations placed on a list, *L*, for processing in a future pass. The major benefit of this approach over the greedy algorithm (as well as the lazy and estimating variants) is that it produces hierarchies with logarithmic height. Thus, the hierarchy can always be traversed depth first, from root to leaf, in logarithmic time. For example, the hierarchy built for the bunny model using the greedy or lazy algorithm has roughly 100 levels, whereas the hierarchy built using the independent algorithm has roughly 50 levels. However, because the independence criterion causes some higher-cost operations to be performed before lower-cost alternatives, it often produces output meshes with more triangles for a given error bound, as seen in Figure 2.23.

```
1  for each possible operation op
2      L->insert(op)
3  while L not empty
4      while L not empty
5          op = L->removeNext()
6          ComputeCost(op)
7          op->independent = true
8          Q->insert(op)
9      while Q not empty
10         op = Q->extractMin()
11         if (op->independent == true)
12             ApplyOp(op)
13             for each neighbor operation i
14                 op->independent = false
15         else
16             L->insert(op)
```

Figure 2.25   The independent queuing algorithm for ordering mesh operations.

2.4.6 INTERLEAVED SIMPLIFICATION OPERATORS

Simplification of the geometry and topology are sometimes viewed as two distinct stages in the simplification pipeline. In such a setting, geometry simplification alternates with topology simplification. This is motivated by the observation that each simplification stage allows the mesh to be simplified more aggressively than if only one kind of simplification had been applied. In particular, topology simplifications by small amounts can often enable large overall simplifications (e.g., by closing the small holes of the brake rotor in Figure 2.18).

An example of such alternating topology and geometry simplifications appears in Figure 2.26, based on work in El-Sana and Varshney [El-Sana 98]. Here the object complexity is reduced as follows: (a) original object had 756 triangles; (b and c) genus reduction removed the two holes on the side and followed this by geometry simplification; (d and e) a second-level, genus-preserving simplification removed a hole at the top and was followed by a geometry reduction; (f) to yield a final object with 298 triangles.

Clearly, such interleaved ordering of different mesh simplification operators can become fairly complicated, since one could conceivably use any of the previous schemes (nonoptimizing, greedy, lazy, estimating, and independent) or any combination of them to choose the order of the different simplification operators. The simplest is the nonoptimizing approach for both simplification operators ApplyOp1() and ApplyOp2(), shown in Figure 2.27.

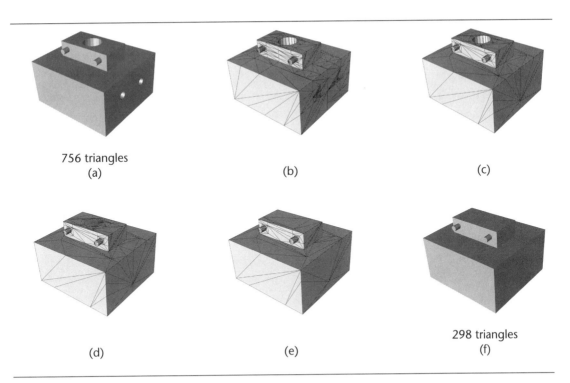

756 triangles
(a)

(b)

(c)

(d)

(e)

298 triangles
(f)

Figure 2.26   (a–f) Alternating topology and geometry simplifications [El-Sana 98]. Copyright ©
1998 IEEE.

```
1  for each level of hierarchy
2      for each possible independent operation op
3          ApplyOp1(op)
4      for each possible independent operation op
5          ApplyOp2(op)
```

Figure 2.27   The nonoptimizing queuing algorithm for ordering multiple mesh-simplification
operators.

2.5 CONCLUSIONS

We can characterize a mesh simplification according to the optimization algorithm, simplification operator, and error metric that it uses. In this chapter we have examined two of these elements in detail: the various simplification operators, both local and global, and the various simplification optimization processes. The choice of the simplification process and simplification operator largely depend on the constraints imposed by the target application, ease of coding, and the nature of the input data sets. In Chapter 3, we turn to the major remaining ingredient of a simplification algorithm—the simplification error metric.

SIMPLIFICATION ERROR METRICS

We have studied mechanisms for and approaches to mesh simplification, but so far we have glossed over a crucial component—the measurement of the output quality. The way we measure error both during and after the simplification process can have a dramatic impact on the visual appeal and usefulness of our simplified models. However, it is often this component that baffles the reader of a conference or journal article on polygon simplification. For some algorithms, error measurement may involve complex geometrical constructs, and error minimization may rely on solving nontrivial algebraic problems. In this chapter, we will examine some of the key elements of measuring simplification quality at a high level, looking to several of the published algorithms to see the range of possible approaches to the problem.

3.1 WHY MEASURE ERROR?

Before we move on to the *how* of simplification error metrics, let us first consider the *why*. In the domain of manually created levels of detail, the only error metric is the judgment of a human modeler. The modeler decides how to create a simple version of a detailed model and may also decide how small it must be on the screen before it looks good. In some respects, this is an excellent error metric, because it uses the human visual system and human intuition to make intelligent decisions. In other respects, however, this human error metric falls short—it is labor intensive and thus not appropriate for any LOD system more complex than the use of a few discrete levels of detail. We will next discuss several important reasons for the development of automatic, quantitative measures of simplification error for the domain of automatic simplification.

3.1.1 GUIDE AND IMPROVE THE SIMPLIFICATION PROCESS

Just as a human modeler uses visual criteria to decide the best way to create a simpler version of a model, so does our simplification algorithm need to make decisions about the best way to simplify a model. As we have seen in Section 2.3, many simplification algorithms look like a nested optimization problem. The outer optimization is often a greedy process that chooses the best available simplification operation to perform next. The inner optimization seeks to make each simplification operation work as well as possible. A consistent, quantitative error metric is useful for both of these optimization problems.

In the outer optimization problem, we are given a large number of possible simplification operations to choose from, and we wish to choose the "best" of these operations to apply to the current model. For many algorithms, this best operation is defined with respect to a simplification error metric. The better the simplification error metric, and the tighter our bounds are on this error, the better the choices we will make throughout the simplification process. Although this greedy process does not guarantee optimal results, experience has shown that better greedy choices improve the output quality of the simplification.

Optimizing an appropriate error metric in the inner optimization problem improves the quality of the choices available to the outer optimization problem. Thus, the use of a good error metric here also improves the final quality of the simplification output.

3.1.2 KNOW THE QUALITY OF THE RESULTS

Polygonal levels of detail have a number of uses besides rendering acceleration. For instance, they may speed up computations, such as in collision detection and finite element analysis. In each of these cases, it is important to know the accuracy of the simplified models. In addition, polygon simplification can be used as a form of lossy compression. In this scenario, the user expresses the desired compression as an error tolerance, the system simplifies the model until it reaches the specified error tolerance, and the user discards the original model in favor of the simplified model.

Sometimes we will want to apply an error metric to evaluate the quality of the results after simplification is complete, separately from the simpler metric or heuristic used to guide the simplification process. For example, if the goal is to produce a small set of discrete LODs, it may prove practical to use a tool such as Metro [Cignoni 98b] to measure the true simplification error after the fact (we return to Metro in Section 3.3.3). Similarly, if the goal is to produce a single level of detail with a given number of polygons (e.g., for lossy compression), this approach may work well. However, when generating a large number of levels of detail (as in the case of a hierarchy for view-dependent adaptation), it may prove more sensible to measure the error during the actual simplification process.

3.1.3   KNOW WHEN TO SHOW A PARTICULAR LOD

One of the primary ways to use LOD for multiresolution rendering is to reduce the resolution of all the models in an environment to a specified quality level. More formally stated, we are given a screen-space error tolerance, and we wish to choose levels of detail to minimize the number of polygons while respecting the specified error tolerance. To accomplish this, we need to know the screen-space error of a particular level of detail when viewed from a given viewpoint. By knowing the error of every level of detail we create, computing the screen-space error from a given viewpoint and choosing the level of detail to render are straightforward. This approach applies not only to discrete per-object LODs, but also to dynamic view-dependent level of detail of an object or environment.

3.1.4   BALANCE QUALITY ACROSS A LARGE ENVIRONMENT

The other common way to use LOD is to reduce the quality across an entire rendered environment by just enough to achieve a desired polygon count or frame rate. In this case, we are given the desired polygon count, and we wish to choose the levels of detail to minimize the error while respecting the specified polygon budget. As we will see in Chapter 4, this problem amounts to solving a type of knapsack optimization problem [Funkhouser 93b]. As in the fidelity-driven LOD selection scheme, this budget-driven LOD selection scheme applies in both the contexts of discrete and continuous levels of detail. The better the screen-space error metric we have to work with, and the more closely it corresponds to perception of fidelity by the human visual system, the better the visual quality our system will produce for a given polygon budget.

3.2 KEY ELEMENTS

Several key conceptual elements are common to the error metrics for a number of simplification algorithms. Most simplification error metrics incorporate some form of object-space geometric error measure, which is often stored and converted to a screen-space distance by the run-time multiresolution display algorithm. In addition, many modern simplification algorithms also incorporate some measure of attribute errors, including color, normal, and texture coordinate attributes. These geometric and attribute errors may be combined in a number of ways during the simplification process and later in the run-time rendering system. We next discuss these conceptual elements in preparation for discussion of several error metrics from actual simplification systems in Section 3.3.

3.2.1 GEOMETRIC ERROR

The polygonal surfaces we see in computer graphics are embedded in a 3D object space, and their vertices are specified by 3D coordinates. Simplifying a polygonal surface reduces the number of vertices, changing the shape of the surface as a result. Measuring and minimizing a 3D geometric error as we perform the simplification allows us to preserve the original shape as best we can. If we consider this shape preservation in the screen space, it helps the object cover the correct pixels on the screen and maintain an accurate silhouette.

Euclidean geometry defines a measure of the distance between two points. For two points $p_1 = (x_1, y_1, z_1)$ and $p_2 = (x_2, y_2, z_2)$, the distance d between them is

$$d = \sqrt{(x_1 - x_2)^2 + (y_1 - y_2)^2 + (z_1 - z_2)^2}$$

However, finding the distance between two surfaces is more involved. We can think of each surface as an infinite set of infinitesimal points. Then conceptually, finding the distance between the two surfaces involves matching up pairs of points, computing their distances, and tabulating all the results. In practice, we may exploit the polygonal nature of our surfaces to allow us to use small, finite sets of points, or we can compute conservative bounds or estimates on these distances rather than taking many pointwise measurements.

Hausdorff Distance

The Hausdorff distance is a well-known concept from topology, used in image processing, surface modeling, and a variety of other application areas. The Hausdorff distance is defined on point sets, but because a surface may be described as a form of a continuous point set, it applies to surfaces as well. Given two point sets, A and B,

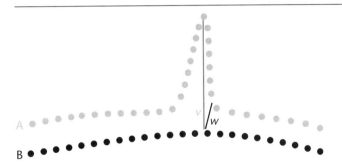

Figure 3.1   The Hausdorff distance between two surfaces. The one-sided Hausdorff distances are
h(A, B) = ‖v‖ and h(B, A) = ‖w‖. The two-sided Hausdorff distance is H(A, B) =
max(‖v‖, ‖w‖) = ‖v‖.

the Hausdorff distance is the max of min distances between points in the two sets.
In other words, for every point in set *A*, we find the closest point in set *B*, and vice
versa. We compute the distance between all these closest point pairs, and take the
maximum. We can express this algebraically as follows:

$$H(A, B) = \max(h(A, B), h(B, A))$$

where

$$h(A, B) = \max_{a \in A} \min_{b \in B} \|a - b\|$$

h(A, B) finds for each point in *A* the closest point in *B* and takes the maximum. This
function, called the one-sided Hausdorff distance, is not symmetric. Every point in
A has been paired with a single point in *B*, but there may be unpaired (and multiply
paired) points in *B*. Thus, h(A, B) ≠ h(B, A). The Hausdorff distance (or two-sided
Hausdorff distance), however, is constructed to be symmetric by considering both of
the one-sided Hausdorff distances and reporting the maximum. This is illustrated in
Figure 3.1.

Mapping Distance

The Hausdorff distance is, by construction, the tightest possible bound on the maximum distance between two surfaces. However, for the purpose of polygon simplification, it has a number of shortcomings. It does not provide a single set of pointwise
correspondences between the surfaces, but rather relies on two potentially conflict-
ing sets of correspondences. In addition, each of these sets of correspondences may

have discontinuities, regions of the point sets with no correspondences, and regions of the point sets that have multiple correspondences. These limitations of the Hausdorff distance mapping make it difficult to carry attribute values from the original surface to the simplified surfaces in a continuous fashion.

As an alternative to the Hausdorff distance, we consider a continuous, one-to-one, and onto mapping (called a *bijection*) between the two surfaces, and measure the distance with respect to this mapping.

Given such a continuous mapping

$$F : A \to B$$

we define this mapping distance as

$$D(F) = \max_{a \in A} \|a - F(a)\|$$

So D is the distance between corresponding points in *A* and *B*, where the correspondence is established by the mapping function F. If this mapping is accomplished via correspondences in a 2D parametric domain, such as a texture map, we call this mapping distance a *parametric distance*. Such a correspondence is illustrated in Figure 3.2. In this case, we might express the distance as

$$D(F) = \max_{x \in P} \|F_{i-1}^{-1}(x) - F_i^{-1}(x)\|$$

Here *x* is a point in the 2D parametric domain and each of the F^{-1} functions maps this 2D point onto a 3D mesh, either before or after a particular simplification operation.

Because there are many such mappings, there are many possible mapping distances. Conceptually, the theoretically minimum possible mapping distance is simply

$$D_{min} = \min_{F \in M} D(F)$$

where *M* is the set of all such continuous mapping functions. Note that although D_{min} and its associated mapping function may be impossible to explicitly compute, *any* continuous mapping function F provides an upper bound on D_{min} as well as on the Hausdorff distance. If our simplification goal is to provide a guaranteed bound on the maximum error, any such function will accomplish this. However, if the bound is very loose, we might use many more polygons than necessary to provide a specified quality. Similarly, if our goal is to optimize the quality for a fixed polygon budget, we would like the bound to be as tight as possible to ensure the best real quality in our rendered scene.

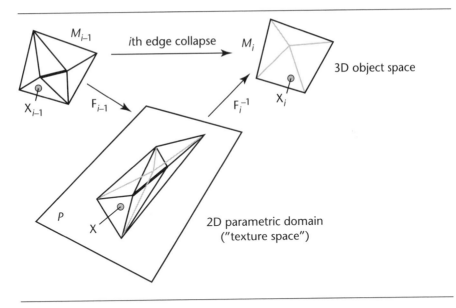

Figure 3.2   Correspondences established in a 2D parametric domain. The points X_i and X_{i-1} correspond to the same point, x, in the parametric domain [Cohen 98a].

Maximum versus Average Error

Both the Hausdorff distance and the general mapping distance compute the final distance between two surfaces as the maximum of all the pointwise distances. This is a valid choice, but there are other reasonable choices as well. Rather than taking the maximum of the pointwise distances (known as the L_∞ norm), we could take the average (the L_1 norm), the root mean square (the L_2 norm), or some other combination.

The advantage of the maximum error is that it provides what is often referred to as a *guaranteed error bound* (this term has been somewhat overloaded, so the meaning should be considered carefully for a particular usage). For some applications such as medical and scientific visualization applications, knowing that the error is *never* more than some specified tolerance may be desirable.

The average error, on the other hand, can be an indication of the error across the entire surface as opposed to a few particularly bad locations. Anecdotal evidence indicates that the maximum error may be 10 times larger than the average error for many models [Erikson 00]. Thus, a system that focuses entirely on minimizing the maximum error may ignore large increases in the average error. Similarly, heuristics that have been shown to do well in terms of minimizing average error may exhibit erratic behavior when gauged according to their maximum error. Ideally, a system should show some compromise between the two, bounding the maximum error without allowing the average error to grow in uncontrolled fashion. Such systems are currently rare in practice.

Screen-Space Error

All of the geometric error measures we have described thus far measure surface deviation in a 3D object space. However, when we render the surface using perspective projection, our run-time level of detail manager can make better use of a screen-space error bound. Given a set of viewing parameters (viewpoint, field of view, etc.) and an LOD created with a bound ϵ on the 3D surface deviation of the simplified model from the original, we can compute a bound on the screen space deviation p measured in pixel units. Figure 3.3 depicts a particular view of an LOD within a rendering application. In this figure, θ is the total field of view, d is distance in the viewing direction from the eye point to the level of detail (or its bounding volume), and x is the resolution of the screen in pixels. We denote by w the width of the viewing frustum at distance d. For the LOD enclosed by the bounding sphere, c is the center and r is the radius. Notice that we place an error vector of length ϵ just in front of the level of detail and orthogonal to the viewing vector. This will enable us to compute a convenient approximation to the projected size of the error in pixels. It is correct when the level of detail is at the center of the screen, but it underestimates the size as the object gets farther off center. (A more accurate computation would orient the error vector orthogonal to the vector from the eye to the level of detail rather than orthogonal to the primary view vector.) The level of detail may actually be an entire object (in the case of a discrete level of detail system) or just a small portion of a surface (in the case of a continuous level of detail system).

We see from the diagram, using the properties of similar triangles, that

$$\frac{\epsilon}{w} = \frac{p}{x}$$

which we then solve for p:

$$p = \frac{\epsilon x}{w} = \frac{\epsilon x}{2d \tan \frac{\theta}{2}} \tag{3.1}$$

Given this formulation, it is easy to compute this bound p on the screen-space deviation for a given level of detail at a given viewing distance. We compute d as

$$d = (c - eye) \cdot v - r$$

where v is the unit view vector. We then need just one more multiplication and one division to compute p from the other known constants using Equation 3.1.

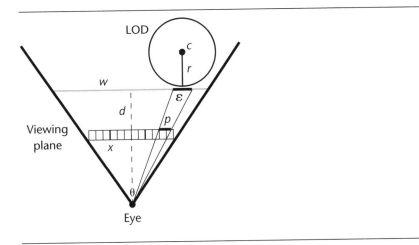

Figure 3.3 Converting object-space geometric error ϵ to screen-space geometric error p measured in pixels of deviation [Cohen 98a] [Cohen 98b].

In a discrete level of detail system, we may want to quickly choose the appropriate level of detail from a sequence of possibilities so that we render the minimum the number of triangles while meeting a tolerance bound, $t \geq p$, on the maximum allowable screen-space error. Solving Equation 3.1 for ϵ yields:

$$\epsilon = p \frac{2d \tan \frac{\theta}{2}}{x} \leq t \frac{2d \tan \frac{\theta}{2}}{x}$$

Now, rather than converting ϵ for a particular LOD from object space to screen space and comparing to the tolerance, we are essentially converting the tolerance from screen space to object space and comparing to the ϵ for each candidate LOD (notice that we have eliminated the division in this case). The application chooses to render the LOD whose ϵ is as large as possible, while still small enough to satisfy the inequality; this is the LOD with the smallest number of triangles for the error tolerance.

3.2.2 ATTRIBUTE ERROR

Many of today's interesting polygonal models comprise not only geometric coordinates but other attributes as well. Colors, normals, and texture coordinates are the most common attributes; they may be specified on faces, vertices, or corners. A corner attribute is one that is specified at a particular (face, vertex) pair. This allows vertices to have multiple attribute values, describing attribute discontinuities across adjacent faces when desired. For example, an object with a sharp crease may represent the vertices along the crease as having two normals.

Simplification algorithms vary widely in their support for these attribute fields. Some algorithms, especially the earlier ones, offer no support for attributes. The inputs to these algorithms are purely geometric models. If desired, we can compute face normals for the simplified models using cross products of the triangle edges and compute a weighted average of these face normals to compute vertex normals. This allows for flat or smooth shading of the simplification output.

Other algorithms support attributes to the extent that they "carry" them through the simplification process. For algorithms whose simplified vertices are a subset of the input vertices—for example, algorithms using the vertex removal or half-edge collapse operators—this amounts to just retaining the attribute values of the input vertices. For algorithms that produce new vertices—for example, those algorithms using the full-edge collapse operator—this generally entails interpolating the attribute at the new vertex from the attributes of the vertices that contribute to it.

Another option is to carry the attribute value but also to measure the attribute error incurred by the simplification operation. One approach is to use the same correspondences method from the geometry error measurement to determine which attribute values to compare. This error measurement can then be used in the computation of an operation's priority for the purpose of guiding the choice of operations. In this case, we are leaving the minimization of attribute error up to the outer optimization loop that chooses the operations in a greedy fashion.

Finally, an algorithm can both measure and optimize the attribute error. This allows us to actually reduce the attribute error for a given simplification operation as part of the inner optimization by carefully choosing the attribute values for the newly created vertices.

We will next briefly consider the issues that arise with measuring and optimizing error for color, normal, and texture coordinate attributes.

Colors

The colors of a polygonal model are typically stored as (r, g, b) triples with each value in the range $[0, 1]$. The most straightforward way to measure color error is to treat the RGB space (in which red, green, and blue form the orthogonal basis vectors of the coordinate system) as a Euclidean space and compute the RGB distance between corresponding points as

$$d_{color} = \sqrt{(r_1 - r_2)^2 + (g_1 - g_2)^2 + (b_1 - b_2)^2}$$

In optimizing the color error, we can actually think of the r, g, and b values over the mesh as three separate scalar fields and optimize each scalar value separately.

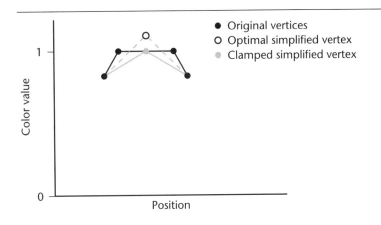

Figure 3.4   The optimized color value of a simplified vertex may lie outside the valid color range. Clamping the value to [0,1] keeps it in range (and increases the color error).

A frequently ignored problem with this approach is that this RGB space is perceptually nonlinear. Thus, equal-sized distances in different portions of the RGB color cube appear to the human visual system as different distances. It is possible, however, to evaluate the error in a more perceptually linear space, such as the CIE-L*u*v* space [Rigiroli 01].

A harder-to-ignore problem results from the optimization of this color distance. When choosing the color value for a new vertex to minimize the overall color error, the resulting color value may very well lie outside the [0,1] range of valid color values. Such a situation is illustrated in Figure 3.4. The hollow vertex indicates the optimal color value to minimize the maximum color error, but it is unfortunately greater than 1. A reasonable solution to this problem is to clamp the value to the [0,1] range, as indicated by the solid gray vertex.

Normals

The natural space for normal vectors is on the Gaussian sphere—a unit radius sphere centered at the origin, on which each point represents a normal vector [Carmo 76]. The proper measure for distance between two normal vectors is an angular distance,

$$d = \arccos\left(\left(n_{1_x}, n_{1_y}, n_{1_z} \right) \cdot \left(n_{2_x}, n_{2_y}, n_{2_z} \right) \right)$$

Some algorithms optimize normals at a gross level by preventing foldovers (see Figure 2.3). Such a foldover may be detected by comparing the normal of a triangle before

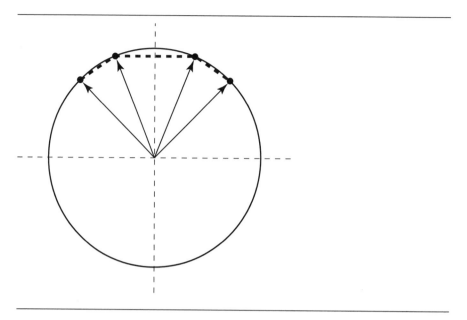

Figure 3.5   Four normal vectors and their associated points on the Gaussian sphere. The thick dashed lines indicate Euclidean-space interpolation of normal vectors.

a simplification operation to the normal of a corresponding triangle after the operation. If the angle is more than some threshold, the operation may be disallowed.

Algorithms may also minimize the normal error by choosing the best normal vector at newly created vertices. Because optimization in the true normal space of the Gaussian sphere is difficult, a common approach is to optimize the normals as if they live in a standard Euclidean space. Thus, we can consider the normal vectors as standard 3D points. If necessary, interpolated normals across a triangle may be interpreted using a Euclidean linear interpolation, as indicated by the thick dashed lines in Figure 3.5. Optimizing normals in a Euclidean normal space generally requires us to renormalize the resulting normal, which projects it back onto the Gaussian sphere.

Texture Coordinates

Texture coordinates for polygonal surfaces are represented as (u, v) coordinate pairs that define a mapping of vertices to points in a 2D texture space. As with the color space, this texture space generally uses values in the range [0,1], so the same issues

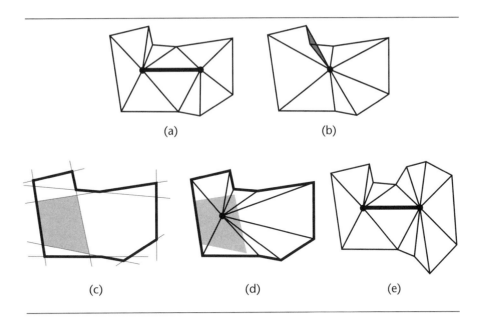

Figure 3.6   Edge collapse viewed in the 2D texture space. (a) Bold edge and vertices to be collapsed. (b) Collapsing to the edge midpoint causes folding in the texture space.
(c) The gray *kernel* of the polygon defines the safe region for placing the texture
coordinates of the new vertex. (d) Valid edge collapse in the texture space. (e) Edge
with an empty kernel. The edge cannot be collapsed without causing a texture fold.

with optimized values going out of range apply, and clamping remains a viable solution (see Colors section, above).

However, unlike the color space, the u and v values should not be considered as
totally independent. The difference here is that the texture coordinates are intended
to describe a bijection (one-to-one and onto mapping) between the polygonal surface
and the texture space. The simplification process should take care to avoid creating
folds in the texture space, causing the same texture space location to map to multiple locations on the surface. (This will appear as an odd local texture warping on
the rendered surface.) As seen in Figure 3.6, we can avoid such folds during an edge
collapse operations by placing the new texture coordinate within the edge neighborhood's *kernel*, defined by the intersection of its boundary edge half spaces. Note that
for some edges, the kernel is empty, meaning that any choice of texture coordinates
for the new vertex will cause a fold (this also applies to other simplification operations
that would remove either of the edge's vertices, such as a vertex removal or half-edge
collapse). In such cases, the simplification algorithm should disallow or penalize the
operation.

3.2.3 COMBINING ERRORS

As we have seen, a simplification algorithm can measure the geometry error plus a host of other attribute errors during the process of evaluating a potential simplification operation. For priority-based simplification algorithms, such as the optimization schemes presented in Section 2.4, we need to compute a single number to be used as the priority key for a given operation. In general, we compute some combination of the individual error terms to arrive at a single error value. For example, we can take a weighted linear combination of the error terms, with the weights chosen empirically [Hoppe 96]. It is also possible to weight the terms according to other factors, such as whether the operation causes topological changes or affects discontinuities of the original model. Currently, little consensus exists on the most meaningful way to combine an arbitrary set of error terms. Although the terms are combined for the purpose of prioritization of simplification operations, it is possible to also track the individual errors through the entire process to make them available to the rendering system as part of the simplification output.

3.2.4 INCREMENTAL AND TOTAL ERROR

Most simplification algorithms involve iteratively simplifying the surface, so the triangles we simplify with a particular operation may themselves be the result of some previous simplification operations. With this in mind, it is important to consider whether we are measuring and optimizing the *incremental error* or the *total error*. The incremental error is the error between triangles being simplified by an operation and those that result from the operation. The total error, on the other hand, is the error between the triangles of the original surface and the triangles resulting from an operation.

In many cases, the incremental error is more efficient to measure and optimize. However, the total error is the more useful measure as part of the simplification output. It may be used for operation prioritization as well as for determining switching distances at rendering time. Interestingly, Lindstrom and Turk have demonstrated that using only the incremental error for the prioritization can still produce measurably good simplifications [Lindstrom 99]. This can be very useful if we never need to know the total error, or if we only need to know it for a few discrete levels of detail (as opposed to requiring it for every simplification operation for use in a dynamic LOD system).

The direct approach to computing total error measures it directly from the original surface. If this is required for each simplification operation, then the simplification operations become increasingly time consuming as the surface becomes more and more simplified. This occurs because increasingly coarse triangles correspond to more and more of the original triangles, so a direct error computation takes longer for coarser triangles.

An alternative approach computes bounds on the total error instead. For example, we can store a spatial data structure, such as a sphere, box, or other simple 3D volume, with the simplified mesh elements. Here, the simple volume indicates the size and locality of the total error thus far. We then accumulate the new incremental error with the previous total error by growing the volume to contain the new incremental error. We compose two volumes by computing the position and size of a new volume that contains all the various component volumes (a type of 3D analog of interval arithmetic). The error bounds produced by this type of approach may be less tight than those produced by direct measurement, but at least the measurement will not slow down as simplification proceeds.

3.3 RANGE OF APPROACHES

Having considered many of the issues surrounding simplification error metrics, we now examine a number of simplification algorithms from the literature. There are so many published algorithms that we can only discuss a small proportion of them; those we present were chosen to encompass a broad range of approaches to the measurement and optimization of simplification error.

Our emphasis in this discussion is not on providing a detailed description of the various algorithms, but on understanding their error metrics and how these metrics are applied. We will revisit some of these approaches in Chapter 5. For each algorithm, we wish to consider issues such as what type of error is measured, how tight a bound it computes on this error, how easy the metric is implement, and to what class of models it applies. We therefore organize the algorithms according to which geometric elements they use to construct the correspondences for measuring error. The categories we discuss are vertex–vertex, vertex–plane, vertex–surface, and surface-surface approaches. Finally, we discuss the use of image-space metrics as opposed to object- and attribute-space metrics.

3.3.1 VERTEX–VERTEX DISTANCE

The simplest approach to measuring the error of a simplified model is to measure the distances between the original vertices and simplified vertices. How we choose the vertex–vertex correspondences and the specific simplification operators involved determine the accuracy of results. Take, for example, the four vertices shown in Figure 3.7. Starting with the two triangles ABC and ACD, we swap the diagonal edge to get the triangles ABD and BCD. Although we have not changed the vertices, the surface has changed, perhaps dramatically. If we measure the Hausdorff distance between the vertices only, we get a distance of 0, but the distance at the interior points of the surface is much greater.

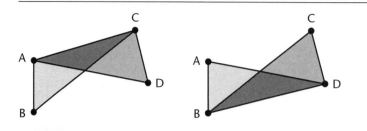

Figure 3.7   Measuring vertex–vertex error may not capture the error between surfaces. Here the four vertices remain unchanged, as do the four boundary edges of this surface patch, but the surfaces have some unmeasured geometric deviation between them.

Having said that, there are circumstances where we can consider only the distances between vertices and still compute a useful bound on the distance between surfaces. In particular, during vertex merging operations (edge collapse, cell collapse, etc.) we can find an appropriate mapping between vertices to achieve a conservative distance bound.

Uniform Grid-Based Vertex Clustering

The grid-based vertex clustering algorithm of Rossignac and Borrel [Rossignac 92] [Rossignac 93] is one of the fastest and most robust simplification algorithms known. A uniform spatial grid is imposed on the space of the polygonal input surface (a simple example is shown in Figure 3.8). Within each grid cell, all vertices are collapsed to a single representative vertex, which may be one of the input vertices or some weighted combination of the input vertices (see Section 5.1 for more implementation details). As a result of this collapse operation, some triangles degenerate to edges or points, which are discarded if they coincide with the remaining triangles.

This clustering of two or more vertices lends itself to a *natural mapping* [Cohen 97] between the input and output surfaces, shown in Figure 3.9. Each of the input triangles is stretched as a result of the vertex merging. Given the correspondences of these triangle vertices before and after the merge, we can assign correspondences to the interior points of the triangles using linear interpolation. This linear interpolation also applies to the distance that all the surface points move. Thus, the greatest distance moved by any point of the surface must occur at a vertex, and the maximum geometric distance of this mapping is the maximum distance between corresponding vertices.

The clustering algorithm and associated natural mapping are quite general. They apply not only to meshes as in Figure 3.9 but also to arbitrary vertex merges on triangle sets. Note, however, that this distance measure may be quite conservative, as

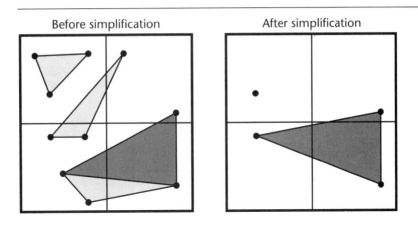

Figure 3.8   The vertices of each grid cell are collapsed to a single representative vertex, leaving only the dark gray triangle and a disconnected point [Luebke 97].

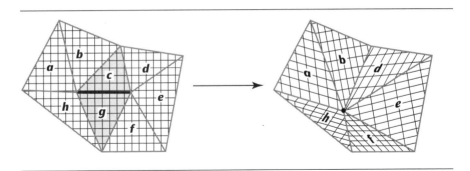

Figure 3.9   The natural mapping for vertex clustering operations. Most triangles map to triangles. Some triangles (the gray triangles, *c* and *g* in this case) degenerate to edges, and some edges degenerate to points. The maximum error according to this map is the maximum 3D distance any vertex moves [Cohen 98a].

shown in Figure 3.10. In fact, an even more conservative error measure is typically used in practice—the diagonal length of the grid cell, which is an upper bound on the distance any merged vertex may have moved. Given that this approach was originally used to compute a discrete level of detail, this conservative distance may be reasonable, because the largest error over *all* the cells will probably be used to determine the error for the level of detail.

    In terms of dealing with attributes, the original algorithm recomputes vertex normals for the simplified vertices from the simplified triangles and does not mention

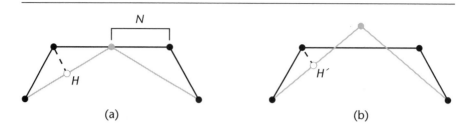

Figure 3.10   Distances for merging two vertices. (a) Vertex position chosen to minimize N, the natural mapping distance, which is more conservative (i.e., longer) than H, the Hausdorff distance. (b) Vertex position chosen to minimize H', which is now even smaller than H.

color. However, when a representative vertex is chosen from among the input vertices, carrying color attributes through the simplification is straightforward.

The cell diagonal length is guaranteed to bound the total error from the original surface to the simplified surface. Thus, if multiple levels of detail are created, it is acceptable to start from the current level of detail to compute the next simpler one using a coarser, nested grid. The cell acts in some sense as our spatial data structure to bound both the incremental error and the total error to the original surface.

Hierarchical Grid-Based Vertex Clustering

Luebke and Erikson perform simplification using a hierarchical grid in the form of an octree [Luebke 97]. This vertex tree (each octree node is associated with a vertex) allows for dynamic, view-dependent adaptation of the level of detail. Their algorithm makes the vertex clustering method even more general, allowing a single hierarchy to perform drastic simplification across an entire environment, with no notion of individual objects.

This algorithm uses the same object-space geometric error bound as Rossignac and Borrel [Rossignac 92], but it allows local, view-dependent adaptation of the model according to screen space geometric deviation. The cell size is projected to screen-space to determine the error caused by *folding* (merging) or *unfolding* (splitting) an octree node. Note that it would be straightforward for this algorithm to incorporate a somewhat tighter, more local error bound than the cell size. For example, the maximum distance from a cell's representative vertex to all of the original vertices contained in the cell may produce a tighter bound for some cells.

In addition, the algorithm provides for more sophisticated handling of normal error. In one variant of the tree construction, a *normal cone* is constructed to measure the maximum normal vector deviation of each simplified vertex. These normal cones are used at run-time to detect silhouettes, enabling the use of different screen-space error thresholds for silhouette and nonsilhouette regions. Much more detail on view-dependent simplification is provided in Section 4.4.

Floating Cell-Based Vertex Clustering

Low and Tan present a modified vertex clustering algorithm using *floating cells* rather than a uniform grid [Low 97]. Their algorithm provides quantitative and qualitative improvements to the simplification algorithm of the grid-based approach.

As in the algorithm of Rossignac and Borrel [Rossignac 92], the floating cell algorithm begins by *grading* the original vertices to see which are best to retain as representative cell vertices (for more on grading, see Section 5.1.2). However, the cells are now chosen to surround these representative vertices, rather than choosing the vertices according to the cells. The vertices are prioritized according to their grades. Then, in priority order, a vertex is chosen, surrounded by a fixed radius cube or sphere, and the other vertices in that radius are merged to the chosen vertex. We can think of this as using a bounding volume approach rather than a spatial partitioning approach to perform the clustering. From the standpoint of the optimization approaches presented in Section 2.3, floating-cell clustering uses the greedy high-level algorithm rather than the nonoptimized high-level algorithm.

An immediate quantitative advantage of this approach is a tighter error bound: whereas the grid-based approach used the cell diameter as a conservative bound on the distance vertices could move, the floating-cell approach can use the cell radius, in effect halving the error bound while supporting roughly the same number of vertices in the output model. The floating cell approach also removes the sensitivity of the grid approach to the placement of the grid, and reduces the occurrence of some qualitatively undesirable cases. In terms of attribute handling, Low and Tan also incorporate thick lines rendered with view-dependent, cylinder-based normals as opposed to single-pixel-width lines rendered with a fixed normal. We expand on the features and implementation of floating-cell clustering in Section 5.1.6.

3.3.2 VERTEX–PLANE DISTANCE

The distance between a point and a plane is even more computationally efficient than the distance between two points. Given a plane with unit normal n, and signed distance from the origin D, the shortest distance from point $p = (x, y, z)$ to the plane is

$$d = n \cdot p + D = n_x x + n_y y + n_z z + D$$

Because our models are composed of planar polygons rather than infinite planes, the vertex–plane distance methods do not really provide a bound on the maximum or average distance between models. Measuring the error of a simplified mesh thus requires another metric or a tool such as Metro. However, simplification methods based on vertex–plane distance generally work well in practice: they are fast and moderately accurate, tending to produce LODs with measurably low error for a given polygon count. These methods have generated a great deal of interest in recent years due to their speed and empirically demonstrated accuracy.

Maximum Supporting Plane Distance

The algorithm of Ronfard and Rossignac [Ronfard 96] follows the greedy high-level algorithm using edge collapse operations. It measures for each potential edge collapse the maximum distance between the simplified vertex and each of its *supporting planes*. Each vertex of the original mesh has one supporting plane for each adjacent face. When an edge is collapsed, the set of supporting planes for the resulting vertex is the union of the set of supporting planes from the two edge vertices (thus, the sets are merged and the duplicates removed). This set of planes grows larger and larger as the simplified vertices cover more and more of the original mesh. We write this error metric as

$$E_v = \max_{p \in planes(v)} (p \cdot v)^2$$

where $v = (x, y, z, 1)$ and $p = (n_x, n_y, n_z, D)$. E_v is a total distance measure rather than an incremental distance. This measure may underestimate the maximum error between the surfaces for several reasons. First, the vertex–plane distance for some planes may be much smaller than the actual distance to the supporting polygon from the original mesh, and the maximum vertex–plane distance may also underestimate the actual distance (see Figure 3.11). In addition, the maximum distance between the two surfaces may not occur at one of the simplified vertices at all, but at the interior of some triangle or along some edge. However, Ronfard and Rossignac use an auxiliary plane at sharp corners of the mesh to guarantee that the measured bound is off by no more than a factor of $\sqrt{3}$ from the maximum error.

Error Quadrics

Garland and Heckbert [Garland 97] follow a similar approach. However, they modify the error metric of Ronfard and Rossignac [Ronfard 96] to make it faster and more compact in storage space. In addition, they extend its application to the class of vertex pairing operations, which can merge nearby but nonadjacent vertices to produce topological changes. This topology merging can have quantitative as well as qualitative benefits, reducing the number of triangles for a given error bound. The quadric

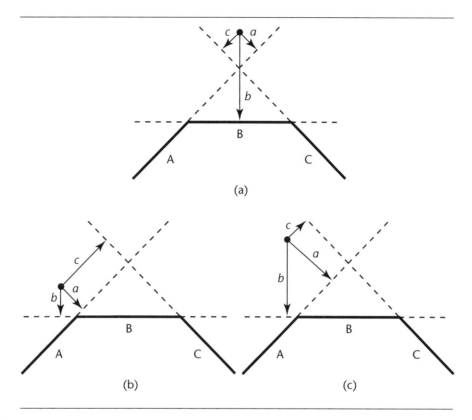

Figure 3.11   Distance from a simplified vertex to some supporting planes. (a) The maximum vertex–plane distance, *b*, is the shortest distance to the supporting polygons. (b) The maximum vertex–plane distance, *c*, overestimates the shortest distance to the supporting polygons. (c) The maximum vertex–plane distance, *b*, underestimates the shortest distance to the supporting polygons.

error metric replaces the maximum of squared vertex–plane distances, used above, with the sum of squared vertex–plane distances as follows:

$$E_v = \sum_{p \in planes(v)} (p \cdot v)^2 = \sum_p \left(v^{\mathrm{T}} p\right)\left(p^{\mathrm{T}} v\right) = v^{\mathrm{T}} \left[\sum_p \left(pp^{\mathrm{T}}\right)\right] v = v^{\mathrm{T}} \sum_p Q_p v = v^{\mathrm{T}} Q_v v$$

Given the initial substitution of the sum for the maximum, followed by a few algebraic manipulations, we find that each plane *p*'s contribution to E_v amounts to Q_p, a *quadratic form* (or *error quadric*). This quadratic form is a 4x4 symmetric matrix, computed as pp^{T} and represented using 10 unique floating point numbers. The

Figure 3.12   Ellipsoids (level surfaces of error quadrics) illustrate the orientation and size of the error quadrics associated with a simplified bunny [Garland 97]. Copyright © 1997 Association for Computing Machinery, Inc.

contribution of multiple planes is computed by summing their matrices, for example, summing all the Q_ps to arrive at Q_v. Thus, as we combine two vertices during the simplification, we compute the new quadric as the sum of the two previous quadrics. To evaluate the error for a vertex v, we perform the matrix-vector multiplication $Q_v v$ and take the dot product of the result with v. Thus, neither the storage nor the computation requirements grow as the simplification progresses, allowing for extremely efficient management of an approximate total error metric. Figure 3.12 shows graphically how the size and orientation of these quadrics reflect the shape of the bunny's surface as it is simplified.

Boundary edges are preserved by incorporating additional planes perpendicular to the edges to be preserved. Lindstrom [Lindstrom 01b] employs a similar approach in the context of out-of-core models, but applies these constraints to every edge. The edge planes of adjacent or nearly adjacent triangles will cancel each other out, while those of boundary edges retain their full weight. This is useful for models where adjacency information is unknown.

In addition, it is possible to choose v to minimize E_v by solving a small system of linear equations. The main computational cost in solving this minimization problem is to invert the 4×4 matrix Q_v. Lindstrom and Turk [Lindstrom 98] [Lindstrom 99] provide an alternate solution to the computation of v. They constrain the choice of v to preserve the volume enclosed by the surface and the local area around the boundary edges, then choose v to minimize the error subject to these constraints. Interestingly, they choose not to store a quadric with each vertex of the mesh, but compute their edge collapses based only on the incremental error. Thus, the quadric for a simplified vertex is defined by the planes of its triangles at their current simplified resolution. They demonstrate that this *memoryless* approach to simplification still produces quantitatively good results.

Several different approaches to attribute handling are possible in the domain of error quadrics. Garland and Heckbert propose the use of higher-dimensional quadrics to track and minimize the error of models with attributes [Garland 98]. For example, a model with 3 vertex coordinates, 3 color values, 3 normal coordinates, and 2 texture coordinates would use quadrics operating in an 11-dimensional space. This is a mathematically elegant approach that directly extends the mechanics of dealing with the geometry-space quadrics to the problem of attiributes. However, the storage requirements for an n-dimensional quadric, represented as an $n \times n$ symmetric matrix, an n-vector, and a constant are

$$\frac{n(n+1)}{2} + n + 1$$

resulting in the storage of 78 floating point values for the 11-dimensional quadric. In addition, the optimization of the vertex values requires the inversion of an $n \times n$ matrix. However, most models do not have colors, normals, *and* texture coordinates. The more common cases are six-dimensional and possibly eight-dimensional, requiring only 28 floating point values.

Hoppe proposes a different quadric constructed based on separating the geometric error from the attribute error [Hoppe 99b]. In his formulation, the geometric optimization results in the same values that would result if no attributes were present, and the attribute errors are determined with this geometric correspondence in mind. The required attribute quadric for this formulation also contains an $n \times n$ matrix, an n-vector, and a constant, but the $n \times n$ matrix is sparse, and the total space dependency on the number of attributes is only linear rather than quadratic. For example, the 11-dimensional quadric for geometry, colors, normals, and texture coordinates requires only 43 nonzero values rather than 78. He demonstrates that not only does this approach require less storage and computation, but it produces better-looking results.

In both of these approaches to incorporating attributes into quadrics, color values and texture values are clamped, normal values are normalized, and texture folding is ignored. Because of the popularity and importance of quadric error metrics, we will revisit the above topics in some detail in Section 5.3.

3.3.3 VERTEX–SURFACE DISTANCE

The vertex–surface distance metric is a sampled approach to mapping one surface to another. In this case, the vertices of the original model are mapped to their closest points on the polygons of the simplified surface (Figure 3.13). This approach may be entirely appropriate for models whose existence begins as a set of point samples that are then triangulated. For such models, one can argue that it is the input vertices that

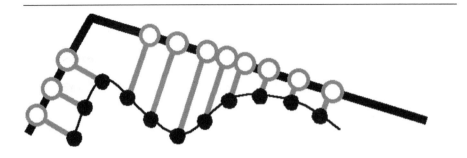

Figure 3.13   The original, curvy surface is mapped to a highly simplified surface. The black points are the vertices of the original surface, and the hollow points are associated closest points on the simplified surface. The lengths of the gray lines are pairwise distances.

are the true data to be preserved rather than the input surface. In fact, the approach may be generalized by resampling the input surface to any desired resolution to more finely optimize the distance between the two surfaces. Vertex–surface approaches are generally much slower than vertex–plane approaches because suitable mappings must be found for the many input vertices, each of which ultimately adds terms to the optimization function.

Mesh Optimization and Progressive Meshes

Hoppe's well-known progressive mesh algorithm [Hoppe 96] provides continuous LOD. It does not produce a small, discrete number of LODs, but rather a more continuous spectrum of detail, stored as a simple base mesh and a series of refinement operations. These refinement operations lend themselves to storing, rendering, and transmitting meshes in a progressive manner. They also support smooth morphing between different level-of-detail approximations, mesh compression, and selective refinement (Figure 3.14).

The progressive mesh algorithm follows a greedy edge collapse algorithm, minimizing the change to an energy function with each successive edge collapse. Although the high-level optimization process differs from Hoppe's previous mesh optimization algorithm [Hoppe 93], the two algorithms share the same geometric error metric. For a proposed edge collapse, the following procedure is performed:

1. Choose an initial value for the position of the new vertex v (e.g., an edge vertex or midpoint).

2. For each original vertex, map it to the closest point on one of the simplified triangles.

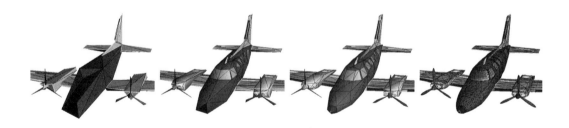

Figure 3.14   Progressive mesh levels of detail containing 150, 500, 1000, and 13,546 triangles, respectively [Hoppe 96]. Copyright © 1996 Association for Computing Machinery, Inc.

3. Optimize the position of v to minimize the sum of squared distances between the pairs of mapped points (solve a sparse, linear least-squares problem).

4. Iterate steps 2 and 3 until the error converges.

Notice that when the vertex v is moved in step 3, the mappings we had found in step 2 are no longer closest point pairs, so we must re-map them and re-optimize the system until it converges.

   In some cases, this system will never converge, because the optimal vertex position may be at infinity. This is possible because the vertex–surface metric is an approximation to a one-sided, surface-to-surface distance rather than the two-sided distance. It may be that none of the input samples map near to the vertex, so moving the vertex farther away does not negatively impact the metric (and may in fact benefit it). To deal with this problem, Hoppe introduces a spring energy term to the geometric error function. Conceptually, all the edges around v act as springs, applying some force that pulls v toward its neighboring vertices. The force of these springs is reduced as the number of samples mapped to v's adjacent faces increases. Thus, the forces are stronger at the start of the simplification process and decrease over time. As in the vertex–plane algorithm of [Ronfard 96], the work per edge collapse increases as the number of points mapped to the edge's adjacent faces increases, and the error measured is a total error rather than an incremental error.

   The progressive mesh algorithm also introduced the first sophisticated handling of attribute values. Edge collapses are prioritized according to how they affect the following energy function:

$$E(M) = E_{\text{dist}}(M) + E_{\text{spring}}(M) + E_{\text{scalar}}(M) + E_{\text{disc}}(M)$$

E_{dist} and E_{spring} refer to the geometric error and spring energy terms described above. E_{scalar} refers to color distances and other scalar value errors. These are optimized using the pointwise correspondences determined for the geometric error, and do not affect the iterative process of finding these correspondences. Another sparse, linear least-squares problem is solved to determine these scalar attribute values at v. The algorithm also preserves discontinuity curves in the attribute fields (such as normal creases or sharp edges in the mesh coloring) by assigning a penalty, E_{disc}, to the final error value of operations that alter the discontinuity. Normal vectors are simply carried through the simplification by assigning v the normal value from its initial position in step 1.

Metro

Metro is not a simplification algorithm but a tool for measuring the output quality of simplification algorithms using a point–surface distance metric [Cignoni 98b]. Metro takes as input two polygonal models and a sampling distance. One of the input models is sampled by points spaced at the specified distance. Each point is mapped to a closest point on the second model; a uniform spatial grid accelerates the task of finding the nearest polygons to a given point. The (possibly signed) distance is computed between these closest point pairs. The program outputs the maximum and average distance from the first model to the second model, as well as producing visual output to show how the distance function is distributed across the model. A two-sided distance function may also be computed by swapping the order of the models and running the algorithm again. The tool has been used in several research papers to report on the relative merits of various simplification algorithms [Cignoni 98a] [Lindstrom 99].

3.3.4   SURFACE–SURFACE DISTANCE

A surface–surface distance metric can provide the strongest guaranteed bounds on the error of a simplified surface. By definition, such a metric considers all points on both the original and simplified surface to determine the error at a given stage of the simplification process. These methods generally choose to minimize the maximum error, perhaps because finding a guaranteed maximum bound on the simplification error is the whole point of using such a rigorous (and sometimes painstaking) approach. Applications for which such bounds may be especially useful include medicine and scientific visualization. One can also make an argument for using a surface–surface metric for scanned models: although the raw scanned data may take the form of points or vertices, implying that a vertex–surface metric may suffice, great effort is often put into creating a high-quality surface reconstruction from these points. Thus, it may make sense to minimize the error from this entire reconstructed surface during the simplification process. We now present several algorithms based on surface–surface distance metrics.

Simplification Envelopes

The simplification envelopes algorithm [Varshney 94a] [Cohen 96] uses a nonoptimizing high-level queuing to compute each discrete level of detail. It uses an intuitive
and conceptually compelling method to bound the maximum geometric deviation
between the original and simplified surfaces. It first constructs inner and outer *envelope* surfaces that together enclose the original surface. These envelopes are modified
offset surfaces, constructed by displacing the original vertices by a distance of $\leq \epsilon$
along their normal vectors. Some vertices are displaced by less than ϵ to prevent self-
intersections among the envelope polygons. By construction, all points within the
envelopes are within distance ϵ of the original surface. Examples of these envelope
surfaces are shown in Figure 3.15.

   The input to the algorithm is a manifold triangle mesh (possibly with borders)
and an error tolerance; the output is a simplified mesh with a maximum error that
is as close as possible to the tolerance without exceeding it. The algorithm places all
the original vertices in a queue for removal, and attempts a vertex removal operation
for each one, filling the resulting holes using greedy triangle insertion. If a candidate
triangle intersects an envelope surface (or the rest of the simplified surface), it is
invalid and may not be used to fill the hole. The process is applied iteratively until
none of the remaining vertices may be successfully removed. Such a simplification
is depicted in 2D in Figure 3.16. The source code for the simplification envelopes
algorithm is available on the Web site accompanying this book.

   One interesting aspect of this algorithm is that it performs an overall distance
computation using only conservative intersection tests, so little information is known
about the error of the triangles except that they do not violate the given error tolerance. We should therefore classify this as a nonoptimizing algorithm in the simplification frameworks terminology of Section 2.3. The error tolerance may be specified
for each individual vertex, if desired, rather than for the model as a whole, generating
a manifold surface with bounded maximum error that varies across it, as shown in
Figure 3.17. For example, this can be used to favor regions with greater perceptual
importance, such as eyes or faces.

   Borders are preserved within the specified tolerance in a similar fashion to the
entire surface. *Border tubes,* essentially a set of non–self-intersecting, piecewise cylindrical tubes surrounding the edges of the border, are used to constrain the deviation
of the border edges as the simplification progresses.

   Because this algorithm uses vertex removal operations, attributes are easily carried through the process. Of course, the use of vertex removal operations also leaves
less freedom for optimizing the error. The error for each vertex removal operation is
a binary value—either it satisfies the bound or it violates the bound. There is some
room to optimize combinatorially by searching for a tessellation of a vertex's hole
that does not violate the bound. Varshney and Cohen experiment briefly with an *exhaustive hole-filling* approach that tries all possible tessellations, if necessary, to find
a satisfactory one.

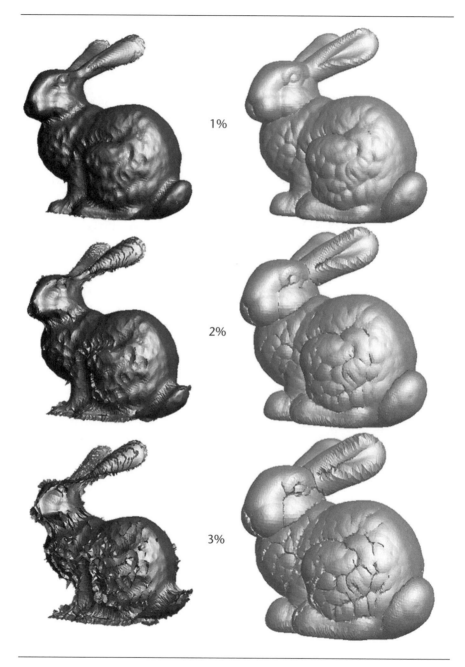

Figure 3.15   3D inner and outer envelope surfaces for the bunny model at three different settings of the error tolerance ϵ [Cohen 96]. Copyright © 1996 Association for Computing Machinery, Inc.

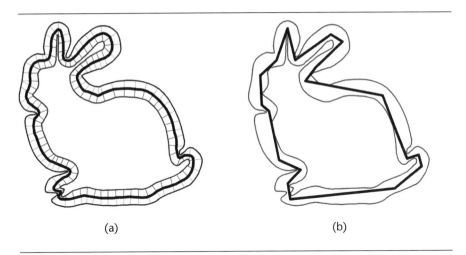

(a)   (b)

Figure 3.16   2D example of simplification using envelopes. (a) Original black surface is displaced by ϵ along normal vectors to compute inner and outer envelope surfaces. (b) Simplification is performed by staying within the envelopes.

To compute multiple discrete LODs, we may either simplify the original model several times with different error thresholds, or *cascade* the simplifications. In a cascaded simplification, the first level of detail is simplified to produce the second, the second to produce the third, and so on. In the former scheme, ϵ specifies the total error bound, while in the latter it specifies an incremental error bound. To compute a total error bound for the cascaded simplifications, we add the errors of successive levels of detail.

Mappings in the Plane

Bajaj and Schikore's plane mapping algorithm [Bajaj 96] employs a greedy framework, using a priority queue of vertex removal operations to simplify a mesh while measuring the maximum surface–surface error at each step of the simplification. The measure of error used here is the maximum pointwise mapping distance, where the mapping function is locally defined by orthogonally projecting the affected set of triangles before and after the vertex removal operation onto the same plane. Points of each surface that project to the same location on the plane are corresponding point pairs.

Bajaj and Schikore begin evaluating a vertex removal operation by orthogonally projecting to a plane the triangles surrounding the vertex to be removed. Working in this planar domain is equivalent to considering this local piece of mesh as a height field, where the "vertical" direction is the chosen direction of projection (typically

Figure 3.17   An adaptive simplification for the Stanford bunny model. ϵ varies from 1/64% at the nose to 1% at the tail [Cohen 96]. Copyright © 1996 Association for Computing Machinery, Inc.

the average face normal). In this plane, the vertex is removed and the planar polygon retriangulated. The mutual tessellation of the original vertex neighborhood with the new triangulated polygon is then computed, as shown in Figure 3.18.

Every point inside this polygon in the plane now corresponds to two points in 3D—one on the mesh before the vertex removal and one on the mesh after the removal. The error function is the maximum pointwise distance between these mapped points. For each subpolygon of this mutual tessellation, the distance function varies linearly. Thus, the maximum distance must occur at one of the subpolygon vertices. These subpolygon vertices are just the projection of the removed vertex and the

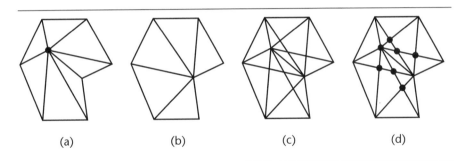

Figure 3.18   Mapping a vertex neighborhood in the plane. (a) The neighborhood of a removal vertex. (b) The vertex has been removed and the hole triangulated. (c) A mutual tessellation of the two sets of triangles. (d) Edge crossing points for error measurement [Bajaj 96].

edge–edge crossings between the two tessellations. To compute the maximum error across the entire local mesh neighborhood, we just compute the distance between these special point pairs and take the maximum. The maximum error is stored at each triangle of the mesh as an interval ranging from the greatest error below the triangle to the greatest error above the triangle. The same mapping can be used to measure the error in scalar fields, such as colors and texture coordinates that vary across the triangles.

The planar mapping method is extended by Cohen, Manocha, et al. [Cohen 97] for use with the edge collapse operation. They propose a simple algorithm for testing a direction of projection to see if it produces a valid, fold-free projection to the plane, as well as a rigorous algorithm based on 3D linear programming to find a valid direction if one exists. They then employ similar algorithms in 2D to find a valid placement of the new vertex in the plane (placing the vertex in the planar polygon's *kernel;* see Figure 3.6). Given this 2D vertex placement, Cohen, Manocha, et al. compute the mutual tessellation shown in Figure 3.19. Finally, they optimize the placement of the new vertex along the plane's normal vector to minimize the maximum incremental error using a 1D, linear programming algorithm. In this algorithm, an axis-aligned bounding box is associated with each triangle of the simplified mesh to propagate the total error from one simplification operation to the next. (Plots of the total error versus the number of triangles for the bunny model using this metric are shown in Figure 2.23.) The same planar mapping is also used to carry texture coordinates of the original mesh through the simplification process.

Local Error and Tolerance Volumes

Like the simplification envelopes algorithm, Guéziec's approach to simplification [Guéziec 95] [Guéziec 99a] uses a bounding volume approach to measuring simplification error. However, his error volumes are measured locally and grown iteratively.

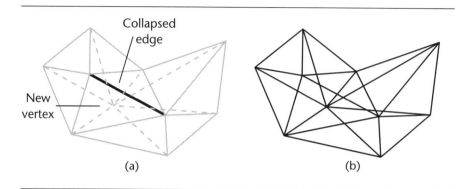

Figure 3.19   (a) Edge neighborhood and generated vertex neighborhood superimposed. (b) A mapping in the plane, composed of 25 polygonal cells. Each cell maps between a pair of planar elements in 3D [Cohen 97] [Cohen 98].

This makes the approach highly suitable for measuring and optimizing the error of each individual operation as well as for producing a continuous progression of guaranteed-quality levels of detail.

The algorithm uses the *estimated* high-level simplification framework (see Section 2.3). It employs a priority queue of edge collapses ranked by maximum error. However, for the purpose of prioritization, edge collapse error bounds are initially computed using a fast—but less tight—method. When the edge is actually collapsed, a more expensive but accurate method may be applied.

A bound on geometric error is tracked using an error volume (see Figure 3.20). A sphere with zero radius is initially centered at each vertex. As the model is simplified, the spheres of the simplified mesh vertices grow at different rates to indicate the maximum local error. This error is defined across the entire surface of the mesh by interpolating the vertex sphere radii across each triangle. The union of these varying radius spheres swept over the entire triangle mesh forms an error volume, and the radius at any given point of the mesh bounds the maximum geometric deviation error at that point.

Using the fast error bound computation, the sphere radii after an edge collapse are determined as follows. All the unchanged vertices surrounding the edge retain their sphere radii. The new vertex is placed at the edge midpoint, and the radius of the new vertex's sphere is chosen to contain the spheres of the collapsed edge's vertices. We can think of this approach as using the natural mapping (see Figure 3.9) to measure the error; it is roughly equivalent to using the weighted edge length as a loose error bound for the purpose of edge prioritization.

When edges are actually chosen to be collapsed, a tighter bound is used to measure and optimize the location of the new vertex. In this computation, the sphere radii of all the vertices surrounding the collapsed edged may grow to produce a more

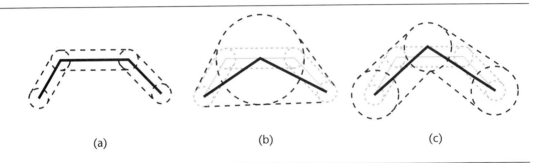

Figure 3.20   2D example of growing an error volume. (a) The solid lines indicate the current mesh. An error sphere with some radius is centered at each vertex, indicating its current error. Sweeping the spheres across the surface and interpolating their radii define the current error volume. (b) For fast error estimation, the new vertex after an edge collapse is placed at the edge center and its sphere contains the two collapsed vertex spheres. (c) For slower, more optimized error computation, all spheres are allowed to change size, and vertex is placed to minimize their sizes while containing the old error volume within the new error volume.

optimal result. A mapping is created between the local mesh before and after the edge collapse. Similar to the mapping used by [Bajaj 96], Guéziec's mapping contains data not only for the vertices of both local meshes, but also for the edge crossings. In this case, however, the mapping is constructed directly on the two surfaces rather than on an arbitrary plane, so the distance measurements may be less conservative. As in Cohen, Manocha, et al. [Cohen 97], the mapping is incremental (between two successive meshes), but here it used to optimize a bound on the total error rather than the incremental error. With all these vertex radii as variables, as well as the position of the new vertex, the new vertex position and the radii are chosen to minimize the error of the mapping (as indicated by the sphere radii) and to preserve the mesh volume. This error sphere approach can also be used to measure and optimize maximum errors in color, normal, and texture coordinate attributes.

Mappings in Texture Space

The appearance-preserving simplification algorithm of Cohen, Olano, et al. [Cohen 98a] proposes a new screen-space error metric for textured models, the 2D *texture deviation*. Intuitively, this texture deviation measures how many pixels a particular texel may shift on the screen from its correct position due to the use of a simplified model. By using parameterized models, with the colors stored in texture maps and the normals stored in normal maps (shown in Figure 3.21), this algorithm preserves the rendered appearance of the model. The primary visual artifact is then a screen-space

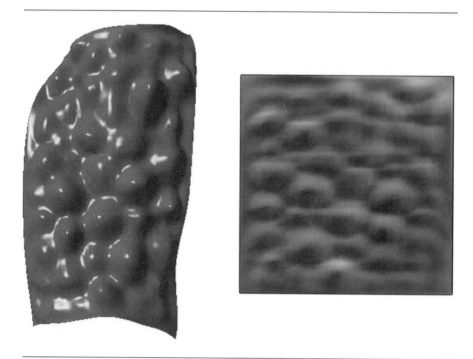

Figure 3.21   Parameterized surface patch and its normal map. The x, y, and z normal components
are stored as red, green, and blue colors, respectively [Cohen 98]. Copyright © 1998
Association for Computing Machinery, Inc.

distortion of the texture and normal maps, which the user can control by choosing
an acceptable tolerance for the texture deviation at run-time.

The simplification algorithm used is quite similar to that of Cohen, Manocha,
et al. [Cohen 97] (see Mappings in the Plane section, above). The primary difference
is that rather than using orthographic projections to produce mappings in a planar
domain, the surface's texture coordinate parameterization is used to establish these
mappings. The parametric error of this mapping is the 3D texture deviation. That
is to say, it measures the maximum distance that any texel moves in 3D as the level
of detail is changed from the original model to the simplified model. This texture
deviation is thus a geometric error measure, and we can apply the same techniques
as for other geometric deviations to convert to a screen-space deviation (see Screen-
Space Error in Section 3.2.1, above). Thus, the texture deviation provides a bound on
other geometric deviations, such as silhouette deviation, while bounding the sliding
motion of the texture (Figure 3.22).

Another contribution of this algorithm in the handling of textures is the detection of valid and invalid texture coordinates for the new vertex after an edge collapse

Figure 3.22   Armadillo model (2 million polygons) simplified using appearance-preserving simplification's texture deviation metric. LODs are shown with 250K, 63K, 8K, and 1K
triangles (from left to right) [Cohen 98]. Copyright © 1998 Association for Computing Machinery, Inc.

operation. If the new texture coordinates lies outside the kernel of the edge neighborhood as seen in the texture plane (as in Figure 3.6), then there will be a folding of the
texture as it is mapped to the surface. Restricting the new texture coordinates to this
kernel eliminates this type of artifact.

The use of texture deviation and normal mapping to provide high-quality, low-
polygon-count, multiresolution surfaces has been explored further in recent works,
such as Lee et al. [Lee 00] and Sander et al. [Sander 01].

3.3.5   IMAGE METRIC

All of the error metrics described thus far have been measured in object space and
attribute space, with the hope of eventually translating these bounds into some meaningful image-space metric. After all, what we typically hope to optimize is the visual
appearance of the models when we view them as images rendered on the screen.
Lindstrom and Turk [Lindstrom 00b] take a more direct approach by actually rendering the model to evaluate the quality of the model output as the simplification
proceeds (see Chapter 5 for more implementation details). They use the lazy high-
level algorithm, with a priority-queue-driven edge collapse scheme. The placement
of new vertices for edge collapses is purely geometry driven, based on the memoryless algorithm of Lindstrom and Turk [Lindstrom 98], but they use an image-space
error metric to prioritize the edge collapses in the queue.

Conceptually, Lindstrom and Turk measure the error for simplification operations by rendering multiple images of the object using a sphere of virtual cameras.
The cameras are placed at the 20 vertices of a dodecahedron. Each camera renders an

image of the original model and of the simplified model, and a root-mean-squared error of pixel luminance values is computed between the two sets of pixels from all the cameras. This RMS error is the edge's key in the priority queue.

This approach has a number of benefits. It naturally incorporates visual errors due to a number of sources, such as motion of the silhouette, and deviation of color, normal, and texture coordinate attributes. It even accounts for factors such as the content of the texture maps and the shading modes used to render the model (such as flat or Gouraud shading).

The image metric is therefore in many ways an excellent one for measuring simplification error, and it promises to work even better as more sophisticated perceptual image-based metrics are developed. However, image-based simplification has disadvantages as well. The algorithm is significantly slower than the slowest geometric algorithms, since rendering and rerendering multiple images for every edge collapse is an intrinsically expensive way to measure error. Since it uses a fixed, relatively small number of camera positions (Lindstrom and Turk use 20 to 30), the algorithm may also make poor choices as a result of undersampling the visual space around the model, or even inside the model. Finally, since LODs are generated with respect to a particular set of rendering parameters (number of lights, flat versus smooth shading, etc.), the LODs may prove suboptimal if the rendering parameters of the scene change. However, for the models and rendering environments tested, the algorithm has been shown thus far to deal well with such problems in practice.

3.4 CONCLUSIONS

To summarize, we have examined the reasons to measure simplification error, the key elements common to many simplification error metrics, and several metrics themselves from the literature. We broadly classified these metrics into vertex–vertex, vertex–plane, vertex–surface, and surface–surface distance measures. These different classes provide a range of characteristic performance in terms of speed, quality, robustness, and ease of implementation.

The vertex–vertex measures are the fastest and most robust, followed by the vertex–plane measures. The vertex–vertex measures do provide guaranteed bounds on quality, but these are typically much looser than we would like. The vertex–plane measures produce much higher-quality models overall, but the latest quadric error measures do not actually guarantee a particular quality, so they do not support fidelity-based simplification systems well. The vertex–vertex measures are quite easy to implement, and the vertex–plane measures are only slightly harder, requiring a few more functions in your algebraic toolbox.

The vertex–surface and surface–surface measures tend to be somewhat slower than the first two classifications. However, the surface–surface measures provide guaranteed error bounds on their output, making them useful for both fidelity-based and budget-based simplification systems. For the highest-quality simplifications, systems based on these measures generally assume a clean, manifold mesh as input and preserve the topology of that mesh throughout the process. The surface–surface measures may be particularly difficult to implement compared to the vertex–vertex and vertex–plane approaches, requiring more geometry-based coding rather than just a few algebraic tools. Some implementations are available, such as the *simplification envelopes* software on this book's accompanying Web site.

We have now studied three of the major components we use for simplification: optimization algorithms, simplification operators, and error metrics. Given this framework for generating LODs, we now move on to applying these LODs in a variety of run-time settings.

PART II

APPLICATION

RUN-TIME FRAMEWORKS

In this chapter we turn from the offline task of LOD creation to the run-time task of LOD management. When using discrete LOD, this task reduces to the selection of which LODs will represent each object each frame. We describe some popular schemes for selecting LOD, ranging from simple distance-to-viewpoint to sophisticated predictive schedulers for maintaining a fixed frame rate. These schemes are easily extended to support continuous LOD, which can be thought of as very fine-grained discrete LOD. However, view-dependent approaches add another level of complexity to run-time LOD management. We describe a generic run-time framework for view-dependent LOD similar to several published approaches, and discuss the subtle but important issue of respecting dependencies in the mesh simplification process. Finally, we examine two run-time techniques to reduce "popping," alpha blending and geomorphs. Both are applicable to both view-dependent and view-independent LOD. These techniques are alpha blending and geomorphs.

87

4.1 LOD SELECTION FACTORS

Clearly the most important question in LOD management is when to switch to a lower or higher resolution model. The basic observation that we need less detail for small or distant objects seems straightforward, but how small or far away should an object be before we transition to a simpler model? The following chapters discuss the various aspects of this problem in detail. Here, we begin by looking at the major frameworks that have been used to modulate LOD.

4.1.1 DISTANCE

A distance-based framework is probably the easiest way to manage level of detail: simply assign a distance to each LOD at which it will be used to represent the object. The underlying theory is obvious. Since fewer high-detail features of a distant object are visible, we can select a lower LOD without greatly affecting the fidelity of the image. Historically, flight simulators were among the first applications to use distance-based LOD heavily [Yan 85] [Schachter 81] [Cosman 81]. These days, it is a common technique available in most graphics APIs and game engines. Figure 4.1 shows an example from the popular *Unreal* game engine. This system provides support for distance-based continuous LOD for 3D models, as well as smooth adaptation of texture map detail [Miliano 99].

Implementing a distance-based scheme simply requires a data structure to store the different levels of detail for each object, and a list of distance thresholds to indicate when each LOD should be used. Given such a structure, a simple pointer switch suffices to select the most appropriate model for any distance. A more subtle issue is the question of which point within the model to use for the distance calculation. This point might be assigned to the object's centroid, assigned directly by the designer, or more accurately calculated as the point closest to the viewer. The LOD node of the VRML97 graphics file format [VRML 97] encapsulates these factors:

```
LOD {
    exposedField    MFNode      level [ ]
    field           SFVec3f     center      0 0 0 # (∞,∞)
    field           MFFloat     range [ ]   # (0,∞)
}
```

The *level* field contains a list of nodes, one for each LOD representation, where the highest detail level is given first. The *range* field specifies the distances at which to switch between the levels of detail in the level array. Finally, the *center* field gives the offset (in the local coordinate system) that specifies the point of the LOD model used for the distance calculations. Therefore, given n levels of detail ($level_1$ to $level_n$) and $n - 1$ range thresholds ($range_1$ to $range_{n-1}$), the appropriate level of detail to use on

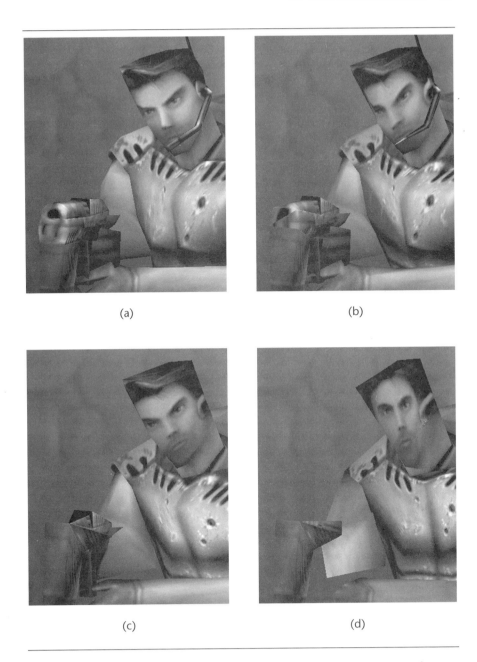

Figure 4.1   Screen shots of an *Unreal* tournament player showing how level of detail reduces as distance increases. The original model (a) contains over 600 polygons (excluding the weapon), whereas (b), (c), and (d) show, respectively, vertex counts reduced to 75%, 50%, and 25%. Copyright © 1999–2001 Epic Games, Inc.

any frame, given a distance d from the viewer position to the center of the LOD node, is computed as:

$$level(d) = \begin{cases} level_1 & \text{where } d < range_i \\ level_i & \text{where } range_{i-1} \leq d < range_i \quad \text{for} \quad 1 \leq i < n-1 \\ level_n & \text{where } d \geq range_{n-1} \end{cases}$$

For example, given a range array of [50, 100] (specified in meters) and three levels of detail, the highest LOD is used when the object's distance is less than 50 m away, the medium LOD is used between 50 and 100 m, and the lowest LOD is used for all distances over 100 m. Often the lowest detail model is made to be an empty set of triangles to allow the object to be culled beyond a certain distance.

Distance-based LOD is both simple and efficient. A few conditional statements suffice to check whether a distance exceeds the predefined thresholds, and the only potentially expensive computation is calculating the 3D Euclidean distance between two points. This normally involves the square root operation, which for example takes about 80 cycles on a Pentium II using the standard C library sqrt() function [King 01]. Various optimizations exist for this calculation, however, such as computing and comparing against the square of the distance thresholds, or using the Manhattan distance (L_1 norm) as an approximation to the Euclidean distance (L_2 norm) [Ritter 90].

Despite its simplicity, distance LOD has some definite disadvantages. Choosing an arbitrary point within the object for all distance calculations introduces inevitable inaccuracy, since the actual distance to the viewpoint can change depending on orientation. This can lead to more obvious popping effects under certain conditions. The best solution is to calculate the distance to the point on the object nearest the viewer. Scaling the object to make it larger or smaller, using a different display resolution, and changing the field of view all invalidate the original distance thresholds. In addition, a pure distance measure does not take into consideration the parameters of the perspective projection used to render all objects. To combat some of these problems, for example, the OpenGL Performer API lets the user specify a scaling factor (PFLOD_SCALE) for all range thresholds. For example, setting PFLOD_SCALE to 2.0 doubles all distance ranges [Silicon Graphics 00a].

4.1.2 SIZE

Distance-based criteria measure the distance from viewpoint to object in world space. Alternatively, the system can use a screen space criterion. Since objects get smaller as they move further away, size-based LOD techniques use the projected screen coverage of an object, and switch between LOD based on a series of size thresholds rather than a series of distances.

Size-based techniques avoid some of the problems with distance-based LOD, since projected size is insensitive to display resolution, object scaling, or field of view.

In addition, size-based LOD selection uses the entire object, rather than requiring the user to select an arbitrary point for the calculation. As a result, size-based LOD techniques provide a more generic and accurate means for modulating LOD than distance-based techniques. However, they can also be more computationally expensive, requiring a number of world coordinates to be projected into screen coordinates. For example, many systems use a bounding box of a bounding box, projecting the eight vertices of an object's bounding box into screen space, and using the 2D bounding box of the eight transformed vertices to quickly estimate the projected area of the object. This requires eight vertex–matrix multiplications, which is certainly more expensive than the viewpoint-to-object distance computation test used for distance-based LOD selection. Nor is this approach rotation-invariant, which presents another disadvantage. The screen-space-projected area of a thin object (e.g., a model of a knife or credit card) can vary drastically when the object rotates on the screen, which may cause some disturbing fluctuations in LOD.

As an example of this, the Open Inventor graphics toolkit from Silicon Graphics provides a means to automatically select different levels of detail based on a screen area criterion. The screen area is calculated by projecting the 3D bounding box for a model onto the viewport and then computing the area of the screen-aligned rectangle surrounding that bounding box [Wernecke 93]. An alternative technique used by many systems is to calculate the projected radius of an object's bounding sphere (see Section 3.2). This approach—in effect a form of distance-based LOD selection that accounts for field of view and object size—provides a very lightweight and effective mechanism for representing the size of an object in screen space. It also provides a rotation-invariant method because the projected radius will be the same length for all object orientations. However, bounding spheres offer a poor fit for some object shapes, which can result in unnecessarily conservative error estimates. Many researchers have investigated or suggested more sophisticated bounding volumes, such as ellipsoids or oriented bounding boxes, that could provide better fits to the geometry (e.g., Luebke and Erikson [Luebke 97]). Figure 4.2 illustrates the use of two different bounding volumes to calculate screen size.

Finally, screen-space LOD techniques have proven particularly popular in continuous and view-dependent LOD systems, such as in the area of terrain visualization. For example, Lindstrom et al. used a screen-space error metric that added further detail until the projected distance between adjacent vertices fell below a predefined pixel threshold [Lindstrom 95]. We discuss view-dependent LOD and terrain LOD extensively in Section 4.3 and Chapter 7, respectively, but pause to note here that this example is subtly different from the previous size-based techniques because it is the size of the error that is being measured rather than the size of the object itself.

4.1.3 PRIORITY

In many environments, some objects are particularly important for preserving the illusion of the scene and the user's acceptance of that illusion. For example, in an

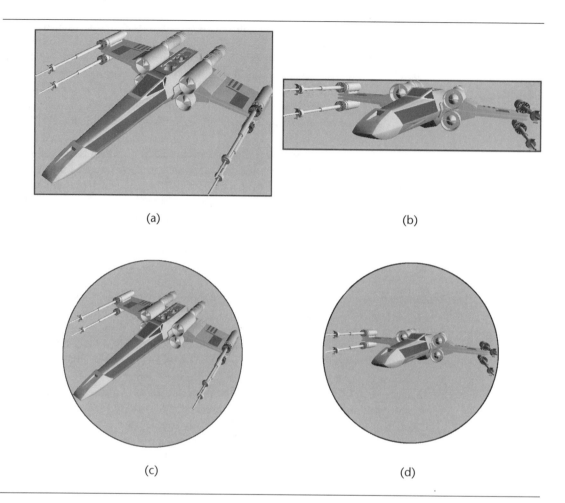

(a) (b)

(c) (d)

Figure 4.2 (a–b) A 3D model shown at two different orientations, illustrating the effect of using a screen-aligned bounding box and (c–d) a projected bounding sphere to estimate screen size. Note that the screen area varies more for the screen-aligned bounding box in this case.

architectural walkthrough system, the walls of a building are crucial to the perception of the scene. If these were to be simplified to the point that they are removed from the scene, then the user's experience will be drastically affected, much more so than if a pencil were to disappear from a desk [Funkhouser 93b]. Similarly, a virtual reality system with a glove-tracking device will typically display a virtual representation of the hand. Reducing the hand to a cuboid, or removing it completely, would seriously impair the user's ability to perform grabbing or other hand–eye coordination tasks.

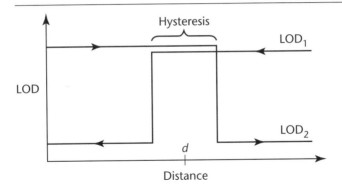

Figure 4.3   Distance-based switching thresholds between two LODs illustrating a period of hysteresis around the threshold distance d [Astheimer 94] [Reddy 97].

Therefore, a number of LOD researchers proposed schemes in which objects receive a priority ranking, so that those objects deemed most important are degraded the least. This is often referred to as a priority- or semantic-based solution.

For example, Richard Holloway implemented a simple priority scheme in his Viper system at the University of North Carolina [Holloway 91]. Two priorities (high and low) were used to define whether an object should always be rendered at the highest level of detail. A representation of the user's hand might be classed as a high-priority object and hence should never be degraded. Funkhouser and Séquin's walk-through system, discussed in detail later, used a benefit heuristic to estimate the contribution any LOD makes to model perception. This heuristic consisted of a number of components, one of which was termed *semantics*. Funkhouser notes that certain types of objects may have inherent importance in the scene. He therefore modulated the benefit value for each LOD by an amount proportional to the object type's semantic importance, as determined by the user [Funkhouser 93a].

4.1.4 HYSTERESIS

In the context of LOD systems, hysteresis is simply a lag introduced into the LOD transitions so that objects switch to a lower LOD slightly further away than the threshold distance, and switch to a higher LOD at a slightly closer distance. This is done to reduce the flickering effect that can occur when an object constantly switches between two different representations as it hovers near the threshold distance. This concept is illustrated in Figure 4.3. In their work, Astheimer and Pöche experimented with hysteresis techniques and found that a hysteresis of 10% of each LOD's distance range produced favorable results [Astheimer 94]. For example, consider two levels of detail of an object, L1 and L2, where L1 is the higher resolution model. If the distance threshold used to switch between L1 and L2 is 100 m, the system may instead choose to switch from L1 to L2 at 110 m and switch back from L2 to L1 at 90 m.

Hysteresis formed another component of Funkhouser's benefit heuristic. Noting that rendering an object at different levels of detail in successive frames could be bothersome to the user, Funkhouser reduced the benefit value for an LOD by an amount proportional to the difference in level of detail from that used in the previous frame. The degree of hysteresis employed could be controlled interactively through sliders on the system's control panel (see Figure 4.4).

Gobbetti and Bouvier introduced a hysteresis factor into their cost/benefit model [Gobbetti 99], although they eventually removed it because they found it unnecessary for most complex scenes. Nonetheless, their model for hysteresis is given as follows, where s is a visible multiresolution object, r is a continuous resolution value between 0 and 1, and n is the number of visible objects:

$$hysteresis(s, r) = 1 - \frac{1}{n} \sum_{i=1}^{n} \left(r_i - r_i^{old} \right)^2$$

4.1.5 ENVIRONMENTAL CONDITIONS

One trick often used to camouflage the switching between levels of detail, or to reduce the range over which models need to be displayed, is to enable atmospheric effects such as haze and fog. For example, the NPSNET group at the Naval Postgraduate School (NPS) performed work regarding the integration of dismounted infantry into their system. They report that their distance-based LOD feature enabled them to increase the number of infantry personnel more than sevenfold, while maintaining a 10- to 15-Hz frame rate [Chrislip 95]. They generated four different levels of detail for each figure and used various environmental conditions to slacken the LOD distance thresholds, including clouds, fog, smoke, and haze. In general, of course, fogging solutions cannot be used for every application, and should not be introduced artificially to cover up LOD artifacts.

4.1.6 PERCEPTUAL FACTORS

Researchers have observed that 3D graphics systems should be based more on how our human visual system works than how a pinhole camera works. A number of perceptual factors that can affect the amount of detail we can perceive under different circumstances are typically ignored in computer graphics. For example, we can perceive less detail for objects in our peripheral vision, or for objects moving rapidly across our gaze. We could therefore imagine reducing the resolution of objects under these circumstances, improving the frame rate without perceptible degradation.

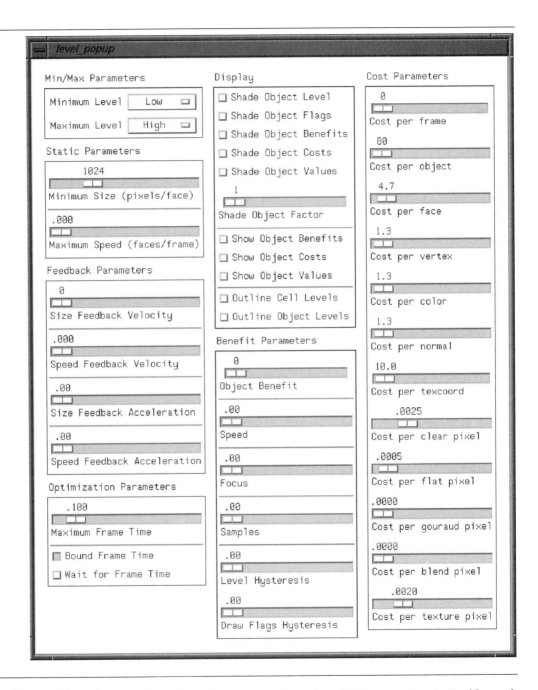

Figure 4.4   The control panel used to manage the various LOD parameters in Funkhouser's architectural walkthough system [Funkhouser 93a].

LOD researchers have indeed studied systems that exploit such perceptual factors; however, we will postpone their discussion to Chapter 8, which is dedicated entirely to perception and LOD.

4.2 Fixed-Frame Rate Schedulers

A naive real-time graphics application is often implemented as a free-running system allowed to take as long as necessary to render each frame. This means that when the current viewpoint contains a few simple objects, the scene can be rendered rapidly, while a viewpoint consisting of complex high-polygon models will take much longer to render. As a result, if a user navigates around a scene in a free-running system, the frame rate will normally vary on a per-frame basis. However, many problems exist with variable frame rate systems. For example, they can affect users' ability to perceive velocities accurately and thus perform temporal coordination tasks. They can cause problems in training simulators where subjects learn to associate a change in frame rate with a certain event, such as an opponent about to enter the scene. Asynchronous visual delays can even cause motion sickness [Uliano 86]. Conventional wisdom therefore dictates maintaining a steady and consistent frame rate for most applications [Hawkes 95] [Helman 96]. Fortunately, level of detail techniques give the graphics developer a powerful tool for managing rendering complexity to maintain frame rates. For example, flight simulators have long used handcrafted LODs to allow the system to produce fixed-frame frames [Clark 76] [Cosman 81]. Chapter 10 investigates more deeply how temporal delays affect user performance. For now, we will look at the various frameworks that have been proposed to produce systems that maintain a fixed frame rate. These include two principal approaches: *reactive schedulers,* (based on the last frame's rate) and *predictive schedulers* (based on estimates of how much work can be done within the current frame).

4.2.1 Reactive Fixed-Frame Rate

The simplest way to implement a fixed frame rate scheduler simply checks how long the previous frame took to render, and assigns LOD settings accordingly. If the last frame was completed after the deadline, detail should be reduced. However, if the last frame finished before the deadline, detail can be increased. This technique does not guarantee a bounded frame rate, but simply adjusts the detail level based on whether the previous frame was rendered within the target frame rate.

Some examples of LOD-based reactive fixed frame rate systems include Airey et al.'s architectural walkthrough system [Airey 90], Hitchner and McGreevy's Virtual Planetary Testbed at NASA [Hitchner 93], and Holloway's Viper system [Holloway 91]. The last is a good example of a very simple reactive system. This attempted to degrade LOD in order to maintain a user-specified fixed frame rate by simply terminating the rendering process as the system became overloaded. This could cause objects to appear with holes in them, or to disappear completely, as the graphics load increased. Holloway noted that if the system adjusted the load as quickly as possible, this introduced abrupt and often oscillating image changes. Instead, Holloway suggested that adapting to the load gradually would provide better results, in essence adding a degree of hysteresis. Viper's top-level main function implemented this, as follows:

```
main()
{
    init();
    read_3D_geometry();
    create_world();
    while ( ! done )
    {
        // calculate the frame rate for the previous frame
        frameRate = calcFrameRate();
        // compare this to the desired frame rate for this frame
        adjustment = evaluateLastFrame(frameRate, DesiredFrameRate);
        // adjust LODs to display
        adjustDisplayList(adjustment);
        // read the tracker, update head and hand positions
        read_tracker();
        // handle any button presses or keyboard commands
        handle_button_events();
        // finally, update the displays (one for each eye)
        update_displays();
    }
}
```

The OpenGL Performer graphics API from Silicon Graphics also supports a reactive fixed-frame-rate model. This is specified using the pfFrameRate() function with a rate parameter. Performer will round this number to the nearest frame rate that corresponds to an integral number of screen refreshes. For example, a value of 33 Hz is rounded to 30 Hz when the screen refresh rate is 60 Hz. If the scene has been modeled with levels of detail (represented in Performer using pfLOD nodes), Performer can automatically reduce or increase scene complexity to attain the specified frame rate. In this case, the system load is calculated as the percentage of the frame period it took to process the previous frame. It is possible that the system can still become overstressed and result in dropped or skipped frames. Figure 4.5 shows a frame-timing diagram with different frame rate scenarios.

It is worth noting that Performer includes support for dynamically reducing *fill rate*, or the rate at which the graphics hardware can rasterize pixels. This highlights a limitation of LOD techniques: when fill rate becomes the system bottleneck, reducing the level of detail of objects in the scene will not generally help, since even the simpler

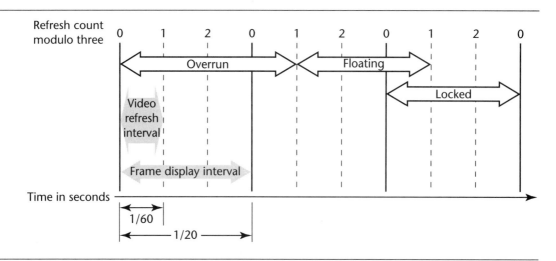

Figure 4.5   A frame-timing diagram showing three frame updates: one that overruns the frame
rate, the resulting out-of-phase frame, and a frame-rate locked frame. In this example, the video refresh rate is 60 Hz and the frame rate is 20 Hz [Performer 00a].

LODs cover roughly the same number of pixels. However, on SGI InfiniteReality
machines, Performer can use the Dynamic Video Resolution (DVR) feature to help
maintain a constant frame rate. The methods in `pfPipeVideoChannel` monitor the
time required to draw each frame. If the frame takes too long to draw because of
fill rate, the size of the viewport is reduced so that fewer pixels must be rendered. The
output video buffer is then scaled up (magnified) so that the image appears to be the
correct size. If the frame requires less time to draw than the frame rate threshold, the
video output is not reduced [Silicon Graphics 00a].

4.2.2   PREDICTIVE FIXED-FRAME RATE

In contrast to reactive fixed-frame-rate schedulers, a predictive scheduler estimates
the complexity of the frame about to be rendered and enforces LOD assignments to
ensure that the update deadline is never exceeded. This approach is substantially more
complicated to implement than a reactive system because it requires an accurate way
to model how long the specific hardware will take to render a given set of polygons.
However, the major benefit of doing this is that the system can maintain a bounded
frame rate even for scenes that vary greatly in detail between successive frames. Under
these circumstances, a reactive fixed frame system could overrun the threshold for a
few frames, dropping below the desired frame rate, until the feedback mechanisms
reduced the scene detail sufficiently to get back under the desired frame time.

View-Independent LOD

Funkhouser and Séquin's architectural walkthrough system employed a predictive fixed frame rate scheduler for selecting discrete LODs [Funkhouser 93b]. They used a cost/benefit paradigm that attempted to optimize the perceptual benefit of a frame against the computational cost of displaying it. That is, given a set S of object tuples (O, L, R) of which each describes an instance of an object O, rendered at LOD L and using rendering algorithm R, the overall image quality for each frame was calculated via the following equation.

Maximize:

$$\sum_S Benefit(O, L, R)$$

(4.1)

Subject to:

$$\sum_S Cost(O, L, R) \leq TargetFrameTime$$

The $Cost(O, L, R)$ heuristic was estimated by assuming a two-stage, pipelined rendering model involving a per-primitive processing stage (e.g., coordinate transforms, lighting, and clipping) and a per-pixel processing stage (e.g., rasterization, Z-buffering, alpha blending, and texture mapping). Assuming a pipelined architecture, only one of these two stages will be the bottleneck to the system. That is, the maximum time of the two is used, as follows, where C_1, C_1, C_1 and are constants specific to the rendering algorithm and target hardware.

$$Cost(O, L, R) = \max \begin{cases} C_1 Poly(O, L) + C_2 Vert(O, L) \\ C_3 Pix(O) \end{cases}$$

The $Benefit(O, L, R)$ heuristic incorporated a number of factors to estimate the object's contribution to model perception. The primary factor was the screen-space size of an object measured in pixels. An accuracy component was also used to estimate the quality of the image produced based on the rendering algorithm used. For example, a textured, lit model would have higher accuracy and thus contribute greater benefit than an untextured, unlit model. Finally, a number of more qualitative factors were applied as scaling factors to these two components: object importance (e.g., priority), focus (eccentricity), motion (velocity), and hysteresis. The weights of these scaling factors were controlled manually through sliders in the user interface (see Figure 4.4). The final benefit heuristic can be given as follows:

$$Benefit(O, L, R) = Size(O) * Accuracy(O, L, R) * Importance(O)$$

$$* Focus(O) * Motion(O) * Hysteresis(O, L, R)$$

Table 4.1   Results for Funkhouser and Séquin's evaluation of four different
LOD models, including their own predictive fixed-frame rate system.

	Compute Time (s)		Frame Time (s)		
LOD Algorithm	Mean	Max	Mean	Max	Std Dev
No LOD	0.00	0.00	0.43	0.99	0.305
Distance LOD only	0.00	0.01	0.11	0.20	0.048
Reactive System	0.00	0.01	0.10	0.16	0.026
Predictive System	0.01	0.03	0.10	0.13	0.008

The accuracy component is further refined as:

$$Accuracy(O, L, R) = 1 - Error = 1 - \frac{BaseError}{Samples(L, R)^m}$$

where *Samples(L, R)* is the number of vertices for Gouraud shading, the number of
polygons for flat shading, or the number of pixels for ray tracing. The exponent *m* is
instantiated to 1 for flat shading and 2 for Gouraud shading. The *BaseError* constant
was set to 0.5.

Given the cost and benefit heuristics, Funkhouser and Séquin's system could
solve Equation 4.1 at each frame in order to choose the best set of object tuples to
render. Unfortunately, this combinatorial optimization problem can be shown to
be NP-complete; it is in fact a variant of the Knapsack Problem (where elements
are partitioned into sets and at most one element from each set may be selected at
any time). Instead, Funkhouser and Séquin used a greedy approximation algorithm
to select LODs. They evaluated their system using a model of an auditorium, UC
Berkeley's Soda Hall, containing 87,565 polygons at full resolution. They tested the
system using four LOD selection algorithms: no LOD, traditional view-independent
(distance-based) LOD, a reactive fixed frame system, and their predictive fixed frame
rate system. Their results are presented in Table 4.1.

Mason and Blake produced a hybrid of Funkhouser and Séquin's predictive
scheduler and Maciel and Shirley's imposters technique [Maciel 95]. This used a
hierarchical LOD concept in which multiple smaller objects in a scene are recursively replaced with a larger single representation [Mason 97]. This view-independent
scheme gracefully handled scenes with many objects by allowing these to be merged
into group imposters. Mason and Blake extended the optimization algorithm of
Funkhouser and Séquin to support hierarchical LOD and incorporated frame-to-
frame coherence within the LOD selection process, incrementally updating the results
from the previous frame rather than recomputing LODs from scratch each frame.
They also performed a number of perceptual experiments to evaluate their system

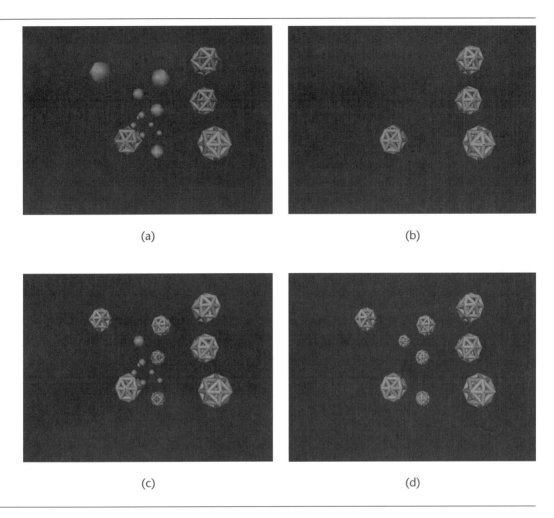

(a)　　　　　　　　　　　　　　　(b)

(c)　　　　　　　　　　　　　　　(d)

Figure 4.6　Images (a) and (b) compare the hierarchical fixed frame rate algorithm versus the nonhierarchical algorithm, respectively, and (c) and (d) show the same comparison for a different level of system stress [Mason 97]. Copyright © 1997 Blackwell Publishers.

against Funkhouser and Séquin's using a stimulus comparison method. This involved 15 subjects comparing a number of pairs of images produced using the two techniques and selecting which image was "better" on a 6-point scale. They found that the images produced by the hierarchical algorithm were perceived as being significantly better than those rendered with the nonhierarchical algorithm, probably because the nonhierarchical algorithm removed objects the hierarchical algorithm was able to preserve with a lower resolution imposter (see Figure 4.6).

Continuous LOD

Building upon the initial work of Funkhouser and Séquin, Gobbetti and Bouvier developed a predictive fixed-frame-rate system that worked with continuous LOD models instead of simply discrete ones [Gobbetti 99]. They performed a constrained optimization at each frame to select the best resolution for each potentially visible object while meeting the specified timing constraint. They used a similar cost/benefit architecture, in which they define $S(\mathbf{r})$ as a parameterized set of visible objects generated at each frame. Each element of the vector $\mathbf{r}$ takes a value between 0 and 1 that represents the degree of simplification to be applied to that object's multiresolution mesh. Given this representation, and a factor W to represent the viewing configuration (camera and lights), they characterize their solution as follows.

Maximize:

$$benefit(W, S(\mathbf{r}))$$

Subject to:

$$cost(W, S(\mathbf{r})) \leq TargetFrameTime$$

Their benefit heuristic provided an estimation of the quality of the image that would be produced when rendering the set of multiresolution objects S at resolutions $\mathbf{r}$. This was given as:

$$benefit(W, S(\mathbf{r})) = \sum_i coverage(S_i W) * focus(S_i, W) * semantics(S_i) * accuracy(S_i, r_i)$$

where $coverage(S_i, W)$ is an estimate of the number of pixels covered by the object, $focus(S_i, W)$ is the distance of the object's projection to the center of the screen, $semantics(S_i)$ is a user-specified importance factor for the object, and $accuracy(S_i, r_i)$ is a factor measuring how well the mesh at resolution r_i approximates the mesh at maximum resolution. This accuracy component was modeled as the square root of the resolution factor, r, times the number of vertices in the highest LOD for the object S. Gobbetti and Bouvier state that they originally introduced a hysteresis factor into their model but eventually removed it because they found it unnecessary for most complex scenes.

This cost heuristic estimated the time required to render a scene of objects at resolutions $\mathbf{r}$ given the viewing parameters W. This included terms to model the graphics initialization phase (e.g., clearing the Z-buffer and setting up initial state), the sequential rendering of each object, and the finalization phase (e.g., buffer swapping). The equation can be given as follows.

$$cost(W, S(\mathbf{r})) = T^{init} + T^{final} + \sum_i T_i^{setup} + \mathbf{t}^{max} \cdot \mathbf{r}$$

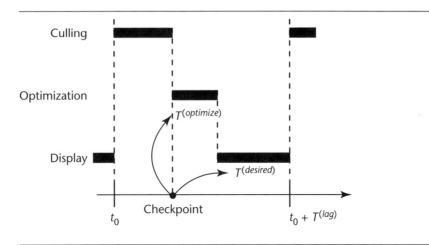

Figure 4.7   The rendering pipeline in Gobbetti and Bouvier's time-critical system, showing the time taken to perform view culling, constrained optimization of the cost/benefit problem, and polygon rendering for each frame [Gobbetti 99].

where T^{init} is the initialization time, T^{final} is the finalization time, T^{setup} is the time to set up the rendering environment for an object, $\mathbf{t}^{max}$ is the vector of maximum rendering time for each mesh (the symbol · represents the inner product). Each entry in the $\mathbf{r}$ vector is determined to be between 1 and the minimal resolution, r^{min}, under which a reduction in resolution does not reduce rendering time. The instantiation of these factors was performed experimentally for the target platform through a benchmarking preprocess.

To find the appropriate level of detail at which to display each object, Gobbetti and Bouvier solved the cost/benefit equation using an interior point algorithm, including the time taken to perform this optimization in the algorithm itself (see Figure 4.7). The authors tested their system on a scene with 166 chairs, totaling 1,393,072 polygons, using a flight path through the scene that produced drastic variations in scene content. They reported that without their adaptive rendering system the frame time would vary between 50 and 1950 ms. However, when they applied their predictive fixed frame rate system, and specified a target frame time of 100 ms, the system never exceeded this threshold.

Need for Perceptual Model

You will have noticed a common thread running through the description of algorithms for LOD selection. Even the most sophisticated fixed-frame-rate schedulers rely heavily on heuristics to estimate the various factors that influence an object's perceptual importance. Funkhouser and Séquin's system, though an important contribution to the state of the art, still used a series of sliders set empirically by the user to control the relative importance of the various benefit factors. Later systems, by Mason and Blake and by Gobbetti and Bouvier, extended the Funkhouser–Séquin model to hierarchical and continuous LOD, but continued to rely on a fundamentally heuristic and ad hoc model of visual importance. Such a system has many drawbacks. For example, a user must have a fair amount of expertise in setting the various sliders, and those settings may not apply correctly to a different 3D scene, rendering scenario, or rendering platform. In Chapter 8 we will return to the problem of managing LOD, and describe more recent attempts by researchers to use models of human perception for a principled approach to this problem.

4.3   View-Dependent LOD

Managing level of detail with discrete LOD reduces to the LOD selection problem: for every frame, choose which LODs will represent which objects. Continuous LOD poses a similar problem: for every frame, choose how much detail to allocate to each visible object. We now turn to view-dependent LOD, which presents a much more complicated task for the run-time system but also offers much more flexibility in how to allocate detail.

Several researchers independently proposed techniques for view-dependent simplification of polygonal meshes at about the same time, including Xia and Varshney [Xia 96], Hoppe [Hoppe 97], and Luebke and Erikson [Luebke 97]. All of these techniques are based on essentially the same concept, a hierarchy of vertex merge operations applied or reversed at run-time according to a set of view-dependent criteria. A single object may span multiple levels of detail. For example, distant portions of a large object may be simplified more aggressively than nearby portions, or silhouette regions may be allocated more detail than interior regions. View-dependent LOD techniques can produce very high-fidelity reductions for a given polygon count, since they allocate polygons exactly where needed. Their continuous fine-grained adjustments also tend to provide smoother transitions between levels of detail, reducing the "popping" artifacts that plague discrete LOD. However, they come at a relatively high computational cost, since the mesh is continuously evaluated, simplified, and refined at run-time. In this section we describe a generic view-dependent simplification framework and relate it to some published schemes. We detail some examples of view-dependent critieria that can be plugged into such a framework, and discuss how to track mesh dependencies to avoid certain simplification artifacts. We close with a discussion of the advantages and disadvantages of view-dependent methods over traditional discrete LOD.

4.3.1   Overview

Most view-dependent simplification approaches encode the model and the gamut of possible simplifications as a single data structure, which we call the *vertex hierarchy*.

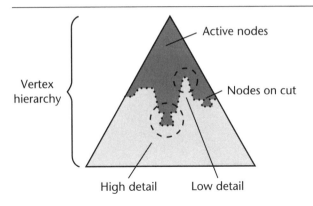

Figure 4.8   A schematic view of the vertex hierarchy. A cut across the hierarchy encodes a particular simplification. Refining a region to high detail pushes the cut down, whereas coarsening a region to low detail pushes the cut up. Note that although we have drawn the hierarchy here as a single rooted tree, it may be generalized to a forest.

As the name suggests, this structure is a hierarchy of vertices from the original model. These vertices are recursively merged during initialization by repeated application of a collapse-based simplification operator (e.g., cell collapse, edge collapse, and triangle collapse; see Section 2.2). Leaf nodes of the vertex hierarchy represent a single vertex from the original model, and interior nodes represent multiple merged vertices. If the hierarchy forms a single tree, the root of that tree represents the entire model clustered together. At run-time, the vertex hierarchy is dynamically and continuously queried to generate a simplified scene. Every possible cut across the hierarchy represents a different simplification, with vertices collapsed according to which nodes are on the cut (Figure 4.8). The algorithm operates by continuously testing nodes on the cut against view-dependent criteria, such as the projected screen-space size or the silhouette status of triangles associated with a cluster, and moving the cut up and down to locally simplify or refine the model according to the result.

4.3.2 THE VERTEX HIERARCHY

Algorithms create the vertex hierarchy by a clustering process in which vertices from the original model are merged into clusters, the clusters then merged into larger clusters, and so on. Any vertex-merging simplification operator can guide this clustering. For example, Luebke and Erikson [Luebke 97] use the cell collapse operator, with a recursive octree providing an adaptive version of the Rossignac–Borrel uniform grid approach. The edge collapse operator, which merges two vertices at a time, provides another common alternative. For instance, the vertex hierarchy might encode the sequence of edge collapses performed by the Garland–Heckbert quadric error metrics

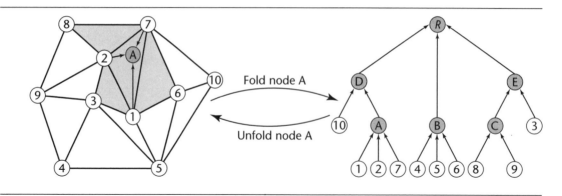

Figure 4.9   Folding and unfolding. Here, nodes 1, 2, and 7 are folded into their parent node A, merging the proxies of those nodes into the proxy of A. Unfolding A splits its proxy vertex into the proxies of its children. Folding A removes the shaded triangles from the model. Unfolding A reintroduces the triangles.

algorithm (see Sections 3.3.2 and 5.3). Note that our generic framework allows a node to cluster any number of vertices; we do not assume a binary tree. We will return to this issue shortly.

Let us define some terminology. In our parlance, a node **N** *supports* a vertex **V** if the leaf node associated with **V** descends from **N**. Similarly, **N** *supports* a triangle **T** if it supports one or more of the corner vertices of **T**. The set of triangles in the model supported by a node forms its *region of support*. Each node stores a representative vertex called the *proxy*. For leaf nodes, the proxy is exactly the vertex, of the original model, that the node represents. For interior nodes, the proxy is typically some average of the vertices supported by **N**. For example, the position of the proxy could be calculated using optimal vertex placement driven by quadrics. *Folding* a node merges all of the vertices supported by that node into the node's single proxy vertex. In the process, triangles whose corner vertices have been merged are removed from the scene, decreasing the overall polygon count. *Unfolding* a node splits its proxy vertex into the proxies of the node's children, reintroducing some triangles into the scene (Figure 4.9).[1] Precomputing and storing with each node the set of triangles to remove and add makes folding and unfolding fast enough to perform dynamically, enabling run-time view-dependent simplification. The cut is the set of folded nodes closest to the root, and is typically encoded with a linked list for efficient traversal, insertion, and deletion.

---

1. Note that *fold* and *unfold* are run-time tasks. We use the terms to distinguish the run-time action from the simplification operators (such as cell collapse or edge collapse), which are chosen and applied during preprocessing.

4.3.3   VARIATIONS ON THE VERTEX HIERARCHY

Some important variations on the general vertex hierarchy structure deserve further mention. Many view-dependent LOD algorithms use repeated application of the edge collapse operator to build a binary vertex hierarchy. For instance, Hoppe's *view-dependent progressive mesh (VDPM)* algorithm extends his influential progressive mesh structure to support view-dependent refinement [Hoppe 97]. Xia and Varshney use a similar binary vertex hierarchy structure, which they term *merge trees* [Xia 96]. The binary hierarchy structure leads to several advantages. The individual nodes require less storage since, for example, nodes need not store the number of children. In addition, a node can avoid storing indices of both children by guaranteeing that sibling nodes are stored in adjacent positions of an array. If a node's left child has index i, the right child will have index $i + 1$, so the node can simply store i. The simple, regular structure of a binary hierarchy also lends itself to efficient traversal. The primary disadvantage of such a binary vertex hierarchy is the very fine granularity it imposes. Since each node represents an edge collapse, folding a node removes only two triangles from the mesh. As a result, the hierarchy will contain many nodes, and many folds and unfolds will be needed each frame to achieve the desired level of detail.

Other algorithms build binary vertex hierarchies but do not require the two vertices merged by a node to share an edge. (Merging two nonadjacent vertices has been given several names: *virtual edge collapse* [Garland 97], *vertex pair collapse,* and *vertex unification* [Popovic 97]; see Chapter 2.) This permits nonmanifold meshes and enables changes to the mesh topology, such as closing holes and merging separate meshes. El-Sana and Varshney [El-Sana 99a] use the term *view-dependence tree* to describe one such binary vertex hierarchy. Still other algorithms, such as Luebke and Erikson's *hierarchical dynamic simplification,* use an octree vertex hierarchy (which they call the *vertex tree*) in which every node has at most eight children [Luebke 97]. One unique feature of this algorithm is its choice of proxy: a cell collapse operation merges all vertices in an octree cell to the single "most important" vertex, so that interior nodes as well as leaves represent vertices of the original model. This reduces the overall storage of the hierarchy at the cost of some fidelity, since the vertices of the simplified LOD cannot be optimized to capture the shape. Octrees are just two of a number of possible spatial subdivision hierarchies that may be used to construct vertex hierarchies [Samet 89a, Samet 89b].

4.3.4   VIEW-DEPENDENT CRITERIA

A vertex hierarchy supports fast local simplification and refinement by folding and unfolding nodes to move the cut up and down. Since different regions of the model can be simplified differently at run-time, vertex hierarchies support view-dependent LOD. Various view-dependent criteria can be used to guide simplification, in effect serving as callbacks that evaluate a node in the vertex hierarchy and returning whether it should be folded or unfolded. We typically require that unfolding be monotonic down the tree: any criterion that would unfold a node should also unfold its parent. Given a set of criteria, a view-dependent LOD algorithm simply traverses the nodes near the cut, evaluating whether to unfold nodes (lowering the cut and increasing local detail) or fold their parents (raising the cut and decreasing local detail).

For example, Luebke and Erikson described three criteria: a screen-space error threshold, a silhouette test, and a triangle budget [Luebke 97]. The screen-space error threshold monitors the projected extent of a node in the vertex hierarchy using a bounding sphere that contains the node's region of support (see Section 3.2), and folds nodes smaller than some user-specified number of pixels on the screen. This results in size-based LOD in which small and distant objects are represented in less detail than nearby objects. Xia, El-Sana, and Varshney [Xia 97] have described an additional criterion of local illumination to guide view-dependent rendering. This criterion increases detail in regions of high illumination gradient and uses normal cones. Other view-dependent criteria include visibility [El-Sana 01] and motion [El-Sana 02].

The silhouette test uses a precalculated *cone of normals* test to determine whether a vertex cluster is currently on the silhouette. This technique associates a cone (which encapsulates the normals of triangles supported by the node) and a sphere (which bounds the vertices supported by the node [Figure 4.10]). The silhouette test dovetails nicely with the screen-space error threshold approach; that is, clusters on the silhouette are simply tested against a tighter screen-space threshold than clusters in the interior. Many other techniques could be used for determining silhouette status. Johnson and Cohen generalize the "cone of normals" concept to *spatialized normal cone hierarchies,* and show their use for several applications beyond silhouette detection [Johnson 01]. Shirman and Abi-Ezzi use a slightly different variant with a cone that contains the geometry [Shirman 93], which Sander et al. have extended to an *anchored cone hierarchy* that gives excellent results [Sander 00]. Using a *normal mask* technique inspired by Zhang and Hoff [Zhang 97], Luebke and Hallen represent the normals spanned by a node with a quantized cube, which they encode as a bit vector that can simply be ANDed with a mask to find silhouette status [Luebke 01]. The result is expensive in memory, but is very fast and less conservative than cone-based methods (Figure 4.11).

Finally, vertex hierarchies support view-dependent budget-based simplification by minimizing an error criterion while staying within a user-specified triangle budget.[2] For example, Luebke and Erikson evaluate the error represented by a node according to the bounding sphere containing the node's region of support, reasoning that vertices cannot move further than the diameter of the bounding sphere. They

---

2. This is the view-dependent analog of predictive fixed frame rate scheduling, discussed in Section 4.3. Although we describe the budget in terms of number of polygons, this could be extended to include factors such as fill rate to give a more accurate estimate of rendering time.

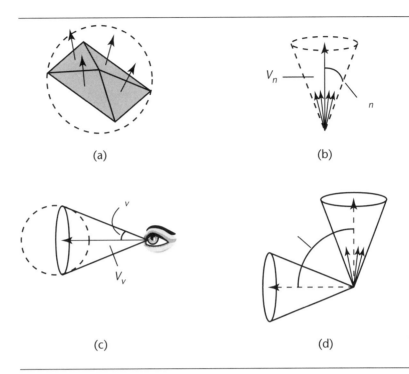

Figure 4.10   Testing silhouette status with a *cone of normals:* (a) A node supporting four triangles (shaded). The arrows represent the normals of the triangles and the dashed circle represents the bounding sphere of the node. (b) The cone of normals for the node, represented as an average vector V_n and semiangle θ_n. (c) The *viewing cone* tightly contains the node's bounding sphere, with center vector V_v from the viewpoint to the center of the sphere and semiangle θ_v. (d) If any vector in the cone of normals is orthogonal to any vector in the viewing cone, the node potentially lies on the silhouette. The node may be classified as backfacing, frontfacing, or silhouette by comparing ϕ, θ_v, and θ_n.

then unfold nodes so as to minimize the screen-space error obtained by projecting this sphere onto the screen. The intuitive meaning of this process is easily put into words: "Vertices on the screen can move as far as x pixels from their original position. Minimize x without exceeding the triangle budget." To implement this, they maintain a priority queue of nodes in the vertex hierarchy, initialized to contain the root node and sorted by screen-space error. The node with the largest error is extracted and unfolded, and its children are placed in the queue. This process iterates until unfolding the top node of the queue would exceed the triangle budget, at which point the maximum error has been minimized.

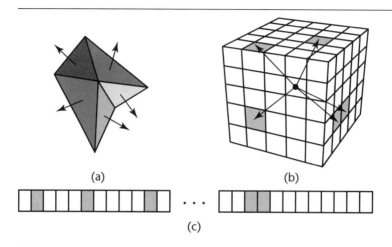

(a)

(b)

(c)

Figure 4.11   Efficient computation of silhouette nodes with the node's *normal mask.* (a) The node's supported triangles. (b) A cell in the normal mask is set if a normal falls within the corresponding range. (c) Each cell corresponds to a bit in a bit vector.

4.3.5   TRACKING MESH DEPENDENCIES

The vertex hierarchy can be viewed as a partial ordering of simplification operators. The preprocessing stage applies these operators one at a time, in effect performing view-independent simplification while recording a history of the operators used. The run-time system applies the operators out of order, according to some set of view-dependent criteria. Clearly some orderings are not possible. For example, we cannot unfold a node unless we first unfold its parent. The arcs connecting parent and child nodes can thus be viewed as dependencies that impose a partial ordering on the simplification operators encoded by nodes in the vertex hierarchy. However, these dependencies are not in general sufficient. That is, we cannot always define a triangulation over these vertices as a cut across the hierarchy and guarantee that the triangulation will not have foldovers or nonmanifold connectivity. In addition to the parent-child arcs, there exist other dependencies among the simplification operands [Xia 97]. Figure 4.12 shows an example of such a dependency.

In this example, A shows the initial state of the mesh. While constructing the merge tree, we first collapsed vertex v_2 to v_1 to get mesh B, and then collapsed vertex v_3 to v_4 to get mesh C. Now suppose at run-time we determined that we needed to display vertices v_1, v_2, and v_4, and could possibly collapse vertex v_3 to v_4. However, if we collapse vertex v_3 to v_4 directly, going from mesh A to mesh D, we get a mesh foldover where there should have been none. It is possible to construct

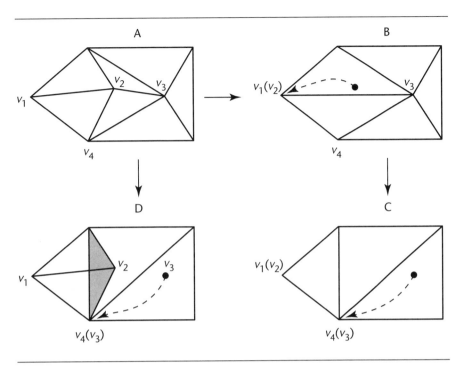

Figure 4.12   Simplification dependencies. The simplification preprocess collapsed v_2 to $v_1(A \rightarrow B)$, then collapsed v_3 to $v_4(B \rightarrow C)$. If at run-time the system folds v_3 to v_4 without first folding v_2 to $v_1(A \rightarrow D)$, a mesh foldover occurs [Xia 97].

procedures for checking and preventing such mesh foldovers at run-time, but these may be computationally expensive. Instead, several researchers have addressed this problem by explicitly storing dependencies in the vertex hierarchies. Although the dependencies may be constructed and stored with any simplification operator, let us trace their evolution in the literature using the simplest case of an edge collapse operator.

Explicit Dependencies

Xia et al. [Xia 96] and Gueziec et al. [Guéziec 98] stored the entire list of vertex neighbors around an edge collapse or a vertex split explicitly. Thus, in Figure 4.13, edge (v_a, v_b) may collapse to the vertex v_{new} only when the vertices $v_0, v_1, \ldots v_k$ exist in the current level of simplification (i.e., are on the cut of the vertex hierarchy) and

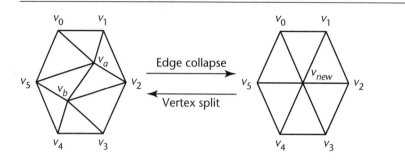

Figure 4.13   Storing the simplification dependencies.

are adjacent to (v_a, v_b). Extending this reasoning further, we can derive the following dependencies that define safe edge collapses and vertex splits:

- Edge (v_a, v_b) may collapse to the vertex v_{new} only when the vertices $v_0, v_1, \ldots v_k$ exist in the current level of simplification and are adjacent to (v_a, v_b).

- Vertex v_{new} may split to create the edge (v_a, v_b) only when vertices $v_0, v_1, \ldots v_k$ exist in the current level of simplification and are neighbors of v_{new}.

These dependency checks are performed during each vertex split or edge collapse during the real-time simplification. These dependencies are explicitly stored as lists of vertices $v_0, v_1, \ldots v_k$ in the vertex hierarchy during its creation. Returning to Figure 4.12, we can now see that the collapse of edge (v_3, v_4) depends on the adjacency of vertex v_1 to v_3. If vertex v_2 is present, then v_1 will not be adjacent to v_3 and therefore v_3 cannot collapse to v_4.

Implicit Dependencies

Such explicit dependencies require extra memory to store and are cumbersome to test at run-time, largely due to the memory overhead of making several nonlocal accesses. These nonlocal accesses ruin cache coherence and may even lead to paging for large data sets or on computers with insufficient memory. Furthermore, it has proven difficult to extend explicit dependencies lists to handle the view-dependent topology simplification. El-Sana and Varshney [El-Sana 99a] have proposed a compact scheme to encode the dependencies implicitly. This scheme uses only local memory accesses.

Implicit dependencies rely on the enumeration of vertices generated after each collapse. El-Sana and Varshney assign the n vertices of a full-resolution mesh vertex IDs $0, 1, \ldots, n - 1$. Every time they collapse an edge to generate a new vertex, they assign the ID of the new vertex to be one more than the maximum vertex ID thus far. This process continues until the entire hierarchy has been constructed. At run-time, the dependency checks now require only a few simple tests based on vertex IDs before each fold and unfold operation, as follows.

- *Edge collapse:* An edge (v_a, v_b) may collapse to the vertex v_{new} if the vertex ID of v_{new} is less than the vertex IDs of the parents of the vertices adjacent to (v_a, v_b).

- *Vertex split:* A vertex v_{new} can be safely split at run-time if its vertex ID is greater than the vertex IDs of all of its neighbors.

El-Sana and Varshney implement the previous checks efficiently by storing two integers with each node in the vertex hierarchy: (1) the maximum vertex ID of its adjacent vertices and (2) the minimum vertex ID m of the parents of its adjacent vertices. For a comprehensive survey of dependencies and their relationships to selective simplification and refinement, the interested reader can refer to the survey paper by DeFloriani et al. [DeFloriani 02].

4.3.6   GLOBAL SIMPLIFICATION

Note that nothing in our definition of vertex hierarchies prevents nodes that merge vertices of separate objects, though a topology-modifying operator must be used to generate such a hierarchy. For example, Luebke and Erikson's hierarchical cell collapse algorithm merges vertices across objects, which enables their system to aggregate small objects and represent them at a distance with a single LOD—a definite advantage for drastic simplification. The ability to aggregate objects coupled with the adaptive nature of view-dependent LOD enable *global simplification,* in which the entire scene is treated as a single model to be simplified in view-dependent fashion. This provides an extremely general and robust visualization solution, since no division of the scene into individual objects is necessary. Such a solution is particularly useful for previewing models such as unsegmented (or poorly segmented) isosurfaces from medical or scientific visualization, or unorganized "polygon soup" CAD models.

The chief disadvantage of view-dependent LOD is the computational load incurred by continuous evaluation, simplification, and refinement of the vertex hierarchy. Another difficulty arises with the representation of the model: modern graphics hardware generally performs best on meshes that have been "compiled" using techniques such as display lists and triangle strips. For this reason, the application of view-dependent LOD techniques is limited today to a few special cases (such as the unorganized models just mentioned, and terrains, which have a long tradition of view-dependent LOD). In Section 5.5 we describe a method for maintaining triangle strips through view-dependent simplification of the underlying mesh, but as this technique incurs additional computation and memory, this only solves part of the problem. However, recent trends in graphics hardware design seem promising. Transform and lighting has moved from the CPU onto the graphics hardware even for commodity systems, and modern chips now provide post-transform-and-lighting vertex caches, which reduce the importance of maintaining triangle strips. Perhaps in the future advances in graphics hardware and the underlying algorithms will make view-dependent LOD techniques more generally applicable.

4.4   BLENDING BETWEEN TRANSITIONS

Often the selection thresholds used for each LOD will not completely minimize or eliminate the visual impact of a switch. The likely result is a noticeable and distracting "popping" during the transition between LODs. To combat these artifacts, researchers and developers have proposed a number of smooth blending techniques with the goal of softening the transitions between levels. The following sections describe two common blending approaches: alpha blending and geomorphs.

4.4.1   ALPHA BLENDING

This technique smooths the abrupt transition between levels of detail by blending one LOD into another, associating an opacity or *alpha* value with the two LODs. An alpha of 1.0 means that the object is opaque; an alpha of 0.0 means that the object is invisible. With each object, the system specifies a fading range centered at the switching distance for each LOD. For example, if the switching distance is 100 m, and a fade range of 10 m is specified, alpha blending will take place between 95 and 105 m. Specifically, as LOD1 moves away from the viewpoint and reaches 95 m, both LOD1 and LOD2 are rendered at the same time, until the object moves beyond 105 m, at which point only LOD2 is rendered. Within the fade region, the alpha value of both levels of detail is linearly interpolated between 0.0 and 1.0 (and vice versa). At a distance of 95 m, LOD1 will have an alpha of 1.0 (opaque), whereas LOD2 will have an alpha of 0.0 (invisible). By 100 m distance, both LOD1 and LOD2 are rendered with an alpha transparency of 0.5. Finally, by the time the object has reached 105 m, LOD1's alpha value will have dropped to 0.0 and LOD2's value is 1.0. Naturally, when an LOD has an alpha value of 0.0, the system need not render that LOD. These concepts are illustrated in Figure 4.14. Note that it is also possible to perform the fade transition over a brief period of time instead of over a distance. This has the advantage of completing the transition process in a timely manner for objects remaining within the fade distance range for extended intervals.

Although alpha blending can produce far smoother LOD transitions, the disadvantage of this approach is that two versions of an object are necessarily rendered within the fade region. The result is an increase in the number of polygons being rendered during the time of the transition. This may be problematic, since the system may well be switching to a lower level of detail precisely to reduce the number

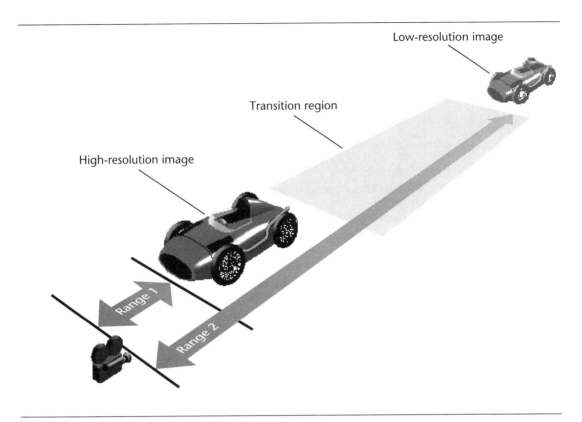

Figure 4.14   Showing the fade range where two levels of detail for an object are blended using alpha transparency [Performer 00a]. Copyright © 2000 Silicon Graphics, Inc.

of polygons. For this reason, it is best to keep the fade region as short as necessary to mitigate any popping artifacts.

Note that ideally each LOD should be rendered as an opaque image, and the resulting images subsequently blended. Rendering the two levels of detail on top of each other as partially transparent will likely cause self-occlusion artifacts [Helman 96]. Many modern graphics platforms offer hardware support for alpha-blending level of detail. For example, SGI's OpenGL Performer API includes a function to control this feature: pfLODTransition() lets the programmer set the distance over which Performer should fade between levels of detail. The distance specified is applied before and after the switch boundary between two LODs, such that the fade between one LOD and another actually occurs over twice the distance value. The default fade distance is 1, and Performer limits the transition distances to the shortest distance between the switch range and the two adjacent switch ranges. Other examples of commercial products that support alpha-blending LOD include the Vega visual simulation system from MultiGen–Paradigm (*www.multigen.com*), and the Rxscene polygon- and spline-based modeler from German company REALAX (*www.realax.com*).

4.4.2   GEOMORPHS

Just as alpha blending performs blending in image space, *geomorphing* blends smoothly between levels of detail in object space, morphing the vertices in one LOD toward those in the next LOD. This is certainly the most complex of the techniques introduced thus far, but it provides a very effective way to switch seamlessly from one level of detail to another. In practice, using geomorphs can make screen-space errors of a few pixels—which would certainly incur visible popping otherwise—appear nearly imperceptible [Hoppe 98a]. Some commercial and public-domain LOD systems support geomorphs. For example, the *Unreal* game engine provides geomorphing as part of its continuous LOD feature.

The first instance of morphing between LODs was demonstrated by Greg Turk for his polygon retiling algorithm [Turk 92]. This algorithm distributed a new set of vertices over the surface of a model and connected them to create a retiling of a surface that was faithful to both the geometry and the topology of the original surface. The vertices of the original and the retiled meshes could then be interpolated so that at one end of the interpolation they all lie on the low-detail mesh, whereas at the other end of the interpolation they all follow the high-detail mesh (see Figure 4.15). Turk notes that a linear interpolation was sufficient to produce smooth transitions between models.

Hoppe applied the term *geomorph* to a similar geometric interpolation between LODs in his progressive meshes algorithm [Hoppe 96]. Recall that progressive meshes encode a series of vertex split operations to refine a coarse version of a mesh into the original high-resolution mesh. Hoppe used geomorphing to smooth the visual transition resulting from a vertex split, or its inverse edge collapse. For example, an edge collapse geomorph simply interpolates the position of two vertices in the finer mesh linearly between their current position and the position of their corresponding parent vertex in the coarser mesh. Thus, in Figure 4.16, a geomorph of the edge collapse operation involves vertex v_u moving toward v_t until they merge, at which point the two vertices are replaced by one, v_s, and the supporting faces f_l and f_r are removed.

Hoppe also performed geomorphing of surface appearance attributes, interpolating vertex attributes in addition to their locations. He noted that any sequence of these smooth transitions can be composed so that geomorphs can be constructed between any two meshes of a progressive mesh representation (Figure 4.17). Hoppe later extended the progressive meshes algorithm to support view-dependent refinement [Hoppe 97], and then applied this technique to the area of terrain rendering

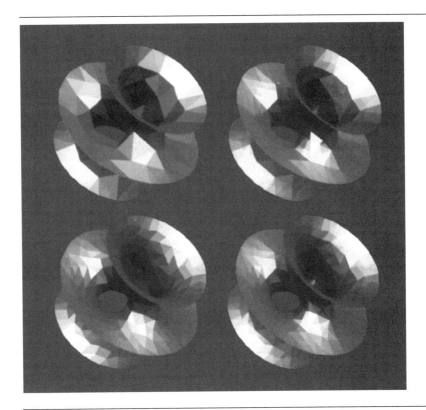

Figure 4.15   An example of the smooth retiling process developed by Turk, showing a transition (starting top left) from low to high detail in a clockwise direction [Turk 92]. Copyright © 1992 Association for Computing Machinery, Inc.

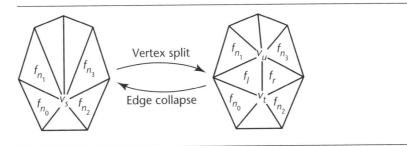

Figure 4.16   The vertex split refinement operation and its inverse, the edge collapse coarsening operation [Hoppe 98a].

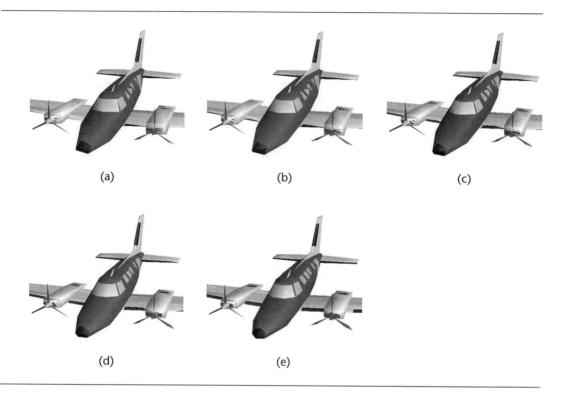

(a) (b) (c)

(d) (e)

Figure 4.17   An example of geomorphing between two meshes (one with 500 faces and the other with 1,000 faces) in Hoppe's progressive meshes algorithm. The geomorph percentages in each case are for images (a) through (e), respectively, 0%, 25%, 50%, 75%, and 100% [Hoppe 96]. Copyright © 1992 Association for Computing Machinery, Inc.

[Hoppe 98a]. In the latter system, geomorphs were created at run-time to gradually transition between edge collapse or vertex-split operations. This was only done for regions visible to the user, since it would be wasteful and unnecessary to geomorph an invisible region of the mesh. Once a geomorph refinement was initiated, it was defined to last over *gtime* frames (Hoppe chose *gtime* to last one second). Geomorph coarsening (smoothing an edge collapse) operated in a similar fashion, except that certain constraints led Hoppe to restrict these geomorphs to occur over only one layer of the vertex hierarchy at a time. He halved the *gtime* parameter for these cases. Fortunately, geomorph coarsening is somewhat unusual, since it usually reflects the infrequent situation of the user receding backward from the terrain. During a 2-minute flyover of the Grand Canyon terrain model, Hoppe reported that 28.3% of vertices underwent geomorph refinement, whereas only 2.2% of vertices underwent geomorph coarsening.

4.5 CONCLUSIONS

In this chapter, we have looked at some of the fundamental run-time concepts for view-independent and view-dependent LOD. In terms of view-independent schemes, we looked at a number of ways to modulate LOD, including distance or size criteria, priority, hysteresis, and environment conditions. The topic of perceptually based LOD was introduced and is covered in greater detail in Part III. We also covered fixed-frame-rate schedulers, learning the distinction between reactive and predictive schedulers. This bridged the discussion into view-dependent LOD, where we described the various run-time factors involved in building a view-dependent LOD system. Finally, we described the concept of smooth blending between LODs to reduce popping effects, both in image space (alpha blending) and geometry space (geomorphs). Whereas this chapter dealt primarily with general run-time concepts, the next chapter focuses on a few specific LOD algorithms, and provides more in-depth discussion of each of these.

A CATALOG OF
USEFUL ALGORITHMS

No single LOD algorithm is fast, robust, simple to code, and capable of both drastic and high-fidelity simplification on all types of models. Instead, in this chapter we describe several LOD algorithms or families of algorithms, each of which excels in some particular respect. Our intent is not to provide an exhaustive list of work in the field of polygonal simplification, nor to select the best published papers, but to describe a few important and useful algorithms that span the gamut of simplification research. You may choose to implement one of these algorithms (or use publicly available code), use another algorithm from the literature, or design your own, but hopefully this book and this chapter will help you make an informed decision.

We begin with *vertex clustering*, a family of algorithms that are fast, robust, and relatively simple. Next we briefly describe an important algorithm for *vertex decimation*, which uses the vertex removal operation described in detail in Chapter 2. Decimation excels at removing redundant detail such as coplanar or nearly coplanar polygons. We then turn to Garland and Heckbert's algorithm using *quadric error metrics,* which strikes perhaps the best balance between speed, robustness, simplicity, and fidelity. We also review *image-driven simplification,* which is quite slow in comparison to the previous algorithms but produces very high-fidelity LODs by guiding simplification with actual rendered images. Finally, we describe two useful auxiliary algorithms, which do not generate LODs but augment the other algorithms presented in this book. First, we introduce *skip strips,* a technique for accelerating rendering of view-dependent LOD meshes. Next, we provide a high-level description of a fast, robust polygon triangulation algorithm for which a publicly available implementation is included on the companion Web site.

5.1 VERTEX CLUSTERING

First proposed by Rossignac and Borrel in 1992, *vertex clustering* remains one of the most useful LOD algorithms to date [Rossignac 92]. Robust, fast, and simple to implement, vertex clustering has provided a springboard for other LOD researchers, such as Low and Tan [Low 97] and Lindstrom [Lindstrom 00a], who have extended or improved Rossignac and Borrel's original algorithm. Multiple graphics packages and toolkits have implemented vertex clustering for simple and efficient LOD generation, and we include a simple implementation (Greg Turk's *plycrunch*) on the companion Web site. Here we describe the original algorithm, as well as some notable later extensions.

5.1.1 OVERVIEW

Vertex clustering begins by assigning a weight or *importance* to every vertex in the model. For example, Rossignac and Borrel assign higher importance to vertices attached to large faces, and to vertices in regions of high curvature (since such vertices are more likely to lie on the silhouette). Next, the algorithm overlays a 3D grid on the model and collapses all vertices within each cell of the grid to the single most important vertex within the cell. The resolution of the grid determines the quality of the resulting simplification. A coarse grid will aggressively simplify the model, whereas a fine grid will perform only minimal reduction. In the process of clustering, triangles whose corners are collapsed together become degenerate and are filtered out.

Clearly the major implementation issues are the choice of an importance metric and the efficient clustering of vertices with the concurrent removal of degenerate triangles. We discuss each of these in the following sections.

5.1.2 VERTEX IMPORTANCE

To evaluate vertex importance, Rossignac and Borrel examine the edges attached to the vertex and assign importance as a weighted sum of two factors. The first factor is the length of the longest attached edge, which reflects the size of the associated faces.

Note that all edge lengths should be normalized to the model size, so that the resulting simplification does not depend on the scale of the model. For example, the developer could divide all edge lengths by the diagonal span of the model bounding box, or by the mean edge length. The second factor affecting vertex importance is the maximum angle between edges, which relates to the local curvature. That is, the maximum angle θ between all pairs of attached edges is small in regions of high curvature. Since high-curvature vertices are more likely to lie on the silhouette, Rossignac and Borrel weight these vertices according to $1/\theta$. In other words, the importance of a vertex is a weighted sum of the length of its longest edge and the reciprocal of the maximum angle between its edges. This can be efficiently computed in a linear-time traversal of vertices and their associated edges.[1]

Other importance criteria are possible. For example, Low and Tan, in their extension of the vertex clustering algorithm (described later), argue that $\cos(\theta/2)$ provides a better estimate of silhouette probability than $1/\theta$ [Low 97]. Depending on the application, one might want to rate vertices on the boundary of the mesh as more important than vertices in the mesh interior. When attributes such as color, normal, and texture coordinates are present, vertices at discontinuities (e.g., a crease in the normal field, or a change in the texture ID) could be of higher importance. One other point of note: since Rossignac and Borrel use the length of incident edges to estimate the size of the polygons associated with a vertex, they calculate vertex importance before triangulation. This avoids inaccurate ratings of small features on large polygons, since vertices at those small features may get associated with long, skinny triangles during triangulation (Figure 5.1).

5.1.3   CLUSTERING VERTICES AND FILTERING DEGENERATE TRIANGLES

The gridded clustering technique of Rossignac and Borrel lends itself to implementation as a spatial hash table. To apply a uniform grid to the vertices, we first find which cell of the grid each vertex occupies, and then find to which entry in the table that cell hashes. A simple hash function (such as the sum of the cell indices in x, y, and z weighted by different prime numbers) suffices. Some implementations optimize this further by converting all vertex coordinates to fixed-point representations and by restricting the grid size to powers of 2. This makes computing the cell indices of a vertex as simple as truncating its fixed-point coordinates to fewer bits.

Given a way to map vertex coordinates to grid cells, the algorithm makes a pass over the model vertices, associating each vertex with the appropriate grid cell and keeping track of the most important vertex in each cell. Next, a pass over the model triangles assigns each triangle corner to the most important vertex in the respective cell, and removes triangles for which two or three corners map to a single vertex.

---

1. This assumes that no vertex has more than a small constant number of edges, which is almost always the case for real-life meshes. Technically, the running time is O($|$V$|$ + M^2), where $|$V$|$ is the number of vertices and M is the maximum valence of any vertex.

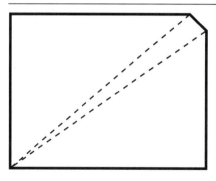

Figure 5.1   An example illustrating why the Rossignac–Borrel algorithm weights vertices by importance *before* triangulation. Triangulating the outlined polygon associates the least important vertices (in the corner cut off) with the longest edges in the triangulated model (dashed lines). This could inflate their importance and lead to poor clustering.

5.1.4   DISPLAYING DEGENERATE TRIANGLES

Rossignac and Borrel also propose a novel technique for displaying simplified meshes—in particular the degenerate triangles created by clustering. Reasoning that a triangle with two collapsed corners is simply a line segment, and a triangle with three collapsed corners is simply a point, they choose to render such triangles using the line and point primitives of the graphics hardware (but filtering out redundant lines and points). Thus, an LOD for a polygonal object will generally be a collection of polygons, lines, and points. The resulting simplifications are therefore more accurate from a schematic than a strictly geometric standpoint. For the purposes of drastic simplification, however, the lines and points can contribute significantly to the recognizability of the object. Objects with long, skinny features (such as the antenna of a car, or the legs of a table) particularly benefit from this. Low and Tan add a clever extension: they keep track of the diameter of collapsed vertex clusters and use the thick-line primitive present in most graphics systems to render degenerate lines as thick edges. By shading these thick edges with dynamically assigned normals, they achieve a cylinder-like appearance at very low rendering cost.

5.1.5   ADVANTAGES AND DISADVANTAGES

Vertex clustering operates at the level of individual triangles and vertices, resulting in a topology-insensitive algorithm that neither requires nor preserves valid topology. Vertex clustering can therefore deal robustly with messy models and degenerate meshes with which other approaches have little or no success. The Rossignac–Borrel algorithm is simple to implement and can be made very efficient, producing one of the fastest algorithms known. However, the method suffers several disadvantages. Since topology is not preserved, and no explicit error bounds with respect to the surface are guaranteed, the resulting simplifications are often less pleasing visually than those of slower algorithms. The algorithm does not lend itself to fidelity-based or budget-based simplification, since the only way to predict how many triangles an LOD will have using a specified grid resolution is to perform the simplification.

The use of a uniform grid for clustering also leads to some specific disadvantages. No correspondence exists between two LODs unless the grid resolution used for one is an even multiple of the resolution used for the other. In addition, changing the resolution or placement of the grid even a small amount can alter the appearance of the resulting LOD considerably, since important vertices may end up in different cells. Similarly, Low and Tan point out that a small addition (such as adding a pot to the tree model in Figure 5.2) can significantly change the simplification of otherwise identical objects by changing the size of the bounding box and distorting the resulting grid [Low 97]. Finally, simplification is sensitive to the orientation of the clustering grid, since two identical objects at different orientations can produce quite different simplifications.

5.1.6 FLOATING-CELL CLUSTERING

Motivated by the disadvantages of uniform-grid clustering, Low and Tan propose an alternative to the original Rossignac–Borrel algorithm. This alternative uses *floating-cell clustering*, as follows:

1. Assign an importance weight to vertices, as in the standard Rossignac–Borrel approach.

2. Sort the vertices by importance (note that this needs to be done only once per model, regardless of the number of LODs generated from that model).

3. Center a clustering cell on the most important vertex in the model and collapse all vertices within the cell to this most important vertex. In the process, delete all vertices in the cell from the list.

4. Repeat step 3 on the most important remaining vertex.

Floating-cell clustering leads to more consistent simplification. Since the importance of vertices controls the positioning of clustering cells, the unpredictable simplification artifacts illustrated in Figure 5.3 are greatly reduced. By using a spherical rather than cubical clustering cell, floating-cell clustering can also avoid the dependence on orientation inherent to uniform-grid clustering. Two similar models are much more likely to produce similar LODs, since the size of the bounding box does not affect simplification.

Implementing floating-cell clustering requires only slightly more work than implementing uniform-cell clustering. The key step is the previously cited step 3, which

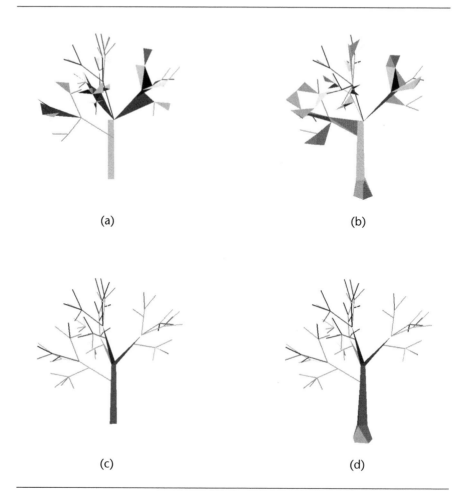

(a)   (b)

(c)   (d)

Figure 5.2   (a–b) Uniform-grid clustering produces substantially different LODs when the bounding box is changed, here by the addition of a small pot. (c–d) Floating-cell clustering
looks better and is more consistent [Low 97]. Copyright © 1997 Association for Computing Machinery, Inc.

finds all vertices within a given radius and collapses them to the center of the cell. To
use spherical cells rather than cubical cells is simply a matter of testing the Euclidean
distance (L_2 norm) between vertices rather than the Manhattan distance (L_1 norm).
It is important, however, that we reduce the number of vertices the algorithm must
check for inclusion in the cell, since a naive implementation that checked all vertices
for inclusion in every cell would require time quadratic to the number of vertices. To

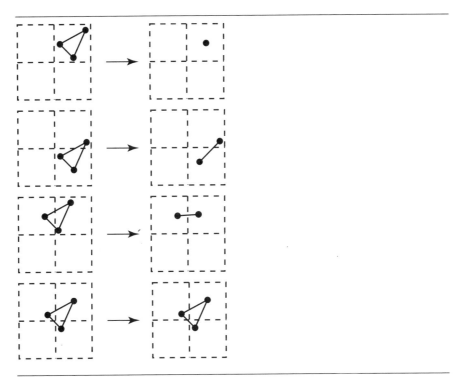

Figure 5.3   A triangle in uniform-grid clustering may be simplified inconsistently, depending on which grid cells it intersects [Low 97].

avoid this slowdown, we can hash vertices into a uniform cubical grid, in which the size of the grid cells equals the user-specified clustering radius. Then, for a clustering cell centered in a given grid cell, only vertices in adjacent cells need be checked—26 adjacent cells for spherical (Euclidean distance) clustering, and even fewer for cubical (Manhattan distance) clustering. In practice this hashing process makes checking vertices extremely efficient.

5.1.7 SIMPLIFYING MASSIVE MODELS

The chief disadvantage of Low and Tan's algorithm is its asymptotic running time. Whereas uniform-grid clustering may be implemented in time linear to the size of the model, floating-cell clustering requires sorting vertices by importance, which raises the running time to $O(n \log n)$. In practice, with a good sorting algorithm (such as *quicksort*), the algorithm remains very fast for all but the largest of models. But what if you have to simplify truly large models, with tens or hundreds of millions of vertices? Here, uniform-cell clustering again has the advantage, since it can be implemented to run in linear time. Lindstrom further extends the Rossignac–Borrel algorithm to support *out-of-core* simplification, in which the memory requirements of the LOD generation do not depend on the size of the original model. By decoupling simplification from input size, Lindstrom is able to create LODs of models much too large to fit in main memory.

Though we do not present Lindstrom's algorithm in detail here, the key idea is worth noting. Lindstrom uses a minor variation of vertex clustering in which the representative vertex for a cluster is synthesized, rather than chosen from the set of clustered vertices. In other words, rather than choosing the most important vertex for a cluster and collapsing all vertices to it, a new vertex is created from the collapsed vertices. For example, the new vertex coordinates may simply be the mean of the clustered vertex coordinates (*plycrunch* uses this approach), or some weighted mean that takes importance into account. Lindstrom uses the *quadric error metric* (see Sections 3.3.2 and 5.3) proposed by Garland and Heckbert to position the new vertex. As it traverses the triangles of the original model, Lindstrom's algorithm stores with each occupied grid cell the cumulative quadric of all triangles with a vertex in that cell. After calculating and accumulating their quadrics, all triangles that do not span three grid cells (i.e., triangles that will be collapsed away by the clustering) are discarded. The coordinates of the final vertices, which will form the new corners of the remaining triangles, are computed from the accumulated quadrics in a more numerically stable variation of Garland and Heckbert's original algorithm. Using quadrics in this fashion allows Lindstrom's algorithm to generate an LOD with a single linear pass through the original model,[2] which can be streamed from disk or from a compressed file, as opposed to the two passes required by Rossignac and Borrel. The resulting algorithm is memory efficient and extraordinarily fast, both crucial attributes for simplifying massive models.

5.2   VERTEX DECIMATION

Like vertex clustering, this seminal algorithm was first published in 1992 and remains heavily used to this day. The original decimation algorithm (by Schroeder, Zarge, and Lorenson) provided a fast topology-preserving LOD technique that excels at removing redundant geometry and has proven well suited to scientific and medical visualization. The algorithm has long been freely available as part of the *Visualization ToolKit* (*VTK*), which also accounts for its wide acceptance in the visualization community. Here we describe the original algorithm, and briefly discuss a later topology-modifying extension for continuous LOD.

---

2. This assumes that the bounding box of the original model is provided in the model file format.

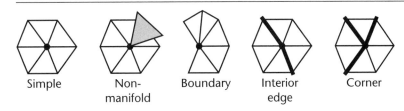

Figure 5.4   Vertices considered for decimation are classified as *simple, nonmanifold, boundary, interior edge,* or *corner* [Schroeder 92].

5.2.1 OVERVIEW

The vertex decimation algorithm uses the vertex removal operation described in Section 2.2. Here we focus on the structure of the surrounding algorithm, which consists of multiple passes over the vertices of a triangulated mesh. During a pass, a vertex is considered for removal by evaluating the decimation criteria described in the following section. Vertices that meet those criteria are deleted, along with all associated triangles, and the resulting hole is retriangulated. The algorithm then increases the threshold at which vertices are removed, and makes another pass. The algorithm terminates when it reaches the desired simplification level, specified as a number of triangles or in terms of the decimation criteria. We discuss each aspect of the algorithm in the following sections.

5.2.2 CLASSIFICATION OF VERTICES

Vertices considered for removal are classified into five categories, illustrated in Figure 5.4: *simple, boundary, interior edge, corner,* and *nonmanifold*. A simple vertex is locally manifold, surrounded by a single complete ring of triangles, each of which shares a single edge with the vertex. Boundary vertices differ in that the set of triangles does not form a complete ring. The algorithm classifies vertices that do not fit either category as nonmanifold, and does not consider them for removal. Simple vertices can be further classified according to the geometry of the surrounding triangles. Two triangles can form a *feature edge,* which Schroeder et al. [Schroeder 92] define by the angle between the triangles, but which could also depend on material attributes such as color or texture coordinates. A simple vertex with less than three feature edges is classified as an interior edge vertex; vertices with three or more feature edges are considered corners.

5.2.3 DECIMATION CRITERIA

Once classified, a geometric error metric is applied to evaluate whether the vertex should be removed. Chapter 3 describes surface error metrics in detail. Here we describe the author's original algorithm. For simple vertices, an *average plane* is computed from the surrounding triangles. The normal of the average plane is an average of the triangle normals weighted by the triangle areas. A point on the average plane is computed by averaging the centroids of the surrounding triangles, also weighted by area. The distance of the vertex from the average plane of its surrounding triangles is used as the decimation criterion. If this distance is less than some user-specified threshold, the vertex is removed. Note that a threshold of zero will remove only vertices in planar regions. The efficiency with which vertex decimation removes coplanar triangles (done in a single linear pass) is especially useful when dealing with algorithms such as Marching Cubes [Lorensen 87], which can produce many such redundant triangles.

Boundary and interior edge vertices are tested against an *average line* formed from the two vertices on the boundary or feature edge. The distance of the candidate vertex from this line is tested against the same threshold, and the vertex is deleted if the distance is under threshold. Corner vertices are assumed to represent important features and are generally not deleted. However, if the mesh is known to be noisy, with many extraneous feature edges, the user may choose to evaluate corner and interior edge vertices against the average plane criterion used for simple vertices.

5.2.4 TRIANGULATION

Schroeder's original algorithm triangulated the polygonal holes resulting from a vertex removal. This triangulation used a recursive loop-splitting procedure, which we do not describe here (see Section 5.6 for discussion of a fast and robust triangulation routine). Instead, we simply mention some special cases. The original vertex decimation algorithm strictly preserves topology, which prevents some vertex removal operations. For example, a series of decimations may reduce an object to a simple closed mesh, such as a tetrahedron. Removing a vertex of the tetrahedron would create two coincident triangles sharing the same three vertices. Similarly, a hole in the mesh may be reduced to a single triangular gap, which would close up upon removal of one of its corner vertices. Both of these operations would change the topology of the mesh. To prevent such operations, the algorithm only removes vertices after verifying that no duplicate edges or triangles would be created during triangulation.

5.2.5 ADVANTAGES AND DISADVANTAGES

Vertex decimation, which simply consists of a few linear passes over the vertices, clearly operates in linear time with respect to the number of vertices. Quite fast in practice, vertex decimation is routinely used in VTK to simplify isosurfaces with millions of polygons. Removing redundant coplanar geometry in a single pass proves particularly useful for the heavily overtessellated models common to many visualization applications. The vertices of a model simplified by the decimation algorithm are a subset of the vertices of the original model. This property is convenient for reusing normals and texture coordinates at the vertices, but it can also limit the fidelity of the simplifications.

As Chapter 4 discusses, the distance-to-average-plane metric described previously may lead to less accurate results than more careful criteria. A developer implementing this algorithm may wish to consider a different metric, and indeed current versions of VTK include decimators based on quadric error metrics (as well as an implementation of Lindstrom's out-of-core vertex clustering algorithm, described in the previous section). Performing vertex removal in multiple passes can make it difficult to specify a target polygon count very exactly, since too high a distance threshold may simplify the model far past the target, and avoiding oversimplification by increasing the distance threshold in small increments may make the algorithm too slow. Finally, the strict topology-preserving nature of the algorithm may be an advantage or a liability, depending on the application. Preserving topology leads to higher fidelity but limits the potential for drastic simplification.

5.2.6 TOPOLOGY-MODIFYING CONTINUOUS LOD

Schroeder addresses several of these limitations in a topology-modifying extension of the original algorithm [Schroeder 97]. In this variation, vertices are ranked and sorted into a priority queue according to the same distance-to-plane and distance-to-line metrics. Vertices are then extracted in order, beginning with vertices whose deletion will introduce least error. Vertices are then classified, and decimated if classification permits. If performing all permitted decimations fails to achieve the user-specified reduction, a *vertex split* operation modifies the mesh topology, separating the mesh along feature edges and at nonmanifold vertices (Figure 5.5). This increases the vertex count by one but permits simplification to continue again, eventually reaching the target polygon count or even eliminating the mesh entirely.

Unlike the original vertex decimation algorithm, which iteratively removes vertices and triangulates the resulting hole, the topology-modifying algorithm uses the half-edge collapse operation, effectively performing a specific type of retriangulation (Figure 5.6a). The algorithm permits edge collapses that introduce topological degeneracies, such the duplicate edge that results from closing a hole (Figure 5.6b). Since the edge collapse is invertible, the sequence of simplifications forms a reversible stream (similar to Hoppe's progressive meshes) that supports continuous LOD. Unlike progressive meshes, however, Schroeder's representation encodes the (also invertible) vertex split operations as well.

The modified decimation algorithm remains quite fast in practice, though maintaining the priority queue brings the asymptotic time to $O(n \log n)$. Changing the

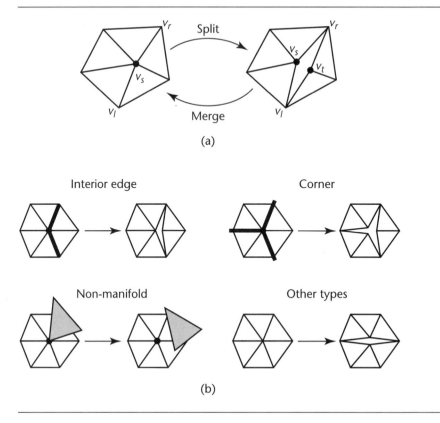

Figure 5.5   Vertex-split operations. (a) A typical vertex split and merge. (b) Splitting various vertex types. Splits are exaggerated [Schroeder 97].

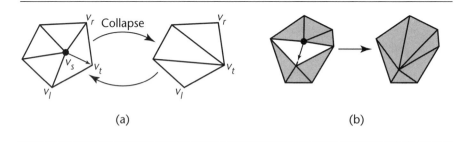

Figure 5.6   (a) A half-edge collapse can be viewed as a constrained vertex removal and triangulation. (b) An edge collapse causing a hole to close [Schroeder 97].

topology using edge collapse and vertex split operations allows the algorithm to reduce a mesh to any desired number of triangles, regardless of the initial genus or any nonmanifold degeneracies that may be present. One disadvantage of the algorithm is that it contains no provision for joining meshes. As a result, fidelity may suffer when performing drastic simplification of a collection of small objects. The decimation algorithm will simply delete the objects one by one rather than merging them into a single, large LOD.

5.3 QUADRIC ERROR METRICS

This algorithm, published in 1997 by Michael Garland and Paul Heckbert [Garland 97], set a new standard for LOD techniques. Though not without flaws, the quadric error metrics algorithm offers a combination of speed, robustness, and fidelity not previously seen. Garland and Heckbert's algorithm is also relatively simple to implement, and source code is publicly available (and included on the companion Web site), making it the most attractive LOD method for many applications. Here we describe the original algorithm, and mention some later improvements and extensions.

5.3.1 OVERVIEW

As described in Chapter 3, the quadric error metric measures the cumulative surface distortion introduced by a series of vertex merge operations. Garland and Heckbert's algorithm iteratively merges pairs of vertices until it reaches the desired level of simplification. The algorithm begins by finding candidate vertex pairs, including all vertices that share an edge. The candidate vertex pairs are entered into a priority queue sorted by their quadric error, and merged in order of increasing resulting error. Merging a vertex pair changes the error associated with other pairs in the local mesh neighborhood. These pairs are reevaluated and reinserted into the priority queue. Simplification terminates when the desired number of polygons is reached.

5.3.2 RECAP: MEASURING SURFACE ERROR WITH QUADRICS

A quadric is a 4×4 symmetric matrix that captures information about one or more planes. In particular, given a vertex coordinate $\mathbf{v}$ and a quadric $\mathbf{Q}$ representing a set of planes, evaluating $(\mathbf{v}^T \mathbf{Q} \mathbf{v})$ gives the sum of the squared distances from the vertex to each plane. Quadrics are additive. That is, the quadric of the union of two sets of planes is the sum of the quadrics of each set. When two vertices $\mathbf{v}_i$ and $\mathbf{v}_j$ with quadrics $\mathbf{Q}_i$ and $\mathbf{Q}_j$ are merged to form a new vertex $\mathbf{v}_k$, the quadric $\mathbf{Q}_k$ is simply $\mathbf{Q}_i + \mathbf{Q}_j$. This enables the algorithm to track sets of planes implicitly with a single matrix. The error associated with this merge operation is $(\mathbf{v}_k^T \mathbf{Q}_k \mathbf{v}_k)$, which represents the sum of the distances from $\mathbf{v}_k$ to all of the planes accumulated in both $\mathbf{Q}_i$ and $\mathbf{Q}_j$. Garland and

Heckbert show how to find a target position for the new vertex v_k that minimizes this error, as follows:

$$
v_k = \frac{1}{2}
\begin{bmatrix}
q_{11} & q_{12} & q_{13} & q_{14} \\
q_{12} & q_{22} & q_{23} & q_{24} \\
q_{13} & q_{23} & q_{33} & q_{34} \\
0 & 0 & 0 & 1
\end{bmatrix}^{-1}
\begin{bmatrix}
0 \\
0 \\
0 \\
2
\end{bmatrix}
$$

This requires inverting the matrix shown. If the matrix is not invertible, they test the error at the two endpoints v_i and v_j and at the midpoint between them, and choose as the target whichever solution produces the least error.

The quadrics at each vertex of the original model are initialized to represent the planes of all triangles that meet at that vertex. If the equation of a given plane is represented by

$$
p =
\begin{bmatrix}
a \\
b \\
c \\
d
\end{bmatrix}
$$

then the *fundamental error quadric* for that plane is the matrix

$$
K_p = pp^T =
\begin{bmatrix}
a^2 & ab & ac & ad \\
ab & b^2 & bc & bd \\
ac & bc & c^2 & cd \\
ad & bd & cd & a^2
\end{bmatrix}
$$

The quadric error metrics algorithm begins by calculating the fundamental error quadric for each triangle in the original model, and initializing the quadric of each vertex in the original model to the sum of the quadrics of its associated triangles. Note that the error at each initial vertex is zero, since the vertex lies at the intersection of the planes of its triangles.

5.3.3 CANDIDATE VERTEX PAIRS

Ideally, the algorithm could consider every possible pair of vertices for contraction, and choose the pair with the least error. In practice, this would require time and space quadratic in the number of vertices. Instead, Garland and Heckbert consider as candidates for collapse all vertex pairs connected by an edge, and optionally all vertex pairs within a threshold distance ϵ of each other. The inclusion of unconnected vertex pairs allows the algorithm to aggregate separate objects, an important feature for high-fidelity drastic simplification. However, it also exposes one of the weaknesses of the algorithm: the number of potential edge collapses in a polygonal mesh will be linear,[3] but the number of vertices within ϵ of each other grows quadratic as ϵ increases. Thus, choosing a value for ϵ is something of an art. Too small a value will prevent useful aggregation, and too large a value will ruin the performance of the algorithm.

5.3.4 DETAILS OF THE ALGORITHM

Once candidate vertex pairs are chosen and quadrics at every vertex initialized, the algorithm computes the target vertex $\mathbf{v}_k$ for every vertex pair $(\mathbf{v}_i, \mathbf{v}_j)$. The cost of merging $\mathbf{v}_i$ and $\mathbf{v}_j$ then becomes $\mathbf{v}_k^T(\mathbf{Q}_i + \mathbf{Q}_j)\mathbf{v}_k$, and the vertex pair is entered into priority queue (implemented as a simple heap) keyed on that cost. The algorithm then iteratively removes the vertex pair with the least cost, merges both vertices to the calculated target vertex, and updates the cost of all vertex pairs associated with the vertices. This update step involves deleting the pairs from the heap, recomputing target vertices and cost, and reinsertion. An LOD is output upon reaching the desired simplification level. If multiple LODs are desired, simplification just continues without restarting.

To preserve boundaries in the simplified mesh, Garland and Heckbert detect boundary edges or interior edges where discontinuities of texture or color occur. At each face containing a boundary edge, they create a "penalty plane" perpendicular to the face. This plane is converted to a quadric, weighted heavily, and added to the initial quadrics of the edge vertices. The resulting quadrics will tend to penalize vertex contractions that pull the mesh away from the boundary, and generate target vertices that lie on the penalty planes. Garland and Heckbert also penalize or prevent mesh foldovers (see Figure 2.11), which they detect by checking the normals of neighboring faces before and after merging a pair of vertices.

5.3.5 ACCOUNTING FOR VERTEX ATTRIBUTES

Though the original quadric error metrics algorithm preserves geometric fidelity nicely, many models define additional attributes at the vertices, such as color, normal, and texture coordinates. We generally wish to account for these attributes during simplification, for two reasons. First, when merging vertices, we must assign attributes to the newly created representative vertex with care. For example, just as simple averaging of coordinates produces generally poor geometric results, simple averaging of colors can produce poor visual results. Second, at times the attribute information should guide simplification. Radiosity-illuminated polygonal models provide a perfect example. Often large patches (e.g., representing walls and floors) are broken up into many small coplanar polygons. Here color is the key attribute. Some of these

---

3. This follows from Euler's formula: $V - E + F = X$. Here V is the number of vertices of a polygonal mesh, E is the number of edges, F is the number of faces, and X reflects the genus of the surface. Note that for a given genus, the number of edges is linear with respect to the number of vertices and faces.

polygons can be simplified away, whereas others are crucial for capturing lighting discontinuities. A simplification algorithm that considers both color and geometry is vital in this case. Chapter 3 provided an in-depth discussion of attribute error metrics. Here we briefly return to two algorithms that extend the original quadric error metrics method to account for vertex attributes.

Garland and Heckbert follow up their first publication with an extension that generalizes the definition of a quadric, effectively treating these attributes as additional spatial dimensions [Garland 98]. For example, a vertex defined by only geometry is represented as a vector $[x, y, z]$; a vertex with associated color is represented by a vector $[x, y, z, r, g, b]$; a vertex with texture coordinates by $[x, y, z, u, v]$, and so on. In the case of a vertex with color (six coordinates), Garland and Heckbert use a 6x6 matrix to represent the associated quadric. Naturally, dealing with these quadrics becomes significantly more expensive in time and memory as the dimension increases. Another disadvantage is that the relative importance of the various attributes is difficult to control, since the representation used by the algorithm essentially captures both geometric and attribute error in an abstract higher-dimensional space.

Hoppe improves on this approach in several ways [Hoppe 99b]. The most substantial change captures attribute error based on a geometric closest-point correspondence in 3D. This leads to a sparse quadric that proves much more efficient in both memory and computational complexity, especially as the number of attributes stored with vertices increases. Hoppe also integrates some concepts from previous work, including a *wedge* data structure for representing attribute discontinuities [Hoppe 98b], and Lindstrom's [Lindstrom 98] memoryless simplification technique (see Section 3.3). The resulting algorithm produces significantly more accurate simplifications of models with attributes.

5.4   RSIMP: REVERSE SIMPLIFICATION

RSimp, published in 2000 by Dima Brodsky and Ben Watson, combines elements from vertex clustering and quadric error metrics along with several new ideas to produce a unique algorithm. The name refers to its "reverse" approach to simplification—a crudely defined initial simplification is iteratively refined. This approach brings particular advantages when simplifying very large models. Shaffer and Garland [Shaffer 01] have since proposed an algorithm for massive models that draws heavily from RSimp, while Choudhury and Watson [Choudhury 02] have also recently completed a version of RSimp specialized for operation on massive models in virtual memory. RSimp's source code is publicly available; see the companion Web site.

5.4.1   OVERVIEW

Like many algorithms, RSimp uses a greedy simplification framework. Its principal data structure is the *cluster*, which represents a surface patch on the input model and a single vertex in the output model. The algorithm creates the first eight clusters simply by splitting the input model's bounding box, and then sorting them into a priority queue using a *normal variation* error metric. The cluster with the greatest normal variation is then split, and the newly produced subclusters are placed into the priority queue. This process iterates until the budgeted number of vertices is reached. At that point, an output vertex is computed for each remaining cluster in the queue using quadric error minimization. As in vertex clustering, the only input faces retained in the output model are those with vertices in three different clusters.

5.4.2   NORMAL VARIATION ERROR METRIC

RSimp's error metric departs from most metrics discussed in Chapter 3 in that it does not measure distance. Intuitively, the goal of RSimp is to split large, curved patches on the model before splitting small, flat patches. In a model with M faces, if a cluster contains N faces and the ith face has area a_i and unit normal n_i, the error metric for the cluster is

$$\frac{\sum_1^N a_i}{\sum_1^M a_i} \left(1 - \frac{\sum_1^N a_i n_i}{\sum_1^N a_i} \right)$$

Here the left factor indicates the relative area of the patch, while the right factor is larger when the faces in the patch are less coplanar. Note that the upper sum in the right factor will equal the lower sum if all the unit face normal vectors are aligned. Despite the fact that this metric does not directly measure distance, it proves quite effective, even when post hoc distance metrics (such as those in Metro) are used to evaluate its output.

5.4.3   CLUSTER SPLITTING

Clusters are split according to the pattern of normal variation. To describe this pattern, RSimp uses principal component analysis (PCA) on the quadric matrices defined by the cluster's faces. PCA is a widely used technique for extracting the directions of maximal change in a data set [Jolliffe 86]. These directions of change are the eigenvectors of a covariance matrix; their relative strengths are described by the matching eigenvalues. As Garland has noted, in this context these directions correspond roughly to the mean normal of the cluster, the direction of maximum curvature, and the direction of minimum curvature [Garland 99]. When all are roughly equal in strength, RSimp splits the cluster into eight new subclusters using three splitting planes orthogonal to the eigenvectors (Figure 5.7a). When only the directions of maximum and minimum curvature are approximately equal in strength, RSimp uses two splitting planes orthogonal to these maximum and minimum directions to produce at most four subclusters (Figure 5.7b). Finally, when none of the strengths are close to each other, RSimp uses just one splitting plane orthogonal to the direction

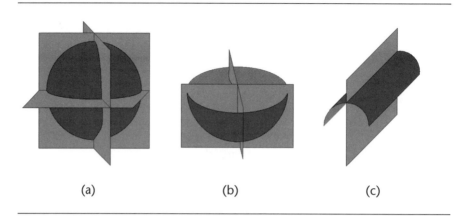

(a)   (b)   (c)

Figure 5.7   Splitting a cluster in RSimp. (a) Normal variation is extreme and the cluster is split with three planes. (b) Normal variation indicates a spherical bump or depression and the cluster is split with two planes. (c) Variation indicates a cylindrical shape and the cluster is split with one plane.

of maximum curvature, producing two subclusters (Figure 5.7c). To ensure that two widely separated surface patches in a new subcluster are not erroneously joined in output, RSimp uses a breadth-first search on the mesh connectivity. If it finds two or more disjoint components, the new subcluster is divided into two or more corresponding subclusters.

5.4.4   ADVANTAGES AND DISADVANTAGES

RSimp strikes a useful compromise between speed and output quality, simplifying models with greater speed and error than Garland's quadric error algorithm, but with less speed and error than Rossignac and Borrel's vertex clustering algorithm. The reverse approach to simplification means that its time complexity is $n \log m$, where n is input size and m is output size. Thus, despite the adaptive nature of its simplification, for a fixed output size it runs in time linearly proportional to the output size. Because it refines rather than simplifies, RSimp builds coarse approximations more quickly than fine approximations. These characteristics prove to be especially valuable when simplifying large or even massive models.

RSimp is very robust, easily handling messy and degenerate meshes. However, because it uses the cell collapse local operator, like vertex clustering, it does not guarantee preservation of input topology. The original RSimp algorithm could not guarantee output quality with fidelity-based simplification, nor could it take special action to preserve mesh boundaries. These latter shortcomings have recently been remedied.

5.4.5 Simplifying Massive Models

Shaffer and Garland [Shaffer 01] exploited the strengths of RSimp to modify it for use with massive models. They used a two-pass approach: The first pass simplified the model to a relatively large size (e.g., 1 million faces) using Lindstrom's out of core quadric-based algorithm. The next pass applied a variation of the RSimp algorithm. Their changes to RSimp used quadrics as the error metric, allowed only two-way splits, and used dual quadrics describing the direction of greatest vertex position change to orient splitting planes. The resulting algorithm was roughly three times slower than Lindstrom's algorithm, but 30% more accurate on average, as measured by Metro.

Choudhury and Watson [Choudhury 02] have also recently improved RSimp for use with massive models. Their strategy is centered on efficient use of virtual memory. They observe that RSimp produces increasingly finer partitions of the input model as it proceeds, with each new partition contained by a preceding partition. They exploit this pattern of execution to build locality of memory use by casting simplification as a sort. As a cluster is split, the faces and vertices corresponding to each new subcluster are sorted into corresponding subranges in the input face and vertex arrays. This simple but powerful improvement shrinks the effective working set continually as execution proceeds, and it enables cluster records in the priority queue to reference matching faces and vertices much more efficiently, hence lowering memory usage. The resulting algorithm is capable of fully adaptive simplification of models containing 56 million faces in 90 minutes on a 1 GHz Pentium III PC with 1 GB RAM. Output simplifications are 25% more accurate on average than Shaffer and Garland's output, according to Metro, with maximum error reduced by a factor of two. Sensitivity to topology allows the new algorithm to preserve mesh boundaries and avoid joining spatially separated model components. The tradeoff for these improvements is slower speed, roughly five times slower than Shaffer and Garland's algorithm.

5.5 Image-Driven Simplification

This novel technique by Lindstrom and Turk guides simplification using rendered images of the resulting simplification [Lindstrom 00b] (see Figure 5.8). Image-driven simplification solves the problem of how to weight appearance attributes such as normals, color, and texture versus geometric distortion of the surface. Other algorithms either ignore attributes or deal with them in an abstract mathematical fashion, such as the quadric error metrics described in this chapter. The unique approach of using image-based rather than geometric metrics to evaluate and direct simplification produces LODs with excellent fidelity. Other advantages of the approach are good silhouette preservation, drastic simplification of hidden portions of the model, and texture-content-sensitive simplification. These advantages come at a cost, however. Image-driven simplification probably ranks as the slowest modern algorithm for producing LODs.

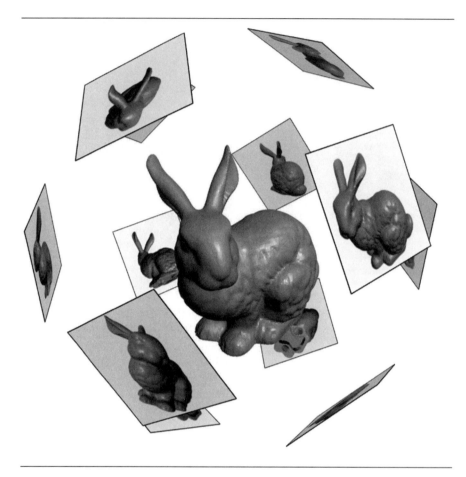

Figure 5.8 Image-driven simplification uses a series of images, rendered from viewpoints uniformly distributed around the model, to guide simplification [Lindstrom 00b]. Copyright © 2000 Association for Computing Machinery, Inc.

5.5.1 OVERVIEW

Image-driven simplification reduces models through a series of edge collapse operations. As in many algorithms (including, for example, the Garland-Heckbert quadrics error metrics algorithm previously described), Lindstrom and Turk store a list of candidate edge collapse operations in a priority queue sorted by an estimate of the error that collapsing the edge would incur. The algorithm computes this estimate by rendering the model from many viewpoints before and after the collapse is applied, and comparing the resulting images (Figure 5.8). A crucial aspect of this work is a clever technique for fast image updates using graphics hardware, which enables the algorithm to calculate edge collapse costs in reasonable time.

Since image-driven simplification depends on rendering the model many times at every level of simplification, it is impractically slow for very large models. Image-driven simplification proves most useful for creating high-quality LODs of medium-size models at drastic simplification levels. Lindstrom and Turk therefore pair the algorithm with a fast geometry-based approach [Lindstrom 98] that "presimplifies" the model to a reasonable level (roughly in the range 5,000 to 50,000 triangles in their examples) before applying image-driven simplification for the final stage of drastic simplification.

5.5.2 IMAGE METRICS

At the heart of image-driven simplification is a method for evaluating the distance between two images—one of the original model and the other of a proposed simplification. The literature of computer graphics, computer vision, and human perception includes many image metrics. Chapter 8 discusses a few examples of such metrics. Although their algorithm could easily be adapted to use any of these image metrics, for efficiency Lindstrom and Turk use a simple metric based on a pixel-by-pixel comparison of the images. Since the human visual system relies primarily on luminance for detection and recognition of form and texture, they reduce the computational expense of the problem further by calculating and working with the luminance channel Y for the images.[4] The final metric is a root-mean-square (RMS) pairwise difference between the pixels of the two images. For two luminance images Y^0 and Y^1 of $m \times n$ pixels, the RMS difference is

$$d_{RMS}(Y^0, Y^1) = \sqrt{\frac{1}{mn} \sum_{i=1}^{m} \sum_{j=1}^{n} (y_{ij}^0 - y_{ij}^1)^2}$$

Each potential edge collapse must be evaluated by rendering multiple images from different viewpoints, since the effect of collapsing the edge will be reduced or missed altogether from many directions. Deciding the number of viewpoints used clearly involves a trade-off between simplification speed and the risk of missing an important effect. Lindstrom and Turk choose to render from 20 viewpoints positioned at the vertices of a dodecahedron. They use a single light source, positioned near the viewpoint so that the model is fully illuminated in each image. Each image is 256×256, rendered using hardware acceleration against a mid-gray background.

---

4. The luminance channel Y of a color image is defined as its monochrome equivalent. The standard formula for the luminance of an RGB pixel (for CRT displays) is: $Y = 0.2125 * R + 0.7154 * G + 0.0721 * B$ [ITU-R 90].

5.5.3   EVALUATING EDGE COST

Once an edge has been collapsed, the error of the edges in its local neighborhood typically increases. Since evaluating this error is relatively expensive, Lindstrom and Turk use the lazy queuing algorithm from Chapter 2. That is, rather than reevaluating the error of each affected edge immediately, they simply mark the edge as "dirty" and proceed with simplification. When a dirty edge reaches the top of the priority queue, they recompute its cost and reinsert it into the queue. Lindstrom and Turk report that lazy evaluation reduces the number of edge cost evaluations by roughly a factor of five, without significantly lowering model quality.

5.5.4   FAST IMAGE UPDATES

Since every potential simplification operation requires rendering multiple images of the resulting model, Lindstrom and Turk develop an extremely efficient technique for updating these images. The key idea is to maintain the images *incrementally*, rendering the entire model only at the beginning and updating only the pixels that may be affected as the algorithm proceeds. To determine which pixels might be affected by an edge collapse, Lindstrom and Turk find the screen-space bounding box of the affected triangles—eight to ten triangles, on average. Unfortunately, it is not sufficient to simply render the simplified triangle set over the presimplified triangles, since changes in silhouette and depth may in principle expose any triangle in the model, even those geometrically and topologically distant from the collapsed edge.

Instead, Lindstrom and Turk implement a clever scheme for quickly finding and rerendering *all* triangles in the affected screen-space bounding box. A set of hash tables T keeps track of which triangles intersect each row and column of pixels. For a screen-space bounding box spanning pixel columns $i..j$ and pixel rows $m..n$, they compute the set of triangles included in those columns from T_{ij} and the set of triangles included in those rows from T_{mn}. The intersection of these sets forms a conservative (but tight in practice) estimate of the set of triangles contained in the bounding box. To accelerate this computation further, Lindstrom and Turk create auxiliary hash tables ΔT for every pixel and row that store only triangles not present in the preceding row or column. In other words, ΔT_{i+1} includes only triangles present in T_{i+1} but not in T_i. The set of triangles intersecting columns $i..j$ thus becomes $T_i \cup \Delta T_{i+1} \cup T_{i+2} \cdots \cup T_{j-1} \cup T_j$. Using these optimizations, Lindstrom and Turk achieve adequate simplification rates of roughly 100 to 300 triangles per second.

5.6   SKIP STRIPS

Triangle strips provide a compact representation of triangular mesh connectivity. An ideal or *sequential* triangle strip encodes a sequence of n triangles using $n + 2$ vertices

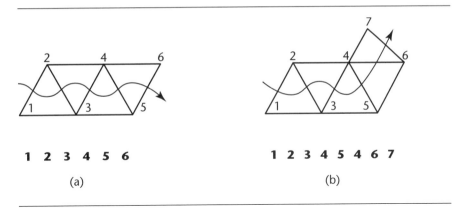

Figure 5.9 (a) A sequential triangle strip encodes n triangles using $n-2$ vertices. (b) A generalized triangle strip can encode "bends" in the strip by repeating vertices, in effect creating zero-area degenerate triangles [El-Sana 00].

(Figure 5.9a). This represents a substantial savings over the more direct encoding of triangles by their three corner vertices, which requires $3n$ vertices per triangle. This savings is reflected in storage size, but more importantly it results in a significant rendering speedup by reducing per-vertex memory bandwidth and computation costs operations such as transformation, lighting, and clipping. A *generalized triangle strip,* usually implemented by repeating vertices in the strip, can encode more complicated mesh structures (Figure 5.9b) at the cost of lesser savings (since repeated vertices represent redundant storage and computation).

Because they reduce storage and accelerate rendering, most high-performance graphics applications break the meshes of their LODs into multiple triangle strips in a postprocessing step (Figure 5.10). Indeed, one benefit of discrete LOD is the ability to create triangle strips of the individual LODs. A number of algorithms have been proposed for stripping triangulated meshes [Akeley 90] [Evans 96] [Xiang 99] [Hoppe 99a], and several publicly available implementations are available. We include one such implementation (STRIPE by Evans and Varshney) on the companion Web site. Unfortunately, for continuous and view-dependent LOD it is less obvious how to exploit the benefits of triangle strips, since the triangles of the underlying model are continuously in flux. In this section we present *skip strips,* an efficient way to update triangle strips in the presence of connectivity changes resulting from view-dependent LOD.

Let us study what happens when folding a node in the vertex hierarchy induces an edge collapse within a triangle strip (Figure 5.11). In this case we can replace both affected vertices with the new vertex. For simplicity, assume a half-edge collapse. We can replace all occurrences of the child vertex in the triangle strip by the parent vertex. In general, to maintain triangle strips under view-dependent changes to the triangle mesh connectivity, we should replace each vertex in a triangle strip by its nearest

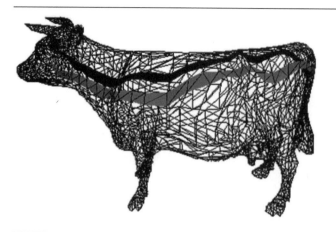

Figure 5.10   A single triangle strip in a model of a cow [El-Sana 00]. Copyright © 2000 Elsevier Science.

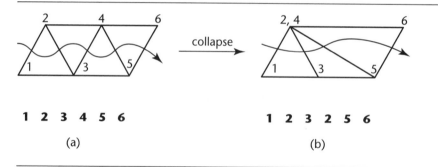

Figure 5.11   A half-edge collapse in a triangle strip. Here the child node (4) collapses to the parent node (2) [El-Sana 00].

unfolded ancestor. In an arbitrarily long sequence of folds, efficient traversal of links to a vertex's ancestors clearly becomes important.

Skip strips are inspired by *skip lists* [Pugh 90], an efficient probabilistic structure for storing and retrieving data. Skip lists rely on efficient compression of pointer paths. Consider a simple linked list. Such a list stores one pointer per node and requires on average $O(n)$ pointer hops to reach a desired node. A skip list stores an additional factor of $O(\log n)$ pointers that probabilistically link to nodes that are 2 away, 4 away, and so on. This enables skip lists to reduce the expected access time to any desired node down to $O(\log n)$.

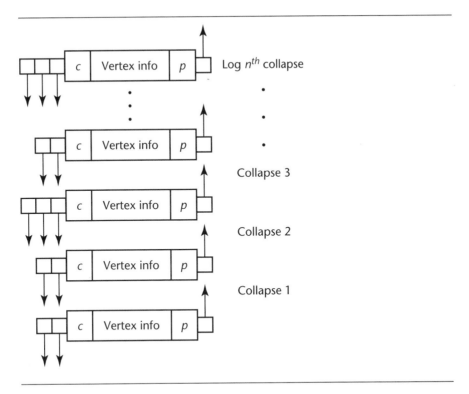

Figure 5.12   The *skip strip* data structure. Parent pointers for each skip strip node in the array are shown on the right, and the list of child pointers on the left [El-Sana 00].

Skip strips use the skip list approach to efficiently access ancestor nodes in a view-dependent LOD vertex hierarchy. The skip strips scheme splits preprocessing into two stages. First, the vertex hierarchy is generated using any appropriate simplification operator (e.g., edge collapse or cell collapse). Second, a triangle-stripping algorithm converts the original full-resolution mesh into a collection of triangle strips. The run-time system loads the vertex hierarchy and triangle strips during initialization, and builds the skip strips from both. At run-time the skip strips are used as the vertex hierarchy. View-dependent simplification and refinement perform vertex-split and edge collapse operations directly on the skip strips, which are used to generate triangle strips of each frame for display.

A skip strip is an array of skip strip nodes, each of which consists of the vertex information, a list of child pointers, and a list of parent pointers. Exactly one of the child and parent pointers is marked as *active* at any time (Figure 5.12). Skip strips are constructed during initialization by allocating a skip strip node for every node in the vertex hierarchy, with parent–child pointers set up to reflect the hierarchy structure. To perform the vertex collapse operation encoded by a node in the vertex hierarchy, we activate the parent pointer and increment the child index of the collapsed node. Deactivating the parent pointer and decrementing the child index reverses the collapse operation. The algorithm maintains a set of *display strips,* which represent the current simplification of the full-resolution triangle strips. Whenever a fold or unfold affects a triangle strip, the corresponding display strips are regenerated by walking the original triangle strip and following parent pointers at each vertex to find the corresponding vertex in the simplified mesh. Figure 5.13 illustrates operations on a vertex hierarchy and the corresponding changes to the skip strip structure.

Note that the simplified triangle strips begin to accumulate identical vertices as the mesh becomes very coarse. Sending such vertices multiple times equates to sending degenerate triangles; that is, they add overhead to the rendering process but do not contribute to the final scene. To avoid this, we detect and skip repetitive sequences of the form (*aa*) or (*ab*)—where *a* and *b* are vertices from the original mesh—when building the display strips.

5.6.1   AN ASIDE: THE VERTEX CACHE

Skip strips bring the important rendering acceleration benefits of triangle strips to view-dependent LOD, but at the cost of some extra memory and computational machinery. It is worth noting that graphics hardware increasingly includes a *vertex cache* that stores a small number of post–transform-and-lighting vertices for reuse. If the application renders a given vertex twice and the result of the previous render is still in the cache, the hardware can avoid the cost of transforming and lighting the vertex a second time. The vertex cache captures much of the rendering benefits of triangle strips, since the primary speedup of using strips results from avoiding the redundant calculation of repeating triangle corner multiple times. As vertex cache hardware becomes ubiquitous it seems likely that the goal of maintaining triangle strips through view-dependent simplification will be generalized to the goal of maintaining good vertex cache coherence throughout view-dependent LOD. This is an important area for future research. The interested reader may wish to consult Hoppe [Hoppe 99a] and Bogomjakov and Gotsman [Bogomjakov 01] for early related work.

5.7   TRIANGULATION OF POLYGONAL MODELS

Since most LOD creation algorithms assume triangle meshes, but many real-world models contain more general polygonal meshes, a triangulation algorithm is often an important component of an LOD system. Simply put, a triangulation algorithm divides a polygon with n vertices into $n - 2$ triangles by inserting $n - 3$ edges or *diagonals* between vertices of the polygon. Sometimes triangulation is straightforward. A model consisting entirely of convex polygons, for example, can easily be triangulated simply by picking a vertex in each convex polygon and forming triangles by

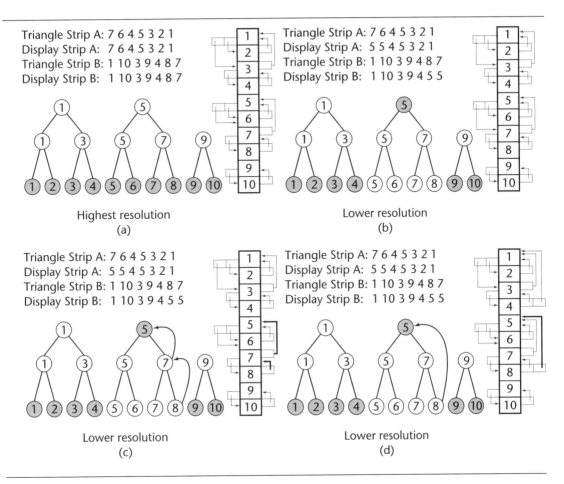

Triangle Strip A: 7 6 4 5 3 2 1
Display Strip A: 7 6 4 5 3 2 1
Triangle Strip B: 1 10 3 9 4 8 7
Display Strip B: 1 10 3 9 4 8 7

Highest resolution
(a)

Triangle Strip A: 7 6 4 5 3 2 1
Display Strip A: 5 5 4 5 3 2 1
Triangle Strip B: 1 10 3 9 4 8 7
Display Strip B: 1 10 3 9 4 5 5

Lower resolution
(b)

Triangle Strip A: 7 6 4 5 3 2 1
Display Strip A: 5 5 4 5 3 2 1
Triangle Strip B: 1 10 3 9 4 8 7
Display Strip B: 1 10 3 9 4 5 5

Lower resolution
(c)

Triangle Strip A: 7 6 4 5 3 2 1
Display Strip A: 5 5 4 5 3 2 1
Triangle Strip B: 1 10 3 9 4 8 7
Display Strip B: 1 10 3 9 4 5 5

Lower resolution
(d)

Figure 5.13   A vertex hierarchy and corresponding skip strip structure. (a) The vertex hierarchy begins at the highest resolution; the triangle strips and display strips are the same. (b) Vertices 6, 7, and 8 have all been folded to vertex 5. The skip strip shows the updated pointers, which are used to derive the new display strips from the triangle strips. (c–d) The pointer traversal. (e) Using multiple parent pointers per skip strip node (akin to the multiple child pointers) provides more efficient pointer traversal [El-Sana 00].

connecting it to all other vertices in that polygon (Figure 5.14a).[5] However, polygons in some models contain concavities and possibly even holes (Figure 5.14b), making them much more difficult to triangulate.

Narkhede and Manocha present a fast and robust algorithm for polygonal triangulation [Narkhede 95] based on Seidel's algorithm [Seidel 91]. This incremental randomized algorithm runs in expected $O(n \log^* n)$ time on a polygon with n vertices, equivalent to linear time for all practical purposes. In practice their implementation seems quite fast enough for use on any real-world graphics data set. Narkhede and Manocha provide source code for their implementation free for noncommercial use, which we in turn have included on the companion Web site.

A full description of Seidel's triangulation algorithm would require a significant background discussion grounded in basic computational geometry. We therefore depart from the detailed descriptions given in the previous sections, and provide only a very high-level sketch of the algorithm. The interested reader may wish to consult Seidel's original paper [Seidel 91], or the source code by Narkhede and Manocha included on the companion Web site, for more details. We also highly recommend Joseph O'Rourke's book *Computational Geometry in C* for a very readable introduction to triangulation (including Seidel's algorithm) and other topics in computational geometry [O'Rourke 94].

The triangulation algorithm consists of three steps (Figure 5.15), as follows.

1. Decompose the polygon into trapezoids.

2. Use trapezoids to decompose the polygon into monotone polygons[6] by drawing a diagonal between opposite-side vertices, forming corners of a trapezoid.

3. Triangulate the resulting monotone polygons.

Decomposing a polygon into trapezoids uses a randomized algorithm that adds segments of the polygon to the trapezoidal decomposition in random order. A clever data structure built during this process supports efficient point-location queries. The authors point out that this structure can be used for efficient point-in-polygon test after triangulation. Seidel shows that the trapezoidal decomposition takes expected time $O(n \log^* n)$ time. The trapezoids are then used to create monotone polygons in linear time by introducing diagonals between any pair of points in a trapezoid that corresponds to vertices from opposite sides of the polygon. The resulting polygons may be easily triangulated in linear time by repeatedly "cutting off" convex corners (Fournier 84).

---

5. Note that many other algorithms exist to triangulate convex polygons, some less prone to creating *sliver* triangles than this approach. Slivers are very thin triangles that can pose numeric problems for some algorithms, such as finite element analysis. However, slivers are typically not a problem in rendering.

6. Informally, a monotone polygon does not "curl back on itself." If a polygon P is monotone, some line L exists for which no perpendicular will cross more than two edges of P.

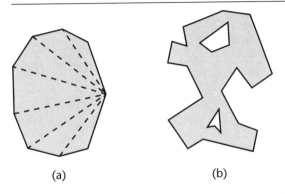

(a)   (b)

Figure 5.14   (a) Convex polygons may be easily triangulated (dashed lines), but (b) polygons with concavities and holes are more difficult.

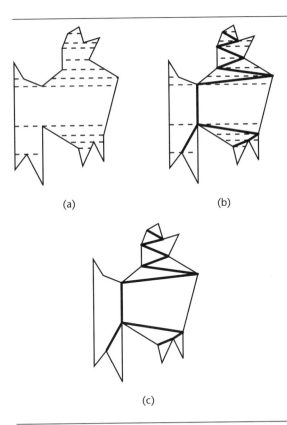

(a)   (b)

(c)

Figure 5.15   Seidel's triangulation algorithm. (a) A polygon is decomposed into trapezoids, then (b) diagonals are introduced that (c) partition the polygon into pieces that are easy to triangulate [Seidel 91].

5.8 CONCLUSIONS

To provide a comprehensive survey of every algorithm published in the mesh simplification literature is well beyond the scope of this book. Instead we have tried to highlight a few important algorithms that will prove useful to the graphics developer. We have reviewed a family of simple, fast, and robust vertex clustering algorithms that use the cell collapse simplification operator. RSimp also employs cell collapse; this algorithm strikes a nice balance between quality and speed, and its coarse-to-fine approach to simplification works well for generating LODs of very large datasets. Another helpful algorithm is vertex decimation, which uses the vertex remove operator and is a particularly common choice for eliminating redundant detail from highly tessellated isosurfaces in visualization applications. Garland and Heckbert's quadric-driven edge collapse approach provides an excellent combination of speed, robustness, and fidelity, and has led to many other important algorithms. Finally, we described Lindstrom and Turk's image-driven approach, which achieves high-quality simplification by choosing edge collapse operations based on actual rendered imagery of the resulting model. We also reviewed two useful auxiliary algorithms. Skip strips help improve rendering performance of view-dependent LODs, and Narkhede and Manocha's triangulation code provides a robust and publicly available tool that is very useful during preprocessing for simplification.

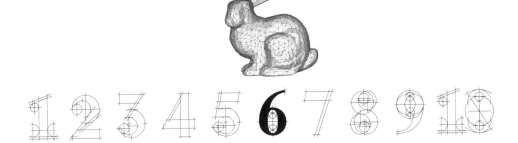

GAMING
OPTIMIZATIONS

Level of detail is of particular importance to developers of game software and hardware. Games push the envelope of advanced real-time techniques harder and faster than other disciplines, and the hardware applied to games is often the first place where important advances occur. In game environments, offline preprocessing of render data is essential for optimum efficiency, and this has a significant impact on our use of LOD. Game techniques such as triangle strips, display lists, instancing of data, skin deformation, and complex shaders can complicate our choice of detail systems. Games operate under tighter memory constraints than any other medium for 3D graphics. A modern video game platform has the processing power of the highest-end workstation, but only 16 megabytes of memory with which to feed its graphics pipeline. Games also give us unique advantages when dealing with detail. Our need for accuracy is less rigorous than, say, medical imaging, which allows our use of approximations or impostors, and because games are interactive, we can incorporate more information about where detail is important to the user based on the situation. This chapter examines and describes the particulars of using LOD in games by applying and refining the techniques discussed elsewhere in this book.

6.1 INTRODUCTION

Interactive gaming is arguably the biggest consumer of "advanced level of detail" techniques. Video game machines impose some of the most severely constrained environments to program in, but consumer demand for realism and complexity is intense. Games are also the most commercial environment using level of detail, so the algorithms must be as robust and visually appealing as possible. This chapter examines the LOD techniques described throughout this text in the context of current and future game platforms.

6.2 THE GAME ENVIRONMENT

Modern 3D gaming platforms rely heavily on dedicated hardware processing to render images. The goal of the game programmer is generally to maximize throughput through these dedicated processors, and to manage the flow of data between the different components of the machine. Other components of the game machine, such as the CPU and main memory, become less critical as the technology advances.

There are actually two different platforms we consider here. We use the term *video games* to refer to specific, closed systems that connect to a user's TV set. Examples include the Sony Playstation, Microsoft XBOX, Nintendo Gamecube, and so on. *Computer games* run on standard personal computers connected to a high-refresh-rate monitor. Each environment poses unique challenges for LOD. Game developers design their engine architecture around the specific capabilities and limitations of their target platform.

A video game system is basically a special-purpose computer designed to efficiently render and display images on a video display. Video game systems are usually less powerful than general computers in terms of their memory, storage, or general processing power, but can be more efficient at tasks such as 3D rasterization, 3D math, and memory manipulation. The primary design consideration for video game hardware is cost, so components are often highly integrated into just one or two chips, and memory (although generally very fast) is often very scarce. Even computer games running on general-purpose hardware, such as a common desktop PC, are moving toward a multiprocessor model that assumes a high-performance graphics co-processor. This graphics co-processor performs the majority of the display management, and has its own command set and local memories.

6.2.1 CONSTANT FRAME RATE

In most genres, a video game is expected to advance at a consistent, fixed frame rate of either 30 Hz or 60 Hz in the NTSC market, or 25 Hz or 50 Hz in PAL markets. Computer games, on the other hand, have typically been less bound to the video-standard refresh rates, and tend to try and achieve the highest possible frame rate up to the maximum refresh rate of the user's monitor, typically between 60 and 100 Hz. If a game drops significantly below this refresh rate, the player will experience noticeably "choppy" response times, as described in Section 10.4. For commercial video games, the hardware vendor has the power to reject games for release if they fail to maintain a minimum acceptable frame rate. Because video game hardware is tied to the television refresh rate, missing the 60 Hz performance target by even a small amount will result in an immediate drop to a 30 frames per second, so the costs of failure are quite high.

This requirement for near-constant refresh makes level of detail simultaneously more critical and more difficult for a game environment. We are forced to avoid methods that require significant periodic recomputation. At the same time, the need to maintain frame rate during different parts of a game requires real-time load balancing methods that can adjust LOD on a per-frame basis in response to instantaneous load measurement.

6.2.2   Very Low Memory

The biggest challenge facing game developers, particularly on video game platforms, is the relatively low amount of available memory relative to the needs of the game content. This forces developers to be very frugal in the use of memory in all areas, including the use of compression when possible. Geometry, the main focus of the algorithms in this book, is generally not the largest user of this precious RAM, but it does require that any level of detail methods used not add considerably to the memory load. LOD methods that can themselves act as a form of compression, such as parametric terrain representations or progressive detail streaming, are therefore highly prized for games.

Most platforms must also deal with the issue of segmented memory, with each dedicated processor having its own local memory pool. This means games must not only manage the total amount of memory they use to implement their systems, but this memory must also reside in the correct memory segment, or be moved there efficiently. This becomes a main concern for LOD algorithms that would endeavor to use the main CPU to manipulate geometry information that will be rendered by the graphics subsystem, so the cost of moving this memory between systems must be factored into the selection of LOD management schemes.

6.2.3   Multiple Instantiations

Games typically include multiple instances of the same model in a visible scene, usually in the form of a number of identical or near-identical "enemies" or "players." The goal of the developer is to share as much data as possible between these instances. When choosing level-of-detail methods, we want to avoid using methods with a high per-instance memory or per-instance computation cost.

Without LOD, most game engines store mesh and model data in a single shared object that can be referenced multiple times at multiple positions in the game. The basic geometry of the object—including vertex position, normal, color, texture placement, and bone influences—is stored in this shared object. Information unique to one instance (such as its current origin position and orientation) and the positions of any key-framed skeletal bones are stored in the per-instance object. The goal is to move as much data as possible into the shared object and instantiate objects with as little memory overhead as possible.

This type of instantiation is typical in many systems and is not unique to games, but games tend to push this memory-saving device further than other applications. Games often use instances not only for the interactive characters that move through the game world, but also for entire rooms, decorative objects, or terrain sections (see Figure 6.1). All this enables the game to present an apparently vast, detailed world within a limited memory budget. Geometry instanced multiple times in a visible scene can also benefit from certain rendering efficiencies. If the models in a scene can be sorted according to their shared geometry, they can be rendered sequentially, which may avoid costly state changes and, most importantly, texture cache misses. On a system with a small high-speed texture cache, this can be a critical optimization.

The primary drawback of using instanced geometry in this way is the difficulty in making per-instance modifications of the geometry. For example, a game that wishes to allow the player to deform the geometry at will by adding, removing, or modifying vertex data would be unable to do so in a purely instanced system.

6.2.4   SCALABLE PLATFORMS

Dealing with wide variations in hardware configurations was one of the first practical applications of LOD in games. Even before 3D hardware became commonplace, games were expected to run equally well on systems with a 90- or 200-MHz processor. This is still a serious concern, but one mainly found on games designed for PC or Macintosh platforms, since dedicated consoles have generally fixed specifications.

With a functional LOD system, using any of the techniques described in this text, the entire platform can be scaled up or down by adding a global bias to the LOD selection algorithm. In more extreme cases, we can also add limits to the maximum LOD the game can select under any circumstance. Capping the LOD can also allow us to scale the memory requirements for the game. If the highest-detail model can never be accessed by the game running on a constrained machine, we can avoid even loading the data. Scaling on such hardware affects not only geometry but texture resolution selection and the enabling/disabling of various effects.

6.2.5   FILL RATE VERSUS TRIANGLE RATE

One major disparity between video games and computer games is the balance between fill-rate and triangle-rate throughput. Computer games typically run at

(a)

(b)

Figure 6.1   Illustrating the use of multiple instantiations of objects such as players, chairs, lights, and so on. Everything in (b), but not in (a), is instantiated, which saves memory.

resolutions of 800 × 600 or higher, and often give the user a choice of different screen resolutions. Video games, however, are generally restricted to resolutions of 640 × 240 or 640 × 480, depending on whether the game is rendering fields or full frames. In field rendering, the game relies on the particulars of the video refresh system, which actually renders a 240-line image twice per frame offset by a single line to give an apparent 480-line image through a process called interlacing. Most consoles allow a 640 × 480 pixel frame buffer, which is re-interlaced by the video encoding device for display. As newer video standards begin to take hold, this disparity will begin to disappear. Some current systems support output at video rates above normal NTSC rates, such as 480p (640 × 480 pixels progressive scanned at 60 Hz) or HDTV resolutions such as 720p (720 lines progressive scan) or 1,080i (1,080 lines interlaced).

In either case, a typical video game system has far fewer pixels to rasterize for each frame, up to a 4X advantage compared to a high-resolution computer game. Because of this disparity, video game applications are more often computationally bound in their ability to transform, light, and set up the rasterization of geometry. In this type of triangle-rate-limited environment, geometric LOD methods yield immediate and significant rewards.

6.2.6 AVERAGE TRIANGLE SIZE

One metric of particular importance to video game developers is the average triangle size. Typical 3D hardware in the gaming segment is constructed as two separate units: a geometry-processing unit (which handles tasks such as triangle setup, lighting, and transformation) and a pixel-processing unit (which manipulates the final frame buffer pixels in response to the output from the geometry unit). These are often referred to as the "front-end" and "back-end" units, respectively. To achieve maximum throughput, these two units need to be carefully load balanced. If the front-end unit is overloaded, the back-end unit will often be idle, awaiting rasterization jobs from the geometry unit. If the back-end unit is overtaxed, the front-end unit must block, waiting for the rasterizer to accept more commands. Because of the complex interplay between these two parallel pipelines, hardware designers often implement parallel pathways through one or both systems, and provide buffering of data between the two.

The metric of average triangle size helps estimate the balance between the loads on these two systems. A small number of large triangles shift more of the burden to the pixel back end, whereas a larger number of tiny triangles will primarily tax the front end. Triangle size in terms of screen pixels therefore provides a convenient estimate of this balance. Ideally, an engine would take steps to ensure that the average screen triangle size remains as close as possible to some optimal balance, no matter how the scene objects or observer change over time. Clearly, the other important factor in this relationship will be the cost of the individual triangle or pixel, which is far from fixed. Generally, hardware vendors will advise developers on the ideal triangle size (often presented graphically from empirical measurements) based on different scenarios for vertex and pixel modes. The ideal size for a triangle that uses multiple dynamic lights or skinned blending would be larger than the size recommendation for a simple unlit triangle, because more pixel operations can be performed between completed triangle computations. Conversely, a more complex pixel operation, perhaps involving more than two texture lookups or blending to the frame buffer, would require smaller triangles at equal levels of performance. Clearly some LOD methods are required to maintain our average triangle size near optimum levels.

6.3 GAME-SPECIFIC DIFFICULTIES WITH LOD

Clearly LOD is very important to game engine design, but the particular needs of gaming make some techniques used in other fields difficult or impossible to implement effectively. This section discusses some of these pitfalls and suggests alternate strategies or simplifications when available.

6.3.1 MODELING PRACTICES

Game models are created using the same tools and workstations used by 3D artists in other disciplines. But rather than using the rendering capabilities of these packages to output fully rasterized frames, game projects use the model geometry itself as the output product from the artist's tool (see Figure 6.2). The process of taking a complex, generalized 3D model from an art package is referred to as "exporting" (or sometimes "compiling") the model, and it shares much in common with how a language compiler turns source code into tightly optimized, compiled object code. The final output from the tool is normally in a format that is highly platform specific. There have been some attempts at standardized game geometry formats, but the rapid rate of hardware change—coupled with the need for this format to mimic, as closely as possible, the preferred input format for the platform's graphics processor—has made most attempts at interchange short-lived. A game that runs across multiple platforms might even compile geometry data differently for each variation of the game, to optimize for the specifics of each targeted machine.

There are some idiosyncrasies in the way game models are constructed, compared to the type of idealized input meshes used to demonstrate classical LOD algorithms.

Vertex Representation

To optimize render speed, interactive game models are normally stored with their vertices in a format that can be directly processed by the hardware. Typically, this means that all data elements for a specific vertex are stored together in a structure, and a number of these vertex structures are stored as a linear array. The alternative, storing each vertex property separately in parallel arrays, is often possible, but generally

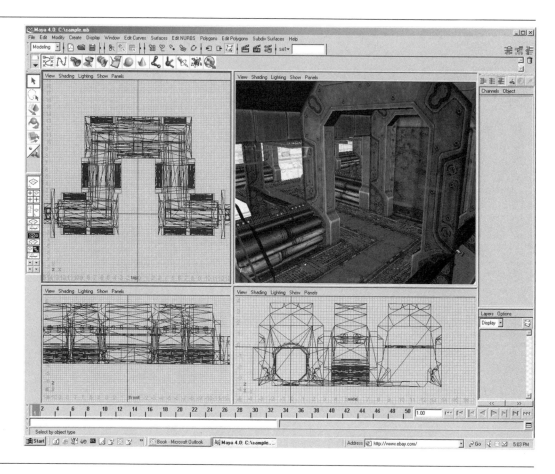

Figure 6.2   An artist's modeling tool used to create game geometry.

requires more work by the CPU or hardware to "gather" the renderable vertex at run-time.

This vertex storage strategy can affect LOD, since as a result vertices that lie along discontinuities in the model have their shared components replicated. The final mesh therefore contains multiple discrete vertices for that position. These discontinuities are typically caused by a normal crease—unsmoothed vertex normals along a faceted edge—or by texture seams due to texture compositing, discussed later. We must give these vertices special consideration when performing mesh simplification. If one shared discontinuous edge collapses to a different destination or at a different step of reduction, a gap can open in the continuous mesh, and further reductions can cause the error to grow.

There are two easy strategies to deal with split vertices of this type. We could simply *harden* the vertices and neighboring edges, excluding them from consideration as collapse candidates when simplifying the mesh. This eliminates all possibility of an inappropriate split, but reduces the maximum effectiveness of our reduction. This method also has a less obvious but potentially advantageous side effect. In game models, texture seams often coincide with important silhouette edges, and discontinuous normals may indicate important visual corners in the model. By preserving these discontinuous edges we sometimes unintentionally guide the LOD scheme to preserve artistically important details. Artists aware of this restriction can also use it to provide manual guidance to the reduction algorithm by intentionally hardening edges or placing texture seams where they can most benefit the model.

The other available strategy is to ensure that any collapse involving the coincident vertices is performed in lock step with their associates. This may somewhat complicate a run-time continuous LOD scheme, since we must store some additional data to indicate which sets of reductions must be treated as atomic operations, but for discrete LOD the export tool can enforce this restriction without any additional costs by not selecting LOD levels that straddle such a pairing.

Texture Compositing

Texture seams are especially commonplace in game models because of a performance-enhancing technique known as texture compositing (see Figure 6.3). The goal of compositing is to create a single texture map that contains all texture information for a single model or even multiple models. This reduces the number of state changes (both texture state and related shader state) required to render the model, and it also allows for larger render batches, since only sets of faces with identical properties can be rendered in a single batch. With consoles that utilize a small texture-memory cache, avoiding texture state changes is one of the most important optimization criteria.

Textures on most game platforms are also restricted to having power-of-two dimensions in both u and v. This leads artists to aggressively pack subtextures into a larger composite to efficiently use all available space in this precious texture resource.

All of these concerns can cause what would normally be a very clean manifold mesh to become a model with frequent discontinuous regions that must be considered during LOD processing.

Nonstandard Geometry

One final noteworthy modeling convention in games is the frequent use of nonclosed or nonmanifold mesh shapes. An open mesh in particular is often used for modeling certain types of character components (e.g., clothing, capes, or teeth), as well as for certain types of effects. Intersecting or folding geometry is sometimes used as a sort of

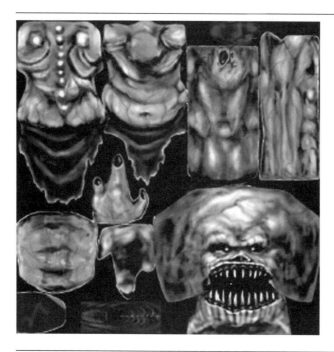

Figure 6.3   Texture compositing optimizes texture memory by creating a single texture map of a number of subtextures.

simplistic volume imposter, such as using two crossed quads with a masked texture to represent a branch of a tree. It is important to consider these cases when selecting an algorithm or metric from those presented in this book. As a general strategy, we attempt to detect these nonstandard constructions in our geometry and exempt them from our chosen LOD scheme. Odd geometric features such as unpaired edges are best preserved intact, since often the visual importance of these features is greater than the geometry would appear to an LOD metric. This is particularly true when such features are used in the area of a character's face or clothing. Nothing makes for amusing bugs more than disappearing eyelids or clothing. In effect, these constructions represent a sort of "manual LOD," an abstraction the artists apply to their art in its initial expression. Such abstractions will generally not benefit from, and will likely be harmed by, additional LOD reductions.

6.3.2 HARDWARE TRANSFORMATION AND LIGHTING

The latest generation of video game hardware contains dedicated hardware units to handle the bulk of the rendering work, including transformation and lighting of geometry. Typically these units can perform fixed-function or near–fixed-function operations much faster than and in parallel with the main CPU. In part for this reason (and in part for the overall desire of hardware producers to minimize costs), the CPU power of a particular console is far inferior to its pixel rendering and vertex-processing power. This is particularly true for Playstation 2 and Gamecube hardware, and somewhat less true for Microsoft's XBOX.

These hardware processing units vary greatly in their flexibility. The vector units on the Playstation 2 are quite flexible and approach the level of a general-purpose processor. The XBOX integrates programmable vertex processing on the same NV2A chip as its pixel pipelines, as does the Gamecube on its "Flipper" GPU. In all of these cases, providing vertex data in one of several preferred formats and using fairly typical processing paths is the key to optimizing geometry throughput. For example, even though the XBOX GPU is capable of processing vertices that have been blended from two sources, deformed by four weighted bones and then lit, the throughput for vertices of this type will be a fraction of those simply transformed and clipped to screen space.

For these reasons, games generally prefer LOD methods that do not require complex or unusual per-vertex operations on a per-frame basis. They tend to avoid continuous blending between LOD sets, or run-time algorithms that require real-time interpolation or modification of vertex data such as the concept of geomorphing introduced in Section 4.4.2.

6.3.3 STATIC AND DYNAMIC GEOMETRY

Not all geometry is created equal when it comes to rendering on game platforms. One thing that characterizes almost all high-performance real-time 3D engines is a large instruction queue placed between the main processor and the graphics processor. Different platforms handle this buffering in different ways, but the main goal is to provide more parallelism between the graphics and main processors for higher performance.

Most games use a combination of dynamically generated geometry data and static geometry. Dynamic geometry is necessary for interactive effects such as particles, explosions, beams, and other secondary effects. To create dynamic geometry and pass it to the graphics processor, the system libraries or game application must construct the command packets in the correct format for the graphics processor and copy them to the command queue for processing. All these operations add to the total processing time for the geometry. Static geometry, on the other hand, can be precompiled into a hardware command stream, and each time the geometry is rendered only some small amount of state information is added to the existing command stream. The exact mechanisms of this static geometry optimization vary between different platforms, but are commonly referred to as "display lists," or often "push buffers," on DirectX hardware. We clearly wish to make our LOD-enhanced geometry engine approach static mesh speeds as much as possible.

6.3.4   CACHE COHERENCE AND TRIANGLE STRIPS

Let us return briefly to the topics of triangle strips and cache coherence, which we have touched on in Section 5.6. Triangle strips as a method to represent geometry more efficiently are not particularly new or novel, but their use on video game platforms is becoming increasingly important. Recall that in a triangle strip, the first three indices define a standard triangle, but from that point on each new triangle is defined by a single new index and an implicit reuse of the two preceding indices. So the sequence "0 1 2 3" defines two triangles formed by indices (0,1,2) and (2,1,3). Most strip implementations reverse the reused vertices in alternating triangles to ensure that all triangles have the same winding order. The most obvious advantage of using strips is their ability to define a triangle with only a single (possibly WORD-sized) index.

In current games, strips are being used less as a compression scheme and more as a way to ensure vertex cache coherence. The XBOX hardware, for example, implements a cache of post-transform vertices based on the index lists. Whenever a vertex exists in this very small cache, the hardware can bypass the entire costly transform and lighting engine; this gives a considerable performance boost, particularly when the vertex processing is complex. Maximizing hits in this cache is one of the most important performance optimizations for that platform. Other platforms benefit as well from vertex reference locality. The Playstation 2, for example, requires packets to be constructed that contain both vertex and index information for rendering. If all references to a particular vertex are contained in a single packet, there will be no need to copy this vertex into a second packet at a later time, and bandwidth will be saved.

Generating optimal strips for a video game console is a complex problem and an area of active research and can only be done adequately as an offline preprocessing step. The optimal strip representation depends directly on the characteristics of the hardware, such as the size of the post-transform cache on the XBOX. This is one case in which model data is likely to be compiled for specific hardware targets.

The desire to generate efficient strips using offline processing is one of the biggest obstacles to using many popular LOD methods on game consoles. Even though it is possible to render nonoptimized triangle index lists on all platforms, the performance reduction might more than offset the LOD gains. In these cases, techniques such as skip strips, described in Section 5.6, could prove particularly valuable.

6.3.5   VECTOR UNIT PACKETIZATION

The Playstation 2 platform is unique in operation because it provides much lower-level access to how data is transferred between different processors in the machine. The basic unit of data transfer is a DMA packet of a fixed size. These packets are buffered and presented sequentially to the vector processing units, where they are processed according to game-specific microcode. When rendering geometry, these packets will include the entire set of vertex and index information needed to render a particular fragment of geometry. Creating these packets can be done either in real-time or offline. Offline packet creation allows for more optimization as well as lower CPU utilization, as the packets are simply streamed from RAM sequentially. The closest analogy is compilation of source code into executable code. The source data of the geometry is processed using complex methods and aggressive optimization that produce the graphical equivalent of optimized executable code. All platforms actually do this to a greater or lesser degree, but not all platforms allow us to do all the compilation offline and present the final "executable" formats directly to the hardware.

The LOD impact of this packetization is the need to avoid, at all costs, dynamically generated geometry that would require real-time processing or packetization. When we must deal with unprocessed data, we should expect a significant performance penalty for doing so. This means LOD schemes that can be processed offline will be more applicable.

6.4 Classic LOD Suitability to Games

Most games use a combination of geometric LOD approaches, but these mainly fall into the broad categories of discrete and continuous LOD. The LOD data for a model is generated as part of the export process that takes the model from 3D tool to in-game format. Because all calculation-intensive processing happens offline, games are free to use any of the more complex metrics for simplification.

View-dependent algorithms have not achieved wide acceptance in the game community. This is probably because they generally have higher run-time computation costs and require more frequent recalculation, since models must be continuously reprocessed as they rotate or move closer or further from the viewer. Games can also be a worst-case environment for view-dependent LOD, since many games implement a camera scheme that rotates the camera around a central player, resulting in frequent changes in viewing angle of the character and the entire scene. View-dependent techniques can, however, be used to great effect in terrain LOD, discussed in the next chapter.

6.4.1 Discrete LOD

As stated earlier, video games can render meshes most efficiently when a considerable amount of offline preprocessing can be performed on the data. Because of the need for preprocessing, many games rely on simple discrete LOD systems, in which each LOD can be aggressively "compiled" before it is loaded into the run-time engine (see Figure 6.4).

Discrete LOD offers other advantages. Most continuous LOD methods assume some continuity in vertex data. For example, a typical vertex removal algorithm assumes that vertices carried over from the previous LOD are unchanged. When simply replacing the LOD, we have the option to replace not only the model topology

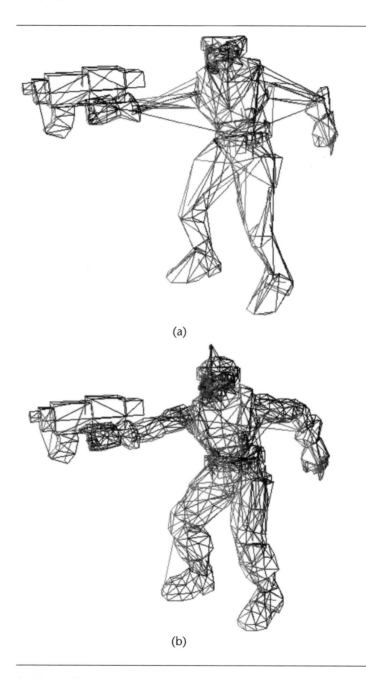

(a)

(b)

Figure 6.4   (a–b) Two discrete LODs for a trooper model.

but to completely rework the vertex data. There are two ways this can be useful. As a model becomes less detailed, it is often useful to replace its (u,v) texture-mapping coordinates. At higher detail levels, some models might contain multiple textures or multiple sets of texture coordinates per vertex (perhaps for lighting, bump mapping, or other effects). As the model reduces, the texturing can be changed to use fewer maps, or even changed to use subtextures from a generic composite.

We can expend significant amounts of offline processing to optimize the final LOD. This may be the most significant advantage of discrete LOD over continuous, progressive, or algorithmic reduction schemes. The trend in high-end hardware is definitely toward additional caching and pipelining. Taking full advantage of this trend requires "compilation" of geometry whenever possible.

Shared Vertex Format

A discrete LOD scheme that uses a shared vertex pool is more restrictive, but also more memory efficient. In this method, the base vertex data is shared between all LOD steps, with each step simply referencing a smaller subset of the original data. The model stores separate versions of the index list that defines the mesh faces for each LOD. Finally, the vertex data can be sorted to appear in detail order, so the less detailed faces reference data residing in a contiguous block.

In this format, the data is ideal for streaming to the hardware. Each time the model is rendered, a decision can be made on the fly to send any of the available index-ordering and vertex-block subsets to the hardware. There is no need to recompute or regenerate any data, which means we can adjust detail on a frame-by-frame basis with no penalty. The memory costs are also modest, since the bulk of the memory cost for a mesh (ignoring textures) is in the vertex definitions. For example, the minimal vertex format used for a game mesh would consist of position, vertex normal, and one set of texture coordinates, for a total uncompressed size of 32 bytes. Compare this to an index list entry, which is often 2 or sometimes 4 bytes in size. Thus, storing multiple sets of index data for a mesh, even a significant number of sets, represents a small percentage of the total memory used.

Separate Vertex Format

If vertices are not shared between LOD levels, the system is effectively just replacing one model with another at different detail levels. This is the simplest and most direct form of LOD management, but it is still a viable method, especially given the constraints of video game hardware.

The advantage of not sharing vertex data in a single pool between all LOD levels is flexibility. Different detail levels can use entirely different vertex formats, different texture coordinates, and so on. The main drawback is obviously the memory cost, which will limit the number of detail levels the game can reasonably store.

Automated Versus Manual Processing

One less obvious advantage of discrete LOD is that each level can be handcrafted and edited by an artist, using manual reduction techniques or a combination of automated methods. Generally even the best automatically generated geometry can benefit from some artistic "tweaking" inside a 3D editing tool.

If the game engine adopts a separate-vertex format, the artist has complete freedom to reshape and simplify a model using a variety of techniques or even by rebuilding the model entirely (usually using the high-detail silhouette as a guide). In a shared-vertex approach, restrictions on the artists can make manual tweaking more difficult. It is possible, if the artist is conscious of the need to reuse existing vertices when creating reduced models, but it is not a type of editing familiar to most artists or directly supported by most tools.

The alternative is of course to use one or more of the automated reduction techniques to algorithmically reduce the model in a way that is pleasing to the artist and end user. Any of the techniques that iteratively remove vertices can be used to generate both continuous and discrete levels of detail. Because the automatic processing is done completely offline, even the most computationally intensive methods can be used to generate the run-time data, and different methods can be selected on a case-by-case basis according to the specific needs of the model or preference of the artists.

6.4.2   CONTINUOUS LOD

At first glance, continuous LOD appears to have good characteristics for games. The algorithm can progressively remove vertices and faces from a model, thereby optimizing the precious bandwidth costs in a game engine.

Although no single canonical implementation of continuous LOD exists, some obvious choices can be made for game rendering. The first restriction we place on our system is that it be strictly based on vertex removal or half-edge collapse, rather than on a more general vertex or topology reduction scheme. This reflects our need to avoid creating or changing the underlying data whenever possible. By making each continuous LOD step a vertex removal or half-edge collapse, we avoid changing or adding to the underlying vertex data, and make only incremental changes to the index list that replace each appearance of one index value with another. After each step, more faces in the index list will become degenerate and can be removed. Since the removal order is computed offline, the vertices and indices can be sorted in order of their removal, allowing us to stream progressively smaller blocks of data to the hardware as the detail level decreases.

Run-Time Processing for CLOD

No matter what type of metric we select for offline preprocessing to determine the collapse or removal order, the run-time processing is the same for the general class of continuous LOD algorithms based on half-edge collapse. In addition to storing the renderable vertex data and the full-detail face index ordering, we store an additional non–render-related data block to facilitate the LOD process. This array is of the same data type as the index list entries (generally WORD or DWORD sized) and represents, for each removable vertex between the maximum and minimum detail, the destination or "collapse-to" vertex index. We also sort the vertex array in order of increasing detail, so the first vertices in the array are those that are part of the minimum LOD set, and those at the end are the first removed. Given these constraints, the collapse-to entry at a given array location can never be greater or equal to that location index, since a vertex cannot collapse to a higher-detail destination.

To change the LOD selection for an instance of a model, we simply recompute a new face index list by iteratively replacing each entry with its collapse-to value, until the resulting value is less than the number of desired mesh vertices. Degenerate faces are detected and removed from the list. We can optimize this process further by reordering the faces in the base index list in order of removal. With this sorting, when our reduction processing encounters the first degenerate face it can assume all remaining faces will likewise be degenerate and exit early.

Although this reprocessing is very straightforward and reasonably fast, it falls short of the "zero-processing," streaming-data model we desire to achieve for maximum speed. However, we can cache the face indexing output by the reduction processing and use it for a number of frames, thus amortizing the LOD processing costs over tens or hundreds of frames. Whenever the desired LOD for a model is unchanged over time, we simply stream the cached index list to the hardware, just as we would the indexing for a discrete LOD or non-LOD model.

Storage costs for this scheme are also quite small. Although each instance of a model must store a private index list, all of the bulkier underlying data—the vertices and even the collapse instructions—will be shared among all instances. This mirrors the data storage schemes used for PC graphics cards, which generally store vertex arrays in video RAM while leaving index lists in system RAM where they can be more efficiently changed at run-time.

Complications with CLOD

In the absence of other types of geometry optimization, such as triangle strip and vertex-cache reordering, this method would appear nearly ideal. However, the problems encountered when dealing with the most optimized types of game geometry can negate the gains possible from continuous LOD.

The most pressing problem is vertex cache coherence. As stated earlier, reordering triangle indices for optimum cache performance can give tremendous performance advantages on hardware such as the XBOX or high-end PC chip sets. We can achieve near-optimal indexing of our geometry via extensive offline processing, but such reordering is not practical at run-time. As vertices are removed from the model and edge collapses change the content of the index lists, our geometry can become nonoptimized and performance will drop, rather than increase, as we make further removals.

A similar problem occurs on systems such as Playstation 2, which require rendering instruction packets that contain both vertex and index data. For a given discrete LOD we can pregenerate these packets and efficiently spool them to the hardware via a dedicated DMA co-processor. But as a continuous LOD scheme removes vertices and changes indices, we must regenerate packets or shift to a "pack on the fly" strategy. Either method will cost precious processing time on the main CPU.

Both methods can benefit from reprocessing the detail level less frequently, so that the one-time costs of reprocessing the data to a new LOD can be amortized over several frames. We can also handle recomputation in a round-robin fashion, ensuring that the potential CPU costs in a given frame will not exceed some fixed budget. Of course, the less frequently we change LOD levels, the closer the visual results become to simple discrete LOD, making the benefits of continuous schemes less clear-cut.

Degenerate Faces

As stated earlier, most game hardware achieves top performance only when processing cache-optimized triangle strips. It should also be noted that the start of each new strip generally involves issuing a new render call, and our goal is to minimize the total number of such calls to the extent possible. In addition, because we are generating strips for a particular cache size, generating the longest strip possible is not our goal, and in fact the strips generated for typical game hardware are considerably shorter than the potential strips if pure index count reduction were the goal.

To process these strips efficiently, the model export stage will intentionally insert degenerate strips intended to "stitch together" disjoint strips without calling the API to start a new strip. Since this is a fairly common optimization, most hardware tries to provide optimized pathways for detecting and rejecting degenerate triangles in a strip without paying the full triangle setup cost for the data.

LOD and Degenerating Strips

In light of this hardware optimization, we can take steps to combine efficient continuous-LOD reduction schemes with optimized triangle lists, and the result is somewhat of a hybrid between shared-vertex discrete LOD and CLOD techniques.

As in discrete LOD, we can generate a highly optimized strip ordering for our indices using offline processing at specific steps along the reduction. At run-time, once we have determined our desired vertex count, we can take the next-larger optimized strip (so for a 500-vertex rendering we could use an index strip generated for 600 vertices, but not one generated at 450) and replace vertices above our target number with their collapse targets, as in the nonstrip case. We then render the geometry using the reprocessed indexing that contains additional degenerate triangles where

(a)

(b)

(c)

Plate 1   (Figure 1.1, p. 4) A variety of large models, all well beyond the interactive rendering capabilities of today's hardware. (a) The UNC Powerplant (≈56 million polygons) (University of North Carolina [Aliaga 99]), (b) the Digital Michelangelo scan of David (≈56 million polygons) (Stanford University [Levoy 00]), and (c) a stream scene rendered from ≈16 million polygons using the system desribed in [Deussen 98] (Courtesy of Bernd Lintermann). Copyright © 1998, 1999, and 2000 Association for Computing Machinery, Inc.

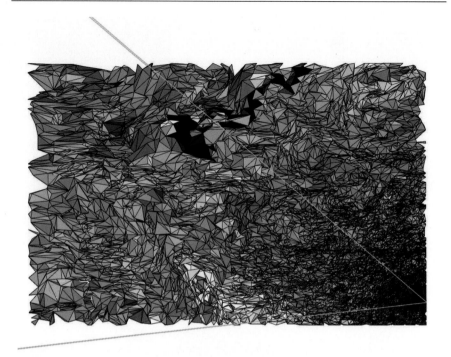

Plate 2   (Figure 1.3, p. 11) View-dependent LOD: a birds-eye view of a terrain model simplified in view-dependent fashion. The field of view is shown by the two lines. The model is displayed at full resolution near the viewpoint and at drastic simplification far away [Luebke 01a]. Copyright © 2001 IEEE.

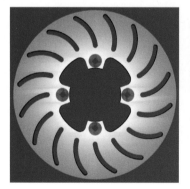
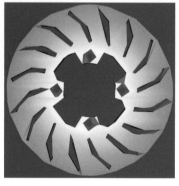
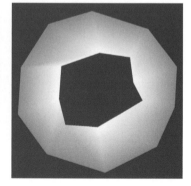

(a) 4,736 triangles, 21 holes   (b) 1006 triangles, 21 holes   (c) 46 triangles, 1 hole

Plate 3   (Figure 1.8, p. 16) Preserving genus limits drastic simplification. (a) The original model of a brake rotor is shown (b) simplified with a topology-preserving algorithm and (c) a topology-modifying algorithm [Luebke 01a]. Copyright © 2001 IEEE. Courtesy Alpha_1 Project, University of Utah.

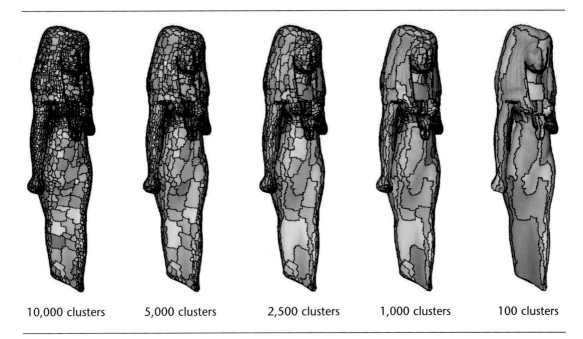

10,000 clusters   5,000 clusters   2,500 clusters   1,000 clusters   100 clusters

Plate 4   (Figure 2.9, p. 27) Face-clustering simplification [Garland 01]. Copyright © 2001 Association for Computing Machinery, Inc.

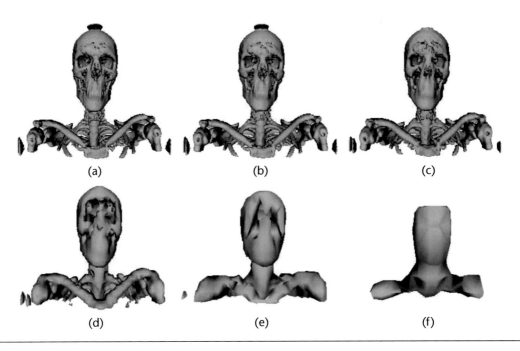

(a)   (b)   (c)

(d)   (e)   (f)

Plate 5   (Figure 2.10, p. 30) LODs of a medical isosurface using volume-domain topology simplification: (a) 334K triangles, (b) 181K triangles, (c) 76K triangles, (d) 17K triangles, (e) 3K triangles, and (f) 568 triangles [He96]. Copyright © 1996 IEEE.

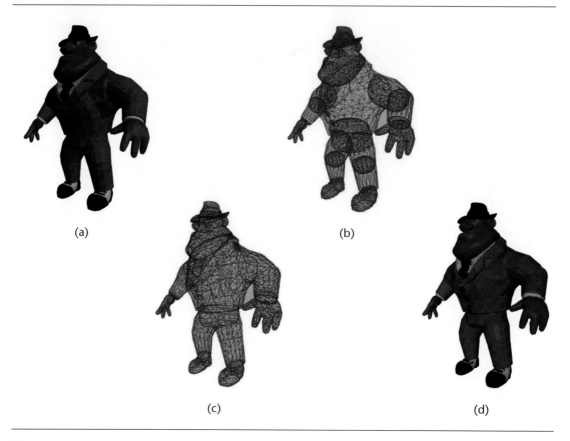

Plate 6   (Figure 2.11, p. 31) Merging multiple components of the Al Capone model: (a) original model, (b) wireframe of the original model, (c) wireframe of the model after conversion to a single manifold, and (d) filled rendering of the single manifold model [Nooruddin 99]. Copyright © 1999 Graphics, Visualization, & Usability Center, Georgia Institute of Technology.

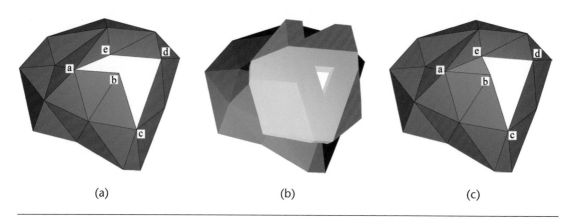

Plate 7   (Figure 2.14, p. 35) Topology simplification by using generalized α-hulls: (a) original mesh, (b) α-grown triangles, and (c) partially filled mesh [El-Sana 98]. Copyright © 1998 IEEE.

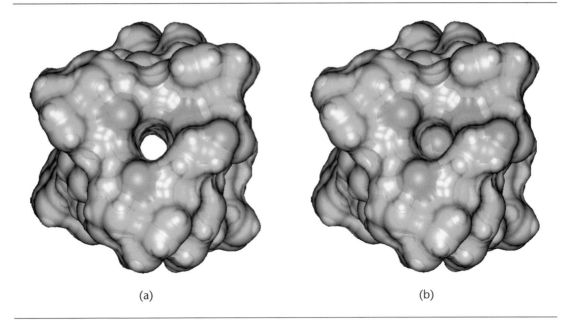

(a)   (b)

Plate 8   (Figure 2.19, p. 38) Gramicidin A's channel accessibility for (a) probe radius < 1.38 Å, and
            (b) probe radius > 1.38 Å.

Plate 9   (Figure 3.12, p. 68) Ellipsoids (level surfaces of error quadrics) illustrate the orientation and
            size of the error quadrics associated with a simplified bunny [Garland 97]. Copyright © 1997
            Association for Computing Machinery, Inc.

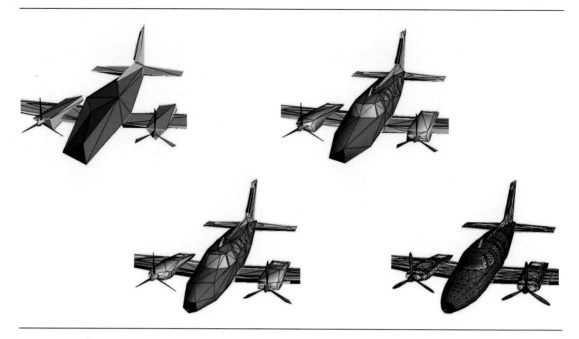

Plate 10   (Figure 3.14, p. 71) Progressive mesh levels of detail containing 150, 500, 1000, and 13,546 triangles, respectively [Hoppe 96]. Copyright © 1996 Association for Computing Machinery, Inc.

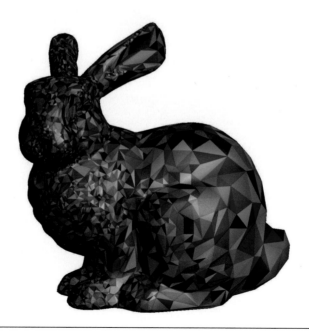

Plate 11   (Figure 3.17, p. 76) An adaptive simplification for the Stanford bunny model. ε varies from 1/64% at the nose to 1% at the tail [Cohen 96]. Copyright © 1996 Association for Computing Machinery, Inc.

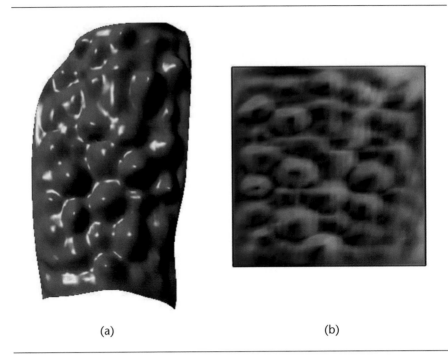

(a) (b)

Plate 12 (Figure 3.21, p. 80) (a) Parameterized surface patch and (b) its normal map. The x, y, and z normal components are stored as red, green, and blue colors, respectively [Cohen 98]. Copyright © 1998 Association for Computing Machinery, Inc.

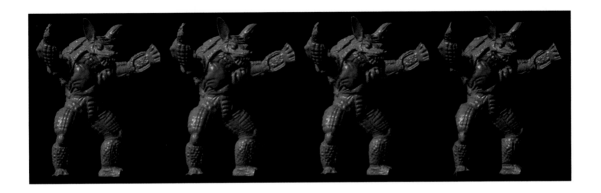

Plate 13 (Figure 3.22, p. 81) Armadillo model (2 million polygons) simplified using appearance-preserving simplification's texture deviation metric. LODs are shown with 250K, 63K, 8K, and 1K triangles (from left to right) [Cohen 98]. Copyright © 1998 Association for Computing Machinery, Inc.

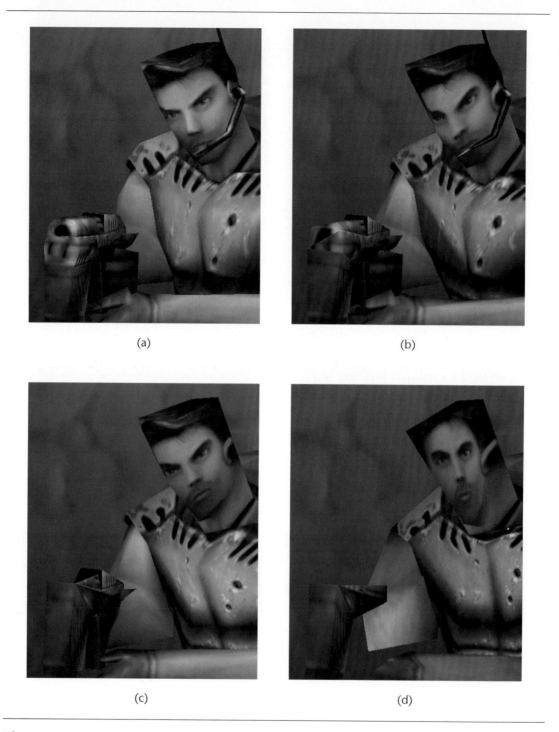

(a)

(b)

(c)

(d)

Plate 14 (Figure 4.1, p. 89) Screen shots of an *Unreal Tournament* player showing how level of detail reduces as distance increases. The original model (a) contains over 600 polygons (excluding the weapon), whereas (b), (c), and (d) show, respectively, vertex counts reduced to 75%, 50%, and 25%. Copyright © 1999–2001 Epic Games, Inc.

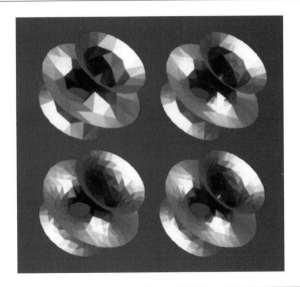

Plate 15   (Figure 4.15, p. 117) An example of the smooth retiling process developed by Turk, showing a transition (starting top left) from low to high detail in a clockwise direction [Turk 92]. Copyright © 1992 Association for Computing Machinery, Inc.

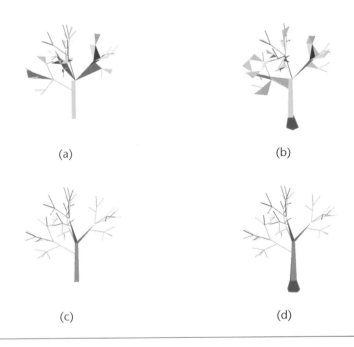

(a)   (b)

(c)   (d)

Plate 16   (Figure 5.2, p. 126) Uniform-grid clustering (a,b) produces substantially different LODs when the bounding box is changed, here by the addition of a small pot. Floating-cell clustering (c,d) looks better and is more consistent [Low 97]. Copyright © 1997 Association for Computing Machinery, Inc.

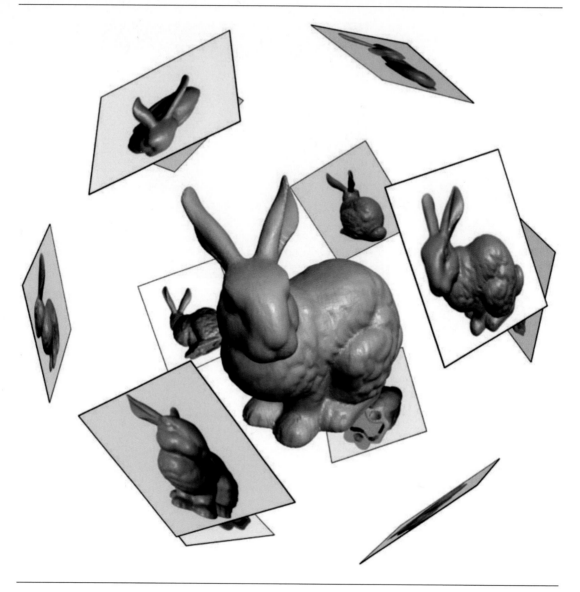

Plate 17 (Figure 5.8, p. 140) Image-driven simplification uses a series of images, rendered from view-points uniformly distributed around the model, to guide simplification [Lindstrom 00b]. Copyright © 2000 Association for Computing Machinery, Inc.

Plate 18   (Figure 7.1, p. 186) Screen shot of the Grand Canyon with debug view—using the Digital Dawn Graphics Toolkit, now incorporated into the Crystal Space portal engine. Courtesy of Alex Pfaffe.

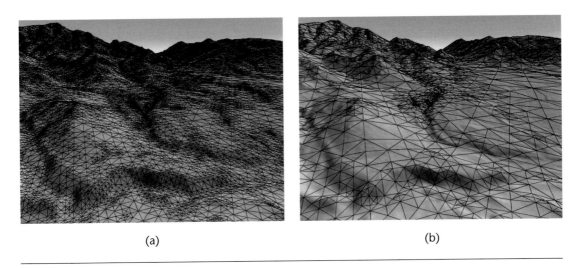

(a)   (b)

Plate 19   (Figure 7.11, p. 202) Terrain surface tessellations for Lindstrom et al.'s system, where (a) corresponds to a projected geometric error threshold of one pixel and (b) corresponds to an error threshold of four pixels [Lindstrom 96]. Copyright © 1996 Association for Computing Machinery, Inc.

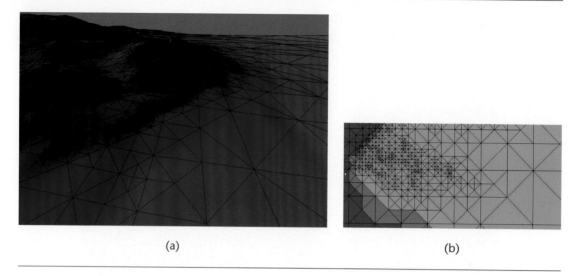

(a)   (b)

Plate 20   (Figure 7.14, p. 205) (a) Example of a ROAM-simplified terrain with the visible mesh edges overlaid. (b) A bird's-eye view of the terrain, where light regions are inside the view frustum, gray are partly inside, and dark regions are outside the view [Duchaineau 97]. Copyright © 1997 IEEE.

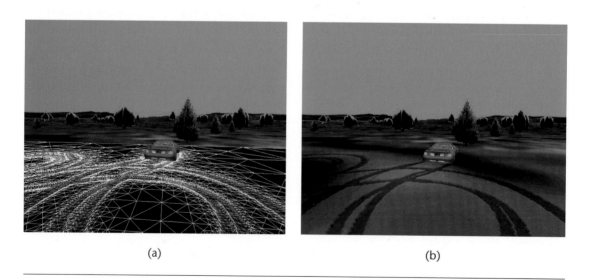

(a)   (b)

Plate 21   (Figure 7.16, p. 207) Real-time dynamic terrain produced by the DEXTER system, where (a) illustrates the simplified terrain mesh that has been deformed, and (b) shows the resulting rendered image [He 00].

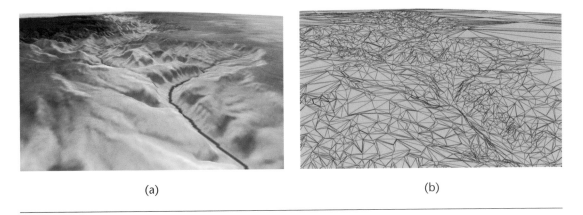

(a)   (b)

Plate 22   (Figure 7.19, p. 211) Screen shot from Hoppe's Grand Canyon model using his VDPM
scheme in which the screen-space error tolerance is 2.1 pixels for a 720×510 window.
The active mesh has 12,154 faces and 6,096 vertices. The two images show (a) a texture-
mapped version of the terrain and (b) the underlying triangle mesh [Hoppe 98a]. Copyright © 1998 IEEE.

(a)   (b)

Plate 23   (Figure 7.23, p. 215) The Puget Sound model used by Lindstrom and Pascucci. The error
thresholds and triangle counts in each case are (a) $\tau = 2$ pixels, 79,382 triangles, and
(b) $\tau = 4$ pixels, 25,100 triangles [Lindstrom 01a]. Copyright © 2001 IEEE.

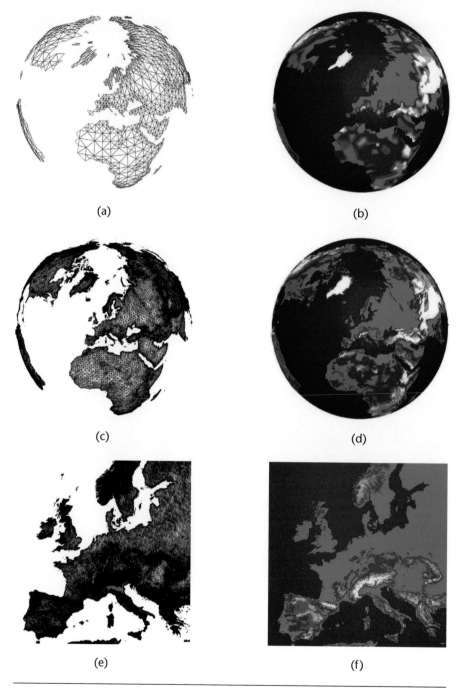

Plate 24   (Figure 7.24, p. 219) The USGS Gtopo30 global elevation data set mapped to a
spherical model of the earth at several resolutions. (a) and (b) show a low resolution version of a globe model. (c) and (d) show the same model at a higher resolution. (e) and (f) show a high-resolution mesh for a region closer to the earth surface [Gerstner 02]. Copyright © 2002 Kluwer Academic Publishers.

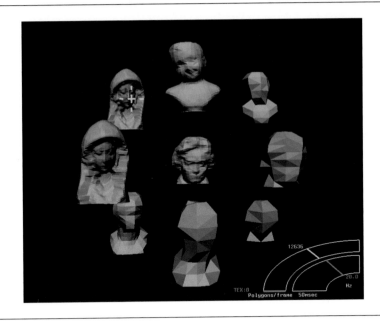

Plate 25   (Figure 8.2, p. 236) Screen shot of Ohshima et al.'s gaze-directed adaptive rendering system, showing reduced detail in the periphery. Courtesy of Hiroyuki Yamamoto.

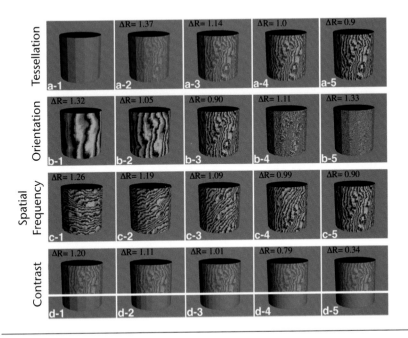

Plate 26   (Figure 8.17, p. 262) Applying Ferwerda et al.'s masking model to predict how texture masking affects the visibility of shading artifacts in a tessellated model. Values of ΔR less than 1.0 indicate a result imperceptible from a nontessellated model [Ferwerda 97]. Copyright © 1997 Association for Computing Machinery, Inc.

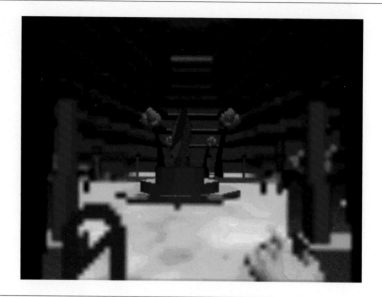

Plate 27   (Figure 9.8, p. 296) Display with reduced fidelity in the periphery as used in
            [Watson 97b].

Plate 28   (Figure 10.27, p. 326) Using IO differencing to manage the tradeoff of visual
            and temporal detail. The full-detail model positioned according to latest input is
            silhouetted at the lower right. Rendering that model (silhouetted upper left) intro-
            duces a temporal error t. Rendering a coarse approximation (shown in polygonal
            form) introduces spatial error s, but eliminates t. In this case temporal error is
            dominant—we should render the coarse model.

edge collapses or vertex removals have caused them to appear. We essentially rely on the hardware to detect and discard these for us, until we reduce to the next pregenerated strip length. Therefore, we have an upper limit on the number of unnecessary degenerate faces sent to the hardware, and this limit can be controlled by generating a greater or lesser number of strips during export. In a sense this approach equates to a limited but hardware-accelerated version of skip strips (Section 5.6).

6.4.3 HIGHER-ORDER SURFACES

The use of higher-order surfaces has gained gradual acceptance in video game applications, but is still nowhere near ubiquitous. The biggest hurdles are not always technical (in fact, some new hardware offers dedicated curve-surface tessellation engines), but are more often artistic. Game art is enjoying the multifold increase in available complexity due to the new hardware chip sets, but the basic modeling strategy is still based on hand-modeled details created with polygonal modeling. Switching to a higher-order surface, such as Bezier patches or displacement surfaces, places restrictions on game artists they are not accustomed to. In addition, even though we have more power at our disposal, we do not yet have anything close to "unlimited" bandwidth, and the greater power is often channeled toward placing more instances of models in a scene or rendering more complex shading equations on our surfaces, and not to smoothing out the edges of each model.

The biggest stumbling block is often texture placement. Game artists are accustomed to aggressively optimizing the use of texture memory, and this is still the case on most platforms. Curved-based modeling does not allow arbitrary stitching and mapping of textures on a per-face basis, and this often leads to artists abandoning the curved methods in favor of traditional polygon modeling at higher face counts. All indications are that future hardware will continue to make curved surfaces easier to process. In particular, subdivision surfaces and the tools to help artists create these models will also mature. Higher-order surface representation will likely never replace polygonal modeling for things such as room interiors or basic objects, but it may gain increasing use for organic characters.

6.4.4 SHADOW LOD

Certain types of game engine operations can also benefit from level-of-detail systems. The most common example is the use of low-detail versions of a model or mesh to enable special effects such as shadowing (see Figure 6.5). Most shadow-generation algorithms rely on rendering some type of silhouette or volume representation of a model without any lighting, texture, or surface details. By keeping a separate low-detail instance for the model, these effects can be accelerated without appreciable artifacts.

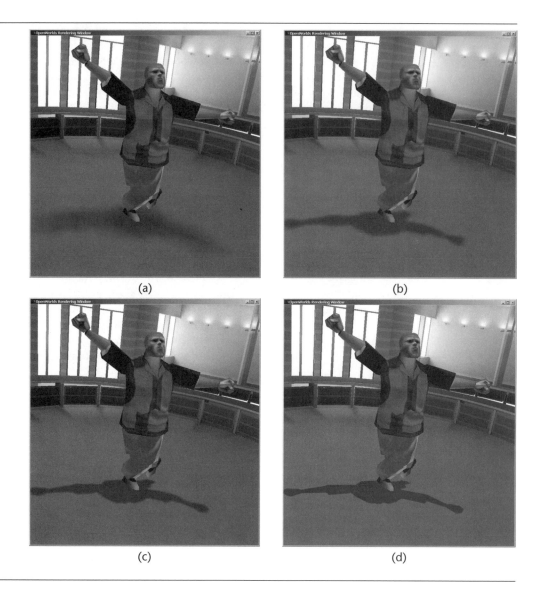

(a)   (b)

(c)   (d)

Figure 6.5   A demonstration of shadow LOD in the OpenWorlds renderer, in which various off-screen buffer sizes are used for rendering the shadow. (a) Detail as a fraction of the current window size = 0.02, frame rate = 12 Hz, (b) detail = 0.1, frame rate = 11.9 Hz, (c) detail = 0.2, frame rate = 10.1 Hz, and (d) detail = 0.5, frame rate = 3.05 Hz.

6.5 NONGEOMETRIC LEVEL OF DETAIL

For games, reducing the complexity of a scene's geometry is only half the battle. Most games approach LOD as something that applies across all of the game's subsystems, from model rendering to shader rasterization, object lighting, and even sound playback. The specific choices made are highly platform and application specific, but some general strategies are presented here.

6.5.1 SHADER LOD

There are two main metrics for which games are generally optimized: geometry processing and pixel fill rate. Most LOD schemes discussed until now attempt to reduce geometry processing costs, but because the reduced geometry is intended to fill the same amount of screen space, pixel fill-rate costs are not affected.

Fortunately, as objects become more distant, the screen space they occupy becomes smaller, thereby reducing fill-rate costs automatically. In cases for which this natural reduction is not enough, shader LOD techniques help fill this gap.

Per-Pixel Costs

Per-pixel costs are highly platform dependent, but we can make some general assumptions. On platforms that support multitexturing, the cost to draw a single pixel goes up more or less linearly with the number of textures referenced. Therefore, a pixel pipeline that accesses four texture maps to paint a single pixel will run at approximately 4X slower than a single-texture setup. Beyond the basic texture mapping, each additional effect applied to a pixel has a more subtle effect. Typical uses for multiple textures include bump mapping, environment or gloss mapping, detail texturing, and so on.

In addition to the per-pixel costs, switching shaders incurs a one-time setup cost, as the rendering pipeline is reconfigured for a new set of parameters. Usually, the cost of this mode change is dependent on the number of changes being made. Changing to a mode that involves multiple texture maps or more complex operations is typically higher.

By progressively disabling the additional passes or features as objects become more distant, we can save on per-pixel rendering costs. Most games include multiple code paths for each shader, and each code path represents a different shader LOD. At extreme distances, the shader can often be reduced to a nontexture color fill, which is typically the fastest way to fill screen pixels and represents the lowest up-front setup cost.

Effect Scaling

Certain visual effects are fairly costly to process at high fidelity. Shadow rendering, for example, can be done in a highly accurate fashion by rendering the object silhouette to a texture and projecting that texture onto nearby objects, but this method involves an additional render pass on both the object and affected geometry. Faster methods to render shadows include using a pregenerated generic silhouette and projecting this, rather than an accurate shape, onto the affected areas, or even rendering a simple round decal to the ground directly beneath the object. All of these are valid shadowing methods, but the more accurate effects are only fully appreciated at close range. Just as the shader applied to an object can be scaled and degraded with increasing distance, so too can the effects applied to an object be degraded or eliminated when the object important is reduced.

Particle effects are also candidates for this technique (see Figure 6.6). A particle field that uses 1,000 billboard sprites to simulate a smoke volume at close range could be equally well represented by 100 larger sprites at a greater distance. As long as the basic shape and color of the final effect are maintained, the exact details are difficult to discern at a distance.

6.5.2   VERTEX-PROCESSING LOD

Although LOD algorithms do a good job of reducing the total number of vertices and faces that require processing, they do not provide ways of reducing the cost per vertex. The sections that follow explore this issue.

Lighting LOD

The most complex per-vertex processing done by most game rendering systems is vertex lighting. The cost of vertex lighting increases linearly with the number of lights considered, with some variation for various types of lights. Games normally select up to a maximum number of closest lights before rendering a mesh to limit this cost. As the model becomes more distant, it is a simple process to reduce this maximum light count until, at great distance, the model is lit only by an ambient average of significant lights. As lights are removed from consideration, their contribution can be added to an average ambient value to reduce visible discontinuities and avoid gradually darkening the object.

A less obvious method often employed is to reduce more complex light types to simpler approximations as the object moves to the background. The effect of spotlights can be converted either to directional lights if the object is entirely inside the umbra or removed altogether if the object is outside the penumbra. Point lights can be converted to directional lights, and eventually to ambient lights. Since ambient light is effectively free, at the lowest level of detail we can eliminate lighting costs altogether.

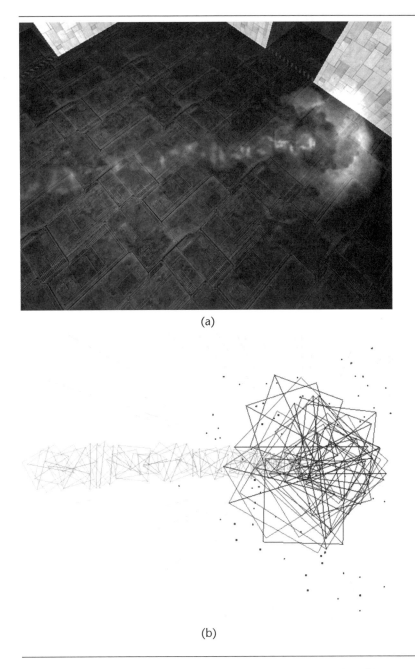

(a)

(b)

Figure 6.6   (a) Illustrating the use of billboard sprites to simulate smoke. (b) A wire frame version.

Transformation LOD

Once lighting is complete, the largest remaining expense to process a single vertex is the transformation and clipping of the vertex positions. Under normal circumstances, this operation (handled by special-purpose hardware pathways) is nominally free. But often a mesh is set up in a way that requires more complex handling. The most common complex transformation scenario is a vertex that uses weighted skin influences. In weighted skinning, each vertex is transformed by a number of bone matrices (usually no more than four), and the results are blended according to blend weights associated with each influence. The resulting position is then clipped and projected as normal. The vertex normals are then blended in a similar fashion. Non-weighted skinning is also common, and in this case each mesh vertex is bound to a single bone matrix. Both of these cases are more complex than the classic rigid mesh, in which a single matrix transforms all mesh vertices.

The mathematics of this type of processing is not significantly more complex than the typical transformation, but because it is a less common pathway it can suffer a greater performance penalty than anticipated. LOD can help with this in two ways. If we are using an LOD system consisting of completely disparate models, the lower LOD versions can be modeled using simpler types of skinning, typically forcing all vertices to attach to a single matrix influence without weight variance. Weighted skinning is most often used to give a natural look to high-polygon surfaces stretched over a joint. Less complex meshes benefit less from the technique. Another option is to gradually ignore some of the weighting information contained in the vertices by dynamically re-weighting during processing. If we determine that a mesh will be rendered at low complexity, the vertex could be forced to weight fully to its more influential bone. If the weights for each vertex were sorted by decreasing influence, this would mean either an abrupt or gradual shift to full weighting on the first referenced bone. Because skinning normally involves very subtle blending effects, this change is not as visually jarring as it might mathematically seem.

6.5.3 OBJECT PRIORITY

One very simple scheme used in games is the concept of geometry priority. In an interactive game, visible objects are normally tied to higher-level abstractions representing game entities, such as enemies, props, decorative detail meshes, or base world geometry. Depending on the purpose these entities serve in the game, they can be handled differently by the LOD systems.

An extreme example of this is how some games handle objects such as "power-ups." These objects interact with the player only at close proximity. The player must touch the object to pick it up and utilize it. Since these objects are small and cannot be used from a distance, some games choose to remove the objects completely after a certain fixed distance, gradually alpha-blending them out of the scene. Similar techniques are used with decorative objects, particularly those that represent close-detail "noise" objects such as rocks or trees on a terrain, small surface details, and similar objects. The game engine can adjust the "draw-in" distance of these objects dynamically, based on performance measurements or estimated render loads in a scene, without much disruption to the player.

6.5.4 LIGHTING

Most interactive games spend a considerable portion of their resources trying to achieve realistic lighting, using a combination of precomputed and real-time techniques. The most common way to render a complex mesh with high vertex density is to calculate the lighting equation at each mesh vertex using a standardized model such as the one used by OpenGL.

Typically games will restrict the maximum number of lights prior to rendering a mesh, based on the intensities and locations of nearby lights. Since the total cost of lighting is at least (numVertices * numLights), reducing the number of lights has a considerable impact on the total cost of rendering.

Lighting is also important because it is the main source of visual discontinuities in the rendered scene for games. When using any type of discontinuous LOD, such as an unsmoothed edge collapse or a swap between discrete LODs, the actual geometry changes generally have a fairly small effect on the rendered image, only shifting the edges of the silhouette slightly. Changes affecting the lighting equation, however, can span many more rendered pixels. If a vertex collapse shifts the vertex normal for a triangle as much as 90 degrees, that could shift the computed lighting color from white to black, a change Gouraud interpolation will then stretch across many pixels on a large face.

There are two methods that can help deal with this problem. First, when we reduce the geometry of a model, we continue to use vertex normals computed from the original high-polygon version whenever possible. When using a vertex removal method, we simply do not recompute vertex normals for the affected faces. When using a discrete LOD replacement scheme, we can either use the original normals from the remaining vertices in a particular level or, if the entire vertex array was replaced, try to compute normals offline that represent the original surface.

Another way to reduce lighting discontinuities in real-time lit meshes is to gradually decrease the influence of directional and point lights in the equation, and shift their contribution to ambient light. Replacing a directional light with an ambient light clearly would cause a visual discontinuity if done immediately, but a gradual blending can hide this. This type of blending, like many others, is often best done based on viewer distance rather than screen depth, as described in Section 6.7.1.

6.6 IMPOSTERS

Video games, and to a lesser degree computer games, present a nearly ideal environment for the use of image-based LODs, known as *stand-ins* or *imposters*. These LODs replace geometric detail with image detail, consisting in their simplest form of an image of the object to be represented, texture mapped onto a single flat polygon. Video game machines generally output to standard television resolutions, which are unsuited to displaying fine details on distant images. Because of this low-resolution output, game machines generally have more excess capacity for pixel processing than vertex processing. Stand-ins represent the most efficient way to fill pixels on-screen for distant objects. Most hardware even has optimized rendering pathways to process screen-aligned quads or "point sprites," which are well suited for rendering stand-ins.

The use of predesigned imposters is almost ubiquitous in games. Often the imposters take the form of *billboards*, imposters whose polygons remain oriented perpendicular to the viewer so that the image is always seen straight-on. Most games use a combination of particle and billboard effects to simulate volumetric effects such as explosions or light volumes. Game engines often use billboards as imposters for trees (see Figure 6.7) or other terrain features. It is sometimes difficult to classify these shortcuts as LOD techniques. It is more often the case that artists or designers improvise ways to generate images that would otherwise be impossible.

When used as stand-ins for more complex objects, the imposter image generally uses an alpha channel, with at least 1 bit of alpha, to store the silhouette of the rendered image. The imposter image is initialized uniformly to zero alpha, and the alpha value is set non-zero for each pixel that represents the object image. It is also important to maintain a 1-pixel buffer at the edge of the image, with zero alpha to avoid artifacts caused by improper wrapping or clamping of the texture. By using an alpha test in our pixel pipeline, we can accurately and efficiently superimpose the object shape using a simple four-vertex quad. The imposter image is created with the object appearing brightly lit, which enables the engine to use vertex coloration to darken the image based on its position in the scene. We can use hardware-based lighting to simulate this lighting automatically if we give our imposter quad vertex normal information approximating a spherical shape. This type of lighting will not accurately light the details of the object being replaced, but it can increase the accuracy appreciably, particularly in environments in which either the imposter or nearby lights are in motion.

6.6.1 PRERENDERED TEXTURE IMPOSTERS

One simple imposter technique for games involves offline rendering of an image or set of images representing a complex character or object. In fact, before real-time 3D games became commonplace, many games achieved a "3D look" using high-end 3D modeling tools to render a series of images or "sprites." To a game player unfamiliar with the underlying technology, this type of 3D is often indistinguishable from real-time rendering.

There are several possible techniques to create these imposter sprites for a real-time 3D game. Our biggest challenges are dealing with the changing appearance of the object due to point-of-view changes and with animation in the character itself.

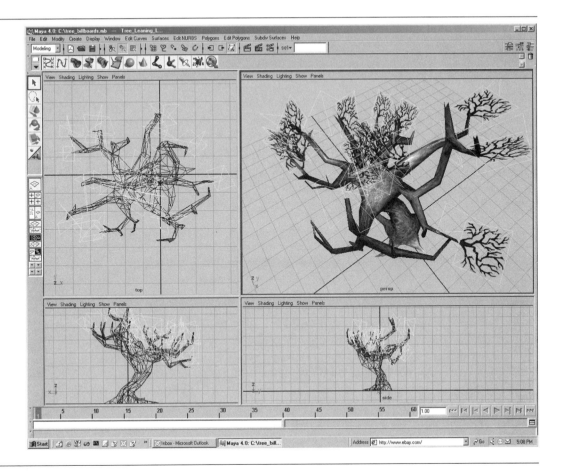

Figure 6.7   Billboards used to create a complex model of a tree.

We can simplify the point-of-view problem by restricting the possible angles to a fixed number around a single axis. Most frequently, we opt for rendering the object at between four and sixteen angles around their vertical axis. If we are using these imposters mainly for distance rendering of upright objects, this is generally adequate. At render time, the engine determines the angle between the viewer and the object's forward axis and selects the proper texture frame to apply to the imposter. If the viewer gets into a position to view the object from an angle significantly higher or lower, we should switch to a geometric version. For small changes in viewing angle, we render the frames on a billboard with a locked vertical axis to approximate the changing perspective. It is possible to expand this scheme to three axes with some additional selection logic and additional frames of storage.

Animation presents a trickier problem. The multiplicative cost of rendering multiple angles and multiple frames of animation is often prohibitive. For this reason, most games opt for a restrictive set of animations for imposters, or restrict certain animations to certain fixed viewing angles, when possible. Often a generic three- or four-frame sequence to provide a general sense of pixel motion is an adequate approximation of more complex animations, so the animation states become effectively "moving" and "not moving."

One interesting option on some hardware is the availability of 3D volume textures. These textures provide a third axis of information that can be used to store multiple angles for an imposter. But more importantly, these textures can benefit from hardware-assisted blending between these frames. At run-time, rather than selecting an integral frame based on the viewing angle we compute a w texture coordinate that will linearly blend between the two nearest frames in the volume. If we are rendering several imposters of the same type, we benefit by avoiding a texture state change that would be required if each frame were a discrete 2D texture. We may further benefit from 3D texture compression techniques.

The MIP mapping capabilities of the hardware can also help us blend between multiple artist-rendered representations as the distance increases, avoiding noise and aliasing that may become apparent when a higher-resolution imposter is used at smaller screen sizes. Perhaps the greatest advantage of using offline-rendered sprites is simply the ability to manually touch up the images before they are used in the game. Filtering and processing the image using more sophisticated offline tools allows the artist to directly control the final look of the imposter on screen.

6.6.2 RENDER-TO-TEXTURE

By rendering a relatively low LOD version of a model to an off-screen texture, we can utilize the same hardware processing that would normally be used to generate the screen image to dynamically create a stand-in image that can be reused, at lower cost, for some number of frames. This method has the ability to generate an image of the model without restricting viewing angle or animation data. It also uses less memory, since we do not devote storage space to any stand-in sprites that are not actively in use. Both video game and computer hardware are moving toward a unified memory model in which the hardware can render equally efficiently to either a visible frame or an off-screen texture.

This type of dynamically rendered stand-in can only improve performance if the resulting image is used over a number of frames. We can further hide discontinuities that result from updating the texture imposter by gradually blending in new images over the older ones using one of two techniques. In the first, we use a set of two textures to represent the imposter during transition, rendering the new image to alternative frames in a round-robin fashion. During the transition, we render our image by blending between the two stored images using common hardware multitexture blend modes. A similar alternative is to use an alpha-blend mode when updating a single texture imposter so that some of the previous content remains. This method is less effective overall but takes up about half as much memory. The round-robin method can also avoid a potential performance penalty on some hardware systems that occurs if a rendered texture image is used immediately after being updated. The hardware might require a complete flush of the rendering pipeline to ensure the image is complete. By adding a one-frame delay between rendering a new imposter and the start of the blend, we can effectively eliminate this possible block. In both cases, because video game platforms have an excess of pixel fill rate, we can afford to blend several passes of stand-in images without impacting performance.

6.6.3 GEOMETRIC IMPOSTERS

Replacing 3D geometry with a flat textured imposter is not the only viable option for high-end 3D hardware. Often replacing a complex, articulated skeletal model with a simple rigid mesh is a better alternative. Using this scheme, the entire model and skeleton are discarded and replaced by a static 3D model based on a single matrix. This is advantageous mainly because it avoids the costs associated with setting the bone matrices and deforming the object skin. When processing normal character meshes, the hardware is able to store a fixed number of matrices simultaneously for processing. Depending on the size of this matrix list, a complex model may have its faces separated into multiple batches. Each time this matrix set needs to be changed, the hardware must process the changes and possibly flush or stall its processing pipelines. In most cases, this cache is too small for single-batch processing of a complex character model, where the total bone count routinely exceeds the hardware limits.

By removing the character bones and thereby freezing the model skeleton in a specific pose, the entire model can be stored relative to a single bone or matrix. In most cases, the vertex processing for this type of rigid positioning is the fastest path in the hardware pipeline, and allows for the most efficient batching of geometry. It also means that when rendering a large collection of similar objects only a single matrix needs to be updated for each instance rendered, and thus bus bandwidth is further reduced.

This type of geometric imposter has several advantages over a texture solution. The object will render a realistic silhouette regardless of viewing angle without storing multiple versions—even from above and below, which are particularly challenging situations for textured billboards. A geometric imposter is also superior when dealing with real-time lighting. A geometric shape can accurately receive directional lighting from its environment, whereas a flat texture would rely on less accurate methods to simulate this lighting. The main shortcoming is in dealing with complex animations, and even in this case it is certainly no worse than a texture-based solution. Additional memory could be used to store multiple "poses" for the rigid model, just as the textured imposter can store multiple frames as a sequence of "flip-book" frames.

6.7 SELECTION AND METRICS

Various methods for selecting LOD are presented elsewhere in this text, and for the most part these apply equally well to interactive gaming as they do to other disciplines (see Figure 6.8). There are a few unique metrics we can apply to interactive games based on a game's knowledge of the situation of the game or scene, which is an advantage other disciplines do not have. The basic strategies for LOD selection are discussed in depth in Chapter 4, but this section revisits some of these ideas with an emphasis on the gaming environment.

6.7.1 DISTANCE SELECTION

Most LOD selection algorithms are based primarily on the distance between the viewer and the object being viewed. In a real-time environment there are a few additional considerations when calculating this distance. First, it is important to base the LOD selection primarily on the true 3D distance between viewer and object, rather than on the screen depth of the object. It is common in a 3D game for the viewer to pivot (yaw) around a fixed view position rapidly. LOD selection based on screen depth might trigger detail-level changes during such a pan, resulting in visual artifacts more likely to be noticed by the player.

It is also advisable to build in some hysteresis (Section 4.1.4), using tolerance factors to avoid changing LOD in response to small changes in viewer distance. Certain games may attach the camera to a moving model or add an explicit "idle" motion to avoid an entirely static screen. These small changes should not trigger repeated LOD changes. Anytime the player is effectively inactive, the LOD should try to avoid making any visible changes, since the lack of overall motion gives us less opportunity to make changes that would go unnoticed by an active player.

6.7.2 GAME-SPECIFIC METRICS

Another simple example is the differentiation between interactive play and noninteractive or "cut-scene" mode. The primary difference between these two modes of play is whether or not the player is actively controlling the camera or player in the scene, or if the player is passively watching a prescripted sequence of events rendered in real time. Maintaining a steady 60-Hz or 30-Hz frame rate is critical for a positive user experience during interactive sequences, particularly when the player is directly controlling the camera view. Rapid user-controlled camera motions at low frame rates have even been found to cause motion sickness in players. However, users are accustomed to viewing passive or noninteractive sequences at frame rates as low as 24 Hz, the frame rate used for film movies. Since the game engine knows when it is presenting scripted or noninteractive content, it can choose to devote available processing or bandwidth to displaying more complex geometry or shaders, while allowing the frame rate to drop to lower levels than it would normally target.

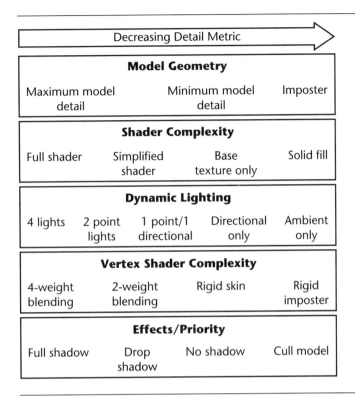

Figure 6.8   A range of potential detail metrics for games.

Another game-specific consideration for LOD is the identification of active (or "targeted") objects in a scene. Depending on the type of game, players commonly interact with only a subset of the objects on screen at a given time. The player may fight one enemy at a time in a combat game, or control only the quarterback during a football play. In cases such as these, the game has a concrete indication of where the user's attention is most likely to be focused, and can bias the selection of LOD based on the likely attentiveness of the viewer.

6.7.3   LOD BLENDING

For games, the metric for which we optimize is quite simply user perception. Our goal is to spend our rendering and CPU budgets on those things the player is focusing his or her attention on, while taking shortcuts to fill the remainder of the screen with convincing supporting elements. One important goal of any game LOD scheme is to avoid distracting the player's focus away from the center of interactivity. The most common cause of visual distraction is an abrupt change in the rendered screen image that occurs during a less active period of the game. Making abrupt changes in detail on visible objects is a common cause of such a change.

One straightforward method to avoid this sort of discontinuity blends gradually to a new representation of a geometry or shader. As described in Chapter 4, this blending can take one of two forms. In its simplest form, we can render two versions of the geometry, gradually cross-fading the alpha values between the two levels. Obviously during this transition we are actually rendering more geometry than either detail level alone, which would tend to work against our goal of decreasing the rendering costs. Fortunately, we need to blend over only a small number of frames to avoid drawing attention to the changeover. We can also exploit some efficiencies when drawing the same geometry multiple times with only incremental topology changes, mainly by avoiding costly hardware state changes such as texture, vertex source, or blend modes.

Geomorphing is a more complex method that involves geometrically blending between two detail levels rather than image-space blending of their resulting images. As with alpha blending, geomorphing temporarily increases the rendering expense during the transition period. In this case, rather than rendering two versions of the geometry, we continue to render the more complex version of the geometry, but we gradually blend the underlying vertex positions between their original and final locations. It is straightforward to program an optimized vertex program or shader to algorithmically blend between two sets of vertex inputs using hardware resources, but it does mean temporarily using a considerably more complex processing path. This method also limits the types of changes we can make between detail levels, and requires us to either create or store a special version of our vertex data to represent the "target" geometry of the blend—one that contains multiple copies of identical vertex entries that represent the destination of blended vertices collapsed by the detail-level transition. This is necessary because typical hardware cannot accept vertex data in random-access or indexed formats. Each atomic processing input, in this case the "start" and "end" vertex positions for the blend, must be streamed to our hardware in tandem, according to our higher-detail index list.

Once blending is initiated, it can proceed based on either time or continuing change in other selection metrics (mainly distance). Although time-based blends have some advantages, such as a guaranteed maximum duration, they can lead to some perceptible errors if the viewer stops moving during such a blend. In that case, a blend may continue for some time after the motion of the scene stops, causing a visible change that can draw the player's attention. It is preferable to base the blend progress on factors that will stop changing if the viewer stops moving, although it might result in the system pausing in mid-blend occasionally.

6.8 CONCLUSIONS

The techniques described in this chapter are merely specific applications of those introduced earlier in this text. The important lesson to be learned here is how a particular set of restrictions and performance characteristics, like those unique to game development, can affect the selection of techniques and the particular application of those techniques. In particular, game platforms provide an interesting case study because they are very constrained in some ways—most notably in regard to memory and processing power—and surprisingly capable in other ways, such as pixel processing power and the ability to implement "down to the metal" access to rendering.

Games are also an interesting case study for LOD because they are affected at so many levels by the concept. Games routinely use billboards and imposters as a first-tier rendering type. Games use polygon-reduction techniques to render not only distant objects, but also shadow projections and volumes for special effects up close. Games must deal with an ever-changing and often unpredictable rendering load while simultaneously being more closely bound to a constant refresh rate than any other commercial graphics application.

It is also worth noting that game developers are notoriously practical engineers when it comes to new techniques. Game programmers are often slow to adopt new research, preferring instead to wait until the techniques "trickle down" and become more proven and turnkey. The fact that, despite all this, game developers are often on the cutting edge of LOD research shows the importance of LOD to that industry as a whole.

The future of LOD in games promises substantial changes. The next generation of hardware will likely introduce increased support for some curved-surface primitives, perhaps using aspects of subdivision surfaces in its hardware pathways. It also seems likely that the processing power available to process vertex data in more complex ways will continue to increase exponentially. Growing adoption of higher resolutions will impact video games, as ATSC resolutions gradually replace NTSC standards to tip the balance between pixel and vertex throughput. All of these changes will affect how game developers select and implement their detail management systems.

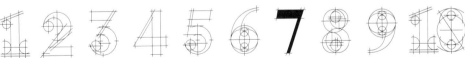

TERRAIN LEVEL
OF DETAIL

In this chapter we deal with the topic of level of detail for terrain visualization. This is a specialized area of LOD, but also one that goes back a long way and has received a large amount of interest. It is of particular importance to realistic flight simulators or terrain-based computer games, as well as to geographic information systems (GISs) and military mission planning applications. In fact, early flight simulators were some of the first systems to use LOD in any practical sense [Vince 93; Yan 85]. For example, in his extensive survey of the early flight simulator field, Schachter discussed the need to optimize the number of graphics primitives representing a scene, and states that it was common to display objects in lower detail as they appeared further away [Schachter 81]. Within the GIS field, the topic of *generalization* has similarly received a lot of interest and is essentially the same thing as LOD (i.e., the simplification of map information at different map scales [Weibel 98]).

185

Figure 7.1   Screen shot of the Grand Canyon with debug view—using the Digital Dawn Graphics Toolkit, now incorporated into the Crystal Space portal engine. Courtesy of Alex Pfaffe.

7.1   INTRODUCTION

A large volume of early work in terrain simplification was done as far back as the late 1970s, and continued through the 1980s and 1990s (e.g., Fowler and Little [Fowler 79], DeFloriani et al. [DeFloriani 83], and Scarlatos and Pavlidis [Scarlatos 92], among many others). Heckbert and Garland provided an excellent review of these early developments in their SIGGRAPH '97 course [Heckbert 97], and a number of further articles contain useful reviews (e.g., Cohen-Or and Levanoni [Cohen-Or 96], DeFloriani et al. [DeFloriani 96], and Youbing et al. [Youbing 01]). In this chapter, we will concentrate on those more recent techniques—focusing on real-time view-dependent solutions—that are of practical value to game developers or to software engineers concerned with accurate visualization of massive, potentially distributed terrain models, such as that shown in Figure 7.1.

In some ways terrain is a much easier case to deal with than arbitrary 3D models because the geometry is more constrained, normally consisting of uniform grids of height values. This allows for more specialized and potentially simpler algorithms. However, terrain data also bring some added complications. For example, because of its continuous nature, it is possible to have a large amount of terrain visible at any point, and for this to recede far into the distance. This makes view-dependent LOD techniques of critical importance for any real-time system. Furthermore, terrain meshes can be extremely dense, requiring paging techniques to be implemented so that they can be viewed on common desktop configurations. As an illustration of this latter point, the U.S. Geological Survey (USGS) publishes the GTOPO30 elevation data set at 30-arc-second resolution (roughly 1 kilometer at the equator). This translates to a height grid of $43,200 \times 21,600 = 933$ million points, and around 1.8 billion triangles over the entire planet. If that does not sound too vast, there is the NASA Earth Observing System (EOS) satellite ASTER, among others, which can gather 30-m resolution elevation data derived from 15-m near-infrared stereo imagery!

7.2 MULTIRESOLUTION TECHNIQUES FOR TERRAIN

We begin this chapter by taking a look at some of the principal variables a developer faces when implementing a terrain LOD algorithm. The bulk of the chapter is devoted to discussions of a few specific techniques that have proved the most valuable over recent years. Following this, we introduce some background on geographic coordinate systems and file formats to help designers interested in producing geographically accurate simulations. Finally, we point out some useful resources on the Web that relate to terrain LOD.

7.2.1 TOP DOWN AND BOTTOM UP

One of the major differentiators of terrain LOD algorithms, as with more general LOD techniques, is whether they are top-down or bottom-up in their approach to the simplification problem. These approaches were discussed in Chapter 2, but we will reprise the essentials here as they relate to terrain. In a top-down algorithm, we normally begin with two or four triangles for the entire region and then progressively add new triangles until the desired resolution is achieved. These techniques are also referred to as subdivision or refinement methods. In contrast, a bottom-up algorithm begins with the highest-resolution mesh and iteratively removes vertices from the triangulation until the desired level of simplification is gained. These techniques can also be referred to as decimation or simplification methods. Figure 7.2 illustrates these two approaches to terrain simplification. Bottom-up approaches tend to be able to find the minimal number of triangles required for a given accuracy. However, they necessitate the entire model being available at the first step and therefore have higher memory and computational demands.

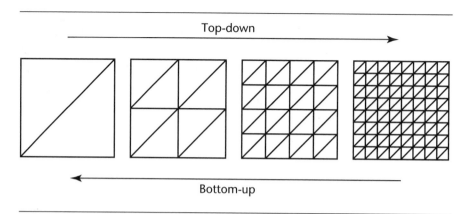

Figure 7.2   Terrain simplification algorithms normally fit into one of the two categories top down or bottom up.

It is worth making an explicit distinction between the preparation-time and run-time sense of bottom-up versus top-down. Bottom-up approaches are almost always used during the initial offline hierarchy construction. However, at run-time, a top-down approach might be favored because, for example, it offers support for view culling. Most interactive bottom-up solutions are usually hybrid in practice, often combined with a top-down quadtree block framework (described later in the chapter). Furthermore, a few systems perform incremental coarsening or refining of the terrain at each frame to take advantage of frame-to-frame coherency. As such, these systems cannot strictly be classified as exclusively top-down or bottom-up.

7.2.2   REGULAR GRIDS AND TINs

Another important distinction between terrain LOD algorithms is the structure used to represent the terrain. Two major approaches in this regard are the use of regular gridded height fields and triangulated irregular networks (TINs). Regular (or uniform) grids use an array of height values at regularly spaced x and y coordinates, whereas TINs allow variable spacing between vertices. Figure 7.3 illustrates these two approaches, showing a regular grid of 65×65 (equals 4,225) height values and a 512-vertex TIN representation with the same accuracy.

TINs can generally approximate a surface to a required accuracy with fewer polygons than other schemes. For example, they allow large flat regions to be represented with a coarse sampling, while reserving higher sampling for more bumpy regions. Regular grids, in comparison, tend to be far less optimal than TINs because the same resolution is used across the entire terrain, at flat places as well as high-curvature regions. TINs also offer great flexibility in the range and accuracy of features that

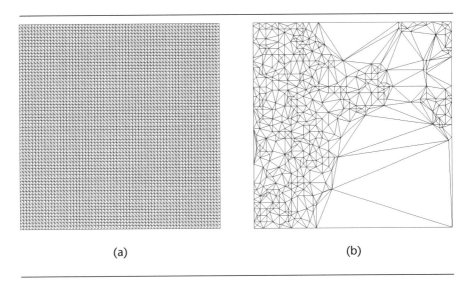

(a) (b)

Figure 7.3   (a) A regular grid terrain representation, and (b) a TIN representation [Garland 95]. Copyright © 1995 Carnegie Mellon University.

can be modeled, such as maxima, minima, saddle points, ridges, valleys, coastlines, overhangs, and caves. However, regular grids offer the advantages that they are simple to store and manipulate. For example, finding the elevation at any point is a simple matter of bilinearly interpolating the four nearest neighbor points. They are easily integrated with raster databases and file formats, such as the DEM,[1] DTED, and GeoTIFF file formats. In addition, they require less storage for the same number of points because only an array of z values needs to be stored rather than full (x, y, z) coordinates. Furthermore, TINs make implementing related functions (such as view culling, terrain following, collision detection, and dynamic deformations) more complex because of the lack of a simple overarching spatial organization. Also, the applicability of TINs to run-time view-dependent LOD is less efficient than regular gridded systems. For these reasons, many contemporary terrain LOD systems favor regular grids over TINs.

It is worth noting that a number of hybrid schemes have been proposed that try to gain the best of both worlds—most notably by using a hierarchical triangulation based on a regular grid. For example, Evans et al. used a representation they call right triangular irregular networks (RTINs), in which a binary tree data structure is used to impose a spatial structure on a triangle mesh. They state that this provides a compact representation similar to a gridded approach yet supports the nonuniform sampling

---

1. Regular grids are sometimes referred to generically as DEMs, or digital elevation models. This term is more normally used to describe the specific elevation data product from the USGS.

feature of TINs [Evans 97]. A further alternative representation scheme was proposed by Gross et al., who used a wavelet transform of gridded data to produce an adaptive mesh tessellation at near-interactive rates [Gross 95].

7.2.3 QUADTREES AND BINTREES

To implement view-dependent LOD for a regular grid structure, we must be able to represent different parts of the grid at different resolutions. This implies a hierarchical representation in which we can gradually refine further detail to different parts of the grid. There are a number of options available for achieving this multiresolution representation. The most common two are the quadtree [Herzen 87] [Samet 92] and the binary triangle tree [Duchaineau 97] [Pajarola 98] [Gerstner 02]. A quadtree structure is where a rectangular region is divided uniformly into four quadrants. Each of these quadrants can then be successively divided into four smaller regions, and so on (see Figure 7.4(a–d)). Quadtrees have been used for a number of terrain LOD systems (e.g., Röttger et al. [Röttger 98], Leclerc and Lau [Leclerc 94], and Falby et al. [Falby 93]). Note that you can still employ a quadtree structure and use triangles as your primitives. You would simply decompose each rectangle into two or more triangles. In fact, a number of different triangulation schemes could be implemented independent of the use of quadtrees or bintrees.

A binary triangle tree structure (bintritree, BTT, or simply bintree) works the same way as a quadtree, but instead of segmenting a rectangle into four it segments a triangle into two halves (note that this is the same as the term RTIN introduced by Evans et al. [Evans 97]). The root triangle is normally defined to be a right-isosceles triangle (i.e., two of the three sides are equal and they join at a 90-degree angle), and the subdivision is performed by splitting this along the edge formed between its apex vertex and the midpoint of its base edge (see Figure 7.4(e–h)). Note that another, more general, term that can be used to describe a bintree is a kd-tree. A kd-tree is a binary tree that recursively subdivides a space such that a k-dimensional kd-tree divides a k-dimensional space with a $(k - 1)$-dimensional plane [Ögren 00]. Systems that have implemented binary triangle tree techniques include Lindstrom et al. [Lindstrom 96] and Duchaineau et al. [Duchaineau 97]. One of the big advantages of bintrees is that they make it easy to avoid cracks and T-junctions (see the next section for more details). Bintrees also exhibit the useful feature that triangles are never more than one resolution level away from their neighbors (this is not true for quadtrees, which often require extra care to preserve this condition). Seumas McNally wrote an excellent piece on bintrees for *GameDev.net*. In that article he presents psuedo code for splitting a triangle in a binary triangle tree while avoiding cracks and T-junctions. The psuedo code follows, including some minor optimizations that have been reported recently [Ögren 00]. In this code, the left and right neighbors point to the triangles on the left and right with the hypotenuse down, and the bottom neighbor is the triangle that meets the hypotenuse. Figure 7.5 illustrates the split progression.

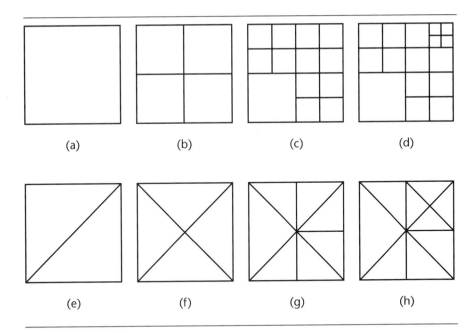

Figure 7.4   Images (a–d) illustrate the recursive refinement of a square-shaped quad-tree structure, and (e–h) illustrate the recursive refinement of a binary triangle tree.

```
Split(BinTri *tri) {
  if tri->BottomNeighbor is valid {
    if tri->BottomNeighbor->BottomNeighbor != tri {
      Split(tri->BottomNeighbor)
    }
    Split2(tri)
    Split2(tri->BottomNeighbor)
    tri->LeftChild->RightNeighbor = tri->BottomNeighbor->RightChild
    tri->RightChild->LeftNeighbor = tri->BottomNeighbor->LeftChild
    tri->BottomNeighbor->LeftChild->RightNeighbor = tri->RightChild
    tri->BottomNeighbor->RightChild->LeftNeighbor = tri->LeftChild
  } else {
    Split2(tri)
    tri->LeftChild->RightNeighbor = 0;
    tri->RightChild->LeftNeighbor = 0;
  }
}

Split2(tri) {
```

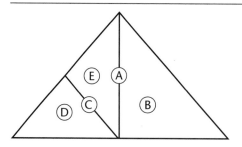

Figure 7.5   The subdivision progression for Seumas McNally's bintree tessellation code. The root triangle is A, with a right child B, and a left child C. C has a right child D, and a left child E.

```
tri->LeftChild = AllocateBinTri();
tri->RightChild = AllocateBinTri();
tri->LeftChild->LeftNeighbor = tri->RightChild
tri->RightChild->RightNeighbor = tri->LeftChild
tri->LeftChild->BottomNeighbor = tri->LeftNeighbor
if tri->LeftNeighbor is valid {
  if tri->LeftNeighbor->BottomNeighbor == tri {
    tri->LeftNeighbor->BottomNeighbor = tri->LeftChild
  } else {
    tri->LeftNeighbor->RightNeighbor = tri->LeftChild
  }
}
tri->RightChild->BottomNeighbor = tri->RightNeighbor
if tri->RightNeighbor is valid {
  if tri->RightNeighbor->BottomNeighbor == tri {
    tri->RightNeighbor->BottomNeighbor = tri->RightChild
  } else {
    tri->RightNeighbor->LeftNeighbor = tri->RightChild
  }
}
tri->LeftChild->LeftChild = 0
tri->LeftChild->RightChild = 0
tri->RightChild->LeftChild = 0
tri->RightChild->RightChild = 0
}
```

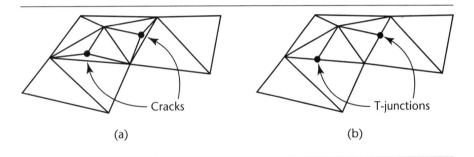

Figure 7.6   (a) Cracks and (b) T-junctions can occur where a mesh changes from one level of refinement to another [Youbing 01].

7.2.4   TEARS, CRACKS, AND T-JUNCTIONS

A common problem when dealing with terrain LOD (particularly when dealing with quadtree- or block-based approaches) occurs when adjacent triangles exist at different levels of detail. In this situation, it is possible to introduce cracks along the edge, where the higher LOD introduces an extra vertex that does not lie on the lower LOD edge. When rendered, these cracks can cause holes in the terrain, allowing the background to peak through. Another undesirable artifact is the T-junction. This is caused when the vertex from a higher LOD triangle does not share a vertex in the adjacent lower LOD triangle. This can result in bleeding tears in the terrain due to small floating-point rounding differences, and visible lighting and interpolation differences across such edges. Figure 7.6 illustrates both of these cases.

There are a number of ways of dealing with cracks. Some of the more common solutions are described in the following.

- The triangles around the crack are recursively split to produce a continuous surface. This will often introduce additional triangles into the mesh but produces a pleasing and continuous result. This approach is often used in bintree-based systems. For example, the ROAM algorithm adopts this solution, along with other systems [Duchaineau 97] [Lindstrom 96]. Figure 7.7 gives an example of this technique. Psuedo code to perform this type of recursive splitting was introduced in the previous section.

- The extra vertex in the higher LOD mesh has its height modified so that it lies on the edge of the adjacent lower LOD mesh. This does not affect the number of triangles or vertices in the model, but it introduces a potentially visible error into the terrain surface unless care is taken that the vertex shift occurs below the accuracy threshold. This method essentially implies introducing a T-junction into the model, which is generally considered harmful to the continuity of the

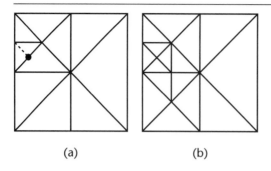

(a)   (b)

Figure 7.7   Eliminating cracks and T-junctions via recursive splitting. The triangle split in (a) highlighted by the dotted line would introduce a T-junction at the indicated point. The mesh in (b) shows the result of recursive splitting to avoid this situation [Evans 97].

mesh, although some systems have used this approach due to its simplicity and compactness [Youbing 01]. A similar solution that avoids the T-junction is to simply skip the center vertex on the higher LOD mesh [Röttger 98].

- An equivalent operation to the previous case is to add an extra vertex to the edge of the lower LOD mesh and assign it the same location as the extra vertex in the higher LOD mesh. This produces a more faithful terrain surface, but at the cost of introducing an extra vertex. A further refinement of this approach is to shift both of the boundary vertices to the average of their two elevations [Leclerc 94].

- A common tool for managing extremely large terrain data sets is to segment them into a number of blocks, or tiles, so that these might be paged into main memory as needed. A simple solution to avoid tears between blocks is to prevent simplification of vertices that lie on the boundary of a block [Hoppe 98a].

- A new triangle is inserted between the two meshes to plug up the gap. Although this results in a continuous mesh, the fill polygons lie in a plane perpendicular to the surface and hence can introduce unnatural-looking short cliffs. This solution also has the disadvantage of using extra polygons to represent the mesh. This solution was implemented by De Haemer and Zyda at the Naval Postgraduate School [De Haemer 91].

7.2.5   PAGING, STREAMING, AND OUT OF CORE

One highly desirable feature of a terrain LOD algorithm is to be able to operate out-of-core; that is, to be able to browse terrain data sets that exceed the size of the available main memory. By adding the capability to page terrain in and out of main memory, it becomes possible to allow streaming of data over the Internet. A number of solutions have been devised for these problems, varying in sophistication and flexibility.

One very simple approach to out-of-core operation was proposed by Lindstrom and Pascucci. Their approach was to optimize the layout of terrain data on disk to improve its spatial coherence. Then the operating system functions for mapping part of the computer's logical address space to a specific disk file were used to implicitly page the data from disk [Lindstrom 01a]. Under UNIX, this means using the `mmap()` function; under Windows the `MapViewofFile()` API call can be used. This approach has the advantage of leaving all of the data paging control to the operating system, which is presumably already robust and efficient. The major design issues to be addressed, therefore, reduce to determining a way to store the raw data that minimizes disk paging events and devising an efficient mechanism to compute the location of a desired vertex element on disk. Their solution achieved good data locality by storing the data in a coarse-to-fine order, where vertices geometrically close are stored close together on disk using an interleaved quadtree structure. Hoppe introduced a similar scheme to this using the Windows operating system's virtual memory functions, `VirtualAlloc()` and `VirtualFree()`, to page blocks of terrain in and out of physical memory [Hoppe 98a]. This approach requires care to commit any pages that might be accessed, but Hoppe's explicit use of blocks makes this very manageable.

A more explicit terrain paging system was developed by Falby et al. as part of the NPSNET simulator at the Naval Postgraduate School [Falby 93]. NPSNET used a 50-km x 50-km terrain model of Fort Hunter-Liggett, California, at 125-m resolution. The entire grid was downsampled to 250-, 500-, and 1,000-m resolutions, and each of these levels were segmented into 1-km x 1-km chunks, or tiles. This scheme is often referred to as a tiled pyramid [Rosenfeld 84]. The total pyramid size was 147 MB, and a heap-sorted quadtree data structure was used to access the tiles. A dynamic terrain-paging algorithm was implemented so that at any one time only a 16-km x 16-km area was resident in main memory. As the user moved around, files corresponding to a 16-km x 1-km strip of terrain were consecutively read into main memory and the opposite 16-km x 1-km strip freed. This design is illustrated in Figure 7.8.

Davis et al. at the Georgia Institute of Technology presented a solution for real-time visualization of out-of-core collections of 3D objects, applying this to both global terrain and the objects that reside on it [Davis 99]. Their solution involved the use of a forest of quadtrees covering the entire earth. Then, at a certain point, the buildings and other objects switched to use a nonquadtree discrete LOD scheme. The VGIS (virtual geographic information system) real-time visual simulation system was extended for this work. VGIS is a multithreaded application with an object server thread that loads pages from disk, and an object manager thread that decides which cells should be loaded [Lindstrom 97]. Davis et al. report that their system can scale to browsing tens to hundreds of gigabytes of data [Davis 99].

The OpenGL Performer library provides support for paging of terrain geometry via its active surface definition (ASD) feature [Silicon Graphics 00b]. This is also

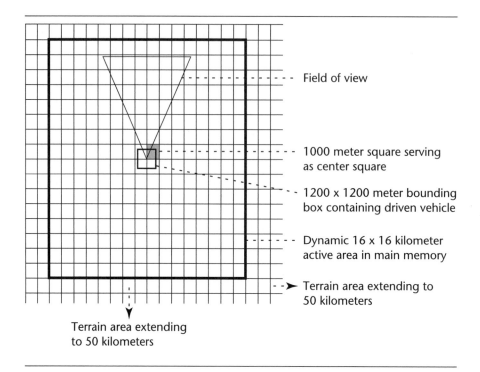

Figure 7.8   The terrain-paging architecture used in the NPSNET simulator [Falby 93].

implemented using tiles of data paged into memory on demand. A further improvement ASD provides is the use of multiresolution tiles so that smaller, high-resolution tiles can be paged in near the viewer, and larger, more coarse data can be paged in for distant regions. This offers a more efficient solution than employing a single tile size, because often a terrain mesh can extend far into the distance, where it obviously requires less detail to be loaded. ASD uses a coarse-to-fine loading order such that the low-resolution tiles are loaded first so that coarse data are always available. This behavior means that when traveling rapidly over a surface, the high-resolution mesh may not have time to load completely, but you still get a coarse representation of the terrain.

All of the techniques described so far deal with paging terrain data from local disk only. Lindstrom and Pascucci's solution, along with Hoppe's, would not scale to paging data over a wide-area network such as the Internet, whereas the system described by Falby et al. could conceivably be extended to read data over a socket instead of just local disk. However, one system that has already implemented this level of capability is SRI International's TerraVision system. Dating back to 1992, TerraVision was designed from the bottom up to browse massive terrain data sets over the Web [Leclerc 94] [Reddy 99]. It used a tiled pyramid approach to store chunks of elevation and tex-

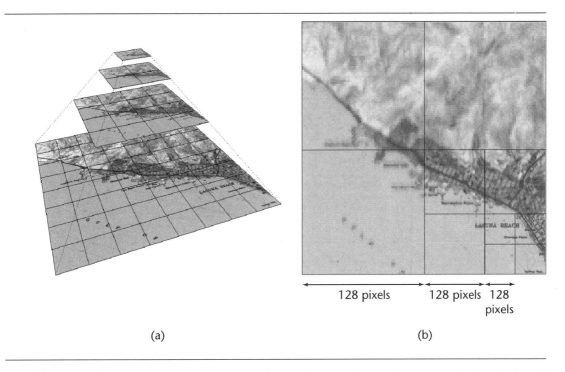

128 pixels   128 pixels   128 pixels

(a)   (b)

Figure 7.9   A tiled pyramid of an image data set showing (a) four different resolution levels and (b) how this structure can be used to produce a view-dependent image [Reddy 99]. Copyright © 1999 IEEE.

ture data over a range of resolutions (see Figure 7.9). A quadtree structure was used to provide coarse LOD management, where the leaf nodes of the quadtree are only allocated as needed so that truly massive terrain models can be accommodated. The system exploits frame coherence, extensive tile caching, and texture-caching management, as well as predictive tile prefetching based on a simple linear extrapolation of the user's position. An important feature of TerraVision is that it was designed to cope with the inherent delays and unpredictable nature of networks. Tiles are requested in a coarse-to-fine manner so that low-resolution data are always available while the higher-resolution tiles are being streamed over the Web. In addition, the rendering and navigation threads were separated from the tile-requesting and tile-reading threads, meaning that the system does not hang while waiting for detail to appear. TerraVision is available for UNIX and Windows platforms at *www.tvgeo.com,* and the Open Source tools for creating and reading the tile pyramid data sets are available at *www.tsmApi.com.*

Also worthy of note is the recent GeoVRML work, which is currently being standardized through ISO (International Organization for Standardization) as part of an amendment to the Virtual Reality Modeling Language (VRML) specification. GeoVRML provides a number of extensions for plain VRML97 to support geographic applications. It includes the GeoLOD node, which provides a simple quadtree LOD capability for terrains. Here, up to four children scenes are dynamically loaded, based on the distance from the viewer [Reddy 00]. An Open Source Java implementation is available from the GeoVRML Working Group web site at *www.geovrml.org.*

7.2.6   TEXTURE-MAPPING ISSUES

It is worth taking the time to talk explicitly about texture-mapping issues for terrain. The LOD literature often passes over texturing issues in order to focus on the management of the terrain geometry. However, there are some extremely important topics to deal with in terms of texturing the terrain skin. In this section, we deal with the issues of managing large texture maps for terrain and how these can be displayed to the user in a realistic manner.

Paging of Large Textures

Supporting paging of texture imagery is at least as important as paging of geometry, given the potentially massive sizes of satellite and aerial images and the often limited amount of texture memory available on contemporary graphics cards. A common way to page large texture maps is to cut the texture into small tiles and then simply load the subset of texture tiles needed at any time. This was illustrated in Figure 7.9.

The simple solution is to cut the image into tiles that are of a power of 2 (e.g., 64, 128, or 512 pixels on side). This approach maps well to the use of texture memory because this memory is normally always a power of 2 in size (e.g., 2,048 by 2,048 pixels). The main disadvantage of this approach is that visible seams can appear when interpolation is used to smooth out textures. This is caused at the edge of texture maps, where no information is available for neighboring textures. It can also be exacerbated by the wraparound behavior of the interpolation, where the first pixel color is used to influence the color of the last pixel in a tile row. This can be significantly reduced by using the texture-clamping features of the graphics API. However, even this does not completely solve the problem, because ultimately the system does not know the color of the next pixel at the end of a tile row. Another solution, therefore, is to still use a power of 2 tile size but to include a single pixel of redundancy on all sides of the texture.

Jonathan Blow, in a 1998 *Game Developer* article, described many of the low-level concerns of producing a texture-caching system [Blow 98]. He described the basic functions of a texture cache and surveyed a number of commercial game systems on their texture cache designs, including Golgotha, Crystal Space, Hyper3D,

Descent 3, KAGE, and Wulfram. Blow also talked about various optimizations that can be implemented to improve the performance of a texture cache, including prefetching textures, using compressed textures, and performing occlusion culling.

Hardware Support for Large Textures

On the topic of texture paging, some graphics systems provide hardware support for paging large texture maps from disk. One such example is the clip mapping support introduced in Open Performer 2.1 for SGI InfiniteReality (IR) workstations [Tanner 98]. This is a patented algorithm that extends the notion of mipmapping to allow the size of each texture level to be clipped to a maximum size in the s, t, and r dimensions, with images caches used to represent levels that exceed this limit. As the user moves around, the clip region is updated incrementally over a high-speed bus so that the new pixels are loaded while the newly invalidated ones are unloaded. No shifting of the old pixels is needed because the clip region coordinates wraparound to the opposite side.

It is worth noting that at least one group has successfully simulated clip mapping in software using multiple textures. For example, the company Intrinsic Graphics has implemented clip mapping, which they claim works on any OpenGL graphics card.

Another hardware technique that may prove useful in managing large texture maps is texture compression. This is a technique in which texture maps can be compressed and therefore use less texture memory on the graphics card. The benefit is of course that more or larger textures can be used. However, the image quality is often adversely affected. Furthermore, current support for texture compression is not ubiquitous (with a number of competing standards), which makes this technique less tenable in the short term.

Detail Textures

Often satellite imagery does not provide sufficient resolution when you are browsing terrain close to the ground. Most publicly available imagery will provide up to 1-m resolution, although some half-meter-resolution satellites are now being launched. However, often we may have to use texture imagery of much lower resolution. This can result in overly blurred surfaces when the viewpoint is close to the ground. One common solution is to blend high-frequency *geotypical* features, such as grass or sand, with the *geospecific* satellite or aerial imagery. This is often implemented using a bitmap mask to specify areas covered with different geotypical ground types. Then the geotypical texture needs to be alpha blended with the geospecific texture, normally using a distance-based function so that the detail texture is faded into and out of use. For more depth on detail textures, see Peter Hajba's May 2001 article "The Power of the High Pass Filter" at *Gamasutra.com.*

7.3 CATALOG OF USEFUL TERRAIN ALGORITHMS

Having described many of the fundamental concepts of terrain LOD, we now describe a number of the most popular algorithms presented in recent years. In this coverage, we try to include those techniques that are of high practical value in real systems or gaming engines. We introduce these in chronological order, as many of the most recent and sophisticated techniques are built upon work in earlier systems.

7.3.1 CONTINUOUS LOD FOR HEIGHT FIELDS

One of the first real-time continuous LOD algorithms for terrain grids was the early work of Lindstrom et al. This algorithm used a regular grid representation and employed a user-controllable screen-space error threshold to control the degree of simplification [Lindstrom 96]. The algorithm is conceptually bottom-up, starting with the entire model at its highest resolution and then progressively simplifying triangles until the desired accuracy is reached. However, in practice, the mesh is broken up into rectangular blocks and a top-down coarse-grained simplification is first performed on these blocks, followed by a per-vertex simplification within the blocks. Bottom-up recursion happens when a vertex changes from active to inactive (and vice versa), at which point forced splits and merges occur. Frame-to-frame coherence is supported by maintaining an active cut of blocks and by visiting vertices only when they could possibly change state between consecutive frames. Cracks are eliminated between adjacent nodes through the use of a binary vertex tree that maintains the dependence between vertices. Although gaps between blocks of different levels of detail were not corrected directly, the authors suggest that adjacent blocks should share vertices on their boundaries.

The simplification scheme devised by Lindstrom et al. involved a vertex removal approach in which a pair of triangles is reduced to a single triangle. This involved identifying a common vertex between a triangle pair, such as that shown in Figure 7.10. Here, the two original triangles are $\triangle$ABD and $\triangle$BCD. These are merged into a single triangle $\triangle$ACD by removing vertex B. The decision on when to perform this merge was based on a measure of the screen-space error between the two surfaces. That is, the vertical distance, δ, between vertex B and the center of line segment AC was computed, and then this segment was projected into screen space to discover the maximum perceived error. If this error was smaller than a given pixel threshold, τ, the triangle simplification could proceed.

The authors also presented a compact data storage structure in which each vertex had associated with it a 16-bit elevation value, an 8-bit compressed δ value, and 7 bits of state. The vertical distance, δ, was compressed using nonlinear mapping to represent values between 0 and 65535 in only 8 bits, with greater precision around the lower end of the range. The formula used is as follows.

$$c^{-1}(x) = \lfloor (x+1)^{1+x^2/255^2} - 1 \rfloor$$

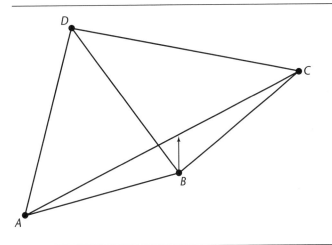

Figure 7.10   Illustrating Lindstrom et al.'s simplification scheme [Lindstrom 96].

Lindstrom et al. presented detailed psuedo code for their implementation and tested this with a 2-m resolution terrain model of the Hunter–Liggett U.S. Army base in California covering 8 × 8 km and containing 32 million polygons (see Figure 7.11). Their system produced a consistent 20-Hz frame rate on a two-processor SGI Onyx RealityEngine², offering polygon reduction factors between 2 times (when $\tau = 0$) and over 6,000 times (when $\tau = 8$) that of the original data. Using an image-based metric, they calculated that at an error threshold of $\tau = 1$ pixels, their algorithm produced only a 2.61% error, in total pixels, from the unsimplified case.

Lindstrom et al.'s algorithm has been implemented in a number of terrain and game systems, including the VGIS (virtual geographic information system) at Georgia Tech. This is a cross-platform multithreaded system that supports visualization of terrain, along with database-driven GIS raster layers, buildings, vehicles, and other features [Koller 95]. Torgeir Lilleskog also produced an implementation of this terrain algorithm at the Norwegian University of Science and Technology. The Virtual Terrain Project (VTP), *www.vterrain.org*, also provides a source code implementation of Lindstrom et al.'s algorithm (referred to as LKTerrain), although the quadtree block mechanism is not implemented and a pure top-down solution was used. Finally, Thatcher Ulrich wrote a Gamasutra article on the terrain algorithm he developed for the game Soul Ride. This was loosely based on Lindstrom et al.'s algorithm, but was augmented in a number of ways, including the use of an adaptive quadtree, a different error metric, and a top-down approach. Ulrich reports that the original screen-space geometric error was not optimal because it ignored texture perspective and depth-buffering errors. Instead, he developed a 3D world-space error proportional to the view distance. This was calculated as follows, where (dx, dy, dz) is the world-space length of the vector between the viewpoint and the vertex, δ is the vertex error, and

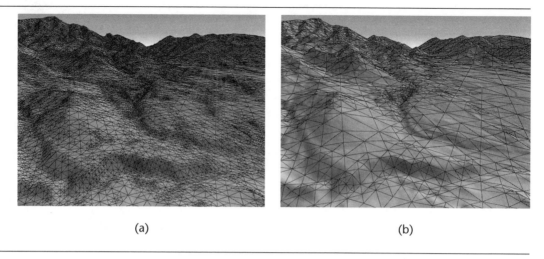

(a)   (b)

Figure 7.11   Terrain surface tessellations for Lindstrom et al.'s system, where (a) corresponds to a projected geometric error threshold of one pixel and (b) corresponds to an error threshold of four pixels [Lindstrom 96]. Copyright © 1996 Association for Computing Machinery, Inc.

threshold is a distance threshold constant (in contrast to the common use of an error threshold).

$$vertex\_enabled = \delta^* threshold < \max(|dx|, |dy|, |dy|)$$

7.3.2   THE ROAM ALGORITHM

A year after Lindstrom et al.'s continuous LOD algorithm was published, Duchaineau et al. of Los Alamos and Lawrence Livermore National Laboratories published the ROAM algorithm [Duchaineau 97]. This has proved to be an extremely popular algorithm, particularly among game developers; it has been implemented for the Tread Marks, Genesis3D, and Crystal Space engines, among others. ROAM (real-time optimally adapting meshes) uses an incremental priority-based approach with a binary triangle tree structure. A continuous mesh is produced using this structure by applying a series of split and merge operations on triangle pairs that share their hypotenuses, referred to as diamonds (see Figure 7.12).

The ROAM algorithm uses two priority queues to drive split and merge operations. One queue maintains a priority-ordered list of triangle splits so that refining the terrain simply means repeatedly splitting the highest-priority triangle on the queue. The second queue maintains a priority-ordered list of triangle merge operations to simplify the terrain. This allows ROAM to take advantage of frame coherence (i.e., to pick up from the previous frames triangulation and incrementally add or remove tri-

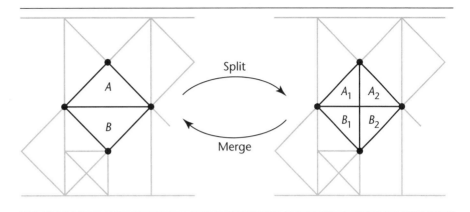

Figure 7.12   The split and merge operations on a binary triangle tree used by the ROAM algorithm.

angles). Duchaineau et al. also note that splits and merges can be performed smoothly by geomorphing the vertex positions during the changes.

The priority of splits and merges in the two queues was determined using a number of error metrics. The principal metric was a screen-based geometric error that provides a guaranteed bound on the error. This was done using a hierarchy of bounding volumes, called *wedgies,* around each triangle (similar to the notion of simplification envelopes). A wedgie covers the (x, y) extent of a triangle and extends over a height range $z - e_T$ through $z + e_T$, where z is the height of the triangle at each point and e_T is the wedgie thickness, all in world-space coordinates. A preprocessing step is performed to calculate appropriate wedgies that are tightly nested throughout the triangle hierarchy, thus providing a guaranteed error bound (see Figure 7.13). At run-time, each triangle's wedgie is projected into screen space and the bound is defined as the maximum length of the projected thickness segments for all points in the triangle (note that under the perspective projection, the maximum projected thickness may not necessarily occur at one of the triangle vertices). This bound is used to form queue priorities, and could potentially incorporate a number of other metrics, such as backface detail reduction, silhouette preservation, and specular highlight preservation.

The ROAM algorithm includes a number of other interesting features and optimizations, including an incremental mechanism to build triangle strips. Modern graphics processing units often provide significant performance gains when triangles are organized into strips. In the original ROAM algorithm, strip lengths of four to five triangles were favored. These strips were incrementally adjusted as triangles were split or merged. The authors report a significant frame time improvement of 72 ms per frame by using triangle strips. Another intriguing feature that was supported was line-of-site (LOS) based refinement. In this case the triangulation is made

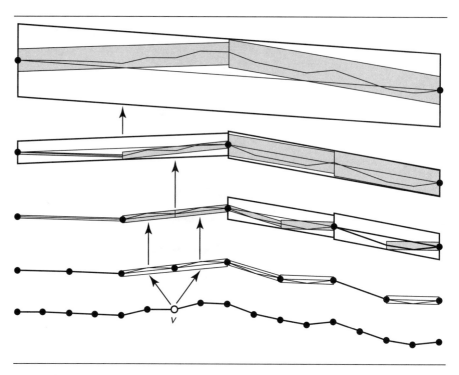

Figure 7.13   Illustrating nested ROAM wedgies for the 1D case, along with the dependents of vertex *v* [Duchaineau 97]. Copyright © 1997 IEEE.

more accurate along a specified line of sight so that correct visibility and occlusion determinations can be made. This is particularly useful for military mission planners and ground-based aircraft testing using synthetic sensor stimulation. Another optimization defers the computation of triangle priorities until they potentially affect a split or merge decision. The authors report that this priority recomputation deferral saved them 38 ms per frame. Finally, the ROAM algorithm can also work toward an exact specified triangle count, as well as support fixed frame rate constraints.

Duchaineau et al. tested their implementation with a USGS 1-degree DEM for Northern New Mexico (about 1,200 × 1,200 postings at 3-arc-second, or roughly 90-m, resolution). They report that on a R10000 Indigo2 workstation they achieved 3,000 triangles within a rate time of 30 ms (5 ms for view-frustum culling, 5 ms for priority queue calculation, 5 ms for split/merge operations, and 15 ms to output the triangle strips). In terms of frame coherence, the authors found that on average less than 3% of triangles changed between frames. Figure 7.14 shows an example of a ROAM-simplified mesh. Extensive implementation nodes and source code have been made available by the authors at *www.cognigraph.com/ROAM_homepage/*.

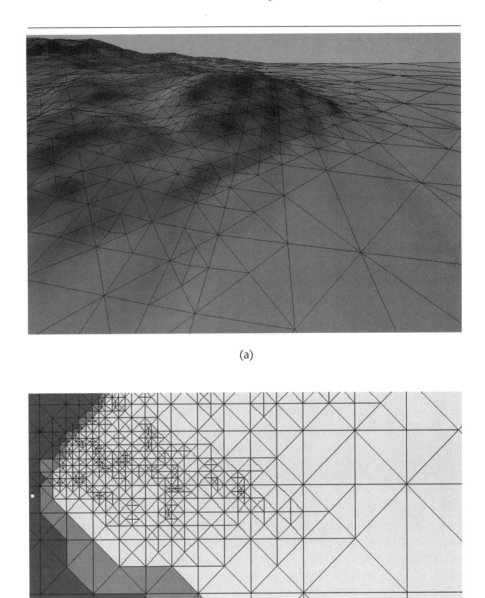

(a)

(b)

Figure 7.14   (a) Example of a ROAM-simplified terrain with the visible mesh edges overlaid. (b) A bird's-eye view of the terrain, where light regions are inside the view frustum, gray are partly inside, and dark regions are outside the view [Duchaineau 97]. Copyright © 1997 IEEE.

The original ROAM algorithm has been improved or modified by a number of researchers and game developers. For example, one simplification sometimes used by game developers is to discard the frame coherence feature, resulting in a "split-only ROAM" implementation (such as that described by Bryan Turner in his *Gamasutra.com* article "Real-Time Dynamic Level of Detail Terrain Rendering with ROAM"). The Virtual Terrain Project (VTP) provides source code for a split-only ROAM implementation, referred to as SMTerrain (for Seumas McNally). This is available at *http://vterrain.org/Implementation/Libs/smterrain.html.*

One noteworthy improvement of the original algorithm was provided by Jonathan Blow at the GDC 2000 conference [Blow 00a]. Blow found that the original ROAM algorithm does not perform well for densely sampled data, and attributed this to the large number of premature recalculations of wedgie priorities that can occur in a well-tesselated high-detail terrain. Blow noted that both Lindstrom and Duchaineau used screen-space error metrics that compressed the 3D geometric error down to a 1D scalar value. Instead, Blow advocated using the full three dimensions of the source data to perform LOD computations and building a hierarchy of 3D isosurfaces to contain all vertices within a certain error bound. (It should be noted that this is simply another way to look at the error function and that Lindstrom et al. also illustrated their error function as a 3D isosurface.) For simplicity, Blow chose spheres as the isosurface primitive, such that each wedgie was represented by a sphere in 3D space. When the viewpoint intersects with the sphere, the wedgie is split, and when the viewpoint leaves a sphere, the wedge is merged. To optimize this process, a hierarchy of nested spheres was used and the algorithm only descends into nodes when the viewpoint intersects a sphere. In addition, spheres could be clustered at any level by introducing extra bounding volumes to provide further resilience to large terrain models (see Figure 7.15). Blow noted that this new error metric produced extremely efficient split and merge determinations for high-detail terrain in cases for which the original ROAM algorithm would stutter visibly. For example, at 640 × 480 resolution with a 3-pixel error threshold, Blow's approach produced a tessellation with 65% less triangles than their ROAM implementation [Blow 00b].

Finally, although the original ROAM work states that the algorithm supports dynamic terrain, such as mudslides and explosion craters, this was not explored extensively in the original paper. However, Yefei He's Ph.D. work produced a system called DEXTER for dynamic terrain visualization based on ROAM [He 00]. Figure 7.16 shows screen shots of this system using a real-time, off-road ground vehicle simulation in which the vehicle deforms the soft ground it drives over, leaving tracks behind it.

7.3.3 REAL-TIME GENERATION OF CONTINUOUS LOD

In 1998, Röttger et al. extended the earlier continuous LOD work of Lindstrom et al. Instead of adopting a bottom-up approach, they chose a top-down strategy, noting that this meant their algorithm needed to visit only a fraction of the entire data set at

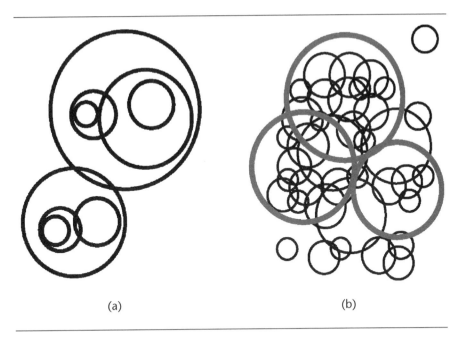

(a)   (b)

Figure 7.15   Image (a) shows the hierarchy of nested isosurfaces used by Blow's adaptation of the ROAM algorithm, and (b) shows an example clustering of isosurfaces using extra bounding volumes [Blow 00b].

(a)   (b)

Figure 7.16   Real-time dynamic terrain produced by the DEXTER system, where (a) illustrates the simplified terrain mesh that has been deformed, and (b) shows the resulting rendered image [He 00].

each frame, but that this also made the addition of features such as silhouette testing problematic because these would require analysis of the entire data set [Röttger 98]. They used a quadtree data structure rather than a binary triangle tree, and dealt with tears between adjacent levels of the quadtree by skipping the center vertex of the higher-resolution edge. To simplify this solution, Röttger et al. implemented a bottom-up process from the smallest existing block to guarantee that the level difference between adjacent blocks did not exceed 1. They also introduced a new error metric that took into consideration the distance from the viewer and the roughness of the terrain in world space. Their metric can be written as follows.

$$f = \frac{l}{d \cdot C \cdot \max(c \cdot d2, 1)}$$

Here, l is the distance to the viewpoint (Manhattan distance was used for efficiency), d is the edge length of a quadtree block, C is a configurable quality parameter that determines the minimum global resolution (a value of 8 was found to provide good visual results), and c specifies the desired global resolution that can be adjusted per frame to maintain a fixed frame rate. The quantity $d2$ incorporates the surface roughness criteria by representing the largest error delta value at six points in the quadtree: the four edge midpoints and the two diagonal midpoints. An upper bound on this component was computed by taking the maximum of these six absolute delta values.

An important feature of Röttger et al.'s system is its direct support for geomorphing of vertices to smooth the transition between levels of detail. This was implemented by introducing a blending function, $b = 2(1 - f)$, clamped to the range $[0,1]$ to morph vertices linearly between two levels of detail. Extra care was taken to avoid cracks that could occur during geomorphing due to adjacent blocks having different blending functions. This was done by using the minimum blending value for edges that were shared between quadtree blocks. The authors state that they were able to associate a single blending value and $d2$-value with each vertex using only one extra byte of storage. Their implementation was evaluated on an SGI Maximum Impact using a terrain model of a region in Yukon Territory, Canada. The c value was dynamically chosen to maintain a frame rate of 25 Hz, which produced roughly 1,600 triangle fans and 15,000 vertices per frame (see Figure 7.17).

7.3.4 VIEW-DEPENDENT PROGRESSIVE MESHES FOR TERRAIN

Hugues Hoppe of Microsoft Research introduced Progressive Meshes (PMs). Hoppe's original algorithm provided a way to incrementally add or remove triangles from an arbitrary mesh [Hoppe 96]. He later extended this work to support view-dependent refinements, naming this View Dependent Progressive Meshes (VDPMs) [Hoppe 97], and then applied this technique to the problem of terrain visualization [Hoppe 98a].

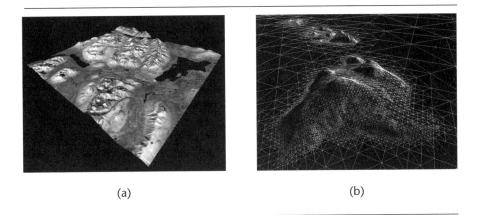

(a)   (b)

Figure 7.17   Textured and wireframe images of Röttger et al.'s continuous LOD algorithm for (a) Kluane National Park south of Haines Junction in Yukon Territory, Canada, and (b) the islands of Hawaii. Courtesy of Stefan Roettger.

In terms of terrain algorithms, VDPMs provide a TIN-based framework instead of the typical regular grid framework. This can provide more optimal approximations because the triangulation is not constrained to produce gridded results, and can potentially handle more complex terrain features such as caves and overhangs. Hoppe cites work stating that the VDPM approach can provide 50 to 75% fewer triangles compared to an equivalent bintree scheme [Lilleskog 98]. More recently, others have reported that regular gridded ROAM implementations offer higher performance than Hoppe's TIN-based approach [Ögren 00]. One further criticism leveled against the application of progressive meshes to terrain is that due to its global optimization approach it becomes difficult to support real-time deformable meshes such as dynamically changing terrain.

Hoppe's algorithm functions out of core by portioning the model into blocks and then recursively simplifying and combining the blocks (see Figure 7.18). Virtual memory is allocated for the entire terrain structure, and the Windows API calls `VirtualAlloc()` and `VirtualFree()` were used to page different blocks to and from physical memory. In his test data set of 4,097 × 2,049 vertices, Hoppe partitioned this grid into 8 × 4 blocks of 513 × 513 vertices. Tears between adjacent blocks are handled by not allowing simplification of those vertices that lie on a block boundary (except for the special case of the top-level single block that has no neighbors). This constraint can produce larger triangle counts. However, Hoppe performed a preprocess in which blocks were hierarchically merged and then resimplified at each

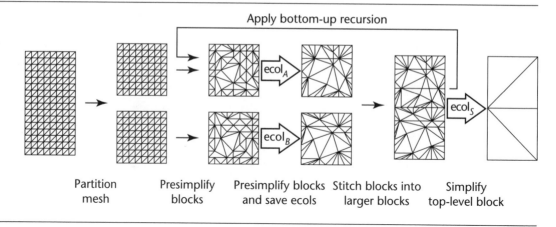

Figure 7.18   Hoppe's hierarchical block-based simplification, performed in a preprocessing step [Hoppe 98a]. Copyright © 1998 IEEE.

step so that the actual polygon increase was small. Hoppe states that a non–block-based scheme only produced 0.8% fewer active faces.

Another noteworthy feature of this system is its elegant support for real-time generation of geomorphs to produce temporally smooth vertex splits and edge collapses. This capability was described in Section 5.3, so we will not replicate that discussion here. The error metric used in the VDPM system was a screen-space criterion that explicitly incorporated geomorph refinements that occur over *gtime* frames. Because these geomorphs will complete their transition a few frames into the future, Hoppe estimates the viewer's position by the time the geomorph completes. A simple linear extrapolation of the viewer's position was implemented by using the current per-frame velocity, Δe. Hoppe's final metric was a simplified version of Lindstrom et al.'s that can be written as

$$\delta_v > k(\mathbf{v} - \mathbf{e} \cdot \vec{e}) \quad \text{where} \quad k = 2\tau \tan \frac{\phi}{2}$$

where δ_v is the neighborhood's residual error (i.e., the vertex's delta value), $\mathbf{e}$ can either be the current viewpoint or the anticipated viewpoint *gtime* frames into the future, $\vec{e}$ is the viewing direction, $\mathbf{v}$ is the vertex in world space, τ is the screen-space error threshold, and ϕ is the field-of-view angle. Hoppe notes that in a view-dependent TIN-based scheme it is not sufficient to measure the maximal vertical deviation by only looking at the original grid points because larger errors can occur between grid points. He therefore introduced a solution to precompute the maximum height deviation between the regular triangulation of grid points and the open neighborhood of

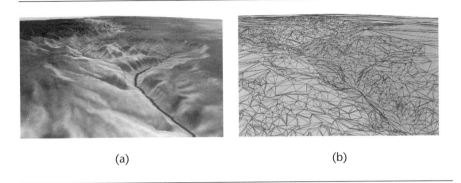

(a)	(b)

Figure 7.19   Screen shot from Hoppe's Grand Canyon model using his VDPM scheme in which the screen-space error tolerance is 2.1 pixels for a 720×510 window. The active mesh has 12,154 faces and 6,096 vertices. The two images show (a) a texture-mapped version of the terrain and (b) the underlying triangle mesh [Hoppe 98a]. Copyright © 1998 IEEE.

each edge collapse. Hoppe also notes that the VDPM framework can produce long, thin triangles that are often considered bad for LOD rendering, but that he observed no such rendering artifacts. The test data set used to evaluate this system was a large model of the Grand Canyon (see Figure 7.19). The model was partitioned into blocks, and these were simplified in a preprocessing step to produce a mesh of 732,722 vertices. At run-time, Hoppe obtained a constant frame rate of 30 Hz by adapting the error tolerance τ from 1.7 to 3.3 pixels to maintain an active triangle count of 12,000. This was done on an SGI Onyx Infinite Reality system. Similarly, fixed frame rates of 60 Hz and 72 Hz were achieved by enforcing triangle counts of 5,000 and 4,000, respectively.

7.3.5   MULTITRIANGULATION

Leila De Floriani and Enrico Puppo of the Geometry Modeling and Computer Graphics group at the University of Genova have made substantial contributions to the literature in regard to terrain simplification. Their recent work has been focused on their notion of multitriangulation, or MT [Puppo 98], which was inspired by previous work on pyramidal and hierarchical terrain models [DeFloriani 89] [DeFloriani 95]. This is essentially an extremely general TIN-based approach, in which an initial TIN is progressively refined or simplified through a series of local updates, such as adding or removing vertices from the mesh and then retriangulating. A dependency relationship is built between all local updates such that C_2 depends on C_1 if some of C_1's triangles are removed by introducing C_2. This dependency relation-

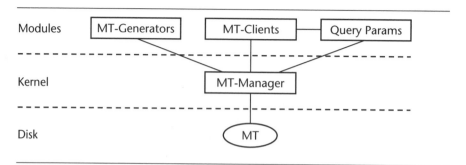

Figure 7.20   The VARIANT system architecture, segmented into a physical disk layer, a system kernel, and an outer layer of extensible modules [DeFloriani 00].

ship can be represented as a directed acyclic graph (DAG) and provides a way to enforce the creation of continuous meshes, by ensuring that all parents of each node are included in any solution. The MT framework has been implemented as a freely available object-orientated C++ library [Magillo 99], and is provided on the companion Web site. This library lets you plug in different generation and simplification libraries, meaning that the MT can be independent of the technique used to build it.

More recently, the MT framework was used to develop the VARIANT (Variable Resolution Interactive Analysis of Terrain) system [DeFloriani 00]. The main purpose of VARIANT was to provide an extensible multiresolution terrain system with support for various terrain analysis and processing capabilities, such as visibility determinations, computation of elevation along a path, contour map extraction, and viewshed analysis. Figure 7.20 presents the architecture of VARIANT, illustrating the system's extensibility model, in which a number of modules are built on top of a core kernel. The kernel, or MT manager, includes basic MT construction, query, and I/O functions. The extensible modules can be MT generators that incrementally modify a TIN through a sequence of local updates, MT clients that perform basic spatial queries or operations, or query parameter modules that customize the generic query operations within the kernel for specific spatial queries (such as point-based, line-based, circle-based, or wedge-based queries).

In terms of terrain LOD functions, the VARIANT system supports the definition of a region of interest (ROI) through a focus function that can be applied to each triangle and return either true or false. The use of the wedge-based query module as a focus function effectively provides the capability to perform view-frustum culling. An LOD threshold can also be defined, implemented as a function applied to each triangle that returns true only if its level of detail is considered sufficient. The LOD threshold function is particularly flexible and can depend on a number of properties, such as a triangle's position, size, shape, elevation approximation error, and slope approximation error. These generic functions provide the capability to perform the

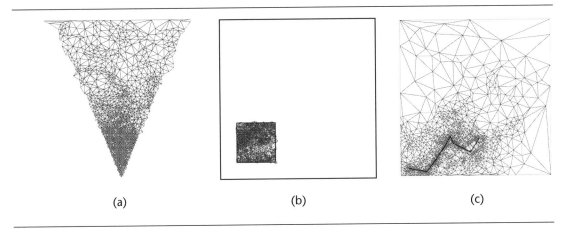

(a)   (b)   (c)

Figure 7.21   Examples of different types of TINs extracted from an MT using the VARIANT
system where (a) shows view-frustum culling, (b) shows the result of a rectangular
subset query, and (c) shows higher resolution in relation to a polyline [DeFloriani
00]. Copyright © 2000 Kluwer Academic Publishers.

usual view-frustum culling and distance-based LOD operations that we are familiar
with by now, but they also allow for more general capabilities, such as returning
a rectangular subset of the terrain at full resolution or producing a TIN in which
resolution is high only in the proximity of a polyline (see Figure 7.21). De Floriani et
al. report that the VARIANT implementation offered interactive frame rates (more
than 10 Hz) on PC-based hardware in 2000.

There are a number of further features of particular note in the VARIANT system.
First, the MT manager provides three different algorithms for extracting a TIN from
an MT. Those algorithms are static (each query is solved independently of any previous queries), dynamic (each query is solved by updating the solution of a previous
query), and local (suitable for queries on a restricted subset of the MT). In effect, the
dynamic algorithm provides a frame coherence feature, using the mesh from the previous frame as a starting point for the current frame. The authors also note that they
have already developed a technique to page part of a large MT from disk as needed for
solving any given local query [Magillo 00], thus effectively providing an out-of-core
capability.

7.3.6 VISUALIZATION OF LARGE TERRAINS MADE EASY

At Visualization 2001, Lindstrom and Pascucci presented a new terrain LOD approach they claim is simple, easy to implement, memory efficient, and independent

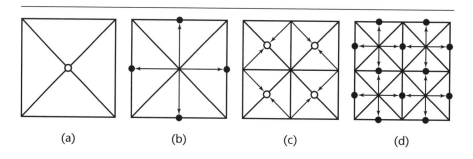

Figure 7.22   The longest-edge bisection scheme adopted by Lindstrom and Pascucci, among others. The arrows in (a–d) designate parent–child relationships [Lindstrom 01a]. Copyright © 2001 IEEE.

of the particular error metric used [Lindstrom 01a]. This work draws on many of the preceding terrain techniques to produce a regular, gridded top-down framework for performing out-of-core view-dependent refinement of large terrain surfaces (see Figure 7.22). Their system provides support for fast hierarchical view culling, triangle stripping, and optional decoupling of the refinement and rendering tasks into two separate threads. Their approach to out-of-core operation organizes the data on disk to optimize coherency and then uses the operating system's memory-mapping functionality to page parts of the model into physical memory space. This has the benefit that the inner rendering loops are as fast as if the data were in memory, and no extra logic is needed to explicitly page in new data. This approach is described in greater detail in Section 7.2.5.

Similar to other view-dependent algorithms we have described, Lindstrom and Pascucci's refinement algorithm recursively subdivided each triangle using longest-edge bisection. This produces right-triangulated irregular network meshes [Evans 97], also known as restricted quadtree triangulations or bintrees. Their algorithm guarantees that a continuous mesh is formed, with no cracks, by enforcing a nesting of error metric terms and hence implicitly forcing parent vertices in the hierarchy to be introduced before their children. They use nested spheres for this, similar in some ways to those used by Blow, as previously described [Blow 00b]. They highlight a number of drawbacks with this concept, such as up-front fixing of the error threshold, dependence on a distance-based error metric, potential introduction of cracks in the mesh, and the need to introduce further clustering of spheres for large sphere forests. They therefore produced a modified approach that avoids many of these undesirable features. Using this nested bounding sphere approach, Lindstrom and Pascucci's framework could accommodate a number of object-space and screen-space error metrics—the important factor being that the position or extent

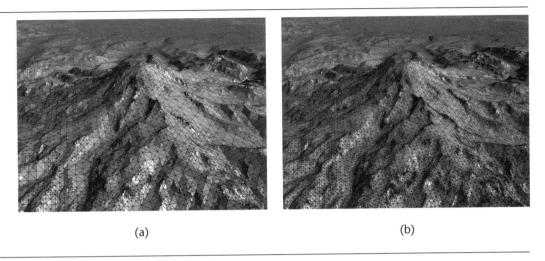

(a)   (b)

Figure 7.23   The Puget Sound model used by Lindstrom and Pascucci. The error thresholds and triangle counts in each case are (a) $\tau = 2$ pixels, 79,382 triangles, and (b) $\tau = 4$ pixels, 25,100 triangles [Lindstrom 01a]. Copyright © 2001 IEEE.

of any error must be able to be used to update the appropriate bounding sphere dimensions.

The authors test their system on three architectures: a two-processor 800-MHz Pentium III PC with NVIDIA GeForce2 graphics card (900 MB RAM), a two-processor 300-MHz R12000 SGI Octane with Solid Impact graphics (900-MB RAM), and a monstrous 48-processor 250-MHz R10000 SGI Onyx2 with InfiniteReality2 graphics (15.5 GB RAM). A 16,385 × 16,385 vertex data set of the Puget Sound area in Washington State was used to evaluate the implementations, totaling 5 GB of disk space (Figure 7.23). They reported sustained frame rates of 60 Hz with 40,000 rendered triangles, and compared this to Hoppe's results of only 8,000 triangles at the same frame rate. Their results also showed an obvious advantage to performing view culling, and a significant advantage obtained through their use of multithreading to decouple the refinement and rendering threads under their multiprocessor platforms (reducing the rendering time between 63% and 88% for a 2816-frame flyover). Finally, in terms of triangle stripping, they observed an average ratio of 1.56 triangle strip vertices per nondegenerate triangle. This was compared to the non–triangle-stripping case of three vertices per triangle.

Lindstrom and Pascucci state that their algorithm can be implemented in as little as a few dozen lines of C code. They expect to release the source code for their implementation by early 2002. The authors have also provided some supplemental notes on their approach at *www.gvu.gatech.edu/people/peter.lindstrom/papers/visualization2001a/*.

Table 7.1 Summary of the major terrain LOD algorithms presented in this chapter (*Continued*)

	Top-down / Bottom-up	Data Structures	Frame Coherence	Memory Cost per Height Value	Tear Handling	Geomorphs?	Out of core?
Lindstrom et al. (1996)	Per-frame incremental blocks followed by bottom-up split and merges	Regular grid-ded bin-tree within quadtree blocks	Yes, via an active cut of blocks and smart vertex visiting	Range from 6 to 28 bytes; 32-bit data structure shown	Implicit remeshing within blocks; no handling between blocks	Possible but not implemented	No
Duchaineau et al. (1997)	Per-frame incremental via dual-queue up-down scheme	Regular grid-ded bintree	Yes, via dual split and merge queues	Crystal-Space/DDG uses height value plus 3 bytes, plus 12 bytes per drawn vertex	Implicit remeshing	Yes	No
Rötter et al. (1998)	Top-down	Regular grid-ded quadtree	None reported	Height value plus 1 byte	Skip center vertex of higher-resolution quadtree level	Yes	No

Table 7.1 *Continued*

	Top-down / Bottom-up	*Data Structures*	*Frame Coherence*	*Memory Cost per Height Value*	*Tear Handling*	*Geomorphs?*	*Out of core?*
Hoppe (1998)	Per-frame incremental with blocks	TIN-based within quadtree blocks	Yes	48 bytes	Vertices on block edges not simplified	Yes	Yes, via VirtualAlloc()
DeFloriani et al. (2000)	Top-down or bottom-up	TIN-based	Yes, with "dynamic" TIN extraction	MT mesh 4 times larger than single resolution model	Implicitly introduce dependent DAG nodes first	Not reported	Yes
Lindstrom and Pascucci (2001)	Top-down	Regular, gridded bintree	None reported	20 bytes for the 5 floats (x, y, z, error, radius)	Implicitly introduce parent vertices before children's	Authors have implemented geomorphing since the article first appeared	Yes, via mmap()

7.4   GEOREFERENCING ISSUES

This section is not strictly related to the simplification of terrains but does address the important area of how to represent terrain models accurately in terms of the real world. This involves the process of *georeferencing;* that is, assigning a precise geographic location (such as a latitude/longitude) to each vertex of a surface. Doing this can have a number of benefits such as incorporating the correct degree of curvature for the earth, correctly integrating multiple data sets into a single model, and accurately representing the co-location of disparate data sets. Figure 7.24 shows an example of real elevation data that have been mapped to a round-earth model.

The reader not well versed in cartographic theory may well be surprised at just how complex the issue of georeferencing is. Most people will be familiar with latitude and longitude. However, the situation is substantially more complex than simply dividing the earth into lines of latitude and longitude. There are issues of earth ellipsoid dimensions, local datums, and geoids to consider. Ignoring these issues can result in errors in the location of points on the order of hundreds of meters or more. On top of that, there are many different coordinate systems in common use today, not just latitude/longitude, and each one has its own particular advantages and disadvantages.

This section explores these issues. However, our treatment is necessarily relatively cursory, and therefore the interested reader is referred to a number of other useful resources. The bible on geographic coordinate systems is Snyder's map projections USGS handbook [Snyder 87]. Further detailed resources that are good references include the U.S. Army Corps of Engineers' *Handbook for Transformation of Datums, Projections, Grids and Common Coordinate Systems* [TEC 96] and Paul Birkel's report on the SEDRIS spatial reference system [Birkel 97]. The GeoVRML specification describes the integration of most of these factors into a real-time 3D graphics system [Reddy 00]. Finally, there is work underway to produce an ISO specification for a spatial reference model that should become the authoritative resource on this topic. It is expected this will be approved by early 2004. Its full designation is ISO/IEC 18026:200x Information technology—Computer graphics and image processing—Spatial reference model (SRM).

7.4.1   ELLIPSOIDS

The earth is commonly approximated as a sphere for visualization purposes. For example, Gerstner used a spherical mapping of global terrain data to produce a hierarchical triangulation over the unit sphere [Gerstner 02]. He also showed how to compensate for pole singularities by using an error indicator that related the area of the planar triangle to the area of the spherical triangle varying with latitude (see Figure 7.25).

Despite this approximation, the earth is not in fact a sphere. The earth can best be modeled geometrically using an ellipsoid of rotation, also known as an

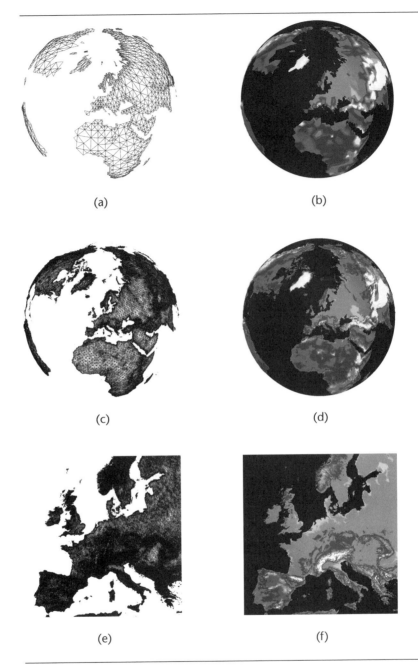

Figure 7.24   The USGS Gtopo30 global elevation data set mapped to a spherical model of the earth at several resolutions (a) and (b) show a low resolution version of a globe model. (c) and (d) show the same model at a higher resolution. (e) and (f) show a high-resolution mesh for a region closer to the earth surface [Gerstner 02]. Copyright © 2002 Kluwer Academic Publishers.

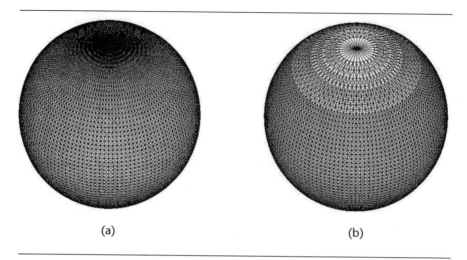

(a)   (b)

Figure 7.25   Compensating for pole singularities in a spherical mapping, where (a) shows a uniform sampling of latitude and longitude, and (b) incorporates an error indicator to vary sampling rate with latitude [Gerstner 02]. Copyright © 2002 Kluwer Academic Publishers.

oblate spheroid. Such an ellipsoid is traditionally specified by two of three variables: the semimajor axis (a), the semiminor axis (b), and the inverse flattening [$1/f = a/(a-b)$]. See Figure 7.26.

Over the past 200 years, as our surveying techniques have gradually improved, many different reference ellipsoids have been formulated, each defining slightly different values for these variables. Table 7.2 presents a small selection of common ellipsoids and their dimensions. These are taken from the SEDRIS spatial reference model [Birkel 97]. The current U.S. Department of Defense standard is defined by the World Geodetic System 1984 (WGS84) such that a = 6378137.0 m and b = 6356752.3142 m.

7.4.2 Geoids

The earth is, however, not a perfect ellipsoid. In regard to the surface of the earth, from which terrain elevations are taken, we find that the earth is actually a fairly bumpy surface referred to as the *geoid*. The geoid is the physically measurable surface corresponding to mean sea level and is related to the earth's gravitational field. This complex, undulating surface varies marginally from the ellipsoid over a range of roughly 100 m across the planet. Figure 7.27 illustrates the relationship between the earth's ellipsoid, the geoid, and undulation of the terrain. Normally, any digital

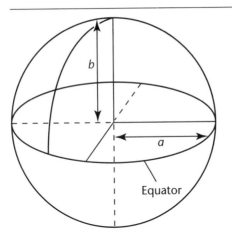

Figure 7.26   The earth represented as an ellipsoid of rotation, where (a) is the semi-major axis and (b) is the semi-minor axis of the ellipsoid. Copyright © 1999 IEEE.

Table 7.2 Definitions for a number of common earth ellipsoids

Ellipsoid Name	Semimajor Axis (meters)	Inverse Flattening (F^{-1})
Airy 1830	6377563.396	299.3249646
Modified Airy	6377340.189	299.3249646
Australian National	6378160	298.25
Clarke 1866	6378206.4	294.9786982
Clarke 1880	6379249.145	293.465
Helmert 1906	6378200	298.3
Hough 1960	6378270	297
International 1924	6378388	297
Geodetic Reference System 1980 (GRS 80)	6378137	298.257222101
South American 1969	6378160	298.25
WGS 72	6378135	298.26
WGS 84	6378137	298.257223563

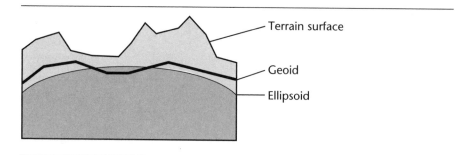

Figure 7.27   The relationships among the geoid, ellipsoid, and terrain undulation. Copyright ©
1999 IEEE.

elevation data are given relative to the geoid; that is, relative to mean sea level, not
the ellipsoid. Once again, there are several slightly different geoid standards (such
as GEOID90, OSU89B, and WGS84), although the WGS84 is becoming a popular
choice in recent years.

7.4.3   DATUMS

A geodetic datum specifies a local or global reference coordinate system for defining
points on the earth, and can be refined to the horizontal datum and the vertical
datum. The horizontal datum specifies the size and shape of the earth, and the origin
and orientation of the coordinate system used to localize points on the earth's surface.
It is typically specified by a reference point on the planet, the azimuth of a line
from that point, and a reference ellipsoid. There are literally hundreds of horizontal
datums in common usage. Practically all of these are local in their extent, such as the
Ordnance Survey Great Britain 1936 datum or the Australian Geodetic 1984 datum.
However, the WGS84 defines a global datum generally accepted as the most accurate
definition now in use. The vertical datum is the surface from which all elevation
values are measured. This is typically taken as mean sea level—that is, the geoid.
Ignoring the datum information when displaying geospatial data can cause positional
errors in the order of tens to hundreds of feet.

7.4.4   COORDINATE SYSTEMS

In general, real-time 3D graphics systems use a right-handed, Cartesian coordinate
system to model all objects in 3D space. In terms of georeferencing, this coordinate

system is most similar to a geocentric coordinate system, in which all locations are specified in units of meters as an (x, y, z) offset from the center of the planet. However, these coordinates tend to be large and can often exceed the accuracy of single-precision floating point values. Since typical single-precision floating point formats have only 23 bits of mantissa, a single-precision coordinate can be accurate to only one part in 8 million $(2^{23} - 1)$; or about 6 or 7 decimal digits of precision, depending on the actual value. Since the equatorial radius of the earth is 6,378,137 m (under the WGS84 ellipsoid), it is not possible to achieve resolutions better than around 0.8 m using single-precision floating point numbers (6,378,137/8,388,607 = 0.8). Below this threshold, various floating point rounding artifacts will occur, such as vertices coalescing and camera jitter. Any terrain visualization system that wishes to deal with global data down to meter accuracy and beyond must therefore address this issue [Reddy 00] [Lindstrom 97].

A further complication is that cartographic data are not normally represented in a geocentric coordinate system. Instead, most georeferenced data are provided in some geodetic or projective coordinate system. A geodetic (or geographic) coordinate system is related to the ellipsoid used to model the earth (e.g., the latitude/longitude system). A projective coordinate system employs a projection of the ellipsoid onto some simple surface, such as a cone or cylinder; as, for example, the Lambert Conformal Conic (LCC) or the Universal Transverse Mercator (UTM) projections, respectively. Therefore, it will normally be necessary to convert from these other coordinate systems into a geocentric representation. The SEDRIS Conversions API provides C source code to perform these transformations at *www.sedris.org/*.

UTM in particular is an extremely common projective coordinate system and is commonly used by the U.S. military and USGS. It is defined by the projection of the earth ellipsoid onto a cylinder tangent to a central meridian. The UTM system is split up into 60 zones, each six degrees wide. Locations are measured with a (*easting, northing*) coordinate in units of meters. The center of each zone has an easting of 500,000. In the northern hemisphere, the equator marks a northing of zero and increases northward, whereas in the southern hemisphere the equator represents a northing of 10 million and decreases southward. Distortion of scale, distance, direction, and area increase away from the central meridian, and the UTM projection itself is only valid over the latitude range 80 degrees south to 84 degrees north. At the poles, the Polar Stereographic projection is often used instead of UTM.

The reason so many different coordinate systems exist is because each was designed for slightly different applications and offers particular advantages and restrictions. For example, some projections can represent only small-scale regions, whereas others are conformal (they preserve angles and have the same scale in every direction), and still others equal area (projected area corresponds to the earth's physical area over the entire projection). Figure 7.28 illustrates some contemporary coordinate systems.

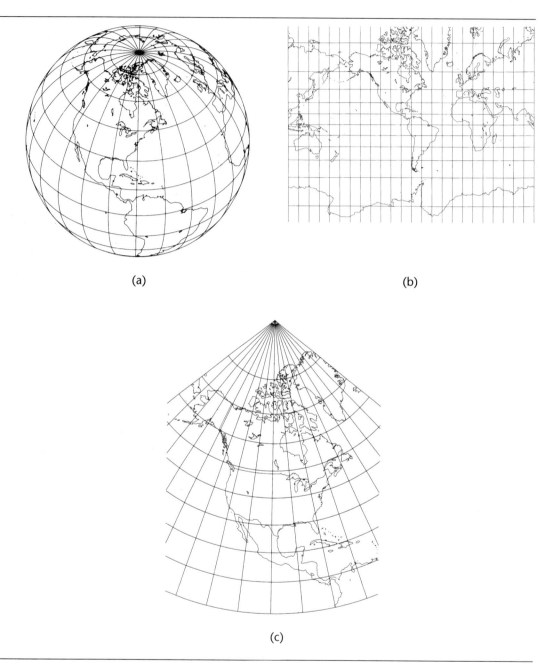

(a)

(b)

(c)

Figure 7.28 Examples of projective coordinate systems. (a) Orthographic projection, used for perspective views of the earth, moon, and other planets; (b) Mercator projection, used for navigation or maps of equatorial regions; (c) and Lambert Conformal Conic, used by the USGS for topographic maps [Snyder 87].

7.5 GEOSPATIAL FILE FORMATS

Terrain data are commonly distributed as regular height grids using any of a number of geospatial file formats. Most readers will be aware of common raster image file formats, such as GIF and JPEG, but may not know much about the available geospatial formats. We therefore take a few moments to introduce a few of these and describe their uses. A geospatial format will normally require a number of capabilities over and above those of a simple image format. First, elevation values must be represented to the required level of accuracy. For example, we may want to represent the height of Mt. Everest, at somewhere over 8,850 m, to meter resolution. Using an 8-bit integer format would be insufficient for this purpose because it can only represent a range of 256 values. We therefore want to be able to store at least 32-bit floating-point numbers, or perhaps 16-bit or 32-bit integers with appropriate scale and offset parameters, to gain submeter accuracy. Second, a geospatial file format will normally include some geographic metadata, such as the coordinate system of the data, the ellipsoid, the lower-left coordinate or bounding box, a time stamp, and so on. Finally, if any data compression is supported, a lossless scheme will normally be favored, because otherwise we lose the accuracy of the original height data. Given these points, the following are explanations of a few of the more common geospatial formats.

- *DEM/STDS:* The USGS digital elevation model (DEM) format is an ASCII representation of elevation values in a raster form. DEMs are sold in 7.5-minute, 15-minute, 30-minute, and 1-degree units [USGS 98]. The 7.5-minute DEMs provide a ground resolution of 30 m and are specified in UTM coordinates. The USGS has mapped much of the United States and provides all of these data in DEM format. More recently, the USGS has moved to a new, more complex, file format called the spatial data transfer standard (STDS), which supports vector as well as raster spatial data, along with attributes, metadata, and a data quality report. See *http://gisdata.usgs.net/*.

- *DTED:* The digital terrain elevation data (DTED) format was developed by the U.S. National Imagery and Mapping Agency (NIMA). As with USGS DEMs, there are a number of different flavors of DTED. DTED Level 0 is publicly available data at 30-arc-second postings (approximately 1 km). DTED Level 1 is the basic medium-resolution elevation data source for all military activities with 3-arc-second postings (approximately 100 m). DTED Levels 2 through 5 provide even higher levels of military resolution, roughly 30-m, 10-m, 3-m, and 1-m resolution, respectively. See *www.nima.mil/*.

- *GeoTIFF:* The GeoTIFF format is an interchange format for georeferenced raster imagery based on the tagged image file format (TIFF). It defines a number of additional tags for the TIFF format to describe the geographic resolution, extent, and coordinate system of the imagery. TIFF was chosen as the base format because it can handle large 32-bit values with lossless compression and because the data can optionally be stored as tiles. A public domain library, called *libgeotiff*, is available for creating software that can read and write GeoTIFF files.

- *BT:* The binary terrain format was developed by Ben Discoe as part of the Virtual Terrain Project (VTP). BT files are simple, compact files that use a file name extension of *.bt*. The 256-byte header sequence includes the grid dimensions, the data type (floating point or integer), the projection (lat/long or UTM), and the bounding box in geographic coordinates. See *www.vterrain.org/*.

- *GeoVRML:* The GeoVRML file format was specifically designed to support precise geospatial applications within the framework of a real-time 3D graphics system. It is essentially an extension of the ISO standard Virtual Reality Modeling Language [VRML 97], with 10 new nodes added to allow the specification of coordinates with respect to geographic coordinate systems such as lat/long and UTM [Reddy 00]. The nodes are implemented in Java and released as Open Source from *www.geovrml.org/*.

For more details on these and other geospatial file formats, see *www.remotesensing. org/*. This includes format specifications, documentation, and software. A similarly excellent resource for Open Source GIS products and data is available from the FreeGIS project at *www.freegis.org/*.

7.6 TERRAIN DATA ON THE WEB

So, you've read through this chapter and have a great idea for a new terrain LOD algorithm that improves on all of the existing solutions, but you need to show your algorithm off with some cool data. So where do you get that great data? To help you in your search, the following list provides a sampling of resources on the Web for digital elevation data or imagery. These links were live and current at the time of publication. However, the URLs may change over time. In addition to this list, some example terrain data are also included on the companion Web site.

- *USGS Landsat 7:* A NASA/USGS satellite used to acquire remotely sensed images of the Earth's land surface and surrounding coastal regions.
  landsat7.usgs.gov/
  landsat.gsfc.nasa.gov/

- *Bay Area Regional Database (BARD):* A collection of USGS digital data for the San Francisco Bay area.
  bard.wr.usgs.gov/

- *USGS Geographic Data Download:* The USGS portal for downloading DEM, DLG, and other digital data.
  http://edc.usgs.gov/doc/edchome/ndcdb/ndcdb.html

- *GTOPO30:* The USGS global digital elevation model DEM with a horizontal grid spacing of 30 arc seconds (approximately 1 km).
  http://edcdaac.usgs.gov/gtopo30/gtopo30.html

- *National Imagery and Mapping Agency (NIMA):* The U.S. government organization tasked with providing timely and accurate imagery and geospatial information to support national security objectives.
  http://www.nima.mil/

- *Earth Info:* NIMA's public imagery portal.
  http://www.earth-info.org/

- *National Ocean Service (NOS) MapFinder:* A portal for images and data from a number of U.S. National Ocean Service (NOS) offices.
  http://mapindex.nos.noaa.gov/

- *Tiger Map Server:* A mapping engine that uses 1998 TIGER/Line data and 1990 Decennial Census data.
  http://tiger.census.gov/cgi-bin/mapbrowse-tbl

- *Virtual Terrain Project (VTP):* A superb resource managed by Ben Discoe, with the goal to foster the creation of tools for easily constructing any part of the real world in interactive, 3D digital form. The Web site includes Open Source software for all stages of the terrain production process, including free, public implementations of several of the LOD algorithms mentioned in this chapter.
  www.vterrain.org/

- *GlobeXplorer:* A provider of satellite images and aerial photography, mostly used in a business-to-business model; for example, with MapQuest and AOL. They boast the world's largest commercial collection of aerial images.
  www.globexplorer.com/

- *Digital Globe:* A company that sells commercial satellite imagery from its Quickbird satellite.
  www.digitalglobe.com

- *Space Imaging:* A company that sells commercial satellite imagery from its IKONOS satellite, the world's first one-meter resolution commercial imaging satellite.
  www.spaceimaging.com/

- *FreeGIS.org:* This site is dedicated to Open Source GIS solutions and contains a list of freely available systems and geodata.
  www.freegis.org/geo-data.en.html

- *Large Models Web Page at GVU:* Contains the Grand Canyon terrain data Hoppe used for his view-dependent progressive meshes work, as well as the Puget Sound model used by Lindstrom.
  www.cc.gatech.edu/projects/large_models/

Note that the original source of the Puget Sound data is the following.
http://duff.geology.washington.edu/data/raster/tenmeter/bil10/

- *Bob Crispen's VRML FAQ:* The Virtual Reality Modeling Language (VRML) Frequently Asked Questions (FAQ) contains an entry on finding VRML models and textures on the web.
http://home.hiwaay.net/~crispen/vrmlworks/models.html

7.7 CONCLUSIONS

This chapter has dealt with the sizeable subtopic of terrain simplification. We began by covering some of the basic concepts, such as top-down versus bottom-up algorithms; regular, gridded data versus triangulated irregular networks (TINs); various hierarchical structures, such as quadtrees and bintrees; dealing with tears between adjacent patches at different resolutions; out-of-core operation; and streaming over the Web. We could not hope to cover every solution that has been developed to date, but instead surveyed a few of the more influential and practical solutions. In this regard, we focused on key solutions that provide real-time, view-dependent support, presenting detailed descriptions of each implementation. This survey included the initial work of Lindstrom et al., the ROAM algorithm developed by Duchaineau et al., Röttger et al.'s continuous LOD work, Hoppe's terrain-specific view-dependent progressive meshes (VDPM) approach, the multi-triangulation work of De Floriani and Puppo, and finally the recent large-scale terrain work of Lindstrom and Pascucci. Table 7.1 provided a concise summary of these approaches in terms of the concepts just mentioned. We then concluded with some auxiliary discussion of geographic coordinate systems, an important topic when considering the development of a terrain visualization system that is highly accurate in real-world terms.

PART III

ADVANCED ISSUES

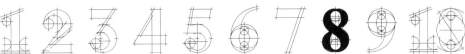

PERCEPTUAL
ISSUES

In this chapter we return to level of detail management, or the question of when to switch between different representations for a model. Since the resulting representations, be they characters in a video game or components in a CAD system, are ultimately presented to the user visually, we must consider the impact of LOD management on the visual system. In particular, reducing the detail of an object too aggressively will produce a noticeable visual change in the image. Such a change may be merely distracting, but in the worst case could impact the user's ability to perform some task, or their sense of presence in a virtual environment. To understand the effect of modulating an object's LOD, we need to understand how the changes made to a model will be perceived by the user, which in turn requires some understanding of the function, efficacy, and limitations of the human visual system. This chapter presents some basic principles of visual perception and describes two examples of systems that manage LOD according to these principles.

8.1 MOTIVATION

Specific reasons LOD researchers and developers should educate themselves about visual perception include the following.

- *Maximize rendering resources:* If we can predict what detail users can perceive, we can remove imperceptible details, and thus save the computational resources that would have been otherwise wasted rendering unnecessary refinements.

- *Minimize popping effects:* Popping effects are caused by a visually noticeable switch in a model's LOD. However, if we remove only those details we predict are imperceptible to the user, the user should not experience these distracting effects. This in turn would obviate the need for techniques from Chapter 4, such as alpha blending, geomorphing, and considering hysteresis during LOD selection.

- *Principled best-effort LOD:* Of course, often removing just imperceptible details will still not achieve the desired frame rate, forcing the system to reduce detail further while accepting that the effect may be perceptible. In this case, we would like to use principles of visual perception to guide our choice of LODs so as to minimize the perceptibility of the resulting simplification.

- *Orthogonal framework:* We have described many potential criteria for selecting LODs, and for guiding simplification when creating LODs. Researchers and developers have generally employed ad hoc heuristics or user-tunable parameters to drive these tasks to for example, balance the importance of geometric fidelity during simplification against preservation of appearance-related attributes, such as color, normals, and texture coordinates [Garland 98] [Erikson 99] [Hoppe 99b], or to trade off the importance of screen-space size with other LOD selection factors such as eccentricity [Funkhouser 93b]. Grounding our choices in a principled perceptual model offers the promise of an orthogonal framework for LOD in which the importance of various factors proceeds naturally from the model.

The next section introduces some prior work on incorporating perceptual factors into LOD systems. We then delve into the visual system, giving a brief overview of the system from eyeball to visual cortex, with particular emphasis on applying this knowledge to LOD. Finally, we describe some recent systems based directly on models of visual perception.

8.2 SOME PERCEPTUALLY MOTIVATED LOD CRITERIA

The simplest and most common criteria used to modulate the LOD of an object are undoubtedly its distance from the viewpoint, or (closely related) its projected size on the display device. The following describe some other LOD criteria researchers have proposed, motivated by the behavior and limitations of our visual system.

- *Eccentricity:* An object's LOD is based on its angular distance from the center of the user's gaze, simplifying objects in the user's peripheral vision more aggressively than objects under direct scrutiny.

- *Velocity:* An object's LOD is based on its velocity across the user's visual field, simplifying objects moving quickly across the user's gaze more aggressively than slow-moving or still objects.

- *Depth of field:* In stereo or binocular rendering, an object's LOD is related to the distance at which the user's eyes are converged, simplifying more aggressively those objects that are visually blurred because the user's gaze is focused at a different depth.

Several computer graphics researchers have proposed systems that take advantage of the fundamental observation that we can perceive less detail in the peripheral field and in moving objects. As far back as 1976, Clark suggested that objects could be simplified further toward the periphery of the field of view, and also that the detail of moving objects could be inversely related to their speeds [Clark 76]. Subsequently, Blake developed metrics to predict the most perceptually appropriate level of detail under circumstances such as the relative motion of objects with respect to the viewer [Blake 89]. More recently, Levoy and Whitaker developed a volume-rendering application that followed the user's gaze and smoothly varied the resolution of the display accordingly [Levoy 90]. Perceptually based models have also been developed to accelerate global illumination algorithms for realistic image synthesis [Myszkowski 01] [Ramasubramanian 99] [Bolin 98]. These frameworks are very sophisticated, but require many seconds or minutes to operate. In subsequent sections we concentrate on those solutions that relate to LOD for real-time polygonal systems.

8.2.1 ECCENTRICITY LEVEL OF DETAIL

Eccentricity LOD selects an object's representation based on the degree to which it exists in the visual periphery, where our ability to perceive detail is reduced. Funkhouser and Séquin incorporated a provision for eccentricity LOD into their architectural walkthrough of Soda Hall (see Figure 8.1) [Funkhouser 93b]. They made the simplifying assumption that the user was always looking at the center of the screen, and let the distance of each object from the screen center influence the detail used to represent that object. The actual relationship between object detail and display eccentricity was controlled manually using a slider.

In concurrent and similar work, Hitchner and McGreevy produced a generalized model of LOD for the NASA Ames Virtual Planetary Exploration (VPE) testbed [Hitchner 93]. Their system modeled object *interest* (a measure of the importance of the object to the user) according to a number of factors, including an eccentricity factor:

$$interest = \gamma_{static}/distance$$

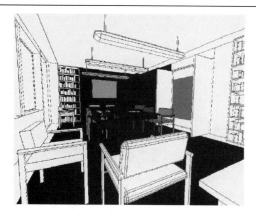 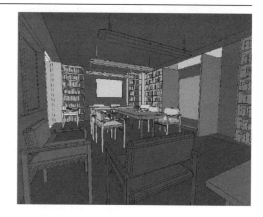

Figure 8.1   Images of Funkhouser's architectural walk-through system showing the relative benefit of objects where the focus (eccentricity) factor is set to (a) 1.0 and (b) 0.01. Darker grayscales represent higher benefit values [Funkhouser 93a].

Here, *distance* to the user's gaze is measured in 2D screen coordinates and γ_{static} is an arbitrary scaling factor. Similarly, Ohshima et al. developed a head-tracked desktop system that could degrade the LOD of objects in the periphery [Ohshima 96]. They modeled the decline of visual acuity with eccentricity using the exponential relationship

$$f(\theta) = \begin{cases} 1 & \text{when } 0 \le \theta \le a \\ \exp\left(-\frac{\theta - a}{c_1}\right) & \text{when } a < \theta \end{cases}$$

where θ is the angular distance between the center of the object to the user's gaze fixation, α is the angle from the center of the object to the edge nearest the user's gaze, and c_1 is an arbitrary scaling factor that the authors simply report they instantiated to 6.2 degrees.

All of the previously discussed systems use eccentricity to affect LOD selection, reducing the resolution of peripheral objects, but none carefully examined the perceptual effect of this reduced resolution. In related research, however, Watson et al. performed a user study to evaluate the perceptual effect of degraded peripheral resolution in head-mounted displays (HMDs) [Watson 95]. Subjects were given a simple search task that required locating and identifying a single target object. The degraded peripheral resolution was implemented by dividing the display into two regions, with a high-detail inset blended into a coarse background field (see Figure 9.8). The inset was always located at the center of the display device. For a number of inset sizes and resolutions, they reported that user performance was not significantly affected by the degraded peripheral display, and concluded that eccentricity LOD should provide a useful optimization tool. Though this study varied display resolution rather than geometric LOD resolution, it remains a promising result.

It is worth noting that view-dependent LOD schemes have an advantage over view-independent schemes when accounting for eccentricity, since resolution can be varied across an object. With view-independent LOD, a large object spanning much of the field of view can exist at only one level of detail, which must therefore be chosen conservatively. For example, if the user's gaze rests on any part of the object, the entire object must be treated as if it were under direct scrutiny, and will probably be rendered at the highest level of detail. A view-dependent LOD scheme can render in high detail where necessary, and smoothly degrade detail away from the center of gaze.

8.2.2   VELOCITY LEVEL OF DETAIL

Velocity LOD selects an object's representation based on its velocity relative to the user's gaze. Again, lacking a suitable eye- or head-tracking technology, some researchers have approximated this with the velocity of an object across the display device. Properly implemented, velocity LOD should automatically support situations with complex motion flows. For example, if the user's gaze tracks an object moving across a stationary background, the object should be rendered in high detail, whereas the background is simplified. However, if the user's gaze stays fixed on the background, the system should simplify the moving object while preserving the detail of background objects.

Funkhouser and Séquin incorporated a velocity term into their architectural walkthrough, reducing the LOD of objects by an amount proportional to the ratio of the object's apparent speed to its average polygon size (their simple but efficient approximation of the spatial detail in an object). Hitchner and McGreevy account for object velocity in their VPE system, similarly to object eccentricity, as

$$interest = \gamma_{\text{dynamic}}/velocity$$

where *velocity* is an estimate of visual field velocity, measured by taking the difference between an object's position in consecutive frames, and γ_{dynamic} is another arbitrary scaling factor. Ohshima et al. modeled the decline of visual acuity with velocity using the following equation:

$$g(\Delta\phi) = \begin{cases} 1 - \frac{\Delta\phi}{c_2} & \text{when } 0 \leq \Delta\phi \leq c_2 \\ 0 & \text{when } c_2 < \Delta\phi \end{cases}$$

Here, $\Delta\phi$ represents the angular distance traveled by the object. The c_2 term, intended to model saccadic suppression (see Section 8.4.5), is an arbitrary scaling factor instantiated to 180 deg/s. See Figure 8.2.

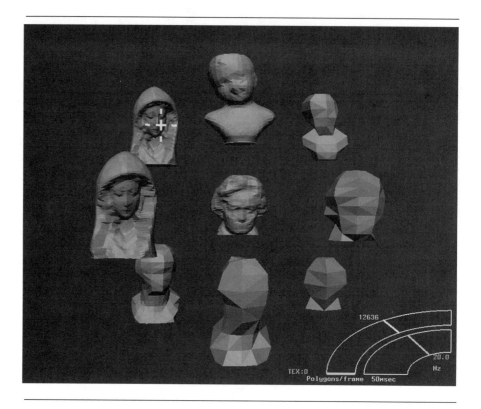

Figure 8.2   Screen shot of Ohshima et al.'s gaze-directed adaptive rendering system, showing reduced detail in the periphery. Courtesy of Hiroyuki Yamamoto.

8.2.3   DEPTH-OF-FIELD LEVEL OF DETAIL

Depth-of-field LOD selects an object's representation by comparing its distance from the user to the distance at which the user's eyes are currently converged. Human binocular vision trains both eyes on an object in order to focus it clearly, a synchronized action known as a *vergence eye movement*. The projection of a verged object on our two retinas is fused by the visual system into a single perceptual image. The depth range over which objects appear fused is called *Panum's fusional area* (Figure 8.3); objects out of this range project to a double image and appear blurred. Ohshima et al. suggest reducing the level of detail of objects that lie outside Panum's fusional area. They use the following formula:

$$h(\Delta\phi) = \begin{cases} 1 & \text{where } 0 \le \Delta\phi \le b \\ \exp\left(-\frac{\Delta\phi-b}{c_3}\right) & \text{where } b < \Delta\phi \end{cases}$$

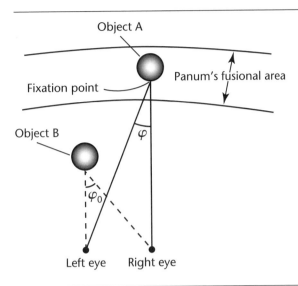

Figure 8.3   Illustrating the depth of field of two objects. Object A lies within Panum's fusional area and is perceived in focus, whereas object B is blurred [Ohshima 96].

Here, $\Delta\phi = |\phi - \phi_0|$, where ϕ_0 is the angle of convergence for the fixation point, ϕ is the angle toward the object, b is the threshold width of the fusional area (assigned the value 0 degrees), and c_3 is a scaling parameter (assigned 0.62 degrees).

Of course, depth of field LOD is most appropriate for stereoscopic displays in which separate images are presented to the user's left and right eyes. Also worth noting is that the perceived blurring of out-of-focus objects is due to two phenomena: vergence eye movements and *accommodation,* or focusing by changing the focal length of the lens. One problem with most stereoscopic displays is that though the user's eyes may verge according to the distance of the virtual object they must still focus to the plane of the display, which is normally at a fixed focal distance [Ware 99]. This produces a conflict between the vergence and focus mechanisms in the eye that can cause eyestrain in users [Wann 95] [Mon-Williams 98]. Ohshima et al.'s depth-of-field LOD may have some merit in this regard, since we can fuse blurred images more readily than sharp ones. Although reducing LOD is not strictly the same as blurring, it can remove high-frequency components and hence may help to abate the vergence-focus problem.

8.2.4   APPLICABILITY OF GAZE-DIRECTED TECHNIQUES

All three of the previously examined criteria may be classed as *gaze-directed* techniques, since they rely on knowledge of the user's gaze to direct LOD selection.

Gaze-directed rendering is a powerful concept with some clear limitations. Without a suitable eye-tracking system, researchers have generally assumed that the user will be looking toward the center of the display, and thus objects will be degraded in relation to their displacement from this point. This approximation is often unsatisfactory. For example, the eye is drawn toward motion, and tends to track moving objects (a visual process called *smooth pursuit*). Clearly, calculating a tracked object's velocity with respect to a fixed point is exactly the wrong thing to do in this case.

Accurately monitoring the user's gaze requires tracking the eye, but eye tracking is still emerging as a commodity technology. Some current systems are fast enough, accurate enough, robust enough, and posses low enough latency for gaze-directed rendering, but no existing eye tracker meets all of these needs at once in an inexpensive package. It seems likely that eye-tracking technology will improve, eliminating these limitations. However, even without eye tracking, gaze-directed rendering may still be a viable option. When allowed free range of head motion, user gaze is almost always restricted to ±15 degrees of head direction [Bahill 75] [Barnes 79]. We can thus substitute head direction for eccentricity simply by subtracting a 15-degree error term.

For multiscreen wide-angle displays, such as video wall or CAVE systems, head-tracked gaze-directed rendering may be a very attractive option. Obviously, multiple viewers can reduce the impact of gaze-directed rendering, since viewers might examine different parts of the display at once. One could handle multiple viewers by calculating worst-case eccentricity, velocity, and so on for each object. For example, the worst-case eccentricity of an object is the minimum distance to any viewer's gaze direction. Such a scenario increases the demand on the eye-tracking system and limits the degree of simplification possible. In a multiscreen wide-angle display scenario, however, most of the scene will still be outside any viewer's point of focus and therefore still eligible for aggressive simplification. Even with head tracking, which forces a more conservative estimate of eccentricity, gaze-directed rendering might prove a powerful technique for managing rendering complexity in such situations.

In the absence of eye or head tracking, it may still be possible to make an informed decision at where the user is looking in a scene. For example, human attention tends to be drawn to bright colors (especially red), movement, objects entering a scene, the foreground, faces, the point where other characters are looking, the center of patterns that can be constructed from geometric shapes in the scene (such as tree branches), familiar characters or characters that stand out in color or behavior, and so on. Obviously, this will not always be exact, but it may provide a tenable low-impact solution for some applications. For example, Yee et al. presented a computational model of visual attention to predict the important regions in an image for cases when eye tracking is unavailable [Yee 01]. Another approach is when the application can direct attention to certain objects. For example, Kosara et al. demonstrated a visualization system using selective blur to visually recede certain objects and direct users' attention to others, such as those chessmen that immediately threaten a user's pieces in a game of chess [Kosara 02].

8.2.5 THE NEED FOR BETTER PERCEPTUAL MODELS

A common thread throughout the perceptually motivated approaches described thus far is the use of ad hoc heuristics and scaling factors to incorporate perceptual criteria. The simple, arbitrary relationships developed empirically by researchers such as Funkhouser and Séquin, Hitchner and McGreevey, and Ohshima et al. achieved the notional goal of reducing LOD according to eccentricity, velocity, and depth of field, but were not founded on principled models of visual perception. The resulting degradation is thus unlikely to be optimal with regard to user perception, especially across a range of models, situations, and applications. This was reinforced by Watson et al., who stated they had no way to predict either the optimal LOD to display or the extent to which LOD could be degraded in the periphery [Watson 95]. Also missing from the early work described so far are results to assess the effectiveness of the various criteria, in isolation and in combination. In general, the evaluation of LOD effectiveness is a difficult problem, especially since it is very application dependent. For example, Funkhouser and Séquin evaluated their system using an architectural walkthrough comprising almost entirely static objects. Here, the velocity of objects is entirely due to user motion, which could affect the usefulness of velocity LOD.

We argue that modulating the LOD of an object based on its perceptual content first requires a principled perceptual model. The first step in developing such a model is to understand the fundamentals of the human visual system, including how it is designed and how it is believed to function. We now describe the anatomy and physiology of the visual system, providing a foundation for the subsequent higher-level perceptual material.

8.3 INTRODUCTION TO VISION

We begin our treatment of the visual system with a brief overview of the anatomy and physiology of the eye and the vision-related parts of the brain.

8.3.1 THE VISUAL SYSTEM

The visual system can be divided into three major processing sites (see Figure 8.4). These are the *eyes* (which act as the input to the visual system), the *visual pathways* (which transport and organize the visual information), and the *visual cortex* (the section within the brain that enables visual perception). We describe the eye and visual cortex in the subsequent sections, but the visual pathways contribute little to the vision process as we are interested in it, so we do not consider them further. We then follow with a discussion of the spatial resolution of the visual system, and how this varies systematically under a number of circumstances.

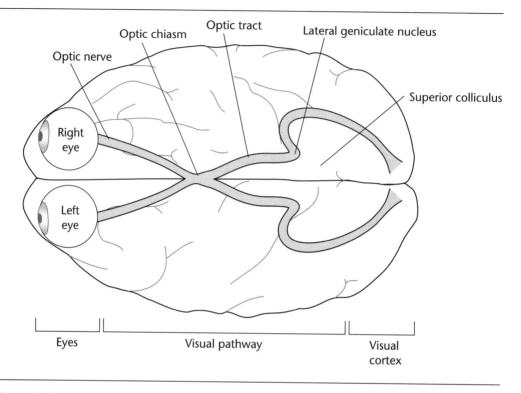

Figure 8.4   Plan view of the brain showing the extents of the three major sites of processing in the human visual system.

8.3.2 THE EYE

The eye is our window onto the external world, an approximately spherical orb around 24 mm in diameter. The inner *vitreous chamber* is enclosed by three layers of tissue. These are the *sclera,* the *choroid,* and the *retina* (see Figure 8.5). The function of these layers is described in the following.

- The sclera is the outermost layer of the eye. It is a white, fibrous tunic that serves to protect the eyeball. On average, the sclera is about 1 mm thick and consists of a dense mosaic of interwoven fibers that creates a strong, tough wall. This becomes transparent toward the front of the eye, where it forms a small bulge known as the *cornea.* It is through the cornea that light enters the eye.

- The choroid is the dark, vascular tunic that forms the middle layer of the eye. It is about 0.2 mm thick on average and provides oxygen, vitamin A, and various other nutrients for the retina via a mesh of capillaries. The dark pigmentation of

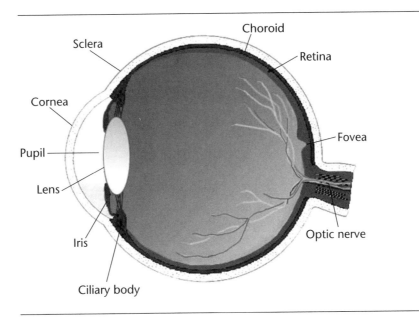

Figure 8.5   Cross-section of a human eye illustrating its major layers and structures [Reddy 97].

the choroid also serves to absorb scattered light in much the same way as the black interior of a camera.

■ The retina is the virtually transparent innermost layer of the eye. It is a very thin tissue consisting of a collection of *photoreceptors* (which detect the incoming light impulses) and a network of neurons, which process these impulses. The output of these neurons form the *optic nerve*, which transmits the optic data to the brain.

Of the three previously cited layers, the retina, where light is first detected and processed, is clearly the most pertinent to our discussion.

The Retina

Light enters the eye through the transparent cornea, is focused by the *lens*, and passes through the vitreous chamber before reaching the retina at the back of the eye. Within the retina itself, light must pass through a number of layers of neurons before finally reaching the *photoreceptor cells*. These are responsible for converting the incident light energy into neural signals that are then filtered back through the network of neurons, consisting of the *collector cells* and the *retinal ganglion cells*. The axons of the retinal ganglion cells form the *optic nerve*, which transports the neural signals to the

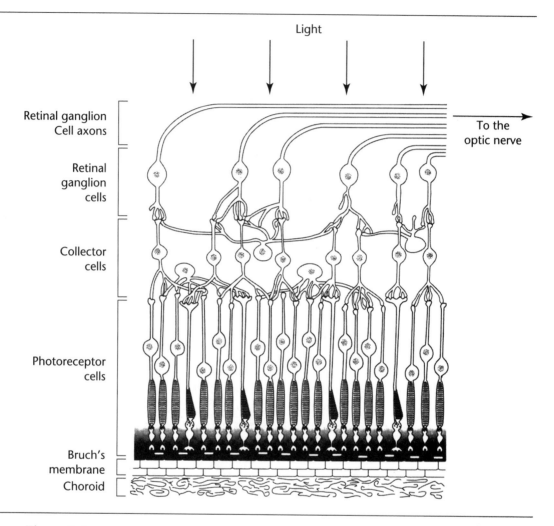

Figure 8.6   A cross-section of the retina, showing the various layers of photoreceptors and neurons that detect and filter incoming light [Sekuler 94]. Note that light must travel through several layers of cells before reaching the photoreceptors [Reddy 97].

visual cortex via the visual pathway. Figure 8.6 illustrates the elements involved in this process.

The *rods* and the *cones* form the two principal classes of photoreceptor cells in the eye. Rods provide high sensitivity in dim light, whereas cones offer high visual acuity in bright light. This duplex arrangement enables humans to see in a wide range of lighting conditions. Both receptor types contain a number of light-sensitive

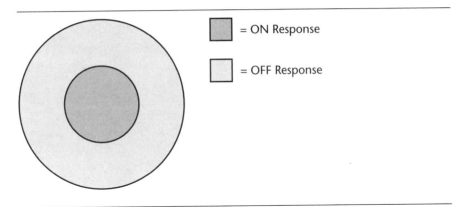

Figure 8.7   Representation of an ON-center retinal ganglion cell. Light falling in the ON-response region causes an increase in cell activity, whereas light falling in the OFF-response region causes a decrease in cell activity [Reddy 97].

molecules, called *photopigments*. Each of these consists of a large protein, called *opsin*, and a vitamin A derivative known as *retinal*. When light strikes the photopigment, it initiates a reaction (occurring in less than one millisecond) that results in the molecule splitting and the subsequent generation of an electric current.

The electrical signals generated in the photoreceptors are transmitted synaptically through the collector cells (incorporating the *horizontal, bipolar,* and *amacrine* cells) and the retinal ganglion cells. Each eye has 100 to 200 million rods and 7 to 8 million cones, but only about 1 million retinal ganglion cells [Ferwerda 01]. Thus the neural network reduces the retinal image into a more concise and manageable representation before it ever leaves the retina, extracting the relevant features of the image that are of particular interest. So which features of the retinal image are relevant? To answer this question we must examine the visual stimuli that evoke a response from the retinal ganglion cells.

The Retinal Ganglion Cells

The inputs of the retinal ganglion cells are arranged in an antagonistic, concentric pattern consisting of a center and a surround region. The ganglion cell is continually emitting a background signal. However, when light strikes the photoreceptors in one region, this stimulates an increased response from the retinal ganglion cell (a so-called *ON response*). Whereas light falling on the other region will generate a reduced response, or *OFF response*. This arrangement is illustrated in Figure 8.7. If the center region is stimulated by an ON response, the retinal ganglion cell is referred to as an

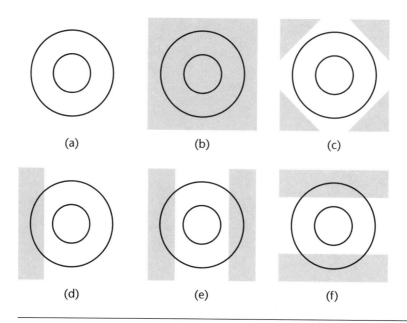

Figure 8.8   Various stimulus arrangements for a single ON-center retinal ganglion cell. Cells (a–c) all generate an equally weak (background) response, whereas cells (d–f) generate a positive response, with cells (e) and (f) responding equivalently [Reddy 97].

ON-center cell. Conversely, if the center region is stimulated by an OFF response, the cell is referred to as an *OFF-center* cell.

The outputs from the ON-response and OFF-response regions are summed to form the net response of the retinal ganglion cell. This means the same luminance presented across the cell will elicit a weak response because of the antagonistic reaction between the center and surround regions. However, if an ON-response region receives light when the corresponding OFF-response region does not, this differential will cause a strong response. An illustration of this operation is presented in Figure 8.8.

Following from the previous observations, we can define the following characteristics of retinal ganglion cells (and hence the first stage of processing, which is performed on the retinal image).

- Retinal ganglion cells are sensitive to edges. They produce a marked response only when there is a contrast gradient across its *receptive field* (the area of the retina the ganglion cell receives input from).

- A light stimulus that falls outside the cell's receptive field will have no effect on the cell's response.

- The size of the cell's receptive field defines the size of the light stimulus it is maximally sensitive to.

- The orientation of a stimulus does not affect the cell's response (because the center and surround regions are circular).

8.3.3 THE VISUAL CORTEX

The visual cortex (also referred to as the striate cortex, Area 17, and V1) is the major center of vision. It is located in the occipital lobe, toward the rear of the brain. As in the retina, the cells of the visual cortex have a receptive field that restricts the sensitivity of the cell to a certain region. The cortical cells respond maximally to gradients of luminance across their receptive fields, rather than to ambient illumination levels. However, unlike the retinal cells, they are also selective on the orientation of a stimulus and the direction of moving stimuli [Blakemore 69].

We can classify the cortical cells into *simple cells* (which are orientation selective to stationary or slow-moving stimuli) and *complex cells,* which respond maximally to moving stimuli of a particular orientation [Hubel 62]. This sensitivity to orientation means the receptive fields of cortical cells are not concentrically circular, as in the retina. For example, the receptive field of a simple cell is an elongated shape with discrete excitatory (ON-response) and inhibitory (OFF-response) zones. Figure 8.9 illustrates some examples of how these zones are arranged in order to achieve their orientation-selective nature. For example, Figure 8.9(b) will be maximally sensitive to a vertical edge and least sensitive to a horizontal edge. In general, a deviation of about 15 degrees from a cell's preferred orientation is enough to render a feature undetectable to that cell [Sekuler 94].

Complex cells are also sensitive to the orientation of a contrast gradient. However, the position of the edge within its receptive field is not as important as it is for simple cells. Edges of the preferred orientation can be detected anywhere within the cell's receptive field. In addition, complex cells respond strongly to the presence of a rapidly moving edge. Often this response is selective for a particular direction of movement through the cell's receptive field.

8.3.4 SENSITIVITY TO VISUAL DETAIL

Knowing the basic physiology of the human visual system, we can take a more detailed look at the implications of this design and their effect on the degree of spatial detail we can perceive.

Spatial Resolution

The size of a cell's receptive field determines the size of stimulus to which it is optimally sensitive. Throughout all three of the vision processing sites we find collections

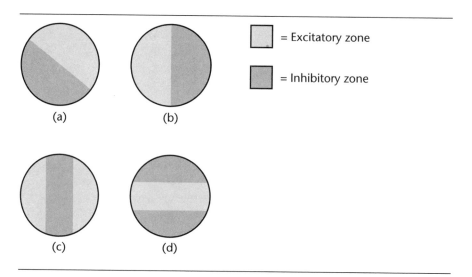

Figure 8.9   (a–d) Example receptive field layouts of four simple cortical cells, illustrating the orientation-selective nature of these cells [Reddy 97].

of cells that exhibit a range of receptive field sizes, thus providing sensitivity to a range of stimulus sizes. Clearly, the smallest receptive field size ultimately determines the limit of resolution of the human visual system. For example, the spacing and pooling of photoreceptors in the retina (which form the inputs to the ganglion cells) will impose the primary limit on how much detail we can perceive. In the most densely packed region of the retina, photoreceptors subtend around 0.5 minutes of *visual arc,* or solid angle, on the retinal surface. Not surprisingly, therefore, we find that the eye can detect detail down to a size of about 0.5 minute of arc [Humphreys 89].

We refer to measures of visual arc frequently throughout this chapter. It is therefore useful to determine the size of a degree of visual arc. One way to define this is that 1 cm at a 57-cm distance subtends 1 degree of arc. This leads to a rough rule (quite literally a "rule of thumb"): one degree is roughly the apparent width of your thumb at arm's length. Remember, 1 degree = 60 minutes of arc.

Variation Across the Retina

The eye's sensitivity to the size of a stimulus is not uniform across the entire retina. Instead, we find that a very small part of the retina, known as the *fovea,* has the ability to resolve the smallest features (see Figure 8.5). However, this ability degrades in proportion to *retinal eccentricity* (angular distance from the center of the retina) such that in the peripheral field the retina has very poor discrimination of fine detail. Our ability to resolve detail is greatest within the central foveal region, which subtends approximately 5.2 degrees of arc [Zeki 93]. Visual acuity drops off significantly, but smoothly, toward the periphery, with about a 35-fold difference between the fovea and the periphery [Nakayama 90]. Within the fovea, there is an even smaller region, known as the *foveola*, that forms the flat pit of the fovea, and subtends only about 1.4 degrees. The foveola contains no rods and is believed to be instrumental in our highly developed analytical skills, such as reading.

This phenomenon means that whenever we wish to focus our attention onto an object we must perform a combination of head and eye rotations so that the light reflected from that object is projected onto the foveae of our retinas. This ensures that we see the object in the highest detail. The peripheral regions of the retina, though less sensitive to visual detail, are more sensitive to movement. This provides humans with a highly adapted balance between acuity and motion sensitivity.

Many physiological features of the visual system vary with retinal eccentricity. These include the following.

- The concentration of cells varies dramatically across the retina. From a total of about 1 million ganglion cells in each eye, about 100,000 of these are located in the fovea [Ferwerda 01].

- The receptive field size of retinal ganglion cells increases linearly with eccentricity [Kelly 84]. This is because the degree of photoreceptor pooling for ganglion cells varies with eccentricity. The 1:1 correspondence between cones and ganglion cells at the fovea increases to 7:1 in the periphery [Cowan 85].

- The visual cortex devotes most of its processing power to the foveal region of the retina. Drasdo estimates that 80% of all cortical cells are devoted to the central 10 degrees of the visual field [Drasdo 77].

Temporal Sensitivity

The human vision system can resolve less detail in a moving object than in an object stabilized on the fovea. The result is the familiar sensation of objects blurring as they move past our point of fixation, or as we pan our head to fixate on another target. Murphy has proposed that the eye's inability to track rapidly moving targets accurately may cause this blurring effect by causing a slippage in the retinal image [Murphy 78]. However, the more recent studies of Tyler [Tyler 85] suggest that the photoreceptors themselves limit our sensitivity to temporal detail [Nakayama 90]. The process of detecting motion implies an integration of a moving object's stimulus energy over time, and this integration process may destroy the visual information for precise features.

8.3.5 THE MULTICHANNEL MODEL

The most widely accepted contemporary theory of spatial vision is that of the *multichannel model*. Developed from the work of Enroth-Cugell and Robson [Enroth-Cugell 66] and Campbell [Campbell 68], this theory essentially proposes that the visual system processes the retinal image simultaneously at several different spatial scales.

Most naturally occurring scenes contain visual information at a number of different scales. For example, in the case of a forest, the outline of all trees provides a coarse degree of detail. We could then focus on each tree individually, or we could concentrate on the finer detail of the leaves on a single tree. The multichannel model suggests that the visual system extracts all of these different scales of information in a scene simultaneously, and that these are later combined by the higher vision processes to assemble our final percept for the particular scene.

This theory agrees with our knowledge of the neural design of the human visual system. As we have seen, the size of a neuron's receptive field defines the size of stimulus to which it is maximally sensitive. Each stage of early vision comprises cells with a wide range of receptive field sizes, and thus able to detect a wide range of detail. In this respect, we can define a *channel* as simply a class of neurons with a certain receptive field size.

It is also believed that the various components of vision—form, color, movement, and depth—are transmitted independently via separate channels to the visual cortex [Livingstone 88]. This behavior helps to describe one of the intriguing dualities of the human visual system—a fine-detail system sensitive to color, and a motion system sensitive to luminance changes but less sensitive to visual detail.

Experts disagree on precisely how many channels exist within the visual system [Heeley 91] [Caelli 85] [Harvey 81] [Wilson 79], but the major point is that the multichannel model predicts that information is analyzed independently by a number of parallel channels, each of which is tuned to a particular level of detail.

8.4 MEASURING VISUAL SENSITIVITY

8.4.1 CONTRAST GRATINGS AND SPATIAL FREQUENCY

A large body of perceptual psychology literature focuses on the perceptibility of visual stimuli. The simplest relation established in this literature is *Weber's law*, which predicts the minimum detectable difference in luminance between a test spot on a uniform visual field. Weber's law states that at daylight levels the threshold difference in luminance increases linearly with background luminance. Interesting scenes are not uniform, however, but contain complex frequency content. Outside a small frequency range, the threshold sensitivity predicted by Weber's law drops off significantly. Since the pioneering work of Schade [Schade 56], the most common experimental device for examining the limits of vision has been the *contrast grating*. This is a regular pattern in which intensity varies sinusoidally between two extreme luminance values, L_{max} and L_{min} (see Figure 8.10). Two principle inde-

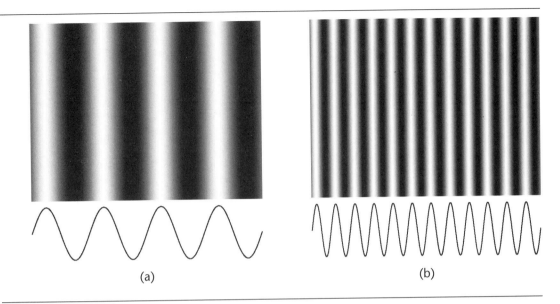

Figure 8.10   An illustration of two contrast gratings displaying: (a) a low and (b) higher spatial frequency. The curve below each of the gratings shows the sinusoidal nature of the intensity distribution. If grating (a) was positioned to occupy 1 degree of visual arc, it would have a spatial frequency of 4 c/deg [Reddy 97].

pendent factors affect the perceptibility of a contrast grating: its *contrast* and *spatial frequency*. Contrast grating studies use *Michaelson contrast*, defined as $(L_{max} - L_{min})/(L_{max} + L_{min})$ and ranging from 0.0 to 1.0, and define spatial frequency as the number of cycles per degree of visual arc. For example, a high spatial frequency implies a short distance between bars, and hence represents a stimulus of high detail.

For a number of different contrast gratings, the limits of human vision can be investigated and recorded in terms of these two parameters. This is normally done by allowing the subject to vary the contrast of a grating until it is deemed to be at threshold. That is, they can no longer resolve discrete bars [Lamming 91a]. Vision researchers have amassed a great deal of empirical evidence about the ability of the visual system to discern detail through contrast grating studies. For example, Fergus Campbell and colleagues studied how our ability to resolve detail varies in relation to the orientation of a contrast grating [Campbell 66b], whereas others have examined how perceptibility of a contrast grating varies with its velocity across the retina [Kelly 79], its eccentricity [Rovamo 79], the level of background illumination [Kelly 75], and the phase of the grating, which turns out to have no effect for a single grating [Lamming 91b].

8.4.2   THE CONTRAST SENSITIVITY FUNCTION

The *contrast sensitivity function* or *CSF* plots contrast sensitivity against spatial frequency, and so describes the range of perceptible contrast gratings. The CSF is essentially a graph of the results from a series of contrast grating tests. It illustrates the threshold of vision for a single or averaged observer at a number of spatial frequencies. Since the region below the CSF curve represents combinations of spatial frequency and contrast that were perceptible to the subject, the CSF is said to describe a subject's *window of visibility*.

Contrast sensitivity is usually defined as the reciprocal of the *threshold contrast*, which is the level of contrast above which a particular stimulus becomes perceptible. For example, a low threshold contrast implies that the stimulus is perceptible, even when its contrast is low, whereas a high threshold contrast implies that a stimulus must contain high contrast before it becomes perceptible.

Figure 8.11 shows a typical CSF curve. Notice that according to this CSF, contrast sensitivity (and thus the ability to resolve detail) peaks about 3 c/deg, and drops off after this peak until no further detail can be resolved. For example (based on the CSF in Figure 8.11), if we presented the subject with a stimulus of 100 c/deg, they would simply not be able to see it; such a stimulus would be invisible to the eye.

The curve in Figure 8.11 is for static detail presented at the observer's fovea. It is produced using the general formula proposed by Mannos and Sakrison and later adopted by Rushmeier et al., among others [Mannos 74] [Rushmeier 95]. This formula can be represented as follows, where α represents spatial frequency in cycles per degree, and $A(\alpha)$ represents Michelson contrast.

$$A(\alpha) = 2.6(0.0192 + 0.144\alpha)e^{-(0.144\alpha)^{1.1}} \qquad (8.1)$$

If we look at the corresponding curves for moving gratings or eccentric gratings, we find that the CSF shifts toward the y axis in both cases [Nakayama 90] [Koenderink 78b]. Effectively, this means that we can perceive fewer high spatial frequencies, and thus less high detail, under these situations.

Given a mathematical equation to represent the shape of the CSF under various conditions, we can compute the highest spatial frequency an observer should be able to see. This provides us with a metric (spatial frequency) and model (contrast sensitivity) to predict the degree of detail the user of a computer graphics system can see.

8.4.3   AN ASIDE: VISUAL ACUITY

We have seen that our ability to resolve spatial detail is dependent on the contrast and relative size (spatial frequency) of a stimulus. This is most accurately represented using the measure of contrast sensitivity. Another common measure of our spatial resolution is *visual acuity*. Visual acuity is a measure of the smallest detail a person can

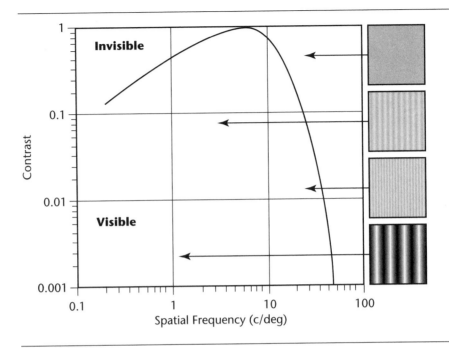

Figure 8.11   An example contrast sensitivity function for static detail produced using Equation 8.1. This represents the size sensitivity of the human visual system in relation to the contrast of the stimulus. The four contrast gratings illustrate the combination of contrast and spatial frequency at certain points in the space.

resolve. It is only a measure of size and does not take into consideration the contrast of a target. Visual acuity is therefore normally assessed under optimal illumination conditions (e.g., black letters on a white background under bright lighting). Generally, contrast sensitivity is a more powerful measure for the following reasons.

1. Of the two, contrast sensitivity provides a more complete model because it takes into consideration the contrast of a stimulus, whereas visual acuity is simply a measure of the smallest resolvable size under ideal illumination conditions.

2. The literature pertaining to contrast sensitivity is more extensive than that for visual acuity. The latter remains a measure of static detail viewed under foveal conditions, whereas much research has investigated effects such as motion and eccentricity on contrast sensitivity.

3. Visual acuity tends to be described in more computationally qualitative terms than contrast sensitivity. The most common measure of visual acuity is the *Snellen fraction*, named after the Dutch doctor, Hermann Snellen, who introduced the

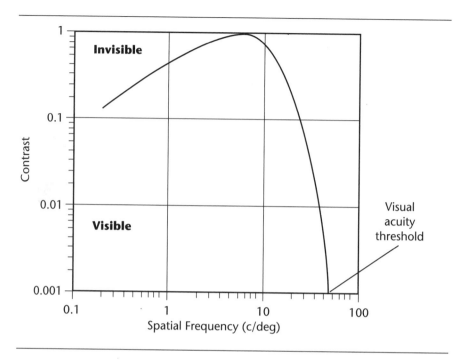

Figure 8.12   A portrayal of how visual acuity can be described in terms of spatial frequency given a subject's contrast sensitivity function.

technique. A Snellen fraction of 20/n is defined as the acuity at which two objects, which subtend 1 minute of arc at n feet, can be perceived as separate at 20 feet [Tipton 84]. Therefore, a person with 20/20 vision is classed as normal, and a person with 20/40 vision can only see a stimulus from 20 feet that a normal person can see from 40 feet. In terms of visual arc, 20/20 vision corresponds to recognizing letters that are 5 minutes of arc [Helman 93].

Note, however, that given an observer's contrast sensitivity we can derive their visual acuity in terms of spatial frequency. This is simply the upper limit of detection; that is, the rightmost point where the CSF meets the x axis. Figure 8.12 illustrates this relationship.

8.4.4   APPLICABILITY OF THE CSF MODEL

We have described the contrast sensitivity function, which provides a simple model of low-level human vision. Later we will describe some systems that apply this model to the LOD process. First, however, we should consider the applicability of the CSF to

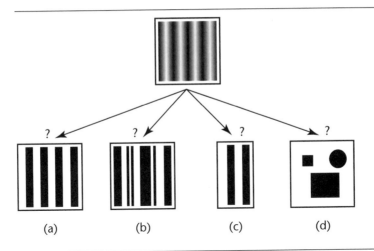

Figure 8.13   How does a simple 1D harmonic contrast grating relate to (a) square-wave gratings, (b) complex gratings, (c) gratings of different periodicity, and (d) 2D gratings [Reddy 97]?

computer-generated imagery. After all, the simple contrast gratings used in CSF experiments bear little resemblance to the images displayed by a 3D computer graphics system. Reddy reviews some of the issues in the use of contrast gratings (also illustrated in Figure 8.13), and argues why the CSF model might reasonably be extended to more complete images [Reddy 97].

- *Modulation:* A contrast grating presents a sine-wave distribution of intensity. However, computer-generated images rarely contain perfectly harmonic features. For example, a simple flat-shaded object would present a square-wave distribution of intensity across the display. We must therefore consider the applicability of a sine-wave grating to square-wave (and other) gratings.

  Beyond the frequency of peak sensitivity, the modulation of a grating has no significant effect on the visibility of that grating. For example, Campbell and Robson found that a square-wave grating is indistinguishable from a sine-wave grating until the third harmonic reaches its own threshold [Campbell 68]. In other words, for the upper regions of the CSF we can analyze a stimulus by referring only to its fundamental harmonic component [Lamming 91b]. Further, the highest perceptible frequency is unaffected by the modulation of a grating. That is, visual acuity is the same in all cases [Campbell 68]. Note, however, that a model based on contrast sensitivity (rather than visual acuity) may need to address this issue for frequencies below the peak, and otherwise may underestimate the correct threshold. Campbell and Robson provide theoretical curves for different waveform modulations.

- *Complexity:* Most computer-generated images involve complex changes of intensity across the display, but a contrast grating is a simple harmonic pattern. However, we can consider the visibility of a complex intensity waveform in terms of the simple harmonic case.

  Campbell and Robson found that the appearance of a compound grating is characterized by the independent contributions from each of the harmonic components. Their results showed that if a compound grating is displayed such that some of its high-frequency components are below threshold, these features will not be perceptible in the compound grating and can be removed without any perceivable change being made to the grating. This finding was one of the major contributing results in the development of the current multichannel model of visual perception. Its implication for our purposes is that the visibility of the component detail in a complex image can be assessed independently in terms of the simple CSF threshold data.

- *Periodicity:* A contrast grating is a periodic sine-wave pattern, normally containing several complete cycles of contrast. However, in applying a perceptual model to computer-generated imagery we will often be concerned with the visibility of an aperiodic region of detail. Can periodicity affect the visibility of a particular spatial frequency? Yes. Coltman showed that the number of cycles in a sine-wave pattern can have a substantial effect on contrast sensitivity [Coltman 60]. This work was later reexamined by Nachmias, who was concerned with the visibility of square-wave patterns at low spatial frequencies (below 10 c/deg) [Nachmias 68]. He found a consistent 60% reduction in sensitivity for single-cycle patterns compared to full gratings. At lower frequencies, then, our sensitivity is reduced for aperiodic gratings. However, our visual acuity is extended for aperiodic versus full gratings. The implication for our work is that the standard CSF data, acquired using extended contrast gratings, may underestimate the sensitivity of a user to detail on a computer screen. Features in a computer-generated image will often represent a half-cycle stimulus; that is, a single peak (or trough) in intensity with respect to the surrounding region. However, [Campbell 69] suggest that the visibility of an aperiodic pattern can theoretically be predicted from that of a sinusoidal grating, and that a simple linear relationship may exist.

- *Dimension:* A contrast grating varies over only one dimension, but images are obviously 2D. We must therefore investigate how to describe features of a 2D image in terms of spatial frequency.

  Spatial frequency, as we have defined it so far, is an inherently 1D measure. It describes the intensity variation over a single cross-section of a display. To describe a 2D feature using this measure, we introduce an orientation parameter for each frequency. A 2D feature is then described by the set of spatial frequencies at all angles (0 to 180 degrees). For example, consider a long, thin object such as a street lamppost. Such an object is considerably taller than it is wide. This object would therefore have a very low vertical frequency (i.e., long vertical distance) and a comparatively high horizontal frequency (i.e., short horizontal distance).

■ *Chromaticity:* Our discussion of the limits of perception has focused on luminance, but clearly computer-generated imagery often includes color. We must therefore ask whether we lose any accuracy by employing achromatic threshold data to our task, and whether we should consider applying color contrast data instead.

We know that the achromatic channel is more effective than the chromatic channels for processing shape [Mullen 85], motion [Anstis 83], and stereoscopic depth [Gregory 77]. For example, Campbell and Gubisch [Campbell 66a] identified the upper spatial limit of the luminance channel as roughly 60 c/deg; whereas Mullen [Mullen 85] found that the red/green upper limit is only about 12 c/deg. This means the achromatic channel can resolve substantially smaller features than the chromatic channels. Thus, although color is clearly an important element of suprathreshold vision [Cavanagh 91], the evidence suggests that ignoring chromatic effects and focusing on luminance is a reasonable approximation, especially when focusing on questions of threshold vision, such as when the user can perceive certain details?

8.4.5 OTHER PERCEPTUAL PHENOMENA

It is important to remember that the CSF model previously described is just that: a model. Human vision is hardly a simple and predictable machine; it is a highly complex, highly nonlinear, imperfectly understood system. The CSF gives us a tool to estimate the perceptibility of visual features, and thus to estimate the ability to distinguish different levels of detail, but it is far from a perfect model of the visual system. Many factors affect our ability to perceive detail, and indeed everybody's visual system is slightly different. In the following sections, we enumerate some of the many factors that affect our perception.

Factors Affecting Visibility

There are many factors beyond eccentricity and velocity that can affect our ability to perceive detail. These are normally dealt with in the vision sciences by introducing the concept of a *standard observer*. This is simply a notional "average" human for whom we can develop general models of perception, normally under optimal conditions.

For example, our contrast sensitivity model pertains only to a standard observer defined as a healthy adult with good vision viewing under good lighting conditions. We justify the notion of a standard observer by noting that most individuals tend to have a visual performance close to this ideal, and that our model reflects a best-case scenario in which perceptibility is nearly maximized. If we use this model to predict visibility in less optimal viewing situations, we will tend to make conservative choices that preserve more detail than necessary.

The following are factors that can affect a user's visual perception. We classify these as *environmental* (related to the state of the environment the user occupies) or *individual* (related to the state of the user's specific visual system) considerations.

Environmental Considerations

- *Background illumination:* The background light intensity used to illuminate a stimulus can substantially affect its visibility. Kelly presents theoretically derived contrast sensitivity functions for an observer under a range of background illuminations [Kelly 75]. These show a degradation of sensitivity in dim lighting conditions. For example, at 3 log cd/m^2 illumination, our visual acuity limit is about 50 c/deg. However, at -3.3 log cd/m^2 it is as low as 2 c/deg. This is equivalent to a drop in visual acuity from 20/10 to 20/300 [Ferwerda 01]. In many applications (e.g., flight simulators) the display environment can be predicted, and the displayed images can be optimized in terms of the user's visual adaptation to this surrounding environment.

- *Light adaptation:* The human eye is sensitive to light intensity over a remarkable range. This is due to the range of photoreceptors in the retina, as well as optical factors such as pupil dilation. Sekuler and Blake offer this example: when entering a dark theater from daylight conditions, your light sensitivity can improve by a factor of about 100,000 [Sekuler 94]. The level of an observer's light adaptation is controlled by the degree of retinal illumination via a feedback system causing a chemical adaptation of photoreceptors. Different photoreceptors take different lengths of time to adapt to a new light intensity. For example, the full dark adaptation period is about 40 minutes for rods, but only about 10 minutes for cones.

- *Stimulus duration:* Stimulus duration has an effect on the contrast sensitivity function. The normal band-pass shape of the CSF occurs at moderate durations of 500 ms, whereas a low pass behavior is found at short durations of 20 ms. Intermediate durations of 50 ms produce a broadly tuned band-pass shape and a shift in the peak toward low spatial frequencies.

- *Display factors:* Since we view computer graphics imagery on a display device, the brightness, contrast, color gamut, and gamma settings of that display will affect the appearance of any stimuli. Clearly the most sophisticated model of human perception is limited by display accuracy, and any attempt to exactly predict perceptibility will be foiled without careful photometric calibration of the display. Fortunately, an approximate estimate of display characteristics (such as the gamma curve) suffices for our purpose, which is simply to guide LOD with a principled perceptual model.

- *Interaction of other senses:* Recent findings have hinted toward complex interactions between the senses. For example, an auditory illusion was reported in *Nature* magazine in which sound affected visual perception under certain circumstances. Subjects were found to incorrectly count a small number of visual stimuli when accompanied by a short beep [Shams 00]. We also know that sound feedback is important for improved perception of virtual events, such as at the point when two virtual objects collide [Astheimer 93].

Individual Considerations

- *Age:* Contrast sensitivity varies as a function of age. For example, an infant's CSF is significantly displaced from an adult's CSF, so that infants see only large, high-contrast objects [Banks 82]. Owsley investigated the contrast sensitivity of adults over a range of ages (20 to 80 years). They found that contrast sensitivity degrades notably over this range. An 80-year-old person, for example, cannot perceive many of the high spatial frequencies perceptible to a 20-year-old [Owsley 83].

- *Color vision:* Color is not perceived equally by everyone. Many people, for example, suffer from color blindness of one type or another. For example, nearly 10% of men have red–green color deficiency [Gregory 90], although this is extremely rare in women [Hurvich 81].

- *Stereoscopic vision:* A surprisingly large percentage of the population cannot perceive depth stereoscopically. That is, they cannot perceive depth as a result of the disparity between the images from each eye. It has been estimated that as many as 1 in 10 people suffer from stereoblindness.

- *Lens aberrations:* Defective vision can result from an eye's inability to accommodate, or adjust the focal length of its lens in order to project a fixated object exactly onto the retina. For example, the lens of a person with *myopic* vision will cause light to converge at a point before the retina. This can cause distortions or blurring of an image, often requiring corrective spectacles.

- *Emotional state:* The emotional state of the observer affects the dilation of their pupils. Since a smaller pupil size reduces the light that can reach the retina, emotional state can cause a drop in the observer's visual acuity [Campbell 65].

- *Experience:* Gregory suggests that our perception of objects may be influenced by a priori knowledge and past experience [Gregory 90]. For example, he speculates that common objects such as oranges and lemons develop a richer and more natural color once they have been recognized as such.

The following sections address certain specific features and anomalies of our visual system, and their impact on our ability to perceive detail.

Hyperacuity

The term *hyperacuity* refers to the paradoxical phenomenon in which certain stimuli can be perceived that are smaller than the size of a single photoreceptor cell. Photoreceptors in the fovea subtend about 25 to 30 seconds of arc (which corresponds to a maximum spatial frequency of about 60 c/deg). However, it has been shown that it

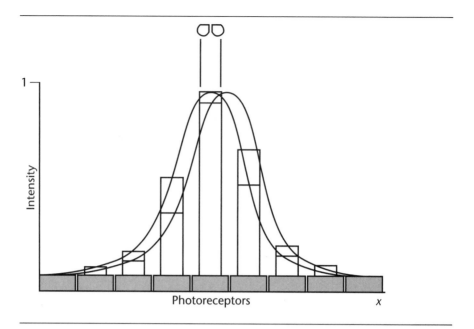

Figure 8.14   Hyperacuity provides highly sensitive position, or phase, discrimination but no greater ability to resolve fine detail.

is possible to discriminate the non–co-linearity of two thick, abutting lines to a resolution of 2 to 5 seconds of arc (referred to as *vernier acuity*). This effect plays an important role in the visibility of aliasing artifacts in computer images. The question therefore arises: need we account for hyperacuity in a perceptual model for guiding LOD?

It is believed that hyperacuity is caused by differences in the mean distribution of light sampled over a number of photoreceptors [Morgan 91]. The effect therefore depends upon the large spatial spread over which two adjacent features extend. Therefore, any isolated feature smaller than a single receptor will still remain undetectable (see Figure 8.14). Thus, hyperacuity gives us a higher positional accuracy between adjacent features (discrimination), but it does not increase the fundamental resolution limit of our visual system (detection).

Since our model predicts the *detection* of features, deciding whether the user can resolve an entire feature, it is largely unaffected by hyperacuity. It is also worth noting that hyperacuity applies chiefly to low-velocity targets at the fovea. For example, Levi et al. [Levi 85] and Schor and Badcock [Schor 85] report that hyperacuity performance degrades rapidly with eccentricity; in fact, more rapidly than contrast sensitivity. Although hyperacuity is an interesting feature of the visual system, it does not invalidate the applicability of the CSF-based model described thus far.

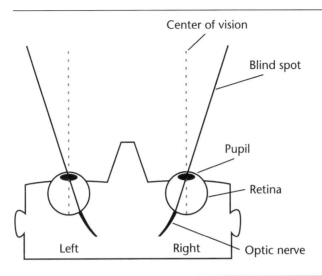

Figure 8.15   The blind spots for both eyes.

The Blind Spot

Another interesting feature of the visual system is the *blind spot,* an area of the retina where all of the axons of the retinal ganglion cells meet to form the optic nerve (see Figure 8.5). There are no photoreceptors in this region, so we cannot detect any light that falls on the blind spot. Furthermore, the angular size of the blind spot is quite large, about 5 degrees [Andrews 91]. This therefore raises the question: could we reduce the detail of objects that fall onto a user's blind spot?

Unfortunately, the answer is "no" under normal stereoscopic vision. The blind spots for both eyes are in different regions of our visual hemisphere (see Figure 8.15). Therefore, any part of a scene within one eye's blind spot will be visible to the other eye. For applications that render a separate image for each eye—such as virtual reality using head-mounted displays or stereo video projection—reducing detail in the blind spot is conceptually possible, but still seems hardly worthwhile. For example, when using discrete LOD, an entire object would have to project onto the blind spot before we could degrade its detail or remove it from the scene.

Saccades

A *saccade* is a rapid movement of the eye to fixate a target onto the fovea (the name comes from the French verb *saccader,* which means "to jerk"). Saccades can occur at velocities of up to 800 deg/s and last for many milliseconds. (A good rule of thumb for the duration of a saccade in milliseconds is 20 plus twice the angular distance traveled (e.g., a 10-degree saccade will last about 40 ms [Robinson 64]). Interestingly, during a saccade we do not experience blurred vision, even though our eyes are moving at very high velocities. This implies we do not perceive detail during a saccade. The term *saccadic suppression* is used to describe this phenomenon. Sekuler and Blake summarize a number of the reasons that have been postulated for this effect [Sekuler 94].

- *Temporal threshold:* We know that certain stimuli become invisible to the eye when they exceed a particular velocity. Perhaps therefore we cannot perceive detail during a saccade simply because the retinal image is moving too fast for our visual system to detect it.

- *Masking:* A large, intense stimulus can affect the visibility of a smaller, dim stimulus if they are presented in the same spatial location closely in time. This effect has been suggested as a reason for saccadic suppression; that is, masking occurs when the eye fixates immediately before and after a saccade.

- *Stimulus uncertainty:* We know that stimuli are more difficult to see if the observer is uncertain of their spatial location. Therefore, if the visual system does not have access to the exact eye position during a saccade, the observer may be unable to correctly resolve the retinal images.

Early 1994 saw a discussion on the USENET newsgroup *sci.virtual-worlds* about the possibility of reducing the detail in a scene during a saccade, on the assumption that the visual system might be unable to detect this change. However, the full benefits are unclear, as is the extent to which we should reduce detail. Our visual system does not "shut down" during a saccade. Gross changes in luminance, such as replacing a scene with a black backdrop, are still noticeable during a saccade.

Ohshima et al. have experimented with this phenomenon, building a system that takes advantage of saccadic suppression [Ohshima 96]. In their approach, the rendering process is simply suspended as the angular velocity of a user's gaze movement exceeds 180 deg/s. However, they do not offer any comment on how visually effective this was, or why they chose the value of 180 deg/s. Despite the work of Ohshima et al., we still lack compelling evidence that LOD systems can effectively exploit saccadic suppression.

Visual Masking

Visual masking describes the perceptual phenomenon that the presence of one visual pattern can affect the visibility of another pattern. For example, a large adjacent stimulus (in time or space) can raise the threshold of a smaller stimulus, meaning that the smaller stimulus must be more intense to be visible. In terms of computer graphics, this means that visual texture can mask small details or aliasing artifacts in an image. For example, Bolin and Meyer illustrated this effect with Figure 8.16,

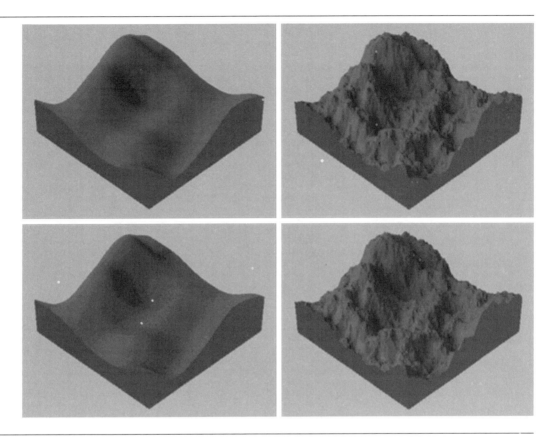

Figure 8.16   Illustrating visual masking of quantization effects by visual texture [Bolin 95]. Copyright © 1995 Association for Computing Machinery, Inc.

in which quantization banding is less apparent on the rough surface than on the smooth surface [Bolin 95]. Similarly, a strongly textured object may be simplified more aggressively than the same object flat-shaded, an effect well known to LOD practitioners.

Visual masking can facilitate detection of stimuli under certain conditions (in particular, when the masking pattern exactly aligns with the stimulus pattern), but generally visual masking increases the detection threshold of stimuli, making them more difficult to see. Therefore, a naive perceptual model that does not incorporate visual masking effects will generally only overcompensate for masked features, conservatively estimating some features to be perceptible when in fact they are masked. We do not ignore visual masking effects for lack of knowledge on how to model them. For example, Ferwerda et al. have described a visual masking model for computer graphics [Ferwerda 97]. Their model predicts how changes in the contrast, spatial

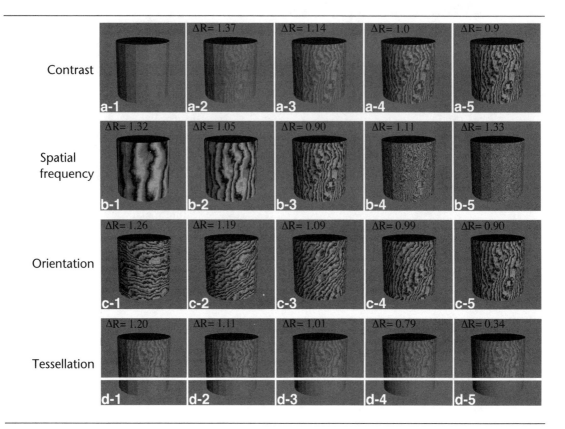

Figure 8.17   Applying Ferwerda et al.'s masking model to predict how texture masking affects the visibility of shading artifacts in a tessellated model. Values of ΔR less than 1.0 indicate a result imperceptible from a nontessellated model [Ferwerda 97]. Copyright © 1997 Association for Computing Machinery, Inc.

frequency, and orientation of a texture pattern alter the masking effect (see Figure 8.17). Unfortunately, current models of visual masking remain too computationally expensive to use in run-time management of LOD. This is an important area for future research, and interested readers may want to refer to Ferwerda [Ferwerda 01] for further discussion of masking issues.

Temporal Thresholds

So far we have considered only the spatial aspects of vision for LOD, but many temporal perceptual issues arise when switching between different representations of a model. The human visual system is sensitive to motion, particularly in the peripheral field where the motion-sensitive rods dominate. This may have developed as an evolutionary need to quickly detect prey (or predators!) moving around us. In any case, we are highly adapted to detect flicker (*flicker sensitivity*) in our peripheral field, and we possess a reflex reaction to turn toward any such sharp visual changes. Related to this is an individual's *critical fusion (or flicker) frequency* (CFF), the highest frequency at which the flicker in a light source can be detected. At frequencies above the CFF, the light source appears to be steady and continuous. For example, fluorescent lights are designed to flicker at 120 Hz, well above the typical CFF, so that the light is perceived as continuous. A related temporal effect is *visual persistence,* in which events tend to blur in time according to the temporal impulse response function. Also note that visual masking can occur in time, with the temporal proximity of a large feature making a smaller feature less perceptible.

All of this raises issues for LOD because the switch between two different levels of detail may be noticeable, even when we predict the actual spatial change to be imperceptible. Unfortunately, there has been much less relevant research done on temporal sensitivity and it is not yet clear how important or relevant this effect is for LOD, or how we can effectively model it in our computer systems. Given a practical formula relating changes in spatial frequency and contrast over different time periods, we could build this into our model and predict whether a sudden switch might be visible, or perhaps guide an alpha-blend or geomorph between models to make the transition imperceptible. At the moment, however, we have no principled way to evaluate the benefit of these techniques, and this is certainly an important area for future research.

8.4.6 FURTHER READING

We have tried to provide some background on the most relevant foundations of perceptual psychology, with a focus on describing a simple model applicable to managing level of detail. Clearly a single chapter can only scratch the surface of vision science and perceptual psychology, or even the topic of perceptual models in computer graphics. The interested reader can refer to a number of other reviews and resources for further reading; we mention a few of them here. James Ferwerda's article "Elements of Early Vision for Computer Graphics" provides an excellent review for computer graphics developers and offers another perspective on many of the topics introduced here [Ferwerda 01]. Colin Ware's book on information visualization provides an essential resource on perceptual issues for data visualization [Ware 99]. Other noteworthy books on the subject of perception include that of Robert Sekuler and Randolph Blake (*Perception* [Sek 94]), Brian Wandell (*Foundations of Vision* [Wandell 95]), and Stephen Palmer (*Vision Science: Photons to Phenomenology* [Palmer 99]).

8.5 MANAGING LOD THROUGH VISUAL COMPLEXITY

We have described a model of contrast sensitivity that can be applied to a computer graphics system. To optimize spatial detail using such a model requires a rendering system that can estimate a scene's perceptual content and quantify the efficacy of an observer's perception. Together, these two facilities enable the rendering system to judge which details a user can perceive in a computer-generated scene. For our CSF-based model, we therefore require the following:

1. An efficient mathematical formulation to predict the contrast sensitivity of a standard observer under various visual conditions (e.g., variable velocity and eccentricity)

2. A mechanism to concisely describe an LOD in terms of its component spatial frequencies (c/deg)

For example, Figure 8.18 shows three different levels of detail for a single die model. In each case we have calculated the spatial frequency content of the LOD for the viewpoint shown, with regions of high frequency (and thus high detail) to the right. The vertical axis denotes the number of features in the image with a particular spatial frequency. In the case of the lowest LOD, the graph contains only three low spatial frequencies. These represent the three visible faces of the die, which are the only features at that level. In the medium LOD, the three low spatial frequencies are joined by a batch of higher spatial frequencies, which represent the spots on the die. Finally, the highest LOD includes the same trends as the other two instances, but also adds some even higher spatial frequencies induced by the added detail of curvature at the edges of the die. The key observation: if this die were presented to a user in a situation in which they could only perceive frequencies below 0.01 c/pixel, we could select the lowest LOD model (Figure 8.18(c)) and the user would be unable to perceive any change.

To reiterate, the two major tasks underlying a perceptually based LOD system are evaluating the user's limit of vision under different visual circumstances and calculating the spatial frequency component of LOD features. We can take two principal approaches to computing the user's limit of vision. The following section presents a mathematical equation for visual acuity that can take into account the peripheral extent and velocity of a feature. This generic model describes an average adult with good vision, and is easily computable in real time. An alternative approach builds a model of a given user's visual performance using a series of psychophysical tests, interpolating this model at run-time. Sen et al. proposed such a model using a set of experimentally acquired acuity data [Sen 95]. To be most accurate, however, the tests should be done on a per-user basis, and should be performed immediately before the simulation so that the same environmental lighting conditions and user adaptation states are effective.

The second task requires evaluating the perceptual content of a model at each frame in terms of spatial frequency. Many simplification systems base their measure

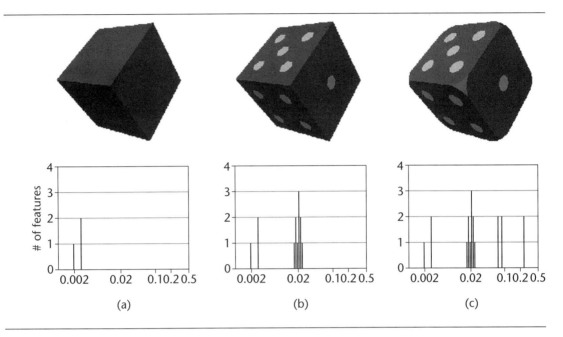

Figure 8.18   (a–c) An example spatial-frequency analysis of three LODs, showing screen-relative spatial frequency in units of c/pixel [Reddy 97].

of perceived detail on the geometry of an object, essentially calculating the projected screen-space extent of an object or feature to determine its spatial frequency [Funkhouser 93b] [Ohshima 96] [Luebke 01]. This has the benefit of being well defined and computable at run-time, but may not incorporate effects such as texture mapping or lighting conditions. On the other hand, some researchers have proposed systems that use an image-based analysis of the rendered image in preprocess [Reddy 97] [Lindstrom 00b]. This has the advantage of acting on the actual stimuli presented to the user's visual system, but can be computationally expensive to calculate and can potentially miss features, since a limited number of viewpoints must be chosen to render and analyze. Chapter 9 deals more with this issue of assessing the spatial complexity of objects.

8.6 Modeling Contrast Sensitivity

As we have seen, the CSF predicts the ability of the human visual system to resolve a stimulus based on its spatial frequency and contrast. However, these curves are produced by interpolating tabulated values obtained through empirical studies. To usefully incorporate these results into a computer graphics system, we may prefer to find a mathematical model to describe the shape of the human CSF. Donald H. Kelly developed a conceptual model to describe the spatial frequency characteristics of retinal receptive fields at high luminance levels, and showed that this can be used to model the sine-wave sensitivity of the visual system [Kelly 75]. Kelly defines the following abstract formula for contrast sensitivity, where α represents spatial frequency in cycles per degree (recall that contrast sensitivity is the reciprocal of threshold contrast).

$$F(\alpha) = \alpha^2 e^{-\alpha} \tag{8.2}$$

With suitable scaling factors, this general equation can be used to model the shape of the CSF under various viewing conditions. We have already seen Mannos and Sakrison's model for static, foveal detail in Equation 8.1, which follows this general formula. Here we examine how to incorporate the effects of velocity and eccentricity.

8.6.1   INCORPORATING VELOCITY INTO THE MODEL

The surface produced by mapping the CSF over a range of velocities is called the *spatiotemporal threshold surface*. This has been investigated by a number of vision researchers over the years. The model presented here is based on one developed at SRI International by Kelly. It is worth noting, however, that Burr and Ross conducted similar experiments to those of Kelly, and that their principal results correlate almost exactly with his [Burr 82].

Kelly made extensive studies of the spatiotemporal surface under conditions of stabilized vision, using a noncontact method of accurately stabilizing the retinal image to enable measurements without the artifacts introduced by uncontrolled eye movements [Kelly 79]. The resulting data indicated that the shape of the CSF remains essentially constant for velocities above 0.1 deg/s, and only undergoes translation with increased velocity. Kelly subsequently extended Equation 8.2 to model, as follows, the spatiotemporal threshold surface for velocities above 0.1 deg/s, where v represents velocity measured in units of deg/s, and α represents spatial frequency in units of c/deg.

$$G(\alpha, v) = (6.1 + 7.3|\log_{10}(v/3)^3|)v\alpha^2 e^{-2\alpha(v+2)/45.9}$$

However, Reddy notes that he was unable to reproduce the empirical data Kelly (and others) presents using this formula [Reddy 97]. He modified Equation 8.8, as follows, to more accurately model his findings.

$$G(\alpha, v) = (250.1 + 299.3|\log_{10}(v/3)^3|)v\alpha^2 10^{-5.5\alpha(v+2)/45.9} \tag{8.3}$$

It is worth noting that Wilson and Manjeshwar's more recent studies lend credence to Reddy's reformulation of Kelly's equation [Wilson 99]. α in Equation 8.3 is plotted in

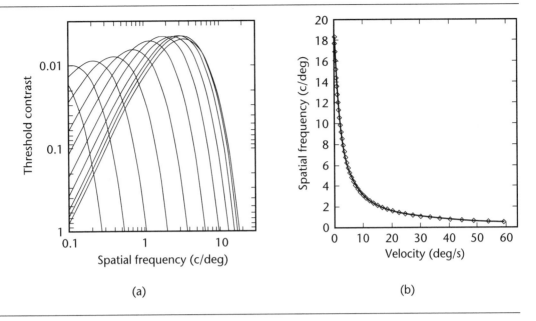

Figure 8.19   (a) Contrast sensitivity functions for velocities of 0.125, 0.25, 0.5, 1, 2, 4, 8, 16, 32, 64, and 128 deg/s (from right to left), calculated using Equation 8.3. (b) The highest perceptible spatial frequency (visual acuity) for a range of velocities; that is, the upper point of intersection with the x axis for each of the curves in (a). The data points represent calculated intersection points, with the curve illustrating the interpolated relationship [Reddy 97].

Figure 8.19(a) for a number of velocities. From this we can observe that the effect of velocity on the CSF is to push the curve further toward the y axis for higher velocities. This matches what we expect. That is, we can see less high detail with increasing velocity. Figure 8.19(b) portrays this relationship more clearly by plotting the highest perceptible spatial frequency for a range of velocities.

8.6.2   INCORPORATING ECCENTRICITY INTO THE MODEL

Contrast sensitivity declines with increasing eccentricity. However, the general shape of the spatiotemporal surface is consistent across the visual field [Virsu 82] [Koenderink 78a] [Kelly 84]. This implies that we can predict the contrast sensitivity for any region of the retina by simply scaling the foveal response with a factor based on eccentricity.

Rovamo and Virsu confirmed this when they showed that visual acuity can be accurately predicted for any eccentricity by applying a constant scaling factor

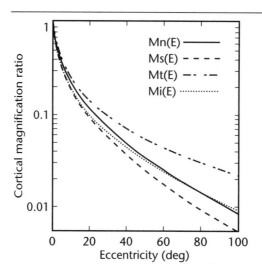

Figure 8.20   A graph of Equations 8.4 through 8.7, which define the cortical magnification factor, M, for each cardinal half-meridian of the retina [Reddy 97].

[Rovamo 79], referred to as the *cortical magnification factor* (M) (see Figure 8.20). To incorporate eccentricity into our model of spatiotemporal contrast sensitivity, we simply need to apply this cortical magnification factor to Equation 8.3.

However, M is not dependent simply on the radial distance from the fovea, because the eye's peripheral sensitivity is not circularly symmetric [Regan 83]. For example, there are marked asymmetries between the nasal and temporal retina beyond 20 degrees [Sutter 91]. Taking this into consideration, Rovamo and Virsu produced the following four equations to characterize M for each principal half-meridian of the retina.

$$\text{Nasal:} \quad M_N = M_0/(1 + 0.33E + 0.00007E^3) \qquad 0 \le E \le 60 \text{ deg} \tag{8.4}$$

$$\text{Superior:} \quad M_S = M_0/(1 + 0.42E + 0.00012E^3) \qquad 0 \le E \le 45 \text{ deg} \tag{8.5}$$

$$\text{Temporal:} \quad M_T = M_0/(1 + 0.29E + 0.0000012E^3) \quad 0 \le E \le 80 \text{ deg} \tag{8.6}$$

$$\text{Inferior:} \quad M_I = M_0/(1 + 0.42E + 0.000055E^3) \qquad 0 \le E \le 60 \text{ deg} \tag{8.7}$$

Here, M_0 is the value of magnification for the most central point in the fovea. We can simply instantiate $M_0 = 1$ because we are treating this as a scaling factor. A sophisticated system might take into account the relevant region of the retina that is being considered and apply the appropriate value of M for that region. Alternatively, to simplify the relationship, we could exclusively use the most sensitive region's M, with the knowledge that the other regions will not exceed this sensitivity; that is, Equation 8.6 (M_T). Furthermore, it would be reasonable to ignore the cubic term in Equation 8.6. This only becomes significant at large eccentricities; and even when E = 100 degrees, there would only be roughly a 1% error [Watson 83] [Kelly 84] [Tyler 85]. We can therefore define the cortical magnification factor for our purposes as

$$M(E) = 1/(1 + 0.29E). \tag{8.8}$$

Incorporating this equation into our model for contrast sensitivity gives

$$H(\alpha, v, E) = G(\alpha, v)M(E) = G(\alpha, v)/(1 + 0.29E).$$

8.6.3 MODELING VISUAL ACUITY

Given a model of contrast sensitivity, we can describe visual acuity in terms of spatial frequency by calculating the high-frequency limit (i.e., the rightmost point in our graphs where the CSF intersects the x axis). Beyond this point, detail is imperceptible regardless of the stimulus contrast. Figure 8.19(b) illustrates this notion by plotting the velocity of a stimulus against the highest spatial frequency perceptible at that velocity. As this figure shows, visual acuity drops precipitously as a stimulus moves with greater velocity, up to about 10 deg/s, and then begins to level off asymptotically. This implies solving the equation $H(\alpha, v, E) = 1$ in terms of α (i.e., finding the spatial frequency when a grating becomes imperceptible at the highest contrast of 1.0, and at the specified velocity and eccentricity). Reddy presents the following such model for visual acuity, based on the previously cited work and various psychophysical studies [Reddy 97] [Reddy 01]:

$$G(v) = \begin{cases} 60.0 & \text{where } v \leq 0.825 \text{ deg}/s \\ 57.69 - 27.78 \log_{10}(v) & \text{where } 118.3 \geq v > 0.825 \text{ deg}/s \\ 0.1 & \text{where } v > 118.3 \text{ deg}/s \end{cases}$$

$$M(e) = \begin{cases} 1.0 & \text{where } e \leq 5.79 \text{ deg} \\ 7.49/(0.3e + 1)^2 & \text{where } e > 5.79 \text{ deg} \end{cases} \tag{8.9}$$

$$H(v, e) = G(v)M(e)$$

8.6.4 INCORPORATING THE DISPLAY INTO THE MODEL

Clearly the resolution of the display device will limit the detail that can be presented to the user's visual system. In essence, we want to take the minimum of the eye's contrast sensitivity function and the display's modulation transfer function (a measure of the faithfulness and clarity with which the display reproduces the detail in the graphics signal). If dealing only with visual acuity, we can calculate the highest spatial frequency (smallest detail) the device can display without aliasing (known in signal processing as the *Nyquist limit*) and use this to threshold all spatial frequency values. In effect, this highest spatial frequency is dictated by the visual arc subtended by a single pixel. We thus augment our model of visual acuity in Equation 8.9 to account for the maximum spatial frequency of the display, ξ (c/deg):

$$H'(v, e) = \begin{cases} \xi & \text{where } \xi \leq H(v, e) \\ H(v, e) & \text{where } \xi > H(v, e) \end{cases}$$

Note that for antialiased or *supersampled* images the Nyquist limit is a function not of pixel density but sample density. In other words, detail smaller than a pixel may still contribute to the final image.

A simple way to calculate the value of ξ for a display is to calculate the highest spatial frequency of a single pixel. For example, if we know that the display has a field of view of 70 x 40 degrees, and the screen resolution is 1,280 x 1,024 pixels, we know that each pixel subtends roughly 0.0547 x 0.0391 degrees. The smallest single complete contrast cycle occupies 2 pixels (a light pixel and then a dark pixel). Therefore, we must halve these angular values to get numbers in units of cycles per degree (i.e., the horizontal and vertical spatial frequencies of a single pixel are 0.0273 x 0.0195 c/deg). We could therefore choose the highest of these two frequencies as the display's highest spatial frequency (i.e., $\xi = 0.0273$ c/deg).

8.6.5   VISUALIZING THE EFFECT OF THE PERCEPTUAL MODEL

With the previously cited models of visual perception taken from the vision literature, we now have mathematical models to assess how much detail a user might perceive under a number of circumstances, but what do these models mean in practice? How much detail do these models predict that we can safely remove from a scene?

Reddy produced a visualization of how much detail we can actually perceive under various circumstances by removing detail in a bitmapped image that our model predicts to be imperceptible [Reddy 01]. The visualization calculates the highest perceptible spatial frequency at each pixel according to its velocity and distance from the fovea. It then blurs that pixel using a Gaussian filter with a kernel size equivalent to the threshold frequency. The resulting image illustrates the degree of detail actually perceptible to the human eye. The visualization code is included on the companion Web site and is publicly available at *www.martinreddy.net/percept/*.

Figure 8.21 applies this visualization to an image of a koala bear [Reddy 01]. Reddy assumed that this image occupies just over half the viewer's visual field, at 150 x 100 degrees. Figure 8.21(a) shows the original image for reference. In Figure 8.21(b), the periphery of the image is degraded according to Equation 8.8, with the user's gaze centered on the koala's nose. Figure 8.21(c) adds the effect of a 50-deg/s velocity component.

(a)

(b)

(c)

Figure 8.21   The effect of combining eccentricity and velocity perceptual optimizations on an image. Image (a) is the original image, (b) includes eccentricity-based blurring, and (c) includes both eccentricity- and velocity-based blurring (50 deg/s) [Reddy 01]. Copyright ©2001 IEEE.

This example shows a noticeable peripheral degradation effect on the detail of the scene, removing subtle nuances of the tree bark and the finer detail of the leaves in the far edges of the image. However, only when we also incorporate the effect of velocity do we see truly drastic reductions in detail that could be usefully taken advantage of in a 3D graphics system. For example, in Figure 8.21(c) we could drastically degrade, or possibly completely remove, many of the leaves and branches around the edges of the scene.

8.7 EXAMPLE IMPLEMENTATIONS

This final section of the chapter examines some recent LOD systems incorporating perceptual factors, based on models of visual perception such as those presented in this chapter.

8.7.1 PERCEPTUALLY MODULATED LOD

Reddy was the first to develop a LOD system based directly on a principled model of visual perception [Reddy 97] [Reddy 98]. The models described in this book derive largely from his work. His implementation, based on a discrete LOD approach, assessed the spatial frequencies in each LOD using a simple image-based metric on images rendered offline from a sphere of cameras, similar to the algorithm detailed in Section 5.4. Reddy used "*just noticeable difference*" models to extract all perceptually atomic features, taking their pixel extents and the display field of view to evaluate the spatial frequency of each of these features. At run-time, these precomputed frequencies were interpolated at each frame to give an estimate of spatial frequency for a specific object orientation. Using Equation 8.9 to model visual acuity, the system selected the highest resolution LOD such that the spatial change it would induce is below the user's threshold frequency for the specific velocity and eccentricity.

Reddy performed a number of psychophysical studies to evaluate the ability of the perceptual models to predict imperceptible details. Using two-alternative forced choice (2AFC) methods, 20 subjects each performed 64 trials testing whether they could perceive various simple stimuli at different sizes, eccentricities, and velocities. The results confirmed the model's ability to predict perceptibility of features. The collected psychophysical data were used to refine the perceptual models and ultimately led to Equation 8.9.

Reddy also performed task performance studies to compare the benefit of the perceptual LOD system versus a system without LOD. Users were navigated through an environment of randomly positioned objects, with their gaze direction offset from their heading direction. The users had to determine whether they were heading to the left or right of the gaze direction, a task that gets easier with larger angular differences. Reddy found that the perceptually based LOD system substantially improved the subjects' ability to perform the task, allowing them to resolve gaze/heading angles three times smaller and decreasing their time to make a choice by a factor of 1.67.

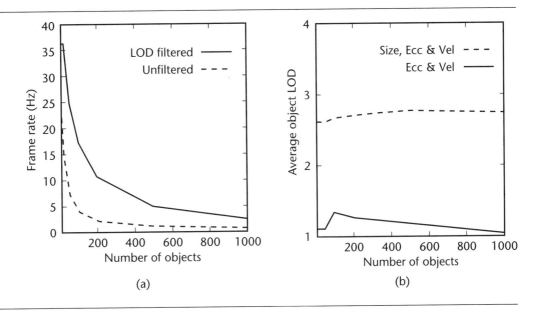

Figure 8.22   (a) Average frame rate for Reddy's system under normal unfiltered conditions (the broken line) and when perceptual LOD optimizations were employed (the solid line). (b) Comparison of average LOD during a trial with and without size optimizations, where 1 is the lowest resolution model [Reddy 97].

These improvements result from the increase in frame rate. Using LOD increased the system frame rate by up to a factor of 5 (see Figure 8.22(a)). Reddy investigated this improvement factor further to examine the extent to which each of the perceptual components—size, velocity, and eccentricity—contributed to the overall improvement in frame rate. He found that using eccentricity or velocity on their own was unprofitable, whereas combining the effect of both of these provided a far greater improvement. Nevertheless, the size component was by far the dominant factor in reducing detail, contributing 90 to 95% of the reduction in the scenario tested (see Figure 8.22(b)). Reddy conjectured that a gaze-directed view-dependent system would provide greater opportunity for the perceptual model to improve the frame rate.

8.7.2   IMPERCEPTIBLE GAZE-DIRECTED SIMPLIFICATION

Luebke et al. developed a view-dependent LOD system augmented with the CSF perceptual model presented in this chapter [Luebke 01]. They extended their view-dependent simplification framework [Luebke 97] to evaluate vertex merge operations according to the worst-case contrast and spatial frequency the merge could induce

Figure 8.23   The Stanford Bunny model, rendered from the same viewpoint with different gaze points. The original model contains 69,591 polygons; the simplified versions contain 34,321 polygons (right) and 11,726 polygons (left). At a field of view of 46 degrees, these simplifications were imperceptible [Luebke 00a]. Copyright ©2000 University of Virginia.

in the final image. Merge operations were only performed when the resulting image was predicted to be indistinguishable from the original. In addition, their system incorporated a silhouette test to account for the high contrast at object silhouettes. As a result, their algorithm preserved silhouettes, providing more detail around the edges of object. This is a desirable attribute in an LOD system, since the human visual system deduces much about an object's shape from its silhouette. Luebke et al. also presented a budget-based mode in which simplifications were ordered according to the distance at which they would become perceptible, allowing perceptual best-effort rendering to a polygon budget. Another interesting aspect of their work was the optional incorporation of an eye tracker to provide gaze-directed rendering.

The authors performed 2AFC user studies to verify the imperceptibility of the resulting simplifications. These experiments provided encouraging indicators of the potential of gaze-directed rendering (see Figure 8.23). They also report that the fine granularity of view-dependent simplification seems to greatly improve on previous results by Ohshima and by Reddy [Ohshima 96] [Reddy 97]. However, they also report that the overall rendering speedup they experienced was less than they believe to be possible. In practice, the LODs created by their system were overly conservative, and could often be reduced by a factor of 2 to 3 while remaining imperceptible. They cite the need for improved perceptual models and more accurate methods to evaluate spatial frequency and contrast in view-dependent LOD.

In other work, Luebke applied the same perceptually driven framework to a completely different rendering paradigm: the point-based rendering system *QSplat*

| (a) | (b) |

Figure 8.24   Image (a) shows Qsplat's high-quality rendering, and image (b) shows a perceptually driven Qsplat. In the latter case, the user's gaze is resting on Lucy's torch. Splats drawn in blue have been simplified [Luebke 00b]. Copyright ©2000 University of Virginia. Stanford 3-D Scanning Repository.

[Rusinkiewicz 00]. Their preliminary results were encouraging. Although QSplat's standard high-quality mode refines the model until each sample is no larger than a pixel, Luebke reports that they were often able to use much larger sample sizes (several pixels across) imperceptibly because of locally low contrast (see Figure 8.24).

8.7.3   PERCEPTUALLY OPTIMIZED 3D GRAPHICS

Reddy revisited his earlier perceptual LOD system in more recent work, describing a view-dependent level-of-detail system for rendering dense terrain meshes using these perceptual models [Reddy 01]. This system refines the terrain at each frame, starting with a single polygon that extends across the entire area. If this polygon was determined to be perceptible to the user, the polygon was broken up into four quadrants and the visibility of each of these smaller polygons was recursively checked. The visibility of a polygon was determined by projecting each of its four vertices into screen coordinates and then transforming these into an extent in units of degrees. Using the eccentricity (degrees), velocity (deg/s), and angular extent of a pixel (degrees), Reddy calculated in pixels the maximum stimulus size that should be perceptible to the user.

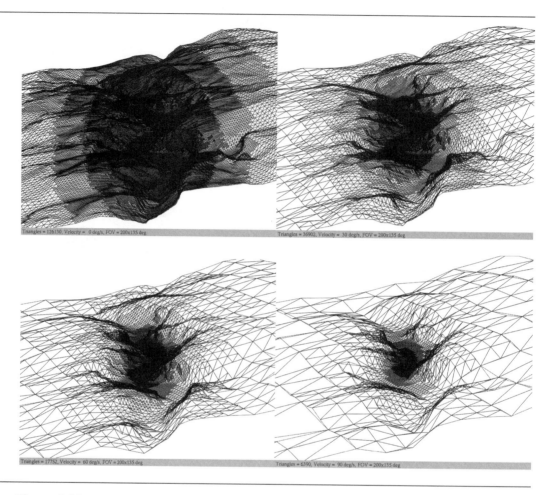

Figure 8.25   Reddy's view-dependent perceptual terrain rendering system with eccentricity optimizations at velocities of 0, 30, 60, and 90 deg/s, respectively [Reddy 01]. Copyright
©2001 IEEE.

If the computed extent of the polygon is smaller than this size, the polygon is assumed
to be imperceptible and no further refinement occurs.

To evaluate this system, Reddy used a large terrain model of Yosemite Valley,
California (1.1 million triangles). For a number of fly throughs of this model, Reddy
recorded the average number of triangles per frame and the average time to render
each frame. The average angular velocity, measured with respect to the center of the
screen, was 50 deg/s. Figure 8.25 shows wireframe renderings of the terrain model

Table 8.1 Comparative performance of the various perceptual optimizations in Reddy's perceptually based view-dependent LOD system.

Optimizations Employed				Average # Triangles Per Frame	Average Frame Time (ms)
Size	Eccentricity	Velocity	View Cull		
No	No	No	No	1,116,720	7,127
No	No	No	Yes	449,828	2,517
Yes	No	No	Yes	59,980	920
Yes	Yes	No	Yes	40,684	650
Yes	No	Yes	Yes	60,850	953
Yes	Yes	Yes	Yes	8,964	161

using the perceptual model to reduce the number of polygons imperceptibly. In the first of these, we see the effect of applying the eccentricity component of our perceptual model, and in the subsequent screen shots we see the added effect of applying global velocities of 30, 60, and 90 deg/s.

Table 8.1 summarizes the results from experiments using different components of the perceptual model. Employing the perceptually based optimizations significantly improved the frame rate of the system. Rendering the full terrain mesh with no optimizations averaged 7,127 ms, whereas applying the viewport culling optimization reduced this by roughly 60%. In terms of our perceptual model, the screen-space size component generated a large increase in performance, improving frame time by a factor of 2.7 over just viewport culling. Adding the eccentricity component to the size-based optimization produced a further 1.4 times improvement, whereas combining velocity and size was not significantly different from using the size criterion alone. However, it is significant to note that combining both velocity and eccentricity with the size component achieves a drastic improvement in frame time: 15 times that of simple viewport culling, and 5.7 times that of the traditional combination of viewport culling and size-based LOD.

8.8 CONCLUSIONS

This chapter has surveyed the workings of the human visual system and has described the *contrast sensitivity function*, or *CSF*, a simple model of low-level vision. This model predicts the ability to resolve spatial detail according to stimulus *spatial frequency* and *contrast*. We have focused on questions appropriate to an LOD system. How much detail can the user perceive? How much detail do we need to display to the user? What other environmental and individual factors can affect perception, and what perceptual factors are not accounted for by this model? We have summarized research on perceptually motivated LOD, including criteria such as *eccentricity* (a measure of the degree to which an object exists in the user's peripheral field), and *velocity* (a measure of the apparent speed of an object across the user's retina). We have also mentioned less-studied criteria such as depth-of-field–based LOD. Using this information, LOD researchers have attempted to measure 3D models in terms of their spatial frequency content, and have applied models of the CSF to decide when certain features should be imperceptible to the user. The most difficult task appears to be measuring or estimating spatial frequencies and contrast within a model. Further research is clearly needed in this area. In the following chapter we will examine this issue from a different angle, considering how to assess the visual fidelity of a computer graphics image.

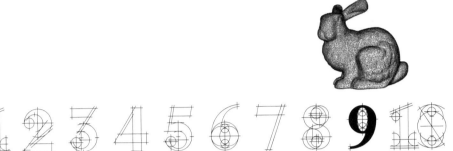

MEASURING VISUAL FIDELITY

Visual fidelity is a fundamental concern in LOD. In simplification, the goal is often to reduce model size while preserving visual fidelity. In run-time LOD, the goal is typically to maintain interactivity while minimizing reductions in visual fidelity. How can visual fidelity be measured? This chapter focuses on this question. In fact, measuring visual fidelity is of importance in many fields related to LOD, including computer graphics, image processing, image compression, and perceptual psychology.

We begin with a review of experimental measures of visual fidelity. The experimental measures set the context for our survey of automatic measures of visual fidelity, which attempt to predict experimental results. Our survey includes measures for static and dynamic imagery, and the 3D models themselves. Measures of dynamic image fidelity are already used in run-time LOD systems, and 3D measures are used for model simplification and in the new field of shape indexing. We conclude with a review of the effectiveness of automatic fidelity measures, and find that even very simple measures work surprisingly well.

279

9.1 WHY MEASURE FIDELITY?

When is a simplification algorithm successful? For many applications, successful simplifications reduce complexity while preserving appearance. A similar definition of success might be adopted for a run-time LOD algorithm. In both cases, the algorithms must define some sort of *automatic measure* of visual fidelity, which they attempt to maximize as they reduce model size or preserve interactivity. We will call such a measure a LooksLike() function.

Most simplification and run-time LOD algorithms use very simple LooksLike() functions, many of which are distance measures and were reviewed in Chapter 3. These error metrics were never intended to be accurate models of visual fidelity, but work fairly well in practice. Still, better LooksLike() functions could be defined, particularly for textured models and preservation of silhouettes and shadows. This chapter reviews many of these proposed improved LooksLike() functions.

9.2 EXPERIMENTAL MEASURES

This section provides a review of several *experimental measures* of visual fidelity that are used to probe the perceptual behavior we wish to model. Some LOD researchers have begun using these experimental measures to answer basic questions about LOD technology. We will consider this research in Section 9.6.

Each of the measures we review here probes different sorts of perceptual behavior. In Chapter 8, we reviewed *low-level* perceptual behavior, involving early processes of the human visual system. *High-level* perception enables identification of what an object is. For a more complete review of experimental methods and measures in perception, see Elmes et al. [Elmes 92]. Throughout this section, we show figures relating experimental measures to visual fidelity. We will discuss the experimental details surrounding these figures in a later section of this chapter.

9.2.1 SEARCH PERFORMANCE

How long does it take a person to find a certain object in an image? Certainly this is fairly directly related to how well that person can see—for example, if the person has forgotten her glasses, it will probably take her longer to find her keys. Measures of search performance rely on this relationship.

In search tasks [Scott 93], a viewer must indicate whether or not a target object is present (and often where it is as well). Like most task measures, search performance has two components: time and accuracy. Time measures the time elapsed between the moment the search began, and the moment it ended. Accuracy measures whether a present target was correctly located, or an absent target correctly determined to

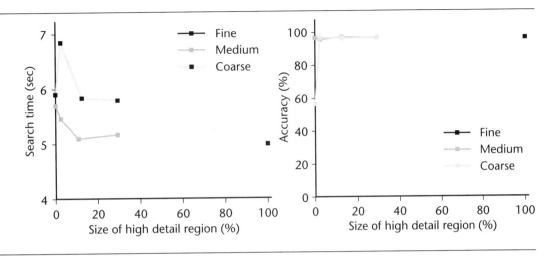

Figure 9.1   Search performance used to measure human response to visual fidelity, as described in [Watson 97d]. (a) shows search time and (b) show search accuracy. A normal, high-detail display was compared to displays with high-detail regions surrounded by low-detail peripheries of various sizes and resolutions. Here, targets were absent.

be missing. If a viewer claims a present target is missing, the trial is termed a *false negative.* If the viewer claims an absent target is present, it is termed a *false positive.*

Generally speaking, good fidelity should allow both low search times and high search accuracy. The faster the search is performed, the lower the resulting accuracy. Searches for present targets are almost always faster than searches for absent targets, since determination of absence requires an exhaustive search of the entire display or scene. We show a typical set of time and accuracy results in Figure 9.1. Here, most of the effect of visual fidelity is captured in the time measure.

While search performance responds strongly to visual fidelity—and it certainly is part of "looking" at something—for some purposes it may be inappropriate. It is not a direct measure of the perceptibility of a fidelity manipulation; rather it quantifies fidelity's impact on a basic, demanding visual task. In many applications such as games, the perceptibility of a fidelity change can be more important than its impact on task or game play.

9.2.2 NAMING TIMES

The naming time measure moves closer from task to perception by asking people to name verbally what they see, and then measuring the amount of time it takes them to do it. There is no "task" per se other than identification.

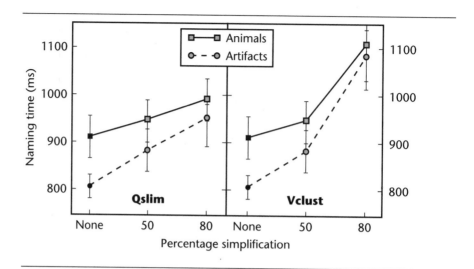

Figure 9.2   Naming times used to measure human response to visual fidelity, as described in Watson et al. [Watson 01]. Naming times increase as fidelity worsens. The two simplification algorithms compared here are *QSlim* by Garland and Heckbert, and Vclust, or vertex clustering by Rossignac and Borrel.

The resulting measure is the time elapsed from the moment an image or object is displayed, until the moment it is correctly verbalized. Because accuracy in naming can be difficult to quantify, it is removed as a factor through the exclusive use of objects that are easily named (e.g., no strange machine widgets). Any experimental trials with incorrectly named objects are discarded. This is usually less than 5% of the total number of trials. Since people typically name objects in less than a second, experimenters must use a voice-terminated timer.

Research shows as image fidelity declines, objects in that image become harder to name, and naming time increases, as shown in Figure 9.2. Naturally there are other influences on naming time, and this figure shows one of them: people name animals more slowly than manufactured artifacts. Current theory holds that this is due to the structural similarity of animals as a class, which requires additional work to disambiguate them [Humphreys 88].

In addition to object type, many other factors can influence naming. Two of particular interest to LOD and graphics researchers are structural similarity and viewpoint [Jolicoeur 85] [Palmer 81] [Bartram 76] [Humphreys 95]. Others of less interest include familiarity with the named object, the frequency of the name's appearance in print, and the number of names commonly in use for the object [Humphreys 88] [Vitkovitch 95].

Naming is a direct probe of perception's outcome. In some sense, it measures the time required to complete the process of perception, from the moment an object is perceived until it is identified (and vocalized). It also has the advantage of

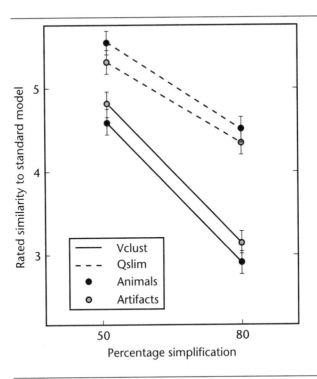

Figure 9.3   Subjective ratings used to measure human response to visual fidelity, as described in Watson et al. [Watson 01]. Ratings decrease as fidelity worsens.

being subconscious, with most naming times well under a second. Nevertheless, for applications focusing on control of the visible effect of a fidelity manipulation, the inclusion of later stages of visual processing, such as structural comparison and naming, may not be appropriate.

9.2.3   SUBJECTIVE RATINGS

Another way of asking people to judge the visual fidelity of an image is to simply ask them to give a number to the "amount" of fidelity they see. Experience in psychology has shown that people responding to surveys make only limited use of available resolution in ratings (using, for example, only 7 of 10 possible values). Experimenters therefore typically allow at most seven different rating responses. This reduces overall response variability and limits variability due to differences among the rating schemes used by viewers. Figure 9.3 shows the results of a study relating viewer ratings to fidelity manipulations.

Presentation format is particularly important when using subjective ratings as an experimental measure. If there is an original or *standard* image, should it be shown to the viewer along with the low-fidelity version? If so, should the standard and the low-fidelity image be present in the same frame, or separated in time by some delay? With a standard, viewers can perform a purely visual comparison, emphasizing visual differences. Without one, viewers must rely on their own mental standard, and the comparison becomes more cognitive. Presentation of standards with delay likely strikes a compromise between these two extremes, with increasing delay causing increased reliance on the mental standard as the memory of the standard image decays. Interestingly, in typical LOD applications users will *never* see high- and low-fidelity versions of displayed imagery side by side; any comparisons must rely on memory.

Ratings have the advantage of being extremely easy for experimenters to collect and for viewers to produce. They are always suspect, however, because they are a conscious sampling of a subconscious perceptual process. (It usually takes viewers at least a few seconds to produce a rating.) Certain viewers may attach special importance to color, while others may emphasize the fidelity of only a particular part of an image. Even worse, these viewer criteria may change over time. This can introduce a great deal of noise into the ratings. Extracting real meaning from the results typically requires very careful instructions to viewers, and the use of a large number of viewers to wash out individual differences in rating strategies.

9.2.4 THRESHOLD TESTING

Threshold testing is the experimental search for the limits of perception, that is, thresholds beyond which a certain stimulus cannot be seen. In the case of visual fidelity, this "stimulus" would be a visible difference in an approximated image. Experimenters repeatedly ask viewers to indicate the presence or absence of such a difference.

In the widely used method of limits, the experimental search becomes quite literal. Whenever the viewer sees a difference, the experimenter reduces the size of the actual difference in the next trial. Whenever the viewer sees no difference, the size of the difference is raised. The search halts when the threshold has been alternatively raised and lowered several times, and the threshold difference is set using a weighted average of the last few difference values. Figure 9.4 diagrams an interleaved staircase approach to the method.

Threshold testing need not only be applied to find the difference between visible and invisible. Through repetitive application, it can be used to find *just noticeable differences* (*JNDs*), the amount of increase in the difference necessary to make the increase itself visible.

Threshold testing is certainly an excellent technique for determining when something can or cannot be seen. However, when image change is visible, even JNDs don't tell the entire story—for example, visual differences in a display affect the viewer's

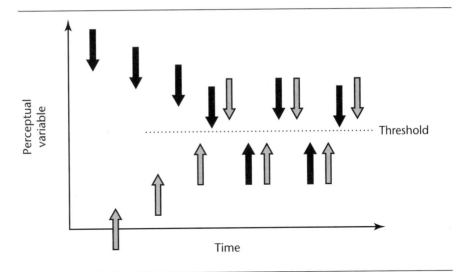

Figure 9.4   An interleaved staircase method for finding thresholds. The two differences are repetitively reduced and raised until they cross one another several times.

higher-level perceptual processes, including the ability to identify an object and find others like it.

9.2.5   COMPARING EXPERIMENTAL MEASURES

The differences among these measures parallel the differences among perceptual psychologists. Psychophysicists are "bottom up," meaning that they focus on the low-level details of visual processing, starting at the cornea and moving through the retina to the early stages of the visual cortex. They prefer threshold tests and very abstract, basic stimuli (e.g., the gratings reviewed in the previous chapter) that have little resemblance to the real world. They may periodically resort to ratings. The critique of pyschophysical research and its measures typically centers on *external validity,* or the extent to which the research has meaning outside of the lab.

Cognitive perceptual psychologists are "top down," and focus on the high-level cognitive abstractions of visual perception. Search performance, naming time, and subjective ratings are commonly used by cognitive psychologists, and their stimuli are usually recognizable real-world objects or scenes. Critiques of cognitive perceptual research often center on *internal validity,* or the extent to which experimental inferences are justified, given the many factors that can influence high-level cognitive task performance.

In fact, research shows that these perceptual fields ignore one another at their peril. Neuroscience confirms definitively that there are "feed-forward" links in the brain from the centers of higher cognition to the centers of lower-level visual processing [Haenny 88]. Experiments also show that higher-level cognitive processes such as attention can have large effects on perceptibility [Suzuki 01].

The measures most appropriate for direct use or for modeling in automatic measures will depend on application context. If the focus is the perceptibility of fidelity manipulations in LOD, thresholds and ratings are likely most appropriate. Certainly if the change in an image cannot be perceived, it will not affect the user at all. But what if the limitations of a system mean that fidelity changes will always be visible? In this case, or if the focus is game play or task performance, a more cognitive approach using search and naming times may be preferred.

9.3 AUTOMATIC MEASURES FOR STATIC IMAGERY

Performing experiments can be a difficult and arduous process, requiring careful experimental design, extensive recruitment and screening of participants, performance of the experiment itself over several days, and finally extensive data analysis. While such experimentation is feasible for those fairly infrequent occasions where different simplification or run-time LOD techniques are being compared, accurate automatic predictors of the experimental results would certainly save time. Of course, any experimentation *during* the execution of an LOD algorithm is out of the question—algorithms require a LooksLike() function.

In the fields of image processing, compression, and half-toning, researchers have been confronting issues of visual fidelity for decades. This section is indebted to the review of automatic measures of visual fidelity put forward by Ahumada [Ahumada 93], and to the distillation of these methods described by Andrew Watson [Watson 00a].

What defines the ideal automatic measure of visual fidelity? The usual algorithmic criteria apply. Certainly such a measure must be *accurate*, in that it reliably predicts the results of experimental measures of fidelity. At the same time, the measure must be *fast*, and ideally so easy to compute that it may be used in real time. Finally, the measure must be *simple*, that is, easily implemented by a designer or developer in his or her system.

9.3.1 DIGITAL MEASURES

Digital measures of visual fidelity in imagery rely solely on processing of the images in their digital form. The most widespread such measure is *root mean squared error* (*RMS error*) [Girod 93], briefly touched on in Section 5.4. In monochrome images, each pixel is represented by a single number indicating luminance. When comparing an original image O and a simplified image S, RMS error is

$$E_{rms} = (\Sigma(O_{xy} - S_{xy})^2)^{1/2}$$

where O_{xy} and S_{xy} are pixels from the original and simplified images. This is sometimes generalized to a Minkowski sum:

$$E_{rms} = (\Sigma(O_{xy} - S_{xy})^n)^{1/n}$$

When $n = 2$, the sum measures Euclidean distance; when it approaches infinity, it becomes a maximum function. As n grows larger, the Minkowski sum gradually increases the effect and importance of local differences in the image.

Digital measures such as RMS error are certainly fast and simple. However, while the error they report increases roughly in proportion to the reduction in fidelity, they differ from the human visual system in their response to visual differences in many respects. For example, if one draws a line across the middle of an image to reduce its fidelity, RMS error will respond only weakly to a very obvious visual artifact. On the other hand, if one decreases luminance by a few steps at every pixel, RMS error responds very strongly to a manipulation that is hardly perceptible.

9.3.2   SINGLE-CHANNEL MEASURES

In the effort to make automatic measure response more like human visual response, a number of researchers have developed measures that model a few early components of the visual system. In this respect they pay particular attention to the results and methods of psychophysical researchers of perception (see Chapter 8). Most of these measures include one or more of the steps in Figure 9.5, or transformations much like them.

The first step, *conversion to contrast,* converts the original and simplified images' arrays of luminance values into descriptions of local luminance change. In its simplest form, if L is the average luminance value of the pixels in an image, the image pixel I_{xy} is converted into contrast C_{xy} with the formula

$$C_{xy} = (I_{xy} - L)/L.$$

The *spatial contrast-sensitivity function (CSF) filter* converts the resulting contrast images into spatial frequencies using a Fourier transform, applies a filter based on the contrast sensitivity function (see Section 8.4.2), and converts the result back into the spatial domain with an inverse Fourier transform. The outcome is two contrast images modulated for the response of the visual system to contrast of varying spatial frequencies. In the final *differencing* stage, a Minkowski sum is used to summarize the difference between the images. Typical values for n in the sum's exponents are 2 and 4.

By adding the conversion to contrast and CSF filter stages, single-channel measures of fidelity incorporate some early behavior of the human visual system and, hopefully, improve accuracy. The conversion to contrast is simple enough, but CSF

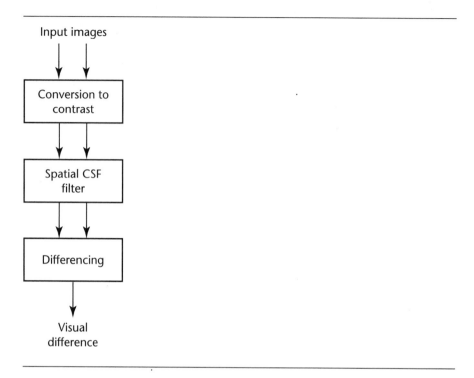

Figure 9.5   The typical transformations employed by single-channel measures of visual fidelity.

filtering requires significant computation. As a result, single-channel automatic measures are impossible to use in interactive settings, and difficult to incorporate into simplification algorithms, which must frequently evaluate the effects of their fidelity manipulations.

9.3.3   MULTI-CHANNEL MEASURES

As discussed in Section 8.3, pyschophysical research suggests that the brain splits the retinal image into several channels, each sensitive to different ranges of spatial frequency and orientation. In a further effort to improve the accuracy of their automatic measures, researchers in image compression and processing have incorporated this model into their automatic visual-fidelity measures.

The measures accommodate the multichannel model with a *channel splitting* stage, which divides each of the two output images from the single-channel measure's spatial CSF filter into a 2D array of images (Figure 9.6). To produce each pair of array images, the input pair are convolved with a band-pass filter. Each array filter is sensitive to a different range of spatial frequency and orientation.

Many automatic measures then add one additional *contrast masking* stage (see Section 8.4), which models the inhibitory effect on response that stimulus in one

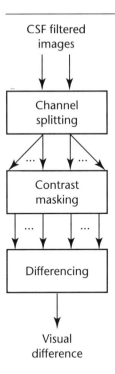

CSF filtered
images

Channel
splitting

...   ...

Contrast
masking

...   ...

Differencing

Visual
difference

Figure 9.6   The typical transformations employed by multichannel measures of visual fidelity.

spatial channel has on neighboring channels. This has the effect of raising the detection thresholds (and reducing visible differences) in each spatial channel. In the final differencing stage, each input pixel pair in a multichannel measure is represented by one pair of coefficients for each frequency and orientation channel. The difference between corresponding coefficients is found and summed in this stage, most commonly with the use of a Minkowski sum.

Multichannel measures improve modeling of the human visual system at great computational expense. Most have at least ten channels, and some approach 100 channels—increasing computation by one or two orders of magnitude. As faithfulness to existing models of visual perception grows, the challenge of implementing these automatic measures grows as well.

9.3.4   EVALUATING MEASURE ACCURACY

Does all of this accuracy in modeling bring accuracy in prediction of experimental measures? Available evidence suggests that it does, but that the point of diminishing returns, at least in applied settings such as LOD, may already have been reached with single channel models.

Rohaly et al. [Rohaly 95] [Rohaly 97] measured the visibility of military targets in natural backgrounds using subjective ratings. They compared these results to three automatic visual-fidelity measures: one digital measure, one single-channel measure, and one multichannel measure (without contrast masking). As input images, they used the background without the target and the background with the target. The multichannel measure was the best predictor, followed by the digital and then the single-channel models. None of the measures reduced prediction error to insignificant levels. However, when corrected by a global contrast-masking factor, the digital and single-channel measures reduced prediction error to insignificant levels, with the digital measure (in RMS form, $n = 2$) performing best. In the case of the digital measure, the contrast factor reduced to dividing the RMS error by the standard deviation of the background image.

Struck by the powerful combination of accuracy, speed, and simplicity promised by these results, Ahamada and Beard [Ahumada 98] followed up this work by adding locality in masking to the digital measure. Without this addition, the global contrast-masking correction might not work well when comparing images that differ greatly in spatial frequency content at each image location. The resulting measure is slower than RMS error but is still completely digital, never requiring a Fourier transform to move into the frequency domain. To our knowledge this measure has not yet been compared to any experimental measures.

Recently the image compression and processing communities gathered to perform a comprehensive evaluation of their automatic measures, dubbed "Modelfest" [A. Watson 00a]. They formed a standard testbed of very basic stimuli (consisting primarily of gratings and similar psychophysical stimuli), and then used experimental threshold measures to find the contrast at which each stimuli became visible against a gray background. They compared these results to five automatic measures. Three were single channel measures with differences calculated using Minkowski sums. In one of these measures, n was selected by using a best fit to the data, while in the other two single channel measures, n was set to 2 and to infinity. The fourth automatic measure was a fairly standard multichannel measure without masking, while the fifth performed the channel split with a simpler, discrete cosine transform (DCT), which is widely used in image and video compression.

The outcome of Modelfest tells a similar story to the Rohaly et al. results. The single-channel model with the Minkowski exponent of infinity (a maximum contrast operator) was a poor predictor. While none of the other four automatic measures reduced prediction error to insignificant levels, they were all still useful, with remaining error only slightly higher than that in the Rohaly et al. study. The standard multichannel measure was only slightly better than the best-fit, single-channel and DCT measures, with the single channel $n = 2$ measure the least reliable of the useful automatic measures. Once again, this time with basic stimuli and threshold experimental measures, lightweight single-channel automatic measures compared well in accuracy with computationally complex multichannel measures.

9.3.5 APPLICATIONS IN GRAPHICS

In computer graphics, a number of researchers have applied automatic measures of visual fidelity to guide adaptive, photorealistic image-generation algorithms such as *path tracers* [Bolin 98] [Ramasubramanian 99] [Volevich 00]. A good review of this work can be found in [McNamara 01]. In a sense, the approach here is the reverse of image compression: rather than removing the pixel with least importance, the image-generation algorithms would like to add the pixel of most importance. Since the standard or ideal image is not available (it is being rendered), rendering is guided by evaluating the difference between two bounding error images, with rendering priority directed toward those regions where current error is most perceptible. Rendering halts when improvements fall below a certain threshold.

All of these researchers used variations of the multichannel automatic measures described by Daly [Daly 93] and Lubin [Lubin 93]. Bolin and Meyer [Bolin 98] in particular, enhanced Lubin's measure to add sensitivity to color, and improved its speed with the use of a wavelet transform at the channel-splitting stage. Although these image-generation researchers all achieved good results, none of them described any comparisons of multichannel to simpler digital or single-channel measures for guiding rendering (although Bolin and Meyer have built a renderer that uses a simpler measure [Bolin 95]). If the results of the evaluations of measure accuracy described above are any indication, use of simpler measures might improve rendering speed at little cost to image quality.

9.4 AUTOMATIC MEASURES FOR RUN-TIME LOD

Run-time LOD takes place in highly interactive, real-time applications. What sorts of automatic measures might successfully be employed in environments like these? Unfortunately, while it certainly provides inspiration and guidance, the image processing and compression community is only beginning to address temporal issues.

A. Watson [Watson 98a] and Daly [Daly 98] have discussed video compression quality. Their efforts to date have focused on Kelly's work in spatiotemporal contrast, discussed in Section 8.6. Myszkowski et al. [Myszkowski 99] [Myszkowski 01] have used Daly's modification of Kelly's relation of contrast sensitivity to velocity to guide rendering of globally illuminated animation sequences. Objects that are relatively still are rendered in high quality, with objects in motion rendered only well enough to achieve an accurately blurry appearance. Yee et al. [Yee 01] add a unique attentional component to the fidelity predictor in their animation renderer, reducing rendering time by an additional factor of 2 or 3. This component makes a view-independent prediction of visual importance based on a bottom-up model. (The authors acknowledge that they ignore significant top-down influences on attention.) There has been very little evaluation of these animation fidelity predictors, though one study [VQEG 01] found that they did not perform much better than weighted MSE at predicting observer ratings.

9.4.1 FIDELITY MEASUREMENT FOR RUN-TIME LOD

Yet the challenges faced by LOD researchers are different and perhaps greater than those faced by researchers in video compression and animation. While accuracy requirements are just as stringent, images must be rendered and their fidelity evaluated in a fraction of a second. Unlike animation, improving visual fidelity reduces temporal detail, which directly impacts the user or viewer (see Chapter 10). Because the system is interactive, it is difficult for systems to extract and anticipate patterns of change such as velocity vectors. There is still a great deal of research required if effective, real-time fidelity management is to become a reality.

While the rendering bottleneck in photorealistic image generators is lighting, polygons are the bottleneck in most interactive applications using LOD. Error introduced by eliminating polygons is precomputed in a view-independent manner, typically by building a detail hierarchy and measuring or estimating the maximum distance between the approximate and original surfaces (see Chapter 3). At run-time, these view-independent errors are projected into the image plane, with perspective-making errors in the foreground particularly important. These projected errors are usually themselves summarized with their maximum.

This *standard* LOD fidelity measure illustrates the paramount importance of real-time performance in interactive applications. Most of the error calculation in this measure is precomputed. The only calculations made at run-time are a very coarse, distance-based approximation of a visual difference image (Figure 9.7), summarized with the maximum difference. This prerendered *error field* is much faster to calculate than even RMS error, since it is sparsely sampled and does not calculate any lighting or color. The tradeoff is poor accuracy, primarily in the failure to sample color and contrast at all, but also in the extremely local emphasis of maximums used both in the detail hierarchy and error field.

9.4.2 CONTRAST SENSITIVITY IN RUN-TIME LOD

Luebke and Hallen [Luebke 01] have proposed an improvement over the standard fidelity measure that maintains real-time performance, but also samples achromatic contrast. Contrast is precomputed with the assumptions that the environment is static (except for the viewer), and all lighting is Lambertian. Like distance, error in contrast is accumulated in the detail hierarchy by taking the maximum at each hierarchy node. At run-time, maximum distance error is projected into the image plane with matching maximum contrast error. A simple calculation converts the distance into a spatial frequency. The new spatial frequency/contrast pair is modulated with an

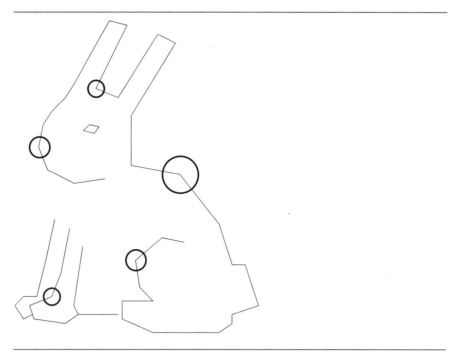

Figure 9.7   A sparsely sampled error field used in run-time LOD, with circles representing uncertainty about vertex location. Most circles are omitted here for clarity of illustration. The underlying bunny shows the eventually rendered approximation.

eccentricity-adjusted, contrast sensitivity function to determine local visibility. The error field is converted into a *visibility field*.

In essence, what Luebke and Hallen have built is an approximate single-channel fidelity measure, enhanced for interactive display with eccentricity-based components. This is certainly a great improvement over the standard LOD fidelity measure. But even putting aside the limitations in color and lighting, there is likely still room for improvement.

First, the measure emphasizes local rather than global differences by using maximum contrast in the detail hierarchy and visibility field. This works well when the maximum contrast is never visible. However, when the demand for interactivity forces the use of visible LOD fidelity approximations, measure accuracy likely declines—witness the very poor performance of the maximizing single-channel operator in the Modelfest study. It may be possible to improve suprathreshold accuracy by using lower-exponent Minkowski operators both in the hierarchy and in the image. In addition, contrast calculation may suffer from the failure of the measure to calculate contrast relative to mean luminance in the current view. It should be a simple matter to calculate this mean luminance, and it may even be possible to make contrast calculation more local with a coarse tiling of the visibility field.

Both the standard LOD fidelity measure and Luebke's measure, with their pressing real-time constraints, ignore the effects of occlusion, contrast with the background, and color and texture maps. It may be possible to capture at least the low-frequency components of these effects if a complete but extremely low-detail, coarse resolution version of the current image could be prerendered. Then, much like adaptive image generation, a similarly coarse error field might be combined with the prerendered image to generate two bounding images, and these could be compared using a very simple automatic measure. The resulting visibility information might then be added somehow into the more finely sampled error or visibility fields.

9.5 AUTOMATIC MEASURES FOR SIMPLIFICATION

Unlike run-time LOD, simplification happens in three dimensions, without prior knowledge of the way the simplified model will be viewed. At the same time, the goal is often to preserve the appearance of the model as much as possible. How can visual fidelity be measured in settings like these? This is a particularly interesting challenge that is also beginning to interest researchers in creating and indexing 3D model databases [Osada 01] [Hilaga 01] [Princeton 01].

We have already reviewed the primarily distance-based measures most commonly used to guide 3D simplification in Section 3.3. Metro [Cignoni 98b] is a tool that implements many of these metrics, but is designed strictly for post-hoc comparisons of simplified models and more indirectly, simplification algorithms. Somewhat surprisingly, given their simplicity, these distance-based measures have proven fairly effective. However, as Li et al. [Li 01] describe, the measures often overlook high-level semantic boundaries on models (e.g., the front of an animal is perceptually more meaningful than the back). This concern led them to develop their semiautomatic simplification tool.

If the viewpoint is not known, one approach to measuring visual fidelity is to sample image fidelity at many viewpoints. We have already seen this approach, used by both Reddy [Reddy 97] and Lindstrom and Turk [Lindstrom 00b]. Reddy precomputed these samples for run-time LOD, while Lindstrom and Turk performed them during simplification in a very intensive computational process. Providing more evidence that a point of diminishing returns in fidelity measure accuracy has been reached, Lindstrom and Turk found a simple RMS error measure to be just as effective as the much more complex multichannel measure by Bolin and Meyer [Bolin 98]. Naturally, this view sampling approach breaks down quickly if the model being simplified is not an object but a complex environment, such as the power plant pictured in Figure 1.1(a).

In the long run, it may prove more effective to perform these types of 3D fidelity comparisons in a 3D cognitive space, rather than an approximated 2D retinal space.

Cognitive researchers of high-level perception have long proposed a 3D structural comparison phase in object recognition [Biederman 87]. The basic idea is that after a viewed 3D structure has been extracted from the retinal image, it is compared to a 3D memory to identify the object itself. Clearly, much interesting research remains to be done on this topic.

9.6 EVALUATION OF LOD TECHNIQUES AND MEASURES

Using comparisons to experimental measures, many researchers have evaluated LOD techniques or automatic measures for LOD. These results suggest possible avenues for future LOD research, and provide indications about how the techniques and measures might best be employed. Examples of this work include Rushmeier et al. [Rushmeier 00], who used subjective ratings to confirm that simplifications in model geometry were not perceptible when hidden with textures with appropriate spatial-frequency content, and Reddy, who used threshold testing on a direction-sensitivity task to confirm that his run-time LOD system was effective (see Section 8.7). In this section, we focus on two research efforts by Watson et al.

9.6.1 SEARCH WITH LOW FIDELITY PERIPHERIES

In a series of studies, Watson et al. [Watson 97a] [Watson 97c] [Watson 97d] used search times to examine the feasibility and methods of perceptible fidelity reductions in the periphery of head-tracked displays. They approximated the effect of geometric LOD in the periphery using texture magnification (Figure 9.8), stretching low resolution imagery across a higher resolution peripheral display. They found that meaningful reductions in peripheral fidelity were possible without harming search performance: time or accuracy (Figure 9.1). In an extension of previous psychophysical research, they also found that for the purposes of peripheral display, head tracking was equivalent to eye tracking with an error of 15 degrees, in both the horizontal and the vertical dimensions.

Finally, in an interesting demonstration of the importance of higher-level, task-related fidelity measures, Watson et al.'s results indicated that the need for supra-threshold detail actually *increased* as search targets moved farther into the periphery (Figure 9.9). Since visual search depends so heavily on the visual periphery, the elimination of any otherwise visible detail proved harmful to search performance.

9.6.2 VISUAL FIDELITY MEASURES AND SIMPLIFICATION

In another series of studies, B. Watson et al. [Watson 00] [Watson 01] studied the relationship of experimental and automatic measures of visual fidelity in the context of

Figure 9.8   Display with reduced fidelity in the periphery as used in [Watson 97d].

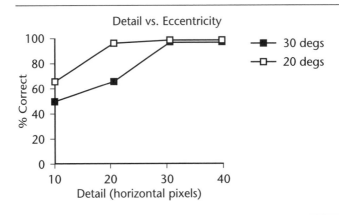

Figure 9.9   Search accuracy as peripheral fidelity and target eccentricity vary. Peripheral fidelity is measured horizontally in the number of pixels across a wide field-of-view display. Search accuracy for targets located at 30 degrees of eccentricity is more, not less, sensitive to peripheral detail.

model simplification. They began by simplifying a suite of 3D models using the *QS-lim* implementation of quadric error metrics [Garland 97] and the vertex-clustering algorithm by Rossignac and Borrel [Rossignac 93] (see Sections 5.1 and 5.3). Figure 9.10 illustrates the fidelity of the resulting LODs. Each model was simplified to two levels. The effect of these fidelity reductions was evaluated with both naming times

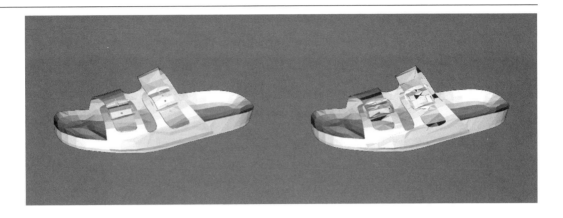

Figure 9.10   The sandal model with half of its polygons removed. Left, as simplified by *QSlim;* right, as simplified by the Rossignac algorithm.

(Figure 9.2) and subjective ratings (Figure 9.3). These experimental data are available as a testbed [Watson 02a].

According to both experimental measures, *QSlim* was better at preserving visual fidelity than Rossignac's algorithm. This is not surprising, considering the greater sophistication and processing time used by the *QSlim* algorithm. Garland [Garland 99] has shown a relationship between his 3D fidelity measure and curvature. Since Rossignac and Borrel's algorithm has no such relationship, these results may be an indication that curvature-based, 3D automatic fidelity measures are more effective.

Both experimental measures also confirmed the widely held belief that simplification algorithms show their mettle during aggressive simplification. When the algorithms removed 80% of the model polygons, both measures indicated a much greater difference between the algorithms than when the algorithms removed only half the polygons. The naming time and subjective rating measures were affected differently by object type (animal versus artifact), with viewers consistently needing more time to name animals, while the effect of object type on ratings depended on the simplification algorithm. This shows one of the differences between these two measures, and suggests simplification algorithms that specialize in models of a certain type.

The study then continued by applying several automatic fidelity measures to the same images and models viewed by the study's participants. These included RMS error and the multichannel measure by Bolin and Meyer [Bolin 98], as well as the mean and maximum 3D distance and volume difference components from Metro. The volume difference measure correlated very poorly with both experimental measures. Other automatic measures all correlated well to experimental ratings, particularly both image measures and the 3D mean-distance measure. Correlations to naming times, however, were particularly weak.

This part of the study provides yet more evidence that multichannel measures may be overkill, with RMS error performing just as well, if not a bit better, than the multichannel Bolin-and-Meyer measure. We are also confronted with the different natures of the naming time measure and the rating measure. Why are naming times modeled poorly?

The authors propose two possible explanations: a "distillation effect" and degree of comparison. The first explanation is suggested by the puzzling fact that the naming time of some models actually dropped as simplification increased—certainly this is not predicted by the automatic measures. Perhaps the simplification algorithms are performing much like caricature artists for these models, distilling the essence of the object from the model and making it easier for viewers to identify. If such an effect could be isolated and quantified, it might be harnessed for very effective use in simplification and even 3D fidelity measurement.

Naming times, unlike ratings, are produced by viewers after looking at one object in isolation. In this study, ratings were produced by viewing two models side by side. Could it be that ratings allowed a much more primitive sort of visual comparison, whereas naming times probed a much more cognitive and complete perceptual process? If so, this might explain the weak correlations of automatic measures to naming times, since the automatic measures are extremely comparative. Confirmation of this conjecture could be quite important, since comparative, side-by-side viewing almost never happens in typical applications. In early reports of a follow-up study, when the authors reduced ease of comparison in ratings by introducing delay between the display of the two compared images, correlations between automatic measures and ratings did indeed decline.

9.7 Conclusions

In this chapter we addressed the measurement of visual fidelity, a fundamental concern in LOD and a number of related fields. We began with a review of experimental measures of fidelity. Many of these measures are in use by LOD researchers as they attempt to validate improvements in simplification methods and run-time LOD management. Automatic measures of visual fidelity strive to predict the results of experimental measures. Measures for comparing single static images are widely used in computer graphics and image processing, and have been applied to simplification, enabling good preservation of appearance with textured models. Automatic fidelity measures for dynamic real-time environments are simpler, but are beginning to approach the complexity of some static measures. Finally, measures of 3D fidelity enable view-independent simplification, and although largely distance based, have proven to be fairly effective for nontextured models.

The latest automatic fidelity measures are quite complex and slow, involving multiple contrast and frequency-based transformations. Fortunately for LOD, although several evaluations of these measures have shown that they bring improvements in accuracy, these improvements seem marginal at best. Simpler and faster digital or single-channel measures work quite well.

Does LOD in fact need improved automatic fidelity measures, that is, a better LooksLike() function? We believe it does. In simplification, these measures would enable more effective simplification of models mapped with textures, normals, or other attributes, and in particular would help determine how to weigh the relative importance of such attributes. In run-time LOD management, the need for improved automatic measures is still clearer. Improved measures would enable sensitivity to textures, color differences, dynamic changes in lighting and shadows, edges due to occlusion and self-occlusion, and more principled suprathreshold approximation. The challenge of run-time LOD, however, is that all this must be accomplished in real time!

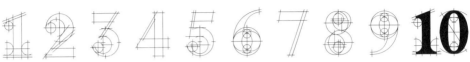

TEMPORAL DETAIL

This chapter focuses on measuring an application's interactivity and how to make it more interactive. We begin with a discussion of methods for characterizing the interactivity or temporal performance of a system, including frame rate as well as other measures such as system latency or lag. We then examine techniques for increasing application interactivity, including LOD, parallelization, prediction, and rendering optimization. The primary reason developers concern themselves with temporal detail is its strong relationship to user performance and satisfaction, and we next investigate that relationship in detail. Unfortunately, there are only a few studies that have directly examined the visual/temporal tradeoff. We review those studies, and conclude by summarizing the implications for developers working in applied settings, such as the surprising indifference of users to constant frame rates.

10.1 INTRODUCTION

Although LOD researchers have always been motivated by the need to achieve temporal control of their applications, the mass of their work focuses on achieving precise

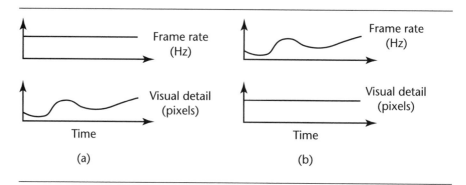

Figure 10.1   The visual/temporal tradeoff. (a) emphasized temporal detail. (b) emphasized visual detail.

visual control. Users of LOD technology are generally left with two options (Figure 10.1): guaranteeing visual accuracy (e.g., within *n* pixels) and leaving interactivity uncertain, or guaranteeing interactivity (e.g., 60 Hz or greater frame rates) and leaving visual error unconstrained. Most commercial interactive applications emphasize interactivity or *temporal detail,* with visual quality reduced as needed to guarantee frame rates of 60 Hz or more. In light of this fact, the sparseness of LOD research dedicated to temporal control is particularly puzzling.

In this chapter, we hope to begin remedying this situation. We start by describing temporal detail itself and listing methods for measuring and controlling it. With this background, we then survey the research studying the relationship between temporal detail and user performance. Surprisingly, there has been little work exploring the three-way relationship of temporal detail, visual detail, and usability (the *TVU relationship*). We conclude by addressing several applied questions in the context of our research survey.

10.2 MEASURING TEMPORAL DETAIL

Temporal detail is most commonly measured with *frame rate,* the number of frames rendered per second (measured in hertz [Hz]). Since frame rate is almost never constant in interactive settings, reported frame rate usually represents some sort of average. As we shall see, variation in frame rate can also be informative. Frame rate has an inverse relationship to *frame time,* the time it takes to display a single frame (measured in ms, Figure 10.2). Frame time is probably the more useful of the two measures, since it has a more intuitive relationship to the passage of time, and therefore human task performance. For example, if the current frame rate is 10 Hz, a 10-Hz improvement moves frame time from 100 milliseconds (ms) to 50 ms, which

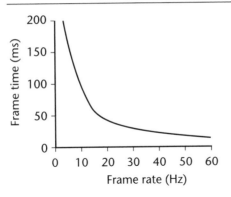

Figure 10.2   The inverse relationship between frame rate and frame time.

can impact human performance significantly. On the other hand, if the current frame rate is 50 Hz, the same 10-Hz improvement changes frame times from 20 ms to 16.67 ms, and if there is any impact on human performance, it will certainly be minimal.

10.2.1 FRAME RATE AND REFRESH RATE

Frame rate should not be confused with *refresh rate*, or the rate at which the graphics hardware displays the contents of the frame buffer. In most current graphic systems, there are two display cycles: the frame rendering cycle of the application and the underlying screen refresh cycle of its display hardware. Since the refresh cycle occupies a lower-level subsystem, refresh rates are constant and unaffected by rendering load. *Single-buffered* systems have only one frame buffer that usually contains two partial frames: one partially rendered frame and the remaining portion of the frame being overwritten. Because the boundary between the partial frames looks like a rip in the image, this artifact is called *tearing* (Figure 10.3).

Double buffering uses two frame buffers to reduce tearing. New frames are rendered in the back buffer while the previous frame contained in the front buffer is displayed. When the new frame is complete, the buffers are swapped and the new frame is displayed. Even in this case, tearing still results if the swap occurs in the middle of a refresh cycle. To finally eliminate tearing, most current graphics cards also use *frame locking*, which synchronizes buffer swaps and the refresh cycle by halting rendering after the new frame is complete, forcing a wait until the next refresh cycle begins.

The use of frame locking is dominant in today's interactive systems. In such systems, refresh rates have a great effect on frame rates. First, the frame rate will never be higher than the refresh rate. Second, frame rates are generally decreased by the

Figure 10.3 Tearing results when there is only one frame buffer or when rendering and refresh cycles are unsynchronized, resulting in simultaneous display of two partial frames.

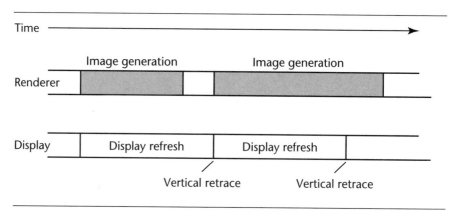

Figure 10.4 In frame-locked systems, frame rate is decreased by the display refresh subsystem. Here the first rendered frame is lengthened to one refresh time, the second to two refresh times.

constant temporal sampling rate of the refresh cycle. For example, a frame that takes 1.1 refresh times to render will not display until the next refresh, and so will have a frame time equal to two refresh times (Figure 10.4). (Refresh time is the inverse of refresh rate.) Effectively, any one frame time will be an integer multiple of the refresh time. Note that similar relationships do not hold for mean frame time or rate, since they summarize many frame samples over time.

What does the frame rendering cycle do when it has completed its frame, but the refresh cycle is still rendering the previous frame? In frame-locked systems, the unfortunate answer is: nothing. The rendering cycle is blocked until the current refresh cycle is completed and frame buffers can be swapped. This troubling fact has led to the development of some *triple-buffered* systems (Figure 10.5) [3dfx 98]

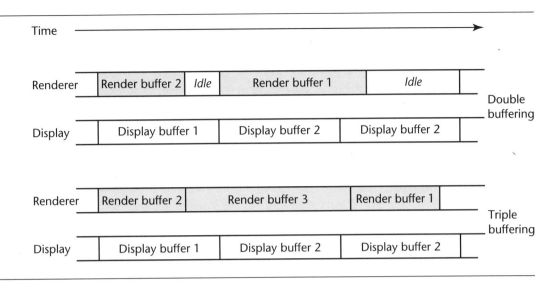

Figure 10.5   Triple buffering can be used to avoid blocking the rendering cycle until the refresh cycle completes.

[McCabe 98]. In these systems, frame rate is improved by using a third frame buffer to avoid blocking the rendering cycle. When the current frame is completely rendered in the back buffer, rendering of the next frame begins immediately in the third buffer. When the refresh cycle completes, the back buffer becomes the front buffer and the current frame is displayed by the refresh cycle. The third buffer becomes the back buffer and rendering of the next frame continues there. The front buffer becomes the third buffer, ready for use when the next frame is completed in the back buffer.

10.2.2   SYSTEM LATENCY AND RESPONSIVENESS

While frame rate measures image continuity, delay or *system latency* measures the age of a displayed input sample, or how current it is. For example, if the user is controlling motion with a mouse, system latency describes how long ago the user's hand was actually in the currently displayed position. System latency includes the time required for the input sample to move through the input subsystem to the rendering subsystem, to be rendered there, and to eventually be displayed on the screen (Figure 10.6). Constant variation in frame time and input gathering ensure that system latency is also very variable. In this text, system latency does not include the additional aging of the sample that occurs while the sample is displayed, although this certainly has some effect on user performance.

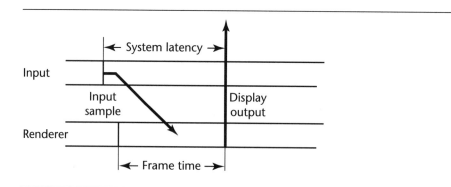

Figure 10.6   System latency measures the time from input sample to eventual display, and includes at least some of frame time.

While frame rate is not affected *by* system latency, it can have a great effect *on* system latency. Thus, a system with poor latencies might have high or low frame rates. But a system with poor frame rates will most likely also have poor latencies. In most systems, system latency includes all of the frame time, since input is used to define the viewing transformation. However, this need not always be the case: input might be sampled only after some animation computation, or sampling of particularly crucial input might be delayed until very late in the rendering cycle. Techniques like these (often called *late sampling*) do not improve frame rate, but can significantly reduce system latency. Triple buffering generally improves frame rate, and therefore reduces latency. However, when triple buffering does not improve the frame rate, it can actually increase latency by sampling input earlier. This occurs whenever the rendering cycle is able to render both the next and the following frames within a single refresh cycle (Figure 10.7).

System latency is not the end of the temporal detail story. *System responsiveness*, the time from user action to system response, is often more meaningful. System responsiveness includes system latency, as well as the additional *sampling delay* between a user's action (or input event) and the sampling of that action (Figure 10.8). For example, a user might be using the mouse to rotate the view to the left, see something of interest, and then change direction to rotate the view to the right. This change in direction is a particularly important input event, one that should be displayed as quickly as possible. While most input subsystems sample very frequently, only one of these samples is used per frame—the rest are discarded. In effect, in most systems the input sampling rate is the frame rate. Since user action is not synchronized with system sampling, on average the system will sample that action after half a frame time (at most one frame time), and respond to it after the additional delay caused by system latency. Variation in system responsiveness is even higher than variation in system latency, since responsiveness includes the additional random delay between user action and sampling.

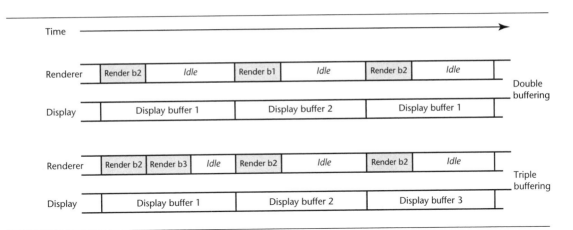

Figure 10.7 When triple buffering does not improve frame rate, it renders both the next and following frames, and then blocks. This process samples input earlier than necessary, and increases system latency.

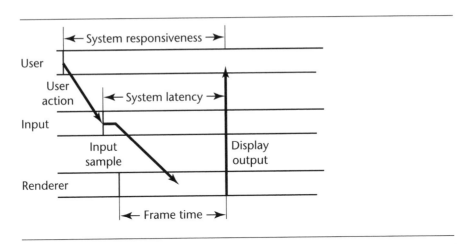

Figure 10.8 System responsiveness measures the time from user action to eventual display, and includes system latency as well as the additional sampling delay.

10.2.3 TWO EXAMPLE SYSTEMS

Consider two fairly simple example systems. The first is a typical desktop system with double buffering and only a mouse for input (Figure 10.9). The mouse defines the rendered view. Assuming that the mouse introduces no delay [MacKenzie 93], at a

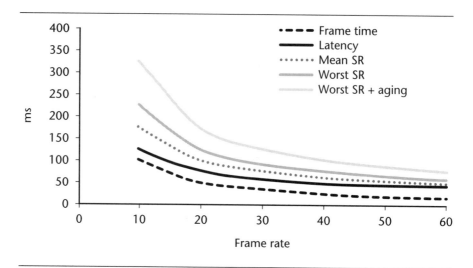

Figure 10.9   Temporal detail in a double-buffered system with a mouse and no input delay. With an excellent 60-Hz frame rate, mean system responsiveness (SR) is 25 ms, a level that can already be perceived. SR worsens rapidly below 30 Hz.

60-Hz frame rate system latency will equal one frame time, or 16.67 ms. The system will respond to an input event within 25 ms on average, and within 33.33 ms at most. Additional aging during display of the frame (certainly users cannot respond at the moment of display) brings response time to 50 ms. As we shall see, 40-ms delays can harm user performance, and even 15-ms delays are detectable. As frame rates drop, system responsiveness climbs, particularly below 30 Hz. LOD managers of systems similar to this one should focus on improving frame rates.

Our second example is a head-tracked virtual reality system with double buffering and monoscopic display (Figure 10.10). Typical tracking-input delay in such systems is 100 ms. Even at a 60-Hz frame rate, the increased input delay raises mean system responsiveness to 125 ms. Input delay dominates temporal detail until frame rates drop below 20 Hz. LOD managers of systems with significant input delay like this one should focus on reducing that delay when frame rates are above 20 Hz. Things would become particularly challenging with stereoscopic display—frame rates are halved!

Real-world systems can become much more complex than these examples, using multiple input devices, such as mice, tracking devices, and voice input, and multiple output devices such as visual, audio, and tactile displays. In systems such as these, each display device has its own display rate (for visual display, this is the frame rate), and each path from input to output (*I/O path*) has its own associated latency and responsiveness. Such systems pose a significant challenge to LOD managers.

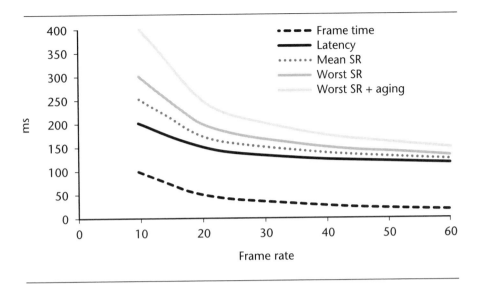

Figure 10.10   Temporal detail in a double-buffered system with 100-ms input delay. Even at a 60-Hz frame rate, mean system responsiveness (SR) is 125 ms, a level that can harm user performance. Input delay dominates frame time effects above 20 Hz.

10.3 CONTROLLING TEMPORAL DETAIL

How can temporal LOD be controlled? Familiarity with these control methods is of paramount importance for application designers. This familiarity will also prove crucial in our study of experiments examining the relationship between temporal detail and human task performance. In this section, we examine those methods. To illustrate them, we will continue using the simple, single I/O-path example systems we described above.

Temporal detail is controlled by reducing or increasing processing times and sampling frequency at various points in an interactive graphics system. We identify three types of points and so three matching types of temporal manipulation: *frame-only*, *latency-only*, and *frame-latency manipulation*. We will call manipulations that improve temporal detail *speedups*, and those that reduce temporal detail *overhead*.

10.3.1 FRAME-ONLY MANIPULATION

Frame-only (FO) manipulation affects frame rate, but not system latency. Typically this involves a change in the amount of calculation made in the rendering sub-system before input is sampled (Figure 10.11). Since it does not affect latency, FO

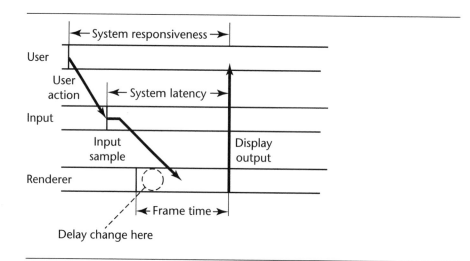

Figure 10.11   Frame-only manipulation affects frame rate, but not system latency. Manipulations are made by changing the amount of calculation made in the rendering system before input is sampled.

manipulation affects system responsiveness only mildly: sampling delay changes on average by half the FO manipulation's frame time change.

Frame-only manipulations will be most effective in systems performing a significant amount of simulation, such as animation and collision detection. Simulation is usually only loosely dependent on user input, and may therefore be performed before input is sampled. Such systems can benefit greatly from schemes that allow rendering of the current frame and simulation of the next to be performed in parallel (Figure 10.12). Care must be taken to avoid synchronization delays, and to match the simulated time to the sampled input time. Similar improvements can be achieved with approaches that use approximation to reduce simulation time. Current research [Carlson 97] [O'Sullivan 01] investigates when and how such approximations in motion and behavior ("animation LOD") can be perceived.

10.3.2   LATENCY-ONLY MANIPULATION

Latency-only (LO) manipulation affects system latency, but not frame rate. Manipulations of this sort are made in the input subsystem, rather than the rendering subsystem (Figure 10.13). System responsiveness changes directly in response to the LO manipulation's system latency.

Latency-only manipulations include filtering, prediction, and late sampling. Filtering of input is typically implemented to smooth a noisy input stream, and is implemented in most 3D tracking hardware. This smoothing can certainly be valuable; however, the calculation required for filtering also increases system latency, and the

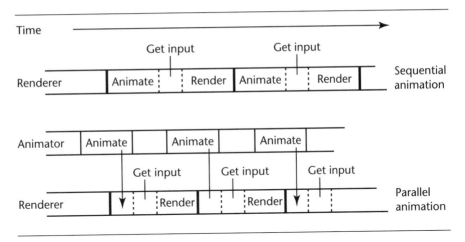

Figure 10.12   Parallelizing simulation to achieve a frame-only speedup.

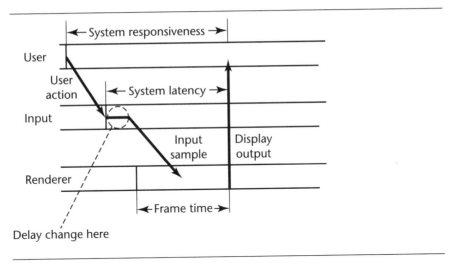

Figure 10.13   Latency-only manipulation affects system latency, but not frame rate. Manipulations are made by changing the amount of calculation made in the input subsystem.

blending of new input with old reduces effective system responsiveness. When system responsiveness is poor, consider using a simpler filtering scheme with a briefer sample history or eliminating filtering altogether.

Prediction [Azuma 94] [Liang 91] is closely related to filtering, and not only smoothes an input stream, but also predicts future values of that stream. If the prediction is accurate, latency is reduced and temporal detail improved, and thus,

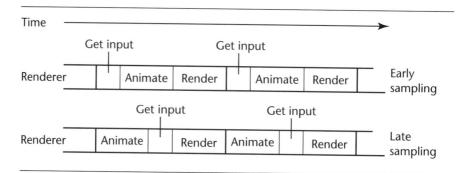

Figure 10.14   Late sampling moves computation from after to before the input is sampled to achieve a latency-only speedup.

the major shortcoming of filtering is overcome. As prediction is extended further into the future, the accuracy of prediction begins to drop, and temporal detail once again worsens. However, an appropriately tuned prediction system can be a very effective tool for improving temporal detail. Unlike filtering, prediction can be very useful even in typical gaming or PC systems, which normally use only mice or joysticks for input.

Late sampling reorganizes computation to perform it before input is sampled. In moving computation from a frame-latency to a frame-only context, frame rate remains constant while system latency and responsiveness improve a latency-only speedup (Figure 10.14). The advantage of late sampling is clear if the reorganized computation has no dependence on input. In situations where there is a limited dependence, it may be possible to segment the computation into input-dependent and input-independent portions. For example, collisions between a game's nonplayer objects might be simulated before input, and collisions between the player and those objects added after input. Some [e.g., Ware 94] have proposed rendering relatively still objects in a scene based on an initial sample of input (possibly coupled with prediction), and rendering more active or user-controlled portions of the scene after a more current sample. The potential disadvantage of this approach is the temporal incoherence that might result from the display in a single frame of two or more input samples.

10.3.3   FRAME-LATENCY MANIPULATION

Frame-latency (FL) manipulation changes both frame rate and system latency. These manipulations are made in the rendering subsystem *after* input is sampled, changing frame time and the length of the I/O path (Figure 10.15). System responsiveness changes on average by 1.5 times the FL manipulation. This SR change has two components: system latency changes directly in response to the manipulation while sampling delay changes by half the manipulation on average.

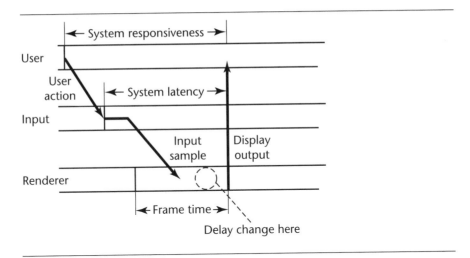

Figure 10.15   Frame-latency manipulation affects both system latency and frame rate. Manipulations are made by changing the amount of calculation made in the rendering subsystem, after input has been sampled.

Frame-latency manipulations include level of detail, the primary focus of this text. LOD reduces rendering computation after the input is sampled, improving frame rate, system latency, and system responsiveness. This reduction in computation often comes at the expense of reduced visual detail, a cost that LOD tries to minimize. In systems that manage the rendering computation very actively (e.g., continuous or view-dependent LOD), it proves beneficial to separate management from rendering and to parallelize them (Figure 10.16).

Any other optimization or speedup of rendering itself is a frame-latency manipulation. These include improved hardware for input or rendering, parallelization [Humphreys 01], triangle stripping [Evans 96], vertex caching [Hoppe 99a] [Bogomjakov 01], texture caching, vertex arrays [Angel 00], frustum culling, and occlusion culling [Luebke 95] [Greene 93]. Since none of these alternative frame-latency speedups introduce visual approximations, they should all be considered for use before LOD is implemented.

10.3.4   COMPARING AND USING MANIPULATIONS

Each of these manipulations varies in its impact on temporal detail. The same reduction in processing time can have drastically different effects on temporal detail. Table 10.1 tabulates these relationships. Each 1-ms speedup in an FO manipulation results in a 1-ms reduction in frame time and an average improvement of 0.5 ms in system responsiveness, without affecting latency. The same millisecond of added speed as an

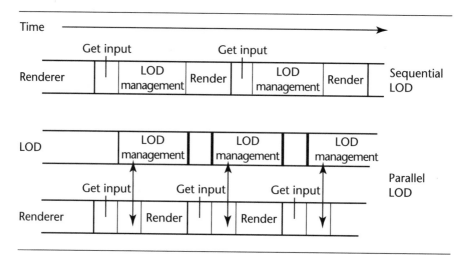

Figure 10.16   LOD reduces computation after input is sampled by using visual approximation, achieving a frame-latency speedup. Here this speedup is improved by parallelizing the management process.

Table 10.1   Summarizing the effects of temporal manipulations of 1 ms on temporal detail. Frame-latency speedups will be most effective. Differences among larger manipulations will be of identical scale.

Manipulation	Frame Time	Latency	System Responsiveness
Frame only (FO)	1 ms	0 ms	0.5 ms
Latency only (LO)	0 ms	1 ms	1.0 ms
Frame latency (FL)	1 ms	1 ms	1.5 ms

LO manipulation results in 1-ms improvements in latency and responsiveness, without improving frame time. Finally, each 1-ms speedup as an FL manipulation results in 1-ms improvements in frame time and latency and an average 1.5-ms improvement in responsiveness.

When improving interactivity in applications, FL speedups are most effective, since they affect temporal detail by all measures and have the largest impact on system responsiveness. LO speedups are typically the next best bet, since they have the next largest impact on system responsiveness. FO speedups are generally least effective, unless user tasks are particularly sensitive to frame time (see below). Conversely, if an application requires additional overhead (e.g., animation or rendering), FO overhead is likely the least harmful, LO overhead is the next preferred option, and FL overhead should be added only if absolutely necessary.

We should add that many of the manipulations reviewed here introduce tradeoffs. For example, LOD trades visual for temporal detail, and filtering speedups trade input smoothness for temporal detail. When improving interactivity, begin with speedups without such tradeoffs. The rendering optimizations discussed above—frustum culling, triangle strips, and so on—are good examples of such speedups, and as FL speedups they are particularly effective. Late sampling is another example of a speedup without an associated tradeoff.

10.4 Temporal Detail and User Performance

Generally, more temporal detail is better. But with LOD, more temporal detail means less visual detail. When is temporal detail particularly important and more appropriately emphasized at the expense of visual detail? In this section, we address this surprisingly complicated question. Humans are extremely complex "systems," and despite centuries of study by psychologists, physiologists, and biologists, only their most basic behaviors and abilities have been modeled with any success. Because this question addresses human satisfaction and task performance, our answers will sometimes be more qualitative than quantitative. Nevertheless, we will strive to be as specific as possible, giving designers of interactive systems a good understanding of the possibilities and tradeoffs they face.

10.4.1 Perceptual Limits

The human perceptual system does have certain limits beyond which additional temporal detail is imperceptible and pointless. The most important, already mentioned in Chapter 8, is the *critical fusion frequency* (*CFF*), beyond which a blinking display (such as the scanned display of your computer monitor) looks continuous. The exact value of this frequency varies from person to person, but for most a frequency of 70 Hz suffices. For this reason, many interactive system designers ensure that their frame rate is maximized and equal to their hardware's refresh rate (typically also set to roughly 70 Hz).

But as we have already explained, frame rate does not measure all aspects of temporal detail: system latency and responsiveness are also very important. It is very possible, for example, to have high frame rates and poor responsiveness. Unfortunately for designers of interactive systems, human sensitivity to latency and responsiveness is very high. Regan et al. have reported that even latencies of 15 ms were perceivable in their head-tracked display [Regan 99]. Wickens has reported that responsiveness of 40 ms consistently harmed task performance [Wickens 86].

Given all this, we can safely say that perceptual limits are of little help with temporal detail. Refresh rates in most displays cap frame rate at levels just above the CFF, and users quickly perceive drops in frame rate below those caps. Even when frame rates are close to maximum at 60 Hz, responsiveness is already perceivable at

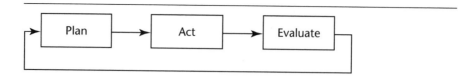

Figure 10.17   In closed-loop tasks, users require frequent feedback, closing the feedback loop. With poor system responsiveness, users take longer to finish tasks.

Figure 10.18   In open-loop tasks, users require little feedback, leaving the feedback loop open.

25 ms and quickly affects user performance as it worsens. System designers will have to find guidance for the temporal detail compromise elsewhere.

10.4.2   OPEN- AND CLOSED-LOOP TASKS

Human factors researchers have identified two basic types of manual tasks [Wickens 00]. *Closed-loop tasks* require users to form a plan, act, evaluate the results of their action, and repeat. These tasks are called closed loop because they close a feedback loop (Figure 10.17). In the real world, closed-loop tasks include driving and watering a garden with a hose. In computer interfaces, they include drawing a straight line with a mouse and steering through a 3D interactive environment.

Open-loop tasks require little or no feedback, and leave the feedback loop "open" (Figure 10.18). These tasks are typically highly practiced and require little attention from the person performing them. Real-world open-loop tasks include assembly line work, pitching, and gymnastics. In computer interfaces, they include typing and moving the mouse pointer to large, well-known icons or buttons.

In fact, these two types of tasks form the ends of a continuum [Wickens 00] spanned by increasing reliance on feedback. Most open-loop tasks were initially closed loop until they were well practiced by the people performing them. Many practiced activities involve both open- and closed-loop behavior. For example, catching a ball involves an initial closed-loop tracking phase, during which the player follows the ball visually and moves to where she predicts it will arrive. As the ball nears the player, visual tracking becomes impossible and the task is completely open loop. Often the feedback continuum corresponds with task difficulty. In computer interfaces, placing the mouse pointer over a large icon is rather simple, enabling very open-loop behavior with little reliance on feedback. If difficulty is increased by making the icon

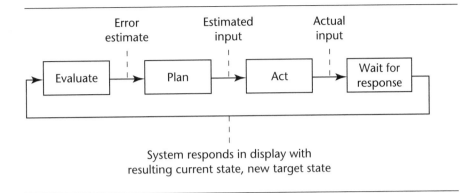

Figure 10.19   Users can be thought of as components in closed-loop dynamic systems.

quite small, several minute adjustments of the mouse are required and reliance on feedback is increased—the task becomes closed loop.

Tasks that are primarily open loop have little sensitivity to temporal detail; display of any sort is largely irrelevant to performance of these tasks. However, closed-loop tasks are profoundly impacted by temporal detail. Tasks that fall in the middle of the open- and closed-loop task continuum are sensitive to temporal detail to the extent that they are closed loop and dependent on feedback. Human factors researchers have long recognized this and have been studying the relationship between temporal detail and closed-loop task performance for decades, particularly in the setting of aviation control. We will briefly review this work here; however, readers interested in details should consult Wickens [Wickens 86] [Wickens 00], to whom we are indebted for our review.

10.4.3   CLOSED-LOOP TASKS AS DYNAMIC CONTROL SYSTEMS

In manual control theory, human factors researchers treat users performing closed-loop tasks as part of a dynamic control system of the sort so often created by engineers. These systems attempt to maintain a certain target state in the face of external disturbances, and perhaps changes in the target state itself. One example of such a system is a device for maintaining a certain temperature in a building. In each iteration, the system compares the target and actual states to derive current error. It then attempts to reduce that error with some sort of actuator. The effect of the system action is then fed back into the system for the next iteration. When humans are part of such systems, their role is to compare the displayed target and actual state to derive error, and through a provided user interface to effect a correction (Figure 10.19). In a racing simulator, for instance, the human compares the desired road position to the actual position and attempts to compensate for the difference by turning the steering wheel.

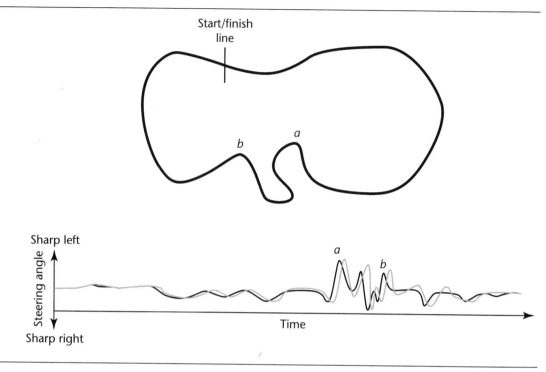

Figure 10.20   Change in target and current system state as time-varying signals with frequencies. Here, target state is defined by a simple race track. Target steering angle is in black, current steering angle in gray. The region from turn *a* to turn *b* requires high-frequency control.

In both system and manual control theory, target and current state are analyzed as time-varying signals with component frequencies. We shall call these two signals the *target* and *output signals.* In a racing simulator, a low-frequency target signal would correspond to a relatively straight track, while a high-frequency signal would correspond to a very twisty, challenging track (Figure 10.20).

When is control successful? Of several criteria, the most obvious is error: successful control stays as close to target state as possible. Another measure of successful control might be the extent to which system activity is minimized, since activity so often corresponds to resource consumption. (Most drivers adopt this measure when their fuel gauge approaches empty.) In manual control, success might also mean minimizing *human* activity, since the human element of a system is often most susceptible to fatigue. Perhaps the most basic measure of successful control is *stability,* or whether the system is able to reliably track target state without oscillating wildly, or even worse, completely diverging from it. Minimization of error and system or hu-

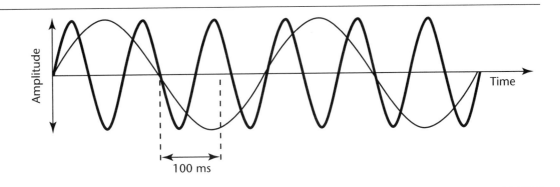

Figure 10.21   Phase lag in a manual control system. As frequency of the target signal increases, phase lag also increases, even though system responsiveness remains constant at 100 ms.

man activity is only possible when stability is achieved. We will define stability more precisely shortly.

10.4.4   DESIGNING FOR SUCCESSFUL DYNAMIC CONTROL

Designers of interactive systems can tune a wide range of elements in their system. The first of these is temporal detail, the focus of this chapter. In manual control, system responsiveness is the preferred measure of temporal detail, since it directly represents the time between a user action and the resulting system response in display. Manual control theorists often relate system responsiveness to task with *phase lag,* which measures system responsiveness in terms of the degrees of phase angle it introduces between the time-varying target and current system states. Figure 10.21 illustrates phase lag in a system with a sinusoidally varying target state and system responsiveness of 100 ms. Note that even when system responsiveness remains constant, phase lag can vary as the frequency of the target signal changes.

Interactive system designers can also tune their user interface controls, which can be zero, first, or second order, depending on their response to user input. *Zero-order* controls map input values to output values. Common zero-order controls are mice, door knobs, and volume dials. *First-order* controls map input values to the rate of output change. Well-known first-order controls include joysticks and steering wheels. We illustrate both of these types of control in Figure 10.22. *Second-order* controls map input values to the acceleration of change in output. Second-order controls are fairly rare, but examples include the thrust controls in spacecraft and in the classic video game *Asteroids.* Controls of any order can also have varying amounts of *gain,* the ratio of output over input, which amplifies (or dampens) user input. Many radios have one high- and one low-gain tuning dial, allowing both coarse and fine tuning. In

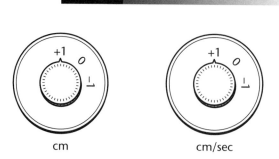

cm   cm/sec

Figure 10.22   Zero- and first-order control in a Pong game. With the zero-order dial, turn 5 degrees and the Pong paddle will move 1 cm and halt. The same turn on the first-order dial will move the Pong paddle 1 cm after one second—and the paddle will keep moving at a constant velocity of 1 cm per second.

many windowed computer interfaces, users can zoom into or out of their document, effectively decreasing or increasing the gain of mouse motion relative to the elements of the document.

In manual control, systems become unstable when phase lag is over 180 degrees and gain is greater than 1. Why these particular values for phase lag and gain? For an intuitive understanding, consider a driving system in which these conditions are fulfilled. The driver sees that the car is headed off the road to the left and steers rightward to correct. However, by the time this correction is implemented, the road has veered to the left, and the rightward correction has worsened a rightward steering error! Making matters worse, because gain is greater than one, error is amplified rather than dampened.

By manipulating phase lag, designers can improve the stability and interactivity of their systems. We have already explored at length the various manipulations that can improve responsiveness and reduce phase lag. But what if these manipulations have already been fully exploited? Fortunately, designers can achieve stability with other approaches. Some of these approaches might be preferable to temporal detail manipulations with associated tradeoffs, such as the visual approximations of LOD.

With *control alteration*, designers tune the user interface controls to achieve stability. To begin, designers might reduce the order of user interface control, such as by switching from a second- to a first-order control. Higher-order controls are less responsive and increase phase lag (zero-order control has no associated lag). Designers might also reduce gain, enabling stable control even when phase lag is larger than 180 degrees. Both of these alterations may have other implications for usability. For example, zero-order control is usually inappropriate for vehicles, and controls with low gain can increase error and make the system seem sluggish. Designers should evaluate these tradeoffs carefully.

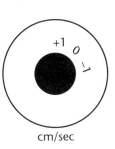

Figure 10.23   Compensating for delay with predictive display. The gray paddle shows the expected position of the actual paddle in 100 ms.

Tasks themselves are also often under designer control. In *task alteration,* phase lag is reduced by reducing task difficulty, usually by reducing required accuracy or speed. Such alterations effectively eliminate high frequency components from the target signal that users must track. For example, in a virtual walk-through, speed in movement might be reduced, and in a shooting game, the size of the target might be increased. Alternatively, the designer might give the user control of these variables— in our example, by giving the user control of navigation speed or of the weapon used. Designers might also reduce randomness and enable repetition, allowing practice to turn a closed-loop task into an open-loop task.

Finally, *display alteration* cannot make theoretically unstable systems stable, but can make nearly unstable systems easier to use. *Previewing display* forecasts future target state, making prediction and early reaction simpler in the face of phase lags. A common example of previewing display is the view of the track ahead in racing games, or (giving an even earlier preview) the inset map of the track that such games often include. *Predictive display* forecasts output state, making use of the same prediction technology reviewed in Section 10.3. However, rather than returning the prediction directly as input, the system displays a more aggressive prediction in the frame. The display of the prediction does not directly affect control, and makes it clear that the prediction is uncertain. Predictive interfaces are most common in applications requiring flying or steering, such as flight simulators, and often take the form of tunnels or rings in the current view. In our simple Pong example (Figure 10.23), we might show a ghostly paddle that indicates its expected position in 100 ms.

10.4.5   TEMPORAL DETAIL AND COMPLEX TASKS

Manual control theory provides a sound theoretical framework for thinking about the relationships among temporal detail, tasks, and user performance, clarifying many of the tradeoffs facing designers of interactive systems. However, it can often be difficult to apply in practice. As the theorists themselves acknowledge [Wickens 86] [Wickens 00], the theory suffers from approximating users as simple linear-system components, ignoring, for example, the perceptual thresholds so prevalent in the human visual system. Real-world tasks have many transient elements that are difficult to represent in the frequency domain, and as we have already discussed, may be partially open loop in nature. Manual control theory also says little about frame rates—of paramount importance here—and tradeoffs in visual detail.

We therefore review research on the relationship between temporal detail and user performance in common interactive tasks. From a manual control perspective, even these common tasks can be complex, containing open- and closed-loop elements, multiple target frequencies, and transient behavior. Many of the studies we will review have examined the effects of different frame rate means and standard deviations, which are of particular importance to designers of interactive systems.

Research on the human effects of temporal detail has focused on three basic types of tasks: *catching, placement,* and *tracking.* We have already discussed catching, which contains an initial, closed-loop, visual tracking phase and a final, predictive, open-loop phase. Shooting or intercepting a moving target are common catching tasks. According to manual control theory, the initial visual tracking phase should only be mildly sensitive to temporal detail, while the final phase should be completely insensitive to it. Catching should be particularly sensitive to changes in frame rate, since these might reduce the number of samples provided for prediction.

Watson et al. [Watson 97a] [Watson 97b] [Watson 98b] and Richard et al. [Richard 96] are the only researchers who have studied catching. Both examined these tasks in 3D virtual-reality displays using FL manipulation. Users caught the target more quickly as responsiveness improved, but catch times stopped dropping after SR improved to 290 ms (Figure 10.24). According to Watson et al., variation in SR made catching more difficult, but only when standard deviations were at least 85 ms. When this was true, low-frequency variations in SR increased catch times, and high-frequency variations did not. Users were particularly sensitive to variation when mean SR was poor (above 290 ms).

In placement tasks, users move something from one location to another. As they move, they refine the direction and speed of their motion so that they arrive at the correct location. Clicking on an icon and picking up or putting down an object are both placement tasks. As a task that depends heavily on feedback and involves less prediction, placement should be extremely sensitive to responsiveness, regardless of the type of temporal manipulation (FL, FO, or LO) that produced it. Naturally, smaller targets should increase difficulty, adding higher frequencies to the target signal and increasing sensitivity to temporal detail.

Bryson [Bryson 93] and MacKenzie and Ware [MacKenzie 93] studied placement in 2D environments. Bryson compared FO to LO manipulations and found that they had similar effects on user performance. Performance continued improving even as system responsiveness reached its best levels. MacKenzie and Ware found similar effects, with placement performance improving even when system responsiveness reached 25 ms. In both studies, increasing the difficulty of the placement increased temporal detail effects.

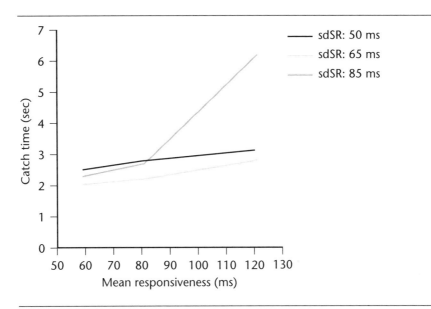

Figure 10.24   The effect of temporal detail on catching times. Here FL manipulation was used to control temporal detail mean and variation. Catching performance improved until mean system responsiveness fell below 290 ms (at a frame time of 85 ms). Variation in responsiveness only affected catching performance at the worst mean responsiveness when it reached a standard deviation of 85 ms (frame time 35 ms).

Watson [Watson 97a] [Watson 97b] [Watson 98b] [Watson 99] and Ware and Balakrishnan [Ware 94] examined placement in 3D environments. Once again, improvements in temporal detail always brought matching improvements in placement performance. Ware and Balakrishnan found no difference among FL, LO, or FO manipulation. When Watson et al. increased placement difficulty, users required improved temporal detail to maintain placement performance (Figure 10.25). Similar to their catching results, they also found that standard deviations in system responsiveness above 85 ms made placement harder, particularly when the frequency of frame time variation was low. In this case, variation had its largest effect when mean responsiveness was already good (not poor, as in catching). This may indicate that users are stressed not by transient changes in sampling rate, but rather in responsiveness itself.

We have already discussed tracking at length in our review of manual control theory. However, it is interesting to examine tracking in more complex settings, including systems with changes in frame rate. Tharp [Tharp 92] and Bryson [Bryson 93] probed the tracking and temporal detail relationship in two small studies—Tharp in 3D and Bryson in 2D—and obtained strikingly similar results. Both compared FO to LO manipulation, and found that user-tracking performance continued to improve through the best levels of system responsiveness (50 ms). FO manipulation had a greater effect than LO manipulation. As the difficulty of the tracking task

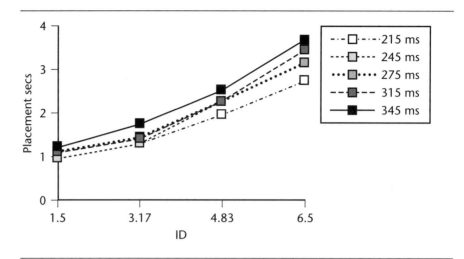

Figure 10.25   The effect of temporal detail (FL) and difficulty (ID) on placement times. Larger ID values indicate increased difficulty. The five curves represent user performance at different levels of mean responsiveness. Improving responsiveness becomes more important as difficulty increases.

was increased, temporal detail became more important to users. Park and Kenyon [Park 99] used a larger study to examine the effects of FL manipulation on tracking in 3D. Tracking performance improved dramatically as mean responsiveness improved. Large, transient variations in responsiveness also had a harmful effect. Difficulty increased the harmful effects on user performance of both mean responsiveness and responsiveness variation.

Overall, the predictions of manual control theory hold up well to this examination of temporal detail effects in more applied and less controlled contexts. In particular, the more closed loop the task, the more sensitive it is to temporal detail, with catching least sensitive and tracking most sensitive. Within task type, as difficulty increases, so does user sensitivity to temporal detail. Manual control theory does not have much to say about frame rates outside of their relationship to responsiveness, but some studies here supported the notion that tasks with a significant element of prediction were especially sensitive to temporal detail changes that adjust frame rates (FL or FO manipulation). More clearly, the studies show that only extreme (standard deviation of 85 ms or more) variation in temporal detail can affect user performance.

10.5   TRADING OFF TEMPORAL AND VISUAL DETAIL

Rendering is a tradeoff between visual and temporal quality (Figure 10.1). On the one hand, an application can have great-looking imagery, but low frame rates. On the

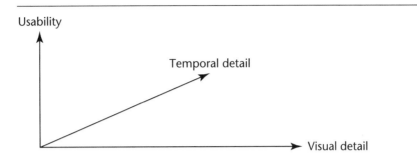

Figure 10.26   TVU space. Application designers must maximize usability by making the best possible tradeoff between visual and temporal detail, finding a surface of optimal usability.

other hand, an application can emphasize high frame rates, resulting in poor image quality. What is the proper balance between visual and temporal detail? The research we have reviewed in this chapter says a great deal about when temporal detail is or is not important to users, providing a good clue as to when it should or should not be sacrificed to improve visual detail. But what if *both* visual and temporal detail are important? What is the three-way relationship—we'll call it the *TVU relationship*—among temporal detail, visual detail, and user performance (Figure 10.26)?

Unfortunately, research on the TVU relationship is extremely sparse. Perceptual science is largely unconcerned with delay, since it is extremely uncommon in the natural world. This makes perceptual research relating to visual detail extremely difficult for system designers to apply. The field of teleoperation studies control of remotely located robots, and has always dealt with delays in robot–operator communication [Sheridan 63]. However, typical teleoperation delays were until recently well over a second, and experience with those delays is not very relevant in today's interactive graphics systems. In one of the few studies to examine the TVU relationship, Ranadive [Ranadive 79] studied teleoperation of an underwater robot as frame rate, spatial resolution, and luminance resolution were varied. He found that successful control was closely related to the amount of information (bits) displayed per second, regardless of whether this information was temporal, spatial, or chromatic. The study was performed under conditions of extreme delay, in a very static underwater environment.

In early and promising work, Meruvia [Meruvia 00] has proposed *IO differencing* to quantify temporal detail in visual terms, enabling direct comparison of temporal and visual detail. As described in further work by Watson et al. [Watson 02b], systems could then minimize the sum of the error introduced by temporal and visual approximation, thereby presumably maximizing user performance. To quantify temporal detail visually, the system measures the difference between the current display state, and current input state as it would be represented in display. For example, if the mouse moves the view from left to right, the current mouse value will specify a view

Figure 10.27   IO differencing to manage the tradeoff of visual and temporal detail. The full-detail model positioned according to latest input is silhouetted at the lower right. Rendering that model (silhouetted upper left) introduces a temporal error t. Rendering a coarse approximation (shown in polygonal form) introduces spatial error s, but eliminates t. In this case temporal error is dominant—we should render the coarse model.

that is different from the currently displayed view. The larger the difference between those views, the larger the IO difference. Systems implementing this approach would use less visual detail whenever temporal error (the IO difference) exceeds visual error (Figure 10.27). The net effect would increased frame rates and coarser visual detail when the user is in motion, decreased frame rates and finer visual detail when the user is relatively still. In a simple rotation task, Meruvia and Watson found that managing LOD with IO differencing improved user performance.

10.6   A Practical Summarization

In this section, we attempt to distill all the detail in this chapter into practical advice for designers of interactive systems. Where this is not possible, we attempt to identify the research that might make it possible. Our approach is to consider a series of questions that might be posed by a typical designer. We should note that most of our answers are based on studies of user performance—not user satisfaction, which might be particularly important in entertainment applications.

How can temporal detail be measured? The three main measures of temporal detail are frame rate, system latency, and system responsiveness.

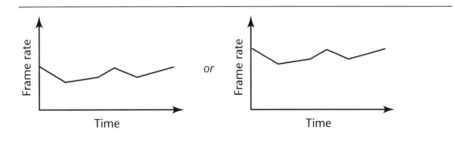

Figure 10.28   How much temporal detail is enough? For example, should mean frame rate always be high, or may it sometimes be low?

How can temporal detail be improved? The three types of manipulations that may be made are frame-only manipulation (including simulation parallelization); latency-only manipulation (including late sampling); and frame-latency manipulation (including rendering optimizations and LOD). Although any improvement in temporal detail is beneficial, frame-latency manipulation has the largest impact on system responsiveness, and so is most effective. Some manipulations are only possible with tradeoffs—for example, using LOD means making compromises in visual detail.

What can be done if temporal detail cannot be improved? Control alteration reduces control order or gain. Task alteration lowers the peak frequencies of the target signal, usually through reducing task accuracy and speed requirements. Display alteration uses previewing or prediction to forecast target or output state.

How is task related to temporal detail? According to manual control theory, tasks demanding high-frequency control are more sensitive to temporal detail. Experimental work in more applied, high-bandwidth task settings confirms this. Ultimately, as phase lag climbs past 180 degrees with gain over one, the manual control system for performing the task becomes completely unstable.

How much temporal detail is enough (Figure 10.28)? If the user's task is largely open loop, it is quite possible to have enough temporal detail, as the ceilings in user performance reached in Watson et al. [Watson 98b] and Richard et al. [Richard 96] show. In this case, designers using LOD might emphasize visual detail with some justification. If the task is instead largely closed loop, and especially when difficulty is high, it is extremely difficult to have enough temporal detail. Studies performed to date show that user performance is harmed even when responsiveness is 40 ms, and delays of 15 ms are perceivable. This is less than one 60-Hz frame time!

How important is temporal detail constancy (Figure 10.29)? Not very. Studies show that standard deviations of up to 85 ms in system responsiveness can be tolerated without harming user performance. Designers therefore need not necessarily go to great lengths to maintain constancy in temporal detail. More specifically, in tasks that emphasize prediction, fairly large variations in frame rate can harm user performance

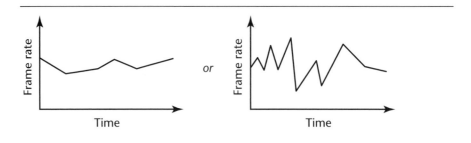

Figure 10.29   How important is temporal detail constancy? For example, should frame rate standard deviation always be small, or may it sometimes be large?

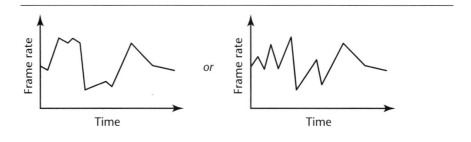

Figure 10.30   Are patterns of change in temporal detail important? For example, when frame rate mean and variation are unchanged, can the pattern of the variation affect users?

when frame rate is already low. Users are already stressed by sample sparseness, and adding variability to the rate at which samples arrive makes prediction harder. In tasks that emphasize feedback, fairly large variations in responsiveness can harm user performance when responsiveness is already good. In cases like these, transient increases in the normally brief time before users receive feedback seem particularly harmful.

Is the pattern of change in temporal detail important (Figure 10.30)? This a very minor concern, according to current evidence. System designers might simply choose to ignore it. Patterns of temporal change have no effect until the amplitude of that change harms performance. Patterns have a limited effect when they are fairly low in frequency or are transient in nature, that is, when the patterns are fairly easily perceived by the user. However, these conclusions should be confirmed in further research.

How important is frame rate outside of its impact on responsiveness? Research shows conclusively that responsiveness has a stronger relationship to user performance than frame rate (aside from the frame rate's own impact on responsiveness). More research is certainly required, but there are indications that frame rate is particularly important in applications requiring significant amounts of prediction. In entertainment, conventional wisdom places great emphasis on high frame rates, perhaps because high frame rates may be required to ensure a pleasing temporal continuity.

Which is more important, visual or temporal detail? No reliable answers to this question currently exist. One promising avenue of research is IO differencing, which intuitively emphasizes temporal detail when input is changing rapidly, and visual detail when input is static.

10.7 CONCLUSIONS

With the conclusion of this chapter, you have now reached the end of the book. Congratulations! We hope that you have found this book to be an illuminating read and a worthy investment of your time. If you have read the book cover to cover and are still hungry for more material, you may want to look at the companion Web site, *www.lodbook.com*, to find software, models, and links to additional resources. We have designed this Web site to act as an up-to-date portal for information relating to this book.

Glossary of Terms

ACCOMMODATION: The faculty of changing the focal length of the eye's lens. This is done to bring a new object into focus, normally in coordination with *vergence eye movements.*

ACTIVE SURFACE DEFINITION (ASD): The name of the terrain level of detail and morphing feature provided by the OpenGL Performer package from Silicon Graphics Inc.

ADVANCED TELEVISION SYSTEMS COMMITTEE (ATSC): Defines a replacement standard for *NTSC* that includes digital encoding using MPEG-2, multiple resolutions, and refresh rates, including higher resolutions referred to as HDTV.

ALPHA BLENDING: An image-based technique for blending between two different levels of detail where transparency is used to fade between the two representations. Within the fade region, one model is faded into view while the other model is faded out. See *geomorphs.*

ANISOTROPIC LOD: Refers to the use of a range of resolution levels across a single object. This term is therefore equivalent to *continuous* or *view-dependent LOD.*

ASD: See *active surface definition.*

ATSC: See *Advanced Television Systems Committee.*

ATTRIBUTE ERROR: Simplification error other than *geometric error*, including possibly color error, normal error, and texture error.

AUTOMATIC FIDELITY MEASURE: An algorithm for predicting the results of an experimental visual fidelity measure. See Chapter 9 for a detailed discussion of automatic and experimental fidelity measures.

BACKFACE SIMPLIFICATION: A view-dependent LOD technique that eliminates polygons facing away from the viewer. This technique assumes that such polygons are not visible, and therefore only applies to closed meshes that have a definite "inside" and "outside." Backface simplification is distinct from *backface culling*, which rejects backfacing polygons on a per-face basis. Backface simplification can accelerate backface culling, since fewer individual polygons need be considered.

BIJECTION: A continuous, one-to-one, and onto mapping. A bijection preserves local neighborhoods. When you map an entire neighborhood of surface points through a bijection, the resulting points still form a neighborhood on the destination surface, and there is no tearing, folding, and so on.

BILLBOARD: A type of dynamic geometry often used in games where an object is given position and dimension, but its rotation is changed dynamically, usually to make it directly face the viewer. The generic term billboard refers to these objects that rotate automatically in one, two, or all three axes. Also sometimes referred to as sprites.

BINTREE: A space decomposition method that recursively partitions the underlying space into equal halves. Also, a hierarchical structure is often used by terrain LOD systems, such as the *ROAM* algorithm. That is, the terrain grid is represented using triangles and these are recursively refined using a longest-edge bisection. See also *quadtree* and *octree*.

BLIND SPOT: The area of the retina, generally assumed to be around 5 degrees, where all of the axons of the *retinal ganglion cells* meet to form the *optic nerve*. There are no *photoreceptor cells* in this region, so we cannot detect any light that falls on the blind spot.

CFF: See *critical fusion frequency.*

CLOSED LOOP TASK: A user task with a tightly closed, feedback loop that requires frequent iterations of a basic "plan, act, and evaluate" subtask sequence. Typical closed-loop tasks include driving, controlling motion in a computer game, and clicking on a small or infrequently used menu item. Closed-loop tasks are particularly sensitive to temporal detail, especially to *system responsiveness.*

COLLECTOR CELLS: The group of cells in the retina that lie between the *photoreceptor cells* and *retinal ganglion cells.* These include the horizontal, bipolar, and amacrine cells. These cells filter the light inputs detected by the photoreceptors such that there are around 120 to 130 million photoreceptors but around only 1 million ganglion cells.

COMPUTER GAME: A game designed for a general-purpose personal computer. Distinct from *video game*, which targets a hardware platform specifically designed for gaming on a television screen.

CONSERVATIVE ERROR BOUND: An upper limit on the potential error of a simplified surface (or, equivalently, a lower limit on its possible quality). This allows us to know something useful even if we cannot measure it exactly. "Conservative" has positive connotations in terms of providing a guarantee, but it can also have negative connotations. A bound that is overly conservative may not be useful since it always reports much higher error than is actually present.

CONTINUOUS LOD: A level-of-detail scheme where surface detail is varied continuously, allowing an object to be represented over many levels of detail. This may also imply *view-dependent LOD*, although this is not necessary, as in the case of progressively streaming a series of discrete detail levels for an object to the display.

CONTRAST: The difference in light intensity between an object and its immediate surroundings.

CONTRAST GRATING: A pattern of alternating light and dark bars generated by varying *contrast* sinusoidally across the display. Used to measure a subject's *contrast sensitivity*.

CONTRAST SENSITIVITY: A measure of an observer's sensitivity to spatial detail in terms of its *contrast*. Defined as the reciprocal of *threshold contrast*.

CONTRAST SENSITIVITY FUNCTION (CSF): A curve that records an observer's ability to resolve detail in terms of *contrast* and *spatial frequency*.

CORTICAL MAGNIFICATION FACTOR: Describes the drop-off in retinal sensitivity out toward the peripheral field. This factor is often given the label M. It has been shown that M^2 is directly proportional to the density of receptive fields of *retinal ganglion cells*.

COST ESTIMATION: A simplification strategy to reduce the total work performed by sometimes replacing an accurate, but expensive computation with a less accurate but faster variant. This requires some care to still produce good simplifications.

CRITICAL FUSION FREQUENCY (CFF): The frame rate at which a sequentially presented series of images appears continuous, or is perceptually fused. Measured in hertz (Hz). For most people, the CFF is roughly 70 Hz. Some speculate that the CFF in the visual periphery is even higher. The term critical flicker frequency is used synonymously.

CSF: See *contrast sensitivity function*.

DECIMATION: See *polygonal simplification*.

DEGENERATE FACE: A polygonal face (typically a triangle) whose corners have been collapsed together by simplification operations. Such a triangle has degenerated to a single point or line segment with no area, and can thus can be removed without affecting the rendered image.

DELAUNAY TRIANGULATION: A *triangulation* scheme that maximizes the minimal angle of all triangles. Constrained Delaunay triangulation forces the triangulation to include a specified set of edges. Conforming Delaunay triangulation extends constrained Delaunay triangulation by adding vertices where necessary to guarantee the Delaunay property.

DELAY: A general term referring to either *system latency* or *system reponsiveness*.

DEM: See *digital elevation model*.

DIGITAL ELEVATION MODEL (DEM): This term has come to mean any regular grid of elevation values. The term DEM is more specifically applied to the digital elevation products produced by the U.S. Geological Survey. See also *triangulated irregular network*.

DIRECT MEMORY ACCESS (DMA): A scheme often used in graphics or *video game* hardware that allows a dedicated processor or device to access system memory without intervention from the other parts of the system, particularly the main CPU. Optimizing data movement using DMA is a key optimization for many platforms.

DISCRETE LOD: An LOD scheme where several discrete versions are created for a complex object at various levels of detail. The system then selects the most appropriate representation to display for an object at each frame. This is also referred to as static or traditional LOD.

DMA: See *direct memory access.*

DOUBLE BUFFERING: The use of two buffers, labeled "front" and "back" to represent the displayed image. The front buffer contains the currently displayed image; each new frame is rendered in the back buffer while the previous frame contained in the front buffer is being displayed. When the new frame is complete, the buffers are swapped. With *frame locking*, double-buffered systems can avoid *tearing.*

ECCENTRICITY: Angular deviation from the center of the retina, often taken as the *fovea.*

EDGE COLLAPSE: A *mesh simplification* technique where the edge of a polygon is collapsed to a single "average" vertex, whose location and attributes are typically chosen to minimize the resulting error in the mesh. After the edge collapse, the local neighborhood of mesh is *retriangulated* and the now-degenerate triangles that shared the edge are removed.

ERROR FIELD: In the standard LOD fidelity measure, the set of projected distances resulting from simplification error.

ERROR METRIC: A self-consistent mathematical framework for evaluating how similar one polygonal model is to another.

EXTERNAL VALIDITY: The extent to which an experimental manipulation has meaning outside the lab (in the real world). Highly controlled experiments can cause one to question external validity.

FALSE NEGATIVE: In a perceptual experiment, a viewer claims that a present object is missing.

FALSE POSITIVE: In a perceptual experiment, a viewer claims that a missing object is present.

FIELD OF VIEW: The solid angular region that is visible to the eye.

FILL RATE: See *pixel fill rate.*

FIRST-ORDER CONTROL: A control that translates each input value into one output velocity. First-order controls include steering wheels (that map input to angular velocity) and joysticks. See also *zero-order control.*

FLOATING-CELL CLUSTERING: A refinement to Rossignac and Borrel's uniform-grid clustering scheme. Proposed by Low and Tan [Low 97] and based on a greedy cell collapse, floating cell clustering iteratively collapses the cell centered at the most important vertex. See Section 5.1.6.

FL: See *frame-latency manipulation*.

FO: See *frame-only manipulation*.

FOV: See *field of view*.

FOVEA: The region of the retina most sensitive to detail.

FRAME: A complete image in an animated sequence. For example, cinematic film uses 24 frames per second. Every element of a frame represents the same moment in time.

FRAME LOCKING: Synchronizing *double buffering* with the display *refresh rate*. If double-buffered swaps are not synchronized with the refresh cycle, swaps can occur in the midst of a screen refresh, resulting in tearing. Frame locking implements this synchronization, effectively blocking rendering until the next refresh cycle begins.

FRAME-LATENCY (FL) MANIPULATION: A system manipulation that affects both *frame rate* and *system latency*. On average, *system responsiveness* changes by 1.5 times the FL change. LOD is a typical method for performing FL manipulation.

FRAME-ONLY (FO) MANIPULATION: A system manipulation that affects *frame rate*, but not *system latency*. On average, *system responsiveness* improves or worsens by half the FO manipulation. A typical manipulation changes animation calculation made before input is sampled.

FRAME RATE: The number of complete images or *frames* displayed per second by an interactive graphics application. Measured in hertz (Hz). Frame rate is primarily a measure of image continuity.

FRAME TIME: The duration, or time of display, for one frame. Frame time is the inverse of frame rate. Measured in milliseconds (ms).

FRAME-TO-FRAME COHERENCE: Coherence during an interactive or animated rendering sequence. Many algorithms take advantage of the fact that changes from frame to frame are usually small in an interactive application.

FRAMELESS RENDERING: A rendering technique that displays each new pixel as it is calculated, rather than waiting for the entire screen to be rendered. To make this effect more visually pleasing, the pixels are updated in a pseudo-random order.

GAIN: A measure of the amplification (or damping) of user input. If O is the output of the control device and I is the input to it, gain is O/I. Gain greater than 1 amplifies input, and gain less than 1 damps (attenuates) input. Gain is often measured in decibels (dB), with positive values corresponding to amplification, and negative values to damping.

GAZE-DIRECTED LOD: Describes the class of techniques that select among level-of-detail representations for an object by exploiting knowledge of the user's gaze, such as gaze direction, the velocity of features across the user's retinae, and ocular vergence (see *vergence eye movement*).

GENERALIZATION: In the field of geographic information systems (GIS), the simplification of map information at different scales. It is analogous to the term *level of detail* in the computer graphics field.

GENUS: Characterizes the *topology* of a surface, in effect providing a count of the number of holes in an closed *manifold*. For example, a sphere and a cube have a genus of zero, while a doughnut and a coffee cup have a genus of one.

GEOMETRIC COMPRESSION: A technique for reducing the storage requirements of a complex surface by compressing the surface representation, such as compressing the list of its vertices and/or polygons. This can also be done in a multiresolution fashion to facilitate the progressive streaming of compressed models.

GEOMETRIC ERROR: Deviation of a simplified surface from the more accurate original surface due to a reduction in the number of (x,y,z) spatial coordinates used to represent the surface.

GEOMETRIC SIMPLIFICATION: See *polygonal simplification.*

GEOMORPHS: A geometry-based technique for blending between two different levels of detail by smoothly interpolating the positions of vertices in one resolution level into the positions of vertices in the subsequent resolution level. See *alpha blending.*

GLOBAL ILLUMINATION: A class of rendering techniques that calculate surface illumination, taking into account interaction among the objects and surfaces in the scene. These algorithms can account for various intersurface lighting effects such as shadows, color bleeding, reflection, and sometimes refraction and caustics. Included are ray tracing, path tracing, and radiosity techniques.

GLOBAL TOPOLOGY: In LOD, the structure of a connected polygonal mesh. The global topology defines the *genus*, or number of holes, of the mesh surface.

GREEDY ALGORITHM: An algorithm that always takes the best immediate or local solution to resolve a problem, that is, it assumes that the path to the best globally optimal solution can be found through a series of locally optimal steps. In terms of simplification, this normally means that some quality measure is used to decide the next operation that will have the least impact on the model. Greedy algorithms are usually quicker but they may not always result in the globally optimal solution.

GUARANTEED ERROR BOUND: See *conservative bound.*

GAUSSIAN SPHERE: The natural space in which to express normal vectors. Each point on the surface of a unit sphere may be interpreted as a unit-length vector from the origin to that point. Distance between two of these normal vectors can be thought of as the arc length required to walk on the sphere from one to the other.

HALF-EDGE COLLAPSE: An *edge collapse* in which one endpoint of the edge is collapsed into the other endpoint, rather than collapsing both endpoints into a newly created "average" vertex. Since this removes one vertex of the edge from the mesh but retains the other, half-edge collapse can be considered a restricted form of *vertex removal.*

HAUSDORFF DISTANCE: The maximum of minimum distances between two point sets. In other words, given two sets of points, each point finds its closest neighbor in the other set, and we record the largest separation between these closest neighbors. This is a form of maximum distance between two points sets, and we can apply it to polygon meshes as well as a way to describe their *object-space error.*

HIERARCHICAL LOD: An LOD scheme in which multiple small adjacent objects in a scene may be replaced with a larger representative object that may in turn be combined with other representative objects and replaced by a still larger LOD. This allows scenes with large numbers of small objects to be drastically simplified into simple fused objects.

HIGH-LEVEL PERCEPTION: The processing at the later stages of the human visual system. Often called "top-down" perception. High-level perception is concerned with how known objects are recognized. The focus of research by cognitive perceptual psychologists. See also *low-level perception.*

HYPERACUITY: The paradoxical phenomenon in which certain visual stimuli can be perceived that are smaller than the size of a single *photoreceptor cell. Vernier acuity* is one such example of hyperacuity.

HYSTERESIS: In the context of LOD, a degree of lag introduced into the switching between levels of detail. Hysteresis is used to avoid the scintillating effect of objects continually switching at the threshold distance.

IMAGE-DRIVEN SIMPLIFICATION: A technique for generating LODs based on rendered imagery. Multiple images are rendered for all candidate edge collapses and an image-based comparison evaluates the resulting error, which is then used to prioritize the edge collapse in a greedy simplification process. See Section 5.5.

IMPOSTERS: See *texture map imposters.*

INTERNAL VALIDITY: The extent to which the conclusions drawn based on a lab experiment are justified. Uncontrolled experimental variables can cause one to question internal validity.

IO DIFFERENCING: An early approach to managing the tradeoff between temporal and visual detail. Temporal detail is measured visually by comparing the currently displayed view to the view that would result according to current input, producing the IO difference. This difference is then summed with the error introduced by LOD techniques. An IO differencing system minimizes this summed error.

I/O PATH: A system path from an input device to eventual display. Many measures of temporal detail include the time required for input to travel along an I/O path. Complex systems may have multiple I/O paths.

ISOSURFACE: In volume data sets, the surface defined as all points at which the value stored in the volume equals a particular value. For example, the bone–tissue interface in a medical CT scan can be expressed as an isosurface at a given density.

ISOTROPIC LOD: Refers to the use of the same resolution level across a whole object. This term is therefore equivalent to *view-independent LOD*.

JUST NOTICEABLE DIFFERENCE (JND): In a perceptual experiment, the level of difference between two stimuli that viewers can reliably sense. JNDs will vary as other variables, such as display luminance, are changed.

KNAPSACK PROBLEM: An optimization problem similar to trying to fill a container of limited capacity with an optimal selection of items so as to maximize the value of the selected items. In the context of LOD management, the container is the allotted rendering budget, and the items are the LODs chosen to represent each object.

KERNEL: The region inside a planar polygon that has an unobstructed view of the entire polygon boundary. These points must lie on the correct side of every polygon edge (more precisely, of the line containing every polygon edge). If we place a vertex inside this kernel, we can connect it to every polygon boundary vertex to create a non–self-intersecting triangulation of the polygon.

LATENCY-ONLY (LO) MANIPULATION: A system manipulation that affects *system latency*, but not *frame rate. System responsiveness* changes directly in response to the LO change. A typical manipulation adjusts filtering in the input subsystem.

LATE SAMPLING: A latency-only manipulation that moves computation from after the input sample to before it. By moving computation from an FL to an FO context, latency and *system responsiveness* are reduced, while *frame rate* is unchanged.

LAZY EVALUATION: A simplification strategy to reduce the total work performed by putting off computations until they are truly necessary. This is a useful strategy when some of the work is redundant and does not contribute to improved results.

LEVEL OF DETAIL: The real-time 3D computer graphics technique in which a complex object is represented at different resolutions and the most appropriate representation chosen in real time in order to create a tradeoff between image fidelity and frame rate. This term is often used interchangeably to refer to both the graphics technique and a single representation of an object.

LOCAL TOPOLOGY: In LOD, the connectivity of a mesh feature (face, edge, or vertex) with its immediate neighborhood.

LOD: See *level of detail*.

LOW-LEVEL PERCEPTION: The processing in the early stages of the human visual system. Often called "bottom-up" perception. Low-level perception begins with the signal from the retina. The focus of research by psychophysicists. See also *high-level perception*.

MANIFOLD: A surface for which each edge belongs to exactly two faces. Topologically, a manifold is everywhere equivalent to a disc. Every vertex in a manifold triangle mesh is adjacent to a single connected ring of triangles. A *manifold with boundary* is a surface where each edge belongs to one or two faces.

MAPPING DISTANCE: The 3D distance between two surfaces measured with respect to some well-behaved, bijective mapping function. The mapping function determines which points on one surface correspond to which points on another surface; we can then measure distances between corresponding points. These distances are always at least as large as the *Hausdorff distance*, but the mappings may better capture the notion that these meshes are surfaces rather than arbitrary collections of points.

MARCHING CUBES: A technique for generating polygonal *isosurfaces* from volumetric data. Proposed by Lorensen and Cline [Lorenson 87], this fast local algorithm has become a de facto standard for this task.

MERGE TREE: A term used by Xia and Varshney [Xia 96] to describe their vertex hierarchy structure for view-dependent LOD. Merge trees are created by an independent high-level simplification framework (see Section 2.4) using edge collapses, and thus form a balanced binary tree.

MESH SIMPLIFICATION: See *polygonal simplification.*

MIP-MAPPING: A simple texture filtering technique widely supported by graphics hardware. Represents textures using an image *pyramid* in which each cell is typically the unweighted average of the four corresponding cells in the next finer level of the pyramid.

MULTICHANNEL MODEL: A widely accepted contemporary theory of spatial vision which proposes that the human visual system processes images simultaneously at different spatial scales, referred to as channels.

NATIONAL TELEVISION STANDARDS COMMITTEE (NTSC): Refers to both the body and the specification it drew up in 1953 that defines the current standard for television transmission and display. The standard defines a display with 525 lines of resolution and an interlaced refresh rate of 60 Hz.

NORMAL CONE: A bounding volume in the space of normal vectors that may be used to solve such problems as silhouette and backface detection. Given a set of normal vectors, a normal cone is a cone guaranteed to contain every vector in the set, while preferably remaining as small as possible. The cone is typically defined by a central axis and an angular extent.

NORMAL MAP: An image analogous to a texture map, except that the pixels represent a surface's normal vectors rather than its colors. The red, green, and blue channels may encode the x, y, and z normal components. We can then shade the surface using these normals rather than using triangle- or vertex-based normals.

NTSC: See *National Television Standards Committee.*

OBJECT-SPACE ERROR: A quantity measured in the 3D object space indicating how far off a simplified model is from its original representation. It may be a scalar, such as the length of some 3D-error vector, a higher-order representation such as a collection of vectors that represents the movement of selected points on the simplified surface, or a volume that lies between the original and simplified representations. See also *screen-space error*.

OCCLUSION CULLING: A class of computer graphics algorithms aimed at quickly discarding geometry that cannot be seen because of intervening objects. In scenes with high-depth complexity, such as architectural walk-throughs, the vast portion of the model cannot be seen from any given viewpoint and can be culled away by these algorithms. This class of algorithms accelerates rendering, complementing level-of-detail approaches: each technique eliminates geometry that the other could not.

OCTREE: A simple hierarchical space-subdivision scheme in which the bounding box of an object or scene is recursively subdivided into eight equally sized octants, which may in turn be subdivided.

OFFSET SURFACE: A new surface generated by displacing all points of some original surface by some distance along individual normal vectors.

OPEN LOOP TASKS: User tasks that require little or no feedback, leaving the feedback loop "open"—the opposite of the *closed-loop task*. Such tasks are typically highly practiced, and require little attention. Tasks that are predominantly open loop include typing, shoe tying, baseball pitching, and clicking on large or well-known menu choices. These tasks are less sensitive to temporal detail, but if they require prediction (often during motion), they can be sensitive to *frame rate* and *system latency*.

OPTIC NERVE: Transports the neural signals from the retina to the visual cortex in the brain. In the retina, the fibers of the optic nerve are formed by the axons of the *retinal ganglion cells*.

OPTIMIZATION: A process for adjusting some variables to seek a state that minimizes or maximizes some objective function. For LOD, we may wish to minimize simplification error.

OUTPUT SIGNAL: In manual control theory, the changes in system state over time, treated as a signal with many component frequencies. A high-frequency output signal corresponds to rapid, high-speed changes in user control of the system.

OUT-OF-CORE SIMPLIFICATION: A *mesh simplification* technique capable of simplifying meshes too large to fit into main memory. Such techniques typically require careful memory management with parts of the model paged in and out of main memory as required.

OVERDRAW: A measure of scene complexity often applied to games that measures how many times, on average, each screen pixel is drawn to achieve the final displayed image. More overdraw capability allows more complex effects in the scene, but requires a greater *pixel fill rate* to achieve an acceptable *frame rate*.

PANUM'S FUSIONAL AREA: The depth range over which objects appear to be fused by the eye for any given point of vergence (see *vergence eye movement*). Objects outside of this range appear blurred.

PARALLEL LOD: A level-of-detail technique where the task of computing the set of polygons to display is partitioned into independent chunks and processed on multiple physical processors at the same time.

PARAMETRIC DISTANCE: A *mapping distance* for which the mapping function is parameterized. This often occurs in the context of texture mapping, where a 2D texture domain is mapped to a surface, allowing color images and other data to be mapped to the surface. If the original and simplified surfaces both maintain texture coordinates, we can use these coordinates to tell us which points on the surfaces correspond to each other.

PATH TRACING: A very high-quality, very computationally expensive global illumination technique that extends ray tracing to allow rendering of diffuse surface-to-surface reflections.

PHASE LAG: A term from manual control theory that relates *system responsiveness* to task. For a given frequency of the target signal, phase lag is the number of degrees of phase that poor system responsiveness introduces between the target and output system signals.

PHOTORECEPTOR CELLS: The cells in the retina of the eye that detect light. There are two different classes of photoreceptors: around 120 million to 130 million rods that are achromatic and sensitive to motion, and around 5 million to 8 million cones that provide color sensitivity. Rods tend to be used for night (scotopic) vision, while cones are used in day (photopic) vision.

PIXEL FILL-RATE: The maximum rate at which the graphics hardware can write to the framebuffer. Expensive pixel-shading operations (e.g., blending between four textures, bump mapping, etc.) reduce the pixel fill rate, often dramatically. If pixel fill rate is the bottleneck in graphics performance, reducing the number of polygons using LOD will not help, since the simpler polygonal models will cover roughly the same number of pixels.

PIXEL SHADER: Defines the processing applied to a rendered pixel before it reaches the frame buffer. A pixel shader generally involves one or more texture lookups, interpolation of vertex properties, and possibly a read-modify-write of the existing frame buffer contents. Pixel shaders are generally hardware specific and are defined as either a set of state switches or pseudo code interpreted by the specific rendering engine.

PM: See *progressive meshes*.

POLYGONAL SIMPLIFICATION: The general term used to describe the action of taking an original set of polygons and producing a second set of polygons that is less complex, that is, contains fewer polygons and/or vertices.

POPPING EFFECT: The noticeable flicker that can occur when the graphics system switches between different levels of detail.

PREVIEWING DISPLAY: A display that forecasts target state, enabling users to more effectively compensate for poor system responsiveness. Common examples include the view of the road ahead in racing games and horizons in flight simulators.

PREDICTIVE DISPLAY: A display that forecasts system state, enabling users to more effectively compensate for poor system responsiveness. Many flight simulators using this technique display the expected position of the aircraft over the current view.

PROGRESSIVE LOD TRANSMISSION: The act of progressively transmitting a large model over the Web. The client receives an initial coarse model and then a stream of updates that add further refinement at each step.

PROGRESSIVE MESHES (PM): A highly influential *continuous LOD* method introduced by Hugues Hoppe and based on *edge collapse* operations. Constructed using a greedy high-level simplification framework, progressive meshes were later extended by Hoppe to *view-dependent progressive meshes.*

PYRAMID: A multiresolution data structure in which a regular grid of data points is represented at a number of levels of detail, where each level is downsampled to half the resolution of the previous one, that is, one quarter the number of vertices. Image pyramids are often used to summarize and filter properties of images.

QSPLAT: A view-dependent rendering system by Rusinkiewicz and Levoy, based on splats rather than polygons and designed for interactive visualization of massive models.

QUADRIC ERROR METRIC: A technique for evaluating the error introduced during simplification that uses the sum of squared distances among vertices of a simplified mesh and the polygons of the original mesh. The quadric can be represented, stored, and accumulated efficiently as a symmetric 4×4 matrix.

QUADTREE: A hierarchical tree structure having four branches that is often used to generate multiresolution terrain meshes. This is normally implemented as a grid structure where each cell can be recursively split into four quadrants. See also *bintree* and *octree.*

RADIOSITY: A global illumination technique that explicitly models radiative transfer among surfaces as a system of equations to be solved. Radiosity assumes a simplistic, diffuse-only lighting model, but unlike other global illumination algorithms (e.g., ray tracing or path tracing) produces a 3D model instead of an image as final output.

REFRESH CYCLE TIME: The time between display refresh events. Refresh cycle time is the inverse of *refresh rate.*

REFRESH RATE: The rate at which the display screen is refreshed, measured in Hz. In most graphics systems, display refresh is accomplished in a hardware subsystem. Refresh rates are therefore constant and independent of *frame rate.*

RETESSELLATION: The process of recalculating the set of polygons over a surface.

RETINAL GANGLION CELLS: The output neurons that encode and transmit information from the eye to the brain. The inputs to these cells come from the *photoreceptor cells* via the *collector cells*. Retinal ganglion cells are organized with circular receptive fields that are classed as either on-center or off-center.

RETRIANGULATION: The process of recalculating the set of triangles over a surface. *Delaunay triangulation*, which minimizes the maximum angle of the triangles created, is one popular technique for calculating the set of triangles over a surface.

RIGID MESH: In game programming, a mesh that does not require any complex skinning; all the mesh vertices are transformed by a single matrix or bone (see *skinned mesh*). These meshes are normally useful to represent rigid and inanimate objects. A rigid mesh is generally the fastest type of mesh to render.

ROAM: Real-time Optimally Adapting Meshes, a *view-dependent* level of detail technique specialized for terrain grids.

ROOT MEAN SQUARED ERROR (RMS):   A common automatic image fidelity measure, based on the root of the summed pixel by pixel squared differences: $E_{rms} = (\Sigma (O_{xy} - S_{xy})^2)^{1/2}$, where O_{xy} and S_{xy} are pixels from the original and simplified images.

SACCADE: A rapid movement of the eye which is made in order to fixate a target onto the *fovea*.

SACCADIC SUPPRESSION: The effect that the visual system seems to shut down to some degree during reflex rapid-eye movements known as saccades. That is, even though our point of fixation moves at very high velocities during a saccade, we do not experience blurred vision.

SAMPLING DELAY: The delay between the completion of a significant user action or input event, and its subsequent sampling by the system. Since input is effectively sampled at the *frame rate*, sampling delay is equal to half of the frame time on average.

SCREEN–SPACE ERROR: A quantity measured in the 2D screen space indicating how far off a simplified model is from its original representation. Convenient units might be pixels, millimeters, and so on. The screen-space error might tell you how many millimeters off an object's silhouette appears on the screen. Some applications balance the tessellation of an entire scene by maintaining a roughly uniform screen-space error for all objects. See also *object-space error*.

SECOND ORDER CONTROL: A control that translates each input value into one output acceleration. Second-order controls are not common, but include control of spacecraft and the thrust control in the video game Asteroids.

SILHOUETTE PRESERVATION: A technique that allocates higher resolution around the visual silhouette of a model. Motivated by the high perceptual importance of silhouettes in human vision, silhouette preservation implies a *view-dependent* LOD algorithm.

SINGLE BUFFERING: The use of only one frame buffer to represent the displayed image. Such systems exhibit *tearing* as new frames overwrite previous frames.

SKINNED MESH: A mesh in which each component vertex is potentially transformed by a different matrix, resulting in final triangles that will deform as these matrices are changed or animated. These transforming matrices are often referred to as the "bones" of the mesh. If each vertex can be transformed by the blended result of multiple matrices, then the skinning is referred to as weighted. These techniques are used to give models a more natural appearance.

SPATIAL FREQUENCY: A measure of the degree of spatial detail that the eye can perceive. This is normally given in units of cycles per degree of visual arc (c/deg).

SPATIOTEMPORAL THRESHOLD SURFACE: The surface that describes the sensitivity of an observer to stimuli of varying spatial and temporal characteristics.

STABILITY: The ability of a dynamic control system—manual or otherwise—to reliably match current system state to target state without wild oscillations or diverging completely from the target state. In control theory, systems are unstable whenever phase lag is over 180 degrees and gain is greater than 1.

STANDARD IMAGE: In a visual fidelity comparison, the original image or unsimplified model.

STANDARD LOD FIDELITY MEASURE: The widely spread run-time LOD measure that projects precomputed distances resulting from simplification error into the image plane, and finds their maximum.

SYSTEM LATENCY (OR LAG): The age of the currently displayed frame, or alternatively the amount of time it takes for an input sample to be displayed in a frame. In systems with more than one I/O path, there will be multiple system latencies. Measured in milliseconds (ms).

SYSTEM RESPONSIVENESS: The time from the moment a user action (such as a change in direction) is executed, until that action is displayed. System responsiveness includes *system latency* as well as an additional delay between the completion of the user action and the moment it is sampled. Measured in milliseconds (ms).

TARGET SIGNAL: In manual control theory, the changes in target state over time, treated as a signal with many component frequencies. A high-frequency target signal corresponds to a challenging task that requires rapid, high-speed user input.

TEARING: The display of two (or more) partial frames at the same time. Typically, one partially complete newer frame is displayed above a now incomplete older frame. The visual (also temporal) boundary between them looks like a "tear" in the image. Tearing is a symptom of single buffering, or systems without *frame locking*.

TEMPORAL DETAIL: Interactivity, or the temporal information presented to the user in an interactive graphics application. This might be measured using *frame rate, system latency,* or *system responsiveness.*

TESSELLATION: The process of subdividing a surface into a mesh of polygons, often triangles or quadrilaterals.

TEXTURE MAP IMPOSTERS: A level-of-detail technique where a number of polygons in a scene are replaced with a simple texture-mapped primitive that represents a rendering of those polygons from a particular viewpoint. Sprites, decal textures, and lightmaps are also examples of imposters. Also referred to as a stand-in.

TEXTURE SEAM: An edge or series of edges of an otherwise continuous mesh where the texture coordinates for the edge vertices are different among the faces that share that edge. A texture seam is necessary when creating a complex mesh using a composited texture, where multiple parts of the image are positioned nonspatially on a single texture to improve efficient use of memory. This practice is very common in game situations.

THRESHOLD CONTRAST: The minimum *contrast* required to see a target.

TIN: See *triangulated irregular network.*

T-JUNCTION: A generally undesirable topological feature where a vertex from a higher LOD triangle lies on the edge of a lower LOD triangle but does not share one of its vertices. This can cause bleeding tears to appear in the mesh due to small floating-point rounding differences.

TOPOLOGY: See *local topology* and *global topology.*

TRADITIONAL LOD: See *view-independent LOD.*

TRIANGULATED IRREGULAR NETWORK (TIN): A surface representation, often used for topographic elevation data, that uses a tessellation of nonoverlapping triangles where the vertices of the triangles can be spaced irregularly over the surface. See also *digital elevation model.*

TRIPLE BUFFERING: The use of a third frame buffer to improve frame rates. After rendering in the second buffer is complete, *double-buffered, frame-locked* systems are blocked until the next refresh cycle begins. Triple-buffered systems can begin rendering in the third buffer, avoiding idle time.

TRIANGULATION: A technique to reduce one or more n-sided polygons into a set of three-sided polygons, that is, triangles.

TVU RELATIONSHIP: The relationship among temporal detail (T), visual detail (V), and their effect on application usability (U). Across platforms and for a fixed task, this would theoretically form a surface; the LOD management system should find the point of maximum usability on this surface.

VDPM: See *view dependent progressive meshes.*

VERGENCE EYE MOVEMENT: The synchronized movement of both eyes to focus on an object at a particular depth. This can either be a convergence or a divergence movement depending upon whether the two eyes rotate toward or away from each other. This process, along with *accommodation*, allows us to focus sharply on a given object.

VERNIER ACUITY: A form of *hyperacuity* where it is possible to discriminate the noncolinearity of two thick abutting lines to a resolution of 2 to 5 seconds of arc. This occurs despite the fact that our *photoreceptor cells* subtend around 25 to 30 seconds or arc.

VERTEX CLUSTERING: A simplification technique in which a single vertex is chosen to represent a group of vertices, normally chosen as the average of all locations. A vertex-clustering operation is a generalization of an *edge collapse*.

VERTEX DECIMATION: An LOD-generation, algorithm-based vertex removal by Schroeder et al., fast and fairly robust in practice. We discuss decimation in detail in Section 5.2.

VERTEX HIERARCHY: A data structure used by *view-dependent LOD* algorithms. A hierarchy of vertex-merge operations encodes a partial ordering of the local simplification operations applied during preprocessing. View-dependent LOD applies these operations according to view-dependent criteria at runtime, tailoring simplification on the fly to the particular viewing parameters. Vertex hierarchies are described in detail in Section 4.3.2.

VERTEX REMOVAL: A local *mesh simplification* operator that removes a vertex and its associated triangles, then *retriangulates* the resulting hole. In a *manifold* mesh, a vertex removal operation will reduce the triangle count by two.

VERTEX SPLIT: A technique to refine a coarser mesh into a more detailed representation by replacing a single vertex with two vertices and thus adding new polygons to the mesh. This can be considered the inverse of an *edge collapse*.

VERTEX SHADER: The type of processing applied to source vertex data to transform, project, clip, light, or otherwise prepare the data for on-screen display. Depending on the platform, vertex shaders might be represented as explicit assembly-language code, a selectable "mode" switch or switches, or a vendor-designed pseudo code that controls the vertex-processing unit.

VERTEX TREE: The term used by Luebke and Erikson [Luebke 97] to describe their vertex hierarchy structure for *view-dependent LOD*. In their algorithm, vertex trees are created by an independent high-level simplification framework using cell collapse operations in an *octree*, so nodes in the vertex tree have at most eight children. Vertices at the top of the vertex tree represent the coarsest resolution.

VERTICAL REFRESH RATE: See *refresh rate*.

VERTICAL RETRACE: See *refresh cycle time*.

VIDEO GAME: Refers to hardware or software specifically designed for fixed-function, low-cost hardware connected to a standard television display. Distinct from *computer game*, used here to refer to games designed for personal computers.

VIEW-DEPENDENCE TREE: The term used by El-Sana and Varshney [El-Sana 99a, 99b] to describe their vertex hierarchy structure for *view-dependent LOD*. View-dependence trees consist of a binary vertex hierarchy created from *edge collapse* and vertex-pair collapse operations applied by a interleaved high-level simplification framework.

VIEW-DEPENDENT LOD: A level-of-detail scheme in which surface detail is varied dynamically, *retessellating* objects on the fly relative to the user's viewpoint, and continuously, allowing a single object to span multiple levels of detail.

VIEW-DEPENDENT PROGRESSIVE MESHES (VDPM): The term used by Hoppe [97] to describe his vertex hierarchy structure for *view-dependent LOD*. VDPM extend Hoppe's *progressive mesh* structure, a binary hierarchy of edge collapse operations created by a greedy high-level simplification framework (see Section 2.4).

VIEW-FRUSTUM CULLING: A graphics acceleration technique based on quickly discarding portions of the scene that lie outside the user's field of view.

VIEW-INDEPENDENT LOD: See *discrete LOD*.

VISUAL ACUITY: A measure of the smallest detail that an observer can resolve under ideal illumination conditions.

VISUAL DETAIL: The visual information presented to the user in an interactive graphics application. This might be measured in a number of ways, including polygon count and spatial accuracy in pixels.

VISUAL MASKING: The perceptual phenomenon that the presence of one visual pattern can affect the visibility of another pattern. For example, a large adjacent stimulus (in time or space) can cause the threshold of a smaller stimulus to be increased, that is, the smaller stimulus needs to be more intense for it to be visible.

VOLUME TEXTURE: A texture that contains three dimensions of pixel information. The format for a volume texture is generally similar to an array of standard 2D textures, but often the hardware can perform texture-filtering operations in this third access. Can be useful when constructing animated textures, multiview imposters, or certain types of lighting and effects.

WEBER'S LAW: States that the change in a stimulus intensity that will be just noticeable is a function of the percentage change in stimulus intensity, not the absolute change in stimulus intensity, that is, the larger the stimulus, the larger the change required for a difference to be perceived.

ZERO-ORDER CONTROL: A control that translates each input value to one output value. Zero-order controls include sliding controls of light level and slider bars in windowed user interfaces. See also *first-order control*.

REFERENCES

Glide 3.0 Programming Guide. 3dfx Interactive, Inc., San Jose, CA. www.bme.jhu.edu/resources/whitaker/doc/Glide3/glide3pgm.pdf. 1998.

Ahumada, A. Computational Image Quality Metrics: A Review. *SID Digest.* vol. 24. pp. 305–308. 1993.

Ahumada, A and B Beard. A Simple Vision Model for Inhomogeneous Image Quality Assessment. *Society for Information Display International Symposium Digest of Technical Papers.* pp. 40.1. 1998.

Airey, J M, J H Rohlf, and Frederick P Brooks, Jr. Towards Image Realism with Interactive Update Rates in Complex Virtual Building Environments. *Proceedings of 1990 Symposium on Interactive 3D Graphics.* pp. 41–50. 1990.

Akeley, K, P Haeberli, and D Burns. *tomesh.c:* (C Program). In *SGI Developer's Toolbox.* CD-ROM. Silicon Graphics, Inc. 1990.

Aliaga, D, J Cohen, A Wilson, E Baker, H Zhang, C Erikson, K Hoff, T Hudson, W Stuerzlinger, R Bastos, M Whitton, F Brooks, and D Manocha. MMR: An Interactive Massive Model Rendering System Using Geometric and Image-Based Acceleration. *Proceedings of 1999 Symposium on Interactive 3D Graphics.* pp. 199–206, 237. 1999.

Andrews, P R and F W Campbell. Images at the Blind Spot. *Nature.* vol. 353(6342). pp. 308. 1991.

Angel, E. Vertex Arrays. In: *Interactive Computer Graphics: A Top-Down Approach with OpenGL.* Addison-Wesley, Reading, MA. pp. 158–160. 2000.

Anstis, S M and P Cavanagh. A Minimum Motion Technique for Judging Equiluminance in Colour Vision. In: J D Mollon and L T Sharpe, eds. *Colour Vision: Physiology and Psychophysics.* Academic Press, London. pp. 156–166. 1983.

Astheimer, P. What You See Is What You Hear: Acoustics Applied in Virtual Worlds. *Proceedings of IEEE 1993 Symposium on Research Frontiers in Virtual Reality.* pp. 100–107. 1993.

Astheimer, P and M-L Pöche. Level-of-Detail Generation and Its Application in Virtual Reality. *Proceedings of VRST '94.* pp. 299–309. 1994.

Azuma, R and G Bishop. Improving Static and Dynamic Registration in an Optical See-Through HMD. *Proceedings of SIGGRAPH 94.* pp. 197–204. 1994.

349

Bahill, A T, D Adler, and L Stark. Most Naturally Occurring Human Saccades Have Magnitudes of 15 Degrees or Less. *Investigative Ophthalmology.* vol. 14. pp. 468–469. 1975.

Bajaj, C and M-S Kim. Generation of Configuration Space Obstacles: The Case of a Moving Sphere. *IEEE Journal of Robotics and Automation.* vol. 4(1). pp. 94–99. 1988.

Bajaj, C and D Schikore. Error-Bounded Reduction of Triangle Meshes with Multivariate Data. *SPIE.* vol. 2656. pp. 34–45. 1996.

Bajaj, C, F Bernardini, and G Xu. Reconstructing Surfaces and Functions on Surfaces from Unorganized 3D Data. *Algorithmica.* vol. 19. pp. 243–261. 1997.

Bajaj, C, V Pascucci, and G Zhuang. Progressive Compression and Transmission of Arbitrary Triangular Meshes. *Proceedings of IEEE Visualization '99.* pp. 307–316. 1999.

Banks, M S. The Development of Spatial and Temporal Contrast Sensitivity. *Current Eye Research.* vol. 2. pp. 191–198. 1982.

Barnes, G. Vestibulo-Ocular Function During Coordinated Head and Eye Movements to Acquire Visual Targets. *Journal of Physiology.* vol. 287. pp. 127–147. 1979.

Bartram, D. Levels of Coding in Picture-Picture Comparison Tasks. *Memory and Cognition.* vol. 4. pp. 592–602. 1976.

Biederman, I. Recognition-by-Components: A Theory of Human Image Understanding. *Psychological Review.* vol. 94. pp. 115–147. 1987.

Birkel, P A. SEDRIS Geospatial Reference Model. *SEDRIS Document Set.* 1997.

Blake, E H. *Complexity in Natural Scenes: A Viewer Centered Metric for Computing Adaptive Detail.* Ph.D. Thesis. Queen Mary College, London University. 1989.

Blakemore, C and F W Campbell. On the Existence of Neurones in the Human Visual System Selectively Sensitive to the Orientation and Size of Retinal Images. *Journal of Physiology.* vol. 203. pp. 237–260. 1969.

Blow, J. Implementing a Texture Caching System. *Game Developer Magazine.* pp. 46–56. 1998.

Blow, J. Terrain Rendering at High Levels of Detail. *Proceedings of Game Developers Conference 2000.* 2000.

Blow, J. Terrain Rendering Research for Games. *Course Notes for SIGGRAPH 2000 Course #39.* 2000.

Bogomjakov, A and C Gotsman. Universal Rendering Sequences for Transparent Vertex Caching of Progressive Meshes. *Proceedings of Graphics Interface 2001.* pp. 81–90. 2001.

Bolin, M R and G W Meyer. A Frequency Based Ray Tracer. *Proceedings of SIGGRAPH 95.* pp. 409–418. 1995.

Bolin, M and G Meyer. A Perceptually Based Adaptive Sampling Algorithm. *Proceedings of SIGGRAPH 98.* pp. 299–309. 1998.

Brodsky, D and B Watson. Model Simplification Through Refinement. *Proceedings of Graphics Interface 2000.* pp. 221–228. 2000.

Bryson, S. Implementing Virtual Reality. *SIGGRAPH 93 Course #43 Notes.* ACM SIGGRAPH 1993. pp. 16.1–16.12. 1993.

Burr, D C and J Ross. Contrast Sensitivity at High Velocities. *Vision Research.* vol. 22. pp. 479–484. 1982.

Caelli, T M and G Moraglia. On the Detection of Gabor Signals and Discriminations of Gabor Textures. *Vision Research.* vol. 25. pp. 671–684. 1985.

Campbell, F W and D G Green. Optical and Retinal Factors Affecting Visual Resolution. *Journal of Physiology.* vol. 181. pp. 576–593. 1965.

Campbell, F W and R W Gubisch. Optical Quality of the Human Eye. *Journal of Physiology.* vol. 186. pp. 558–578. 1966.

Campbell, F W, J J Hulikowski, and J Levinson. The Effect of Orientation on the Visual Resolution of Gratings. *Journal of Physiology.* vol. 187. pp. 427–436. 1966.

Campbell, F W and J G Robson. Application of Fourier Analysis to the Visibility of Gratings. *Journal of Physiology.* vol. 197. pp. 551–566. 1968.

Campbell, F W, R H S Carpenter, and J Z Levinson. Visibility of Aperiodic Patterns Compared with that of Sinusoidal Gratings. *Journal of Physiology.* vol. 204. pp. 283–209. 1969.

Carlson, D and J Hodgins. Simulation Levels of Detail for Real-time Animation. *Proceedings of Graphics Interface '97.* pp. 1–8. 1997.

Carmo, M do. *Differential Geometry of Curves and Surfaces.* Prentice Hall, Englewood Cliffs, NJ. 1976.

Catmull, E E. *A Subdivision Algorithm for Computer Display of Curved Surfaces.* Ph.D. Thesis. Department of Computer Science. University of Utah, Salt Lake City, Utah. 1974.

Cavanagh, P. Vision at Equiluminance. In: J R Cronly-Dillon, ed. *Vision and Visual Dysfunction: Limits of Vision.* CRC Press, Boca Raton, FL. pp. 234–250. 1991.

Chazelle, B. An Optimal Algorithm for Intersecting Three-Dimensional Convex Polyhedra. *SIAM Journal of Computing.* vol. 21(4). pp. 671–696. 1992.

Choudhury, P and B Watson. *Fully Adaptive Simplification of Massive Meshes.* Technical Report. Department of Computer Science, Northwestern University, Evanston, IL.
www.cs.northwestern.edu/~watsonb/school/docs/vmrsimp.tr.pdf. 2000.

Chrislip, C A and J F Ehlert Jr. *Level of Detail Models for Dismounted Infantry in NPSNET-IV.8.1.* Master's Thesis. Naval Postgraduate School, Monterey, CA. 1995.

Cignoni, P, C Montani, and R Scopigno. A Comparison of Mesh Simplification Algorithms. *Computers & Graphics.* vol. 22(1). pp. 37–54. 1998.

Cignoni, P, C Rocchini, and R Scopigno. Metro: Measuring Error on Simplified Surfaces. *Computer Graphics Forum.* vol. 17(2). pp. 167–174. 1998.

Clark, J H. Hierarchical Geometric Models for Visible Surface Algorithms. *Communications of the ACM.* vol. 19(10). pp. 547–554. 1976.

Cohen, J, A Varshney, D Manocha, G Turk, H Weber, P Agarwal, F Brooks, and W Wright. Simplification Envelopes. *Proceedings of SIGGRAPH 96.* pp. 119–128. 1996.

Cohen, J, D Manocha, and M Olano. Simplifying Polygonal Models Using Successive Mappings. *Proceedings of IEEE Visualization '97.* pp. 395–402. 1997.

Cohen, J, M Olano, and D Manocha. Appearance-Preserving Simplification. *Proceedings of SIGGRAPH 98.* pp. 115–122. 1998.

Cohen, J D. *Appearance-Preserving Simplification of Polygonal Models.* Ph.D. Thesis. Department of Computer Science, University of North Carolina at Chapel Hill, Chapel Hill, NC. 1998.

Cohen, J D, D G Aliaga, and W Zhang. Hybrid Simplification: Combining Multi-Resolution Polygon and Point Rendering. *Proceedings of IEEE Visualization 2001.* pp. 37–44, 539. 2001.

Cohen-Or, D and Y Levanoni. Temporal Continuity of Levels of Detail in Delaunay Triangulated Terrain. *Proceedings of IEEE Visualization '96.* pp. 37–42. 1996.

Coltman, J W and A E Anderson. Noise Limitations to Resolving Power in Electronic Imaging. *Proceedings of the Institute of Radio Engineers.* vol. 48. pp. 858–865. 1960.

Cosman, A and R Schumacker. System Strategies to Optimize CIG Image Content. *Proceedings of 1981 Image II Conference.* pp. 463–480. 1981.

Cowan, W B and C Ware. Elementary Colour coding. *SIGGRAPH 1985 Course #3 Notes: Colour Perception.* pp. 55–95. 1985.

Daly, S. The Visible Differences Predictor: An Algorithm for the Assessment of Image Fidelity. In: A Watson, ed. *Digital Images and Human Vision.* MIT Press, Cambridge, MA. pp. 179–206. 1993.

Daly, S. Engineering Observations from Spatiovelocity and Spatiotemporal Visual Models. *Proceedings of Human Vision and Electronic Imaging III, SPIE 3299.* pp. 180–191. 1998.

Davis, D, W Ribarsky, T Y Jiang, N Faust, and S Ho. Real-Time Visualization of Scalably Large Collections of Heterogeneous Objects. *Proceedings of IEEE Visualization '99.* pp. 437–440. 1999.

De Haemer, M, Jr and M J Zyda. Simplification of Objects Rendered by Polygonal Approximations. *Computers & Graphics.* vol. 15(2). pp. 175–184. 1991.

Deering, M. Geometry Compression. *Proceedings of SIGGRAPH 95.* pp. 13–20. 1995.

DeFloriani, L, B Falcidieno, and C Pien-Ovi. A Delaunay-Based Method for Surface Approximation. *Proceedings of Eurographics '83.* pp. 333–350. 1983.

DeFloriani, L. A Pyramidal Data Structure for Triangle-Based Surface Description. *IEEE Computer Graphics and Applications.* vol. 9(2). pp. 67–78. 1989.

DeFloriani, L and E Puppo. Hierarchical Triangulation for Multiresolution Surface Description. *ACM Transactions on Graphics.* vol. 14(4). pp. 363–411. 1995.

DeFloriani, L, L Marzano, and E Puppo. Multiresolution Models for Topographic Surface Description. *The Visual Computer.* vol. 12(7). pp. 317–345. 1996.

DeFloriani, L, P Magillo, and E Puppo. Building and Traversing a Surface at Variable Resolution. *Proceedings of IEEE Visualization '97.* pp. 103–110. 1997.

DeFloriani, L, P Magillo, and E Puppo. Efficient Implementation of Multi-Triangulations. *Proceedings of IEEE Visualization '98.* pp. 43–50. 1998.

DeFloriani, L, P Magillo, and E Puppo. VARIANT: A System for Terrain Modeling at Variable Resolution. *GeoInformatica.* vol. 4(3). pp. 287–315. 2000.

DeFloriani, L and P Magillo. Multiresolution Mesh Representation: Models and Data Structures. In: M Floater, A Iske, and E Qwak, eds., *Principles of Multiresolution Geometric Modeling.* Springer-Verlag, Berlin, New York. 2002.

Standards for Digital Elevation Models. Technical Report. US Department of the Interior, US Geological Survey, National Mapping Division, Reston, VA. January 1998.

Deussen, O, P Hanrahan, B Lintermann, R Mech, M Pharr, and P Prusinkiewics. Realistic Modeling and Rendering of Plant Ecosystems. *Proceedings of SIGGRAPH 98.* pp. 275–286. 1998.

Dörrie, H. *Euler's Problem of Polygon Division.* In: *100 Great Problems of Elementary Mathematics: Their History and Solutions.* Dover, NY. pp. 21–27. 1965.

Drasdo, N. The Neural Representation of Visual Space. *Nature.* vol. 266. pp. 554–556. 1977.

Duchaineau, M, M Wolinsky, D E Sigeti, M C Miller, C Aldrich, and M B Mineev-Weinstein. ROAMing Terrain: Real-Time Optimally Adapting Meshes. *Proceedings of IEEE Visualization '97.* pp. 81–88. 1997.

Dumont, R, F Pellacini, and J A Ferwerda. A Perceptually-Based Texture Caching Algorithm for Hardware-Based Rendering. *Proceedings of 2001 Eurographics Workshop on Rendering.* pp. 249–256. 2001.

Eck, M, T DeRose, T Duchamp, H Hoppe, M Lounsbery, and W Stuetzle. Multiresolution Analysis of Arbitrary Meshes. *Proceedings of SIGGRAPH 95.* pp. 173–182. 1995.

Edelsbrunner, H, D Kirkpatrick, and R Seidel. On the Shape of a Set of Points in the Plane. *IEEE Transactions on Information Theory.* vol. 29. pp. 551–559. 1983.

Edelsbrunner, H and E Mucke. Three-Dimensional Alpha Shapes. *ACM Transactions on Graphics.* vol. 13. pp. 43–72. 1994.

Edelsbrunner, H, D Letscher, and A Zomorodian. Topological Persistence and Simplification. *Proceedings of 41st Annual IEEE Symposium on Foundations of Computer Science.* pp. 454–463. 2000.

Edelsbrunner, H. *Geometry and Topology for Mesh Generation.* Cambridge University Press, Cambridge, New York. 2001.

Edelsbrunner, H and A Zomorodian. Computing Linking Numbers in a Filtration. In: *Algorithms in Bioinformatics (LNCS 2149).* Springer, Berlin, New York. pp. 112–127. 2001.

Elmes, D, B Kantowitz, and H Roediger III. *Research Methods in Psychology.* West Publishing Company, St Paul, MN. 1992.

El-Sana, J and A Varshney. Topology Simplification for Polygonal Virtual Environments. *IEEE Transactions on Visualization and Computer Graphics.* vol. 4(2). pp. 133–144. 1998.

El-Sana, J and A Varshney. Generalized View-Dependent Simplification. *Computer Graphics Forum.* vol. 18(3). pp. 83–94. 1999.

El-Sana, J and A Varshney. View-Dependent Topology Simplification. *Proceedings of Virtual Environments '99.* 1999.

El-Sana, J, F Evans, A Kalaiah, A Varshney, S Skiena, and E Azanli. Efficiently Computing and Updating Triangle Strips for Real-Time Rendering. *Computer-Aided Design.* vol. 32(13). pp. 753–772. 2000.

El-Sana, J, N Sokolovsky, C Silva. Integrating Occlusion Culling with View-Dependent Rendering, *Proceedings IEEE Visualization 2001.* pp. 371–378. 2001.

El-Sana J, O Hadar. Motion-Based View-Dependent Rendering. To be published in *Computer and Graphics* (June). 2002.

Enroth-Cugell, C and J G Robson. The Contrast Sensitivity of Retinal Ganglion Cells of the Cat. *Journal of Physiology.* vol. 187. pp. 517–552. 1966.

Erikson, C and D Manocha. GAPS: General and Automatic Polygonal Simplification. *Proceedings of 1999 ACM Symposium on Interactive 3D Graphics.* pp. 79–88. 1999.

Erikson, C. *Hierarchical Levels of Detail to Accelerate the Rendering of Large Static and Dynamic Polygonal Environments.* Ph.D. Thesis. University of North Carolina at Chapel Hill, Chapel Hill, NC. 2000.

Evans, F, S Skiena, and A Varshney. Optimizing Triangle Strips for Fast Rendering. *Proceedings of IEEE Visualization '96.* pp. 319–326. 1996.

Evans, W, D Kirkpatrick, and G Townsend. *Right Triangular Irregular Networks.* Technical Report 97–09. Department of Computer Science, University of Arizona, Tucson. 1997.

Falby, J S, M J Zyda, D R Pratt, and R L Mackey. NPSNET: Hierarchical Data Structures for Real-Time Three-Dimensional Visual Simulation. *Computers and Graphics.* vol. 17(1). pp. 65–69. 1993.

Ferwerda, J A, S Pattanaik, P Shirley, and D P Greenberg. A Model of Visual masking for Computer Graphics. *Proceedings of SIGGRAPH 97.* pp. 143–152. 1997.

Ferwerda, J A. Elements of Early Vision for Computer Graphics. *IEEE Computer Graphics and Applications.* vol. 21(5). pp. 22–33. 2001.

Fournier, A and D Y Montuno. Triangulating Simple Polygons and Equivalent Problems. *ACM Transactions on Graphics.* vol. 3. pp. 153–174. 1984.

Fowler, R J and J J Little. Automatic Extraction of Irregular Network Digital Terrain Models. *Proceedings of SIGGRAPH 79.* pp. 199–207. 1979.

Funkhouser, T A. *Database and Display Algorithms for Interactive Visualization of Architectural Models.* Ph.D. Thesis. University of California at Berkeley, Berkeley, CA. 1993.

Funkhouser, T A and C H Séquin. Adaptive Display Algorithm for Interactive Frame Rates During Visualization of Complex Virtual Environments. *Proceedings of SIGGRAPH 93.* pp. 247–254. 1993.

Garland, M and P S Heckbert. *Fast Polygonal Approximation of Terrains and Height Fields.* Technical Report CMU-CS-95–181. School of Computer Science, Carnegie Mellon University, Pittsburgh, PA. 1995.

Garland, M and P Heckbert. Surface Simplification Using Quadric Error Metrics. *Proceedings of SIGGRAPH 97.* pp. 209–216. 1997.

Garland, M and P Heckbert. Simplifying Surfaces with Color and Texture Using Quadric Error Metrics. *Proceedings of IEEE Visualization '98.* pp. 263–270. 1998.

Garland, M. *Quadric-Based Polygonal Surface Simplification.* Ph.D. Thesis. Carnegie Mellon University, Pittsburgh, PA. 1999.

Garland, M, A Willmott, and P S Heckbert. Hierarchical Face Clustering on Polygonal Surfaces. *Proceedings of 2001 ACM Symposium on Interactive 3D Graphics.* pp. 49–58. 2001.

Gerstner, T. Multiresolution Visualization and Compression of Global Topographic Data. To be published in *GeoInformatica.* 2002.

Gieng, T S, B Hamann, K L Joy, G L Schussman, and I J Trotts. Constructing Hierarchies for Triangle Meshes. *IEEE Transactions on Visualization and Computer Graphics.* vol. 4(2). pp. 145–161. 1998.

Girod, B. What's Wrong with Mean-Squared Error? In: A Watson, ed. *Digital Images and Human Vision.* MIT Press, Cambridge, MA. pp. 207–220. 1993.

Gobbetti, E and E Bouvier. Time-Critical Multiresolution Scene Rendering. *Proceedings of IEEE Visualization '99.* pp. 123–130. 1999.

Greene, N, M Kass, and G Miller. Hierarchical Z-Buffer Visibility. *Proceedings of SIGGRAPH 92.* pp. 319–326. 1992.

Gregory, R L. Vision with Isoluminant Colour Contrast: 1. A Projection Technique and Observations. *Perception.* vol. 6. pp. 113–119. 1977.

Gregory, R L. *Eye and Brain: The Psychology of Seeing.* 4th ed. Weidenfeld and Nicolson, London. 1990.

Gross, M, R Gatti, and O Staadt. Fast Multiresolution Surface Meshing. *Proceedings of IEEE Visualization '95.* pp. 135–142. 1995.

Guéziec, A. Surface Simplification with Variable Tolerance. *Proceedings of Second Annual International Symposium on Medical Robotics and Computer Assisted Surgery (MRCAS '95).* pp. 132–139. 1995.

Guéziec, A, F Lazarus, G Taubin, and W Horn. Simplical Maps for Progressive Transmission of Polygonal Surfaces. *Proceedings of VRML 98: Third Symposium on the Virtual Reality Modeling Language.* pp. 25–31, 131. 1998.

Guéziec, A. Locally Toleranced Surface Simplification. *IEEE Transactions on Visualization and Computer Graphics.* vol. 5(2). pp. 168–189. 1999.

Guéziec, A, G Taubin, B Horn, and F Lazarus. A Framework for Streaming Geometry in VRML. *IEEE Computer Graphics and Applications.* vol. 19(2). 1999.

Haenny, P, J Maunsell, and P Schiller. State Dependent Activity in Monkey Visual Cortex: II. Retinal and Extraretinal Factors in V4. *Experimental Brain Research.* vol. 69. pp. 245–259. 1988.

Hamann, B. A Data Reduction Scheme for Triangulated Surfaces. *Computer Aided Geometric Design.* vol. 11. pp. 197–214. 1994.

Harvey, L O and M J Gervais. Internal Representation of Visual Texture as the Basis for the Judgement of Similarity. *Journal of Experimental Psychology: Human Perception Performance.* vol. 7(4). pp. 741–753. 1981.

Hawkes, R, S Rushton, and M Smyth. Update Rates and Fidelity in Virtual Environments. *Virtual Reality: Research, Development, and Application.* vol. 1(2). pp. 99–108. 1995.

He, T, L Hong, A Varshney, and S Wang. Controlled Topology Simplification. *IEEE Transactions on Visualization and Computer Graphics.* vol. 2(2). pp. 171–184. 1996.

He, Y. *Real-Time Dynamic Terrain Visualization for Ground Vehicle Simulation.* Ph.D. Thesis. Department of Computer Science, University of Iowa, Iowa City. 2000.

Heckbert, P and M Garland. Survey of Polygonal Simplification Algorithms. *SIGGRAPH 97 Course Notes.* 1997.

Heeley, D. Spatial Frequency Difference Thresholds Depend on Stimulus Area. *Spatial Vision.* vol. 5(3). pp. 205–217. 1991.

Helman, J. Designing Virtual Reality Systems to Meet Physio- and Psychological Requirements. *SIGGRAPH 93 Course Number 23: Applied Virtual Reality.* 1993.

Helman, J. Designing Real-Time 3D Graphics for Entertainment. *SIGGRAPH 96 Course #33.* 1996.

Herzen, B and A Barr. Accurate Triangulations of Deformed, Intersecting Surfaces. *Proceedings of SIGGRAPH 87.* pp. 103–110. 1987.

Hilaga, M, Y Shinagawa, T Kohmura, and T L Kunii. Topology Matching for Fully Automatic Similarity Estimation of 3D Shapes. *Proceedings of SIGGRAPH 2001.* pp. 203–212. 2001.

Hinker, P and C Hansen. Geometric Optimization. *Proceedings of IEEE Visualization '93.* pp. 189–195. 1993.

Hitchner, L E and M W McGreevy. Methods for User-Based Reduction of Model Complexity for Virtual Planetary Exploration. *Proceedings of the SPIE, The International Society for Optical Engineering.* vol. 1913. pp. 622–636. 1993.

Holloway, R L Viper: *A Quasi-Real-Time Virtual-Worlds Application.* Technical Report No. TR-92–004. Department of Computer Science, University of North Carolina at Chapel Hill, Chapel Hill, NC. 1991.

Hoppe, H, T DeRose, T Duchamp, J McDonald, and W Stuetzle. Mesh Optimization. *Proceedings of SIGGRAPH 93.* pp. 19–26. 1993.

Hoppe, H. Progressive Meshes. *Proceedings of SIGGRAPH 96.* pp. 99–108. 1996.

Hoppe, H. View-Dependent Refinement of Progressive Meshes. *Proceedings of SIGGRAPH 97.* pp. 189–198. 1997.

Hoppe, H. Smooth View-Dependent Level-of-Detail control and its Application to Terrain Rendering. *Proceedings of IEEE Visualization '98.* pp. 35–42. 1998.

Hoppe, H. Efficient Implementation of Progressive Meshes. *Computers & Graphics.* vol. 22(1). pp. 27–36. 1998.

Hoppe, H. Optimization of Mesh Locality for Transparent Vertex Caching. *Proceedings of SIGGRAPH 99.* pp. 269–276. 1999.

Hoppe, H H. New Quadric Metric for Simplifying Meshes with Appearance Attributes. *Proceedings of IEEE Visualization '99.* pp. 59–66. 1999.

Hubel, D and T Wiesel. Receptive Fields, Binocular Interaction, and Functional Architecture in the Cat's Visual Cortex. *Journal of Physiology.* vol. 160. pp. 106–154. 1962.

Humphreys, G, M Riddoch, and P Quinlin. Cascade Processes in Picture Identification. *Cognitive Neuropsychology.* vol. 5. pp. 67–103. 1988.

Humphreys, G W and V Bruce. *Visual Cognition: Computational, Experimental and Neuropsychological Perspectives.* Lawrence Erlbaum Associates, Hove, UK. 1989.

Humphreys, G, C Lamote, and T Lloyd-Jones. An Interactive Activation Approach to Object Processing: Effects of Structural Similarity, Name Frequency, and Task in Normality and Pathology. *Memory.* vol. 3. pp. 535–586. 1995.

Humphreys, G, M Eldridge, Buck, G Stoll, M Everett, and P Hanrahan. WireGL: A Scalable Graphics System for Clusters. *Proceedings of SIGGRAPH 2001.* pp. 129–140. 2001.

Hurvich, L M. *Color Vision.* Sinauer Associates, Sunderland, MA. 1981.

Jain, A. *Fundamentals of Digital Image Processing.* Prentice Hall, Englewood Cliffs, NJ. 1989.

Johnson, D and E Cohen. Spatialized Normal Cone Hierarchies. *2001 Symposium on Interactive 3D Graphics.* pp. 129–134. 2001.

Jolicoeur, P. The Time to Name Disoriented Natural Objects. *Memory and Cognition.* vol. 13. pp. 289–303. 1985.

Jolliffe, I. *Principal Component Analysis.* Springer-Verlag, New York. 1986.

Kalvin, A D and R H Taylor. Superfaces: Polygonal Mesh Simplification with Bounded Error. *IEEE Computer Graphics and Applications.* vol. 16(3). pp. 64–77. 1996.

Kelly, D H. Spatial Frequency Selectivity in the Retina. *Vision Research.* vol. 15. pp. 665–672. 1975.

Kelly, D H. Motion and Vision. II. Stabilized Spatio-Temporal Threshold Surface. *Journal of the Optical Society of America.* vol. 69(10). pp. 1340–1349. 1979.

Kelly, D H. Retinal Inhomogenity: I. Spatiotemporal Contrast Sensitivity. *Journal of the Optical Society of America.* vol. A1(1). pp. 107–113. 1984.

King, Y. Floating-Point Tricks: Improving Performance with IEEE Floating Point. In: M DeLoura, ed. *Games Programming Gems 2.* Charles River Media, Hingham, MA. pp. 167–181. 2001.

Klein, R and J Krämer. Multiresolution Representations for Surface Meshes. *Proceedings of Spring Conference on Computer Graphics 1997.* pp. 57–66. 1997.

Koenderink, J J, M A Bouman, A E B de Mesquita, and S Slappendel. Perimetry of Contrast Detection Thresholds of Moving Spatial Sine Wave Patterns. I. The Near Peripheral Visual Field (Eccentricity 0°–8°). *Journal of the Optical Society of America.* vol. 68(6). pp. 845–849. 1978.

Koenderink, J J, M A Bouman, A E B de Mesquita, and S Slappendel. Perimetry of Contrast Detection Thresholds of Moving Spatial Sine Wave Patterns. II. The Far Peripheral Visual Field (Eccentricity 0°–50°). *Journal of the Optical Society of America.* vol. 68(6). pp. 850–854 .1978.

Koller, D, P Lindstrom, W Ribarsky, L F Hodges, N Faust, and G Turner. Virtual GIS: A Real-Time 3D Geographic Information System. *Proceedings of Visualization '95.* pp. 94–100. 1995.

Kosara, R, S Miksch, and H Hauser. Focus+Context Taken Literally. *IEEE Computer Graphics and Applications.* vol. 22(1). pp. 22–29. 2002.

Lamming, D. On the Limits of Visual Detection. In: J R Cronly-Dillon, ed. *Vision and Visual Dysfunction: Limits of Vision.* CRC Press, Boca Raton, FL. pp. 6–14. 1991.

Lamming, D. Spatial Frequency Channels. In J R Cronly-Dillon, ed. *Vision and Visual Dysfunction: Limits of Vision.* CRC Press, Boca Raton, FL. pp. 97–105. 1991.

Leclerc, Y G and S Q Lau. TerraVision: A Terrain Visualization System. Technical Report 540. SRI International, Menlo Park, CA. April 1994.

Lee, A, H Moreton, and H Hoppe. Displaced Subdivision Surfaces. *Proceedings of SIGGRAPH 2000.* 2000.

Levi, D M, S A Klein, and A P Aitsebaomo. Vernier Acuity, Crowding and Cortical Magnification. *Vision Research.* vol. 25. pp. 963–971. 1985.

Levoy, M and R Whitaker. Gaze-Directed Volume Rendering. *Proceedings of 1990 Symposium on Interactive 3D Graphics.* pp. 217–223. 1990.

Levoy, M, K Pulli, B Curless, S Rusinkiewics, D Koller, L Pereira, M Ginzton, S Anderson, J Davis, J Gensberg, J Shade, and D Fulk. The Digital Michelangelo Project: 3D Scanning of Large Statues. *Proceedings of SIGGRAPH 2000.* pp. 131–144. 2000.

Li, G and B Watson. Semiautomatic Simplification. *Proceedings of 2001 ACM Symposium on Interactive 3D Graphics.* pp. 43–48. 2001.

Liang, J, C Shaw, and M Green. On Temporal-Spatial Realism in the Virtual Reality Environment. *Proceedings of 1991 ACM Conference on User Interface Software and Technology.* pp. 19–25. 1991.

Lilleskog, T. *Continuous Level of Detail.* Master's Thesis. Department of Computer Science, Norwegian University of Science and Technology, Trondheim, Norway. 1998.

Lindstrom, P, D Koller, L F Hodges, W Ribarsky, N Faust, and G Turner. *Level-of-Detail Management for Real-Time Rendering of Photoctextured Terrain.* Technical Report TR95–06. Graphics, Visualization and Usability Centre, Georgia Institute of Technology, Atlanta, GA. 1995.

Lindstrom, P, D Koller, W Ribarsky, L F Hodges, N Faust, and G Turner. Real-Time, Continuous Level of Detail Rendering of Height Fields. *Proceedings of SIGGRAPH 96.* pp. 109–118. 1996.

Lindstrom, P, D Koller, W Ribarsky, L F Hodges, A Op den Bosch, and N Faust. *An Integrated Global GIS and Simulation System.* Technical Report Number GIT-GVU-97–07. Georgia Institute of Technology, Atlanta, GA. March 1997.

Lindstrom, P and G Turk. Fast and Memory Efficient Polygonal Simplification. *Proceedings of IEEE Visualization '98.* pp. 279–286. 1998.

Lindstrom, P and G Turk. Evaluation of Memoryless Simplification. *IEEE Transactions on Visualization and Computer Graphics.* vol. 5(2). pp. 98–115. 1999.

Lindstrom, P. Out-of-Core Simplification of Large Polygonal Models. *Proceedings of SIGGRAPH 2000.* pp. 259–262. 2000.

Lindstrom, P and G Turk. Image-Driven Simplification. *ACM Transactions on Graphics.* vol. 19(3). pp. 204–241. 2000.

Lindstrom, P and V Pascucci. Visualization of Large Terrains Made Easy. *Proceedings of IEEE Visualization 2001.* pp. 363–370, and 574. 2001.

Lindstrom, P and C Silva. A Memory Insensitive Technique for Large Model Simplification. *Proceedings of IEEE Visualization 2001.* pp. 121–126. 2001.

Livingstone, M S. Art, Illusion and the Visual System. *Scientific American.* vol. 258(1). pp. 68–75. 1988.

Lorensen, W E and H E Cline. Marching Cubes: A High Resolution 3D Surface Construction Algorithm. *Proceedings of SIGGRAPH 87.* pp. 163–169. 1987.

Lorensen, W. Marching Through the Visible Man. *Proceedings of IEEE Visualization '95.* pp. 368–373, 476. 1995.

Lounsbery, M. *Multiresolution Analysis for Surfaces of Arbitrary Topology Type.* Ph.D. Thesis. Department of Computer Science, University of Washington, Seattle, WA. 1994.

Low, K and T Tan. Model Simplification Using Vertex-Clustering. *Proceedings of 1997 Symposium on Interactive 3D Graphics.* April 27–30, pp. 75–81, 188. 1997.

Lubin, J. A Visual Discrimination Model for Imaging System Design and Evaluation. In: E Peli, ed. *Vision Models for Target Detection and Recognition.* World Scientific 1993. pp. 245–283. 1993.

Luebke, D and C Georges. Portals and Mirrors: Simple, Fast Evaluation of Potentially Visible Sets. *1995 ACM Symposium on Interactive 3D Graphics.* pp. 105–106. 1995.

Luebke, D and C Erikson. View-Dependent Simplification of Arbitrary Polygonal Environments. *Proceedings of SIGGRAPH 97.* pp. 199–208. 1997.

Luebke, D, B Hallen, D Newfield, and B Watson. *Perceptually Driven Simplification Using Gaze-Directed Rendering.* Technical Report CS-2000-04. University of Virginia, Charlottesville, VA. 2000.

Luebke, D, B Hallen. *Perceptually Driven Interactive Rendering.* Technical Report CS-2001-01. University of Virginia, Charlottesville, VA. 2001.

Luebke, D, J Cohen, B Watson, M Reddy, and A Varshney. Advanced Issues in Level of Detail. *Course #41, SIGGRAPH 2000.* 2000.

Luebke, D. A Developer's Survey of Polygonal Simplification Algorithms. *IEEE Computer Graphics and Applications.* vol. 32(13). pp. 753–772. 2000.

Luebke, D and B Hallen. Perceptually Driven Simplification for Interactive Rendering. *Proceedings of 2001 Eurographics Rendering Workshop*. pp. 223–234. 2001.

Maciel, P W C and P Shirley. Visual Navigation of Large Environments Using Textured Clusters. *Proceedings of 1995 Symposium on Interactive 3D Graphics*. pp. 95–102. 1995.

MacKenzie, S and C Ware. Lag as a Determinant of Human Performance in Interactive Systems. *Proceedings of 1993 INTERCHI Conference on Human Factors in Computing Systems*. pp. 488–493. 1993.

Magillo, P. *Spatial Operations on Multiresolution Cell Complexes*. Ph.D. Thesis. Department of Computer and Information Sciences, University of Genova, Genova, Italy. 1999.

Magillo, P and V Bertocci. Managing Large Terrain Data Sets with a Multiresolution Structure. *Proceedings of International Workshop on Advanced Spatial Data Management (2000)*. 2000.

Mannos, J L and D J Sakrison. The Effects of a Visual Fidelity Criterion on the Encoding of Images. *IEEE Transactions on Information Theory*. vol. 20(4). pp. 525–535. 1974.

Mason, A and E H Blake. Automatic Hierarchical Level of Detail Optimization in Computer Animation. *Computer Graphics Forum*. vol. 16(3). pp. 191–199. 1997.

McCabe, D and J Brothers. DirectX 6 Texture Map Compression. *Game Developer Magazine*. pp. 42–46. 1998.

McNamara, A. Visual Perception in Realistic Image Synthesis. *Computer Graphics Forum*. vol. 20(4). pp. 211–224. 2001.

Meruvia, O. *Level of Detail Selection and Interactivity*. Master's Thesis. Department of Computing Science, University of Alberta, Edmonton, Alberta, Canada. 2000.

Miliano, V. Unreality: Application of a 3D Game Engine to Enhance the Design, Visualization and Presentation of Commercial Real Estate. *Proceedings of 1999 International Conference on Virtual Systems and MultiMedia (VSMM '99)*. pp. 508–513. 1999.

Mon-Williams, M and J P Wann. Binocular Virtual Reality Displays: When Problems Do and Don't Occur. *Human Factors*. vol. 40(1). pp. 42–49. 1998.

Morgan, M J. Hyperacuity. In: D Regan, ed. *Spatial Vision*. CRC Press, Boca Raton, FL. pp. 87–110. 1991.

Mullen, K T. The Contrast Sensitivity of Human Color Vision to Red-Green and Blue-Yellow Chromatic Gratins. *Journal of Physiology*. vol. 359. pp. 381–400. 1985.

Muller, D and F Preparata. Finding the Intersection of Two Convex Polyhedra. *Theoretical Computer Science*. vol. 7. pp. 217–236. 1978.

Murphy, B J. Pattern Thresholds for Moving and Stationary Gratings During Smooth Eye Movement. *Vision Research.* vol. 18. pp. 521–530. 1978.

Myszkowski, K, P Rokita, and T Tawara. Perceptually-Informed Accelerated Rendering of High-Quality Walkthrough Sequences. *Proceedings of Eurographics Rendering Workshop 1999.* pp. 5–18. 1999.

Myszkowski, K, T Tawara, H Akamine, and H-P Seidel. Perception-Based Global Illumination, Rendering, and Animation. *SIGGRAPH 2001.* pp. 221–230. 2001.

Nachmias. Visual Resolution of Two-Bar Patterns and Square-Wave Gratings. *Journal of the Optical Society of America.* vol. 58(1). pp. 9–13. 1968.

Nakayama, K. Properties of Early Motion Processing: Implications for the Sensing of Egomotion. In: R Warren and A H Wertheim, eds. *The Perception and Control of Self Motion.* Lawrence Erlbaum, Hillsdale, NJ. pp. 69–80. 1990.

Narkhede, A and D Manocha. Fast Polygon Triangulation Based on Seidel's Algorithm. In: A W Paeth, ed. *Graphics Gems V.* AP Professional, Boston. pp. 394–397. 1995.

Nooruddin, F and G Turk. *Simplification and Repair of Polygonal Models Using Volumetric Techniques.* Technical Report GIT-GVU-99–37. Georgia Institute of Technology, Atlanta, GA. 1999.

Ögren, A. *Continuous Level of Detail in Real-Time Terrain Rendering.* Master's Thesis. Department of Computing Science, University of Umeå, Umeå, Sweden. 2000.

Ohshima, T, H Yamamoto, and H Tamura. Gaze-Directed Adaptive Rendering for Interacting with Virtual Space. *Proceedings of 1996 IEEE Virtual Reality Annual International Symposium.* pp. 103–110. 1996.

O'Rourke, Joseph. *Computational Geometry in C.* Cambridge University Press, Cambridge, New York. 1994.

Osada, R, T Funkhouser, B Chazelle, and D Dobkin. Matching 3D Models with Shape Distributions. *Proceedings of Shape Modeling International 2001.* pp. 154-166. 2001.

O'Sullivan, C and J Dingliana. Collisions and Perception. *ACM Transactions on Graphics.* vol. 20(3). pp. 151–168. 2001.

Owsley, C J, R Sekuler, and D Siemsen. Contrast Sensitivity Throughout Adulthood. *Vision Research.* vol. 23. pp. 689–699. 1983.

Pajarola, R. Large Scale Terrain Visualization Using the Restricted Quadtree Triangulation. *Proceedings of IEEE Visualization '98.* pp. 19–26. 1998.

Palmer, S, E Rosch, and P Chase. Canonical Perspective and the Perception of Objects. *Proceedings of Attention & Performance IX.* pp. 135–151. 1981.

Palmer, S E. *Vision Science: Photons to Phenomenology.* MIT Press, Cambridge, MA. 1999.

Park, K and R Kenyon. Effects of Network Characteristics on Human Performance in a Collaborative Virtual Environment. *Proceedings of 1999 IEEE Virtual Reality.* pp. 104–111. 1999.

OpenGL Performer Getting Started Guide. Technical Report Document Number 007-3560-002. Silicon Graphics, Inc. 2000.

OpenGL Performer Programmer's Guide. Technical Report Document Number 007-1680-070. Silicon Graphics, Inc. 2000.

Popovic, J and H Hoppe. Progressive Simplicial Complexes. *Proceedings of SIGGRAPH 97.* pp. 217–224. 1997.

Workshop on Shape-Based Retrieval and Analysis of 3D Models. Princeton University and NEC Research Institute, Princeton, NJ. 2001.

Pugh. Skip Lists: A Probabilistic Alternative to Balanced Trees. *Communications of the ACM.* vol. 33(6). pp. 668–676. 1990.

Puppo, E. Variable Resolution Triangulations. *Computation Geometry.* vol. 11(3–4). pp. 219–238. 1998.

Ramasubramanian, M, S N Pattanaik, and D P Greenberg. A Perceptually Based Physical Error Metric for Realistic Image Synthesis. *Proceedings of SIGGRAPH 99.* pp. 73–82. 1999.

Ranadive, V. *Video Resolution, Frame Rate, and Gray Scale Tradeoffs Under Limited Bandwidth for Undersea Teleoperation.* Master's Thesis. Massachusetts Institute of Technology, Cambridge, MA. 1979.

Reddy, M. *Perceptually Modulated Level of Detail for Virtual Environments.* Ph.D. Thesis. CST-134-97. University of Edinburgh, Edinburgh, Scotland. 1997.

Reddy, M. Specification and Evaluation of Level of Detail Selection Criteria. *Virtual Reality: Research, Development and Application.* vol. 3(2). pp. 132–143. 1998.

Reddy, M, Y G Leclerc, L Iverson, and N Bletter. TeraVision II: Visualizing Massive Terrain Databases in VRML. *IEEE Computer Graphics and Applications.* vol. 19(2). pp. 30–38. 1999.

Reddy, M, L Iverson, and Y G Leclerc. Under the Hood of GeoVRML 1.0. *Proceedings of Web3D-VRML 2000: The Fifth Symposium on the Virtual Reality Modeling Language.* pp. 23–28. 2000.

Reddy, M. Perceptually Optimized 3D Graphics. *IEEE Computer Graphics and Applications.* vol. 21(5). pp. 68–75. 2001.

Regan, D and K I Beverley. Visual Field Described by Contrast Sensitivity, By Acuity and by Relative Sensitivity to Different Orientations. *Investigative Ophthalmology and Visual Science.* vol. 24. pp. 754–759. 1983.

Regan, M, G Miller, S Rubin, and C Kogelnik. A Real-Time Low-Latency Light-Field Renderer. *Proceedings of SIGGRAPH 99.* pp. 287–290. 1999.

Richard, P, G Birebent, P Coiffent, G Burdea, D Gomez, and N Langrana. Effect of Frame Rate and Force Feedback on Virtual Object Manipulation. *Presence.* vol. 5(1). pp. 95–108. 1996.

Rigiroli, P, P Campadelli, A Pedotti, and N A Borghese. Mesh Refinement with Color Attributes. *Computers & Graphics.* vol. 25(3). pp. 449–461. 2001.

Ritter, J. A Fast Approximation to 3D Euclidean Distance. In: A S Glassner, ed. *Graphics Gems.* Academic Press, Boston. pp. 432–433. 1990.

Robinson, D A. The Mechanics of Human Saccadic Eye Movements. *Journal of Physiology.* vol. 180. pp. 569–590. 1964.

Rohaly, A, A Ahumada, and A Watson. A Comparison of Image Quality Models and Metrics Predicting Object Detection. In: J Morreale, ed. *SID International Symposium Digest of Technical Papers.* Society for Information Display, Santa Ana, CA. pp. 45–48. 1995.

Rohaly, A, A Ahumada, and A Watson. Object Detection in Natural Backgrounds Predicted by Discrimination Performance and Models. *Vision Research.* vol. 37. pp. 3225–3235. 1997.

Ronfard, R and J Rossignac. Full-Range Approximation of Triangulated Polyhedra. *Computer Graphics Forum.* vol. 15(3). pp. 67–76, 462. 1996.

Rosenfeld, A. *Multiresolution Image Processing and Analysis.* Springer-Verlag, Berlin. 1984.

Rossignac, J and P Borrel. *Multi-Resolution 3D Approximations for Rendering Complex Scenes.* Technical Report RC 17687-77951. IBM Research Division, T J Watson Research Center, Yorktown Heights, NY. 1992. Also in: *Modeling in Computer Graphics: Methods and Applications.* Springer-Verlag, Berlin, New York. pp. 455–465. 1993.

Röttger, S, W Heidrich, P Slussallek, and H-P Seidel. Real-Time Generation of Continuous Levels of Detail for Height Fields. *Proceedings of 1998 International Conference in Central Europe on Computer Graphics and Visualization.* pp. 315–322. 1998.

Rovamo, J and V Virsu. An Estimation and Application of the Human Cortical Magnification Factor. *Experimental Brain Research.* vol. 37. pp. 495–510. 1979.

Rushmeier, H, G Ward, C Piatko, P Sanders, and B Rust. Comparing Real and Synthetic Images: Some Ideas About Metrics. *Proceedings of 6th Eurographics Workshop on Rendering (1995).* pp. 82–91. 1995.

Rushmeier, H, B Rogowitz, and C Piatko. Perceptual Issues in Substituting Texture for Geometry. *Proceedings of Human Vision and Electronic Imaging V, SPIE.* vol. 3959. pp. 372–383. 2000.

Rusinkiewicz, S and M Levoy. QSplat: A Multiresolution Point Rendering System for Large Meshes. *Proceedings of SIGGRAPH 2000.* pp. 343–352. 2000.

Samet, H. *Applications of Spatial Data Structures: Computer Graphics, Image Processing, and GIS.* Addison-Wesley, Reading, MA. 1989.

Samet, H. *The Design and Analysis of Spatial Data Structures.* Addison-Wesley, Reading, MA. 1989.

Samet, H and R Sivan. Algorithms for Constructing Quadtree Surface Maps. *5th International Symposium on Spatial Data Handling (1992).* pp. 361–370. 1992.

Sander, P V, X Gu, S J Gortler, H Hoppe, and J Snyder. Silhouette Clipping. *Proceedings of SIGGRAPH 2000.* pp. 23–28. 2000.

Sander, P V, J Snyder, S J Gortler, and H Hoppe. Texture Mapping Progressive Meshes. *Proceedings of SIGGRAPH 2001.* pp. 409–416. 2001.

Scarlatos, L and T Pavlidis. Hierarchical Triangulation Using Cartographic Coherence. *CVGIP: Graphical Models and Image Processing.* vol. 54(2). pp. 147–161. 1992.

Schachter, B J. Computer Image Generation for Flight Simulation. *IEEE Computer Graphics and Applications.* vol. 1. pp. 29–68. 1981.

Schade, O H. Optical and Photoelectric Analog of the Eye. *Journal of the Optical Society of America.* vol. 46. pp. 721–739. 1956.

Schor, C M and D R Badcock. A Comparison of Stereo and Vernier Acuity with Spatial Channels as a Function of Distance from Fixation. *Vision Research.* vol. 25. pp. 1113–1119. 1985.

Schroeder, W J, J A Zarge, and W E Lorensen. Decimation of Triangle Meshes. *Proceedings of SIGGRAPH 92.* pp. 65–70. 1992.

Schroeder, W. A Topology-Modifying Progressive Decimation Algorithm. *Proceedings of IEEE Visualization '97.* pp. 205–212. 1997.

Schroeder, W, K Martin, and W Lorensen. *The Visualization Toolkit.* 2nd ed. Prentice Hall PTR, Upper Saddle River, NJ. 1998.

Scott, D. Visual Search in Modern Human–Computer Interfaces. *Behaviour & Information Technology.* vol. 12(3). pp. 174–189. 1993.

Seidel, R. A. Simple and Fast Incremental Randomized Algorithm for Computing Trapezoidal Decompositions and for Triangulating Polygons. *Computational Geometry: Theory and Applications.* vol. 1(1). pp. 51–64. 1991.

Sekuler, R and R Blake. *Perception.* 3rd ed. McGraw-Hill, New York. 1994.

Sen, R, R B Yates, and N A Thacker. Virtual Reality Based on Cost/Benefit Analysis. *Proceedings of FIVE '95 Conference.* pp. 213–221. 1995.

Shaffer, E and M Garland. Efficient Adaptive Simplification of Massive Meshes. *Proceedings of IEEE Visualization 2001.* pp. 127–134, 551. 2001.

Shams, L, Y Kamitani, and S Shimojo. What You See Is What You Hear. *Nature.* vol. 408(6814). pp. 788. 2000.

Sheridan, T and W Ferrell. Remote Manipulative Control with Transmission Delay. *IEEE Transactions on Human Factors in Electronics.* vol. 4. pp. 25–29. 1963.

Shirman, L A and S S Abi-Ezzi. The Cone of Normals Technique for Fast Processing of Curved Patches. *Proceedings of Eurographics '93.* pp. 261–272. 1993.

Sloane, N J A and S Ploufe. *The Encyclopedia of Integer Sequences.* Academic Press, San Diego, CA. pp. 587. 1995.

Snyder, J P. *Map Projections: A Working Manual.* Professional Paper 1395. US Geological Survey, US Government Printing Office, Washington, DC. 1987.

Sutter, E E and D Tran. The Field Topography of ERG Components in Man. I. The Photopic Luminance Response. *Vision Research.* vol. 32(3). pp. 433–446. 1991.

Suzuki, S. Attention-Dependent Brief Adaptation to Contour Orientation: A High-Level Aftereffect for Convexity? *Vision Reseasrch.* vol. 41(28). pp. 3883–3902. 2001.

Tanner, C C, C J Migdal, and M T Jones. The Clipmap: A Virtual Mipmap. *Proceedings of SIGGRAPH 98.* pp. 151–158. 1998.

TEC. *Handbook for Transformation of Datums, Projections, Grids and Common Coordinate Systems.* Technical Report TEC-SR-7. US Army Corps of Engineers, Topographic Engineering Center, Alexandria, VA. January 1996.

Tharp, G, A Liu, L French, and L Stark. Timing Considerations of Helmet Mounted Display Performance. *Human Vision, Visual Processing, and Digital Displays III, SPIE.* vol. 1666. pp. 570–576. 1992.

Tipton, D A. A Review of Vision Physiology. *Aviation, Space and Environmental Medicine.* vol. 55(2). pp. 145–149. 1984.

Turk, G. Re-Tiling Polygonal Surfaces. *Proceedings of SIGGRAPH 92.* pp. 55–64. 1992.

Tyler, C W. Analysis of Visual Modulation Sensitivity. II. Peripheral Retina and the Role of Photoreceptor Dimensions. *Journal of the Optical Society of America.* vol. A2(3). pp. 393–398. 1985.

Uliano, K, R Kennedy, and E Lambert. Asynchronous Visual Delays and the Development of Simulator Sickness. *Proceedings of Human Factors Society, 30th Annual Meeting (1986).* pp. 422–426. 1986.

Varshney, A. Hierarchical Geometric Approximations. Ph.D. Thesis. Department of Computer Science. University of North Carolina at Chapel Hill, Chapel Hill, NC. 1994.

Varshney, A, F P Brooks Jr, and W V Wright. Computation of Smooth Molecular Surfaces. *IEEE Computer Graphics and Applications.* vol. 14(5). pp. 19–25. 1994.

Vince, J. Virtual Reality Techniques in Flight Simulation. In: R A Earnshaw, M A Gigante, and H Jones, eds. *Virtual Reality Systems.* Academic Press. 1993.

Virsu, V, J Rovamo, P Laurinen, and R Näsänen. Temporal Contrast Sensitivity and Cortical Magnification. *Vision Research.* vol. 33. pp. 1211–1217. 1982.

Vitkovitch, M and L Tyrell. Sources of Name Disagreement in Object Naming. *Quarterly Journal of Experimental Psychology.* vol. 48A. pp. 822–848. 1995.

Volevich, V, K Myszkowski, A Khodulev, and E Kopylov. Using the Visual Difference Predictor to Improve Performance of Progressive Global Illumination Computation. *ACM Transactions on Graphics.* vol. 19(2). pp. 122–161. 2000.

Final Report from the Video Quality Experts Group on the Validation of Objective Models of Video Quality Assessment. http://ftp.crc.ca/test/crc/vqeg/Final_Report_April00.doc. 2001.

The Virtual Reality Modeling Language. Technical Report International Standard ISO/IEC 14772-1:1997. 1997.

Wandell, B. *Foundations of Vision.* Sinauer Associates, Sunderland, MA. 1995.

Wang, S and A Kaufman. Volume Sampled Voxelization of Geometric Primitives. *Proceedings of Visualization '93.* pp. 78–84. 1993.

Wann, J P, S K Rushton, and M Mon-Williams. Natural Problems for Stereoscopic Depth Perception in Virtual Environments. *Vision Research.* vol. 35(19). pp. 2731–2736. 1995.

Ware, C and R Balakrishnan. Reaching for Objects in VR Displays: Lag and Frame Rate. *ACM Transactions on Computer–Human Interaction.* vol. 1(4). pp. 331–357. 1994.

Ware, C. *Information Visualization: Perception for Design.* Morgan Kaufmann, San Francisco. 1999.

Watson, A. Detection and Recognition of Simple Spatial Forms. In: O J Braddick and A C Sleigh, eds. *Physical and Biological Processing of Images.* Springer-Verlag, New York. pp. 100–114. 1983.

Watson, A. Visual Detection of Spatial Contrast Patterns: Evaluation of Five Simple Models. *Optics Express.* vol. 6(1). pp. 12–33. 2000.

Watson, A. Toward a Perceptual Video Quality Metric. *Proceedings of Human Vision and Electronic Imaging III, SPIE.* vol. 3299. pp. 139–147. 1998.

Watson, B, N Walker, and L F Hodges. A User Study Evaluating Level of Detail Degradation in the Periphery of Head-Mounted Displays. *Proceedings of FIVE '95 Conference.* pp. 203–212. 1995.

Watson, B. *Level of Detail Management.* Ph.D. Thesis. College of Computing, Georgia Institute of Technology, Atlanta, GA. 1997.

Watson, B, V Spaulding, N Walker, and W R Ribarsky. Evaluation of the Effects of Frame Time Variation on VR Task Performance. *Proceedings of 1997 IEEE Virtual Reality Annual International Symposium.* pp. 38–44. 1997.

Watson, B, N Walker, and L Hodges. Managing Level of Detail Through Head-Tracked Peripheral Degradation: A Model and Resulting Design Principles. *Proceedings of ACM Virtual Reality Software Technology '97.* pp. 59–64. 1997.

Watson, B, N Walker, L Hodges, and A Worden. Managing Level of Detail Through Peripheral Degradation: Effects on Search Performance with a Head-Mounted Display. *ACM Transactions on Computer–Human Interaction.* vol. 4(4). pp. 323–346. 1997.

Watson, B, N Walker, W Ribarsky, and V Spaulding. Effects of Variation in System Responsiveness on User Performance in Virtual Environments. *Human Factors (Special Section on Virtual Environments).* vol. 40(3). pp. 403–414. 1998.

Watson, B, N Walker, W Ribarsky, and V Spaulding. Managing Temporal Detail in Virtual Environments: Relating System Responsiveness to Feedback. *Proceedings of ACM CHI 99 Extended Abstracts.* pp. 280–281. 1999.

Watson, B, A Friedman, and A McGaffey. Using Naming Time to Evaluate Quality Predictors for Model Simplification. *Proceedings of ACM CHI 2000.* pp. 113–120. 2000.

Watson, B, A Friedman, and A McGaffey. Measuring and Predicting Visual Fidelity. *Proceedings of SIGGRAPH 2001.* pp. 213–220. 2001.

Watson, B. *Visual Fidelity Testbed.* Northwestern University, Evanston, IL. 2002. http://www.cs.northwestern.edu/~watsonb/school/projects/fidelity

Watson, B, D Luebke, C Wooley, C Albrecht-Buehler, and A Dayal. *Breaking the Frame: A New Approach to Temporal Sampling.* Technical Report CS-2002-03. University of Virginia, Charlottesville, VA. 2002.

Weibel, R and C B Jones. Special Issue on Automated Map Generalization. *GeoInformatica.* vol. 2(4). 1998.

Wernecke, J. *The Inventor Mentor: Programming Object-Oriented 3D Graphics with Open Inventor(TM), Release 2.* Addison-Wesley, Reading, MA. 1993.

Wickens, C. The Effects of Control Dynamics on Performance. In: K Boff, L Kaufmann, and J Thomas, eds. *Handbook of Perception and Performance, Volume II.* Wiley, New York. pp. 39.1–39.60. 1986.

Wickens, C and J Hollands. Manual Control. In: *Engineering Psychology and Human Performance.* 3rd ed. Prentice Hall, Upper Saddle River, NJ. 2000.

Wilson, H R and J R Bergen. A Four Mechanism Model for Threshold Spatial Vision. *Vision Research.* vol. 19. pp. 19–32. 1979.

Wilson, D L and R M Manjeshwar. Role of Phase Information and Eye Pursuit in the Detection of Moving Objects in Noise. *Journal of the Optical Society of America, A.* vol. 16(3). pp. 669–678. 1999.

Wood, Z and I Guskov. Topological Noise Removal. *Proceedings of Graphics Interface 2001.* pp. 19–26. 2001.

Xia, J C and A Varshney. Dynamic View-Dependent Simplification for Polygonal Models. *Proceedings of IEEE Visualization '96.* pp. 327–334. 1996.

Xia, J C, J El-Sana, and A Varshney. Adaptive Real-Time Level-of-Detail–Based Rendering for Polygonal Models. *IEEE Transactions on Visualization and Computer Graphics.* vol. 3(2). pp. 171–183. 1997.

Xiang, X, M Held, and J S B Mitchell. Fast and Effective Stripification of Polygonal Surface Models. *Proceedings of 1999 Symposium on Interactive 3D Graphics.* pp. 71–78, 224. 1999.

Yan, J K. Advances in Computer Generated Imagery for Flight Simulation. *IEEE Computer Graphics and Applications.* vol. 5. pp. 37–51. 1985.

Yee, H, S Pattanaik, and D P Greenberg. Spatiotemporal Sensitivity and Visual Attention for Efficient Rendering of Dynamic Environments. *ACM Transactions on Graphics.* vol. 20(1). pp. 39–65. 2001.

Youbing, Z, Z Ji, S Jiaoying, and P Zhigeng. A Fast Algorithm for Large-Scale Terrain Walkthrough. *Proceedings of CAD/Graphics 2001.* 2001.

Zeki, S. *A Vision of the Brain.* Blackwell Scientific Publications, Oxford, Boston. 1993.

Zhang, H and K E Hoff III. Fast Backface Culling Using Normal Masks. *Proceedings of 1997 ACM Symposium on Interactive 3D Graphics.* pp. 103–106. 1997.

Index